OXFORD READINGS IN PHILOSOPHY

TRUTH

TRUTH

Edited by

SIMON BLACKBURN

and

KEITH SIMMONS

OXFORD
UNIVERSITY PRESS

OXFORD
UNIVERSITY PRESS

Great Clarendon Street, Oxford OX2 6DP

Oxford University Press is a department of the University of Oxford.
It furthers the University's objective of excellence in research, scholarship,
and education by publishing worldwide in

Oxford New York

Athens Auckland Bangkok Bogotá Buenos Aires Calcutta
Cape Town Chennai Dar es Salaam Delhi Florence Hong Kong Istanbul
Karachi Kuala Lumpur Madrid Melbourne Mexico City Mumbai
Nairobi Paris São Paulo Singapore Taipei Tokyo Toronto Warsaw

with associated companies in Berlin Ibadan

Oxford is a registered trade mark of Oxford University Press
in the UK and in certain other countries

Published in the United States
by Oxford University Press Inc., New York

British Library Cataloguing in Publication Data

Data available

Library of Congress Cataloging in Publication Data

ISBN 0–19–875251–2 (Hbk)
ISBN 0–19–875250–4 (Pbk)

Typeset in Times
by Best-set Typesetter Ltd, Hong Kong
Printed in Great Britain
on acid-free paper by
Bookcraft Ltd
Midsomer Norton, Somerset

CONTENTS

INTRODUCTION

SIMON BLACKBURN AND KEITH SIMMONS

1. ROBUST THEORIES AND DEFLATIONARY THEORIES

Philosophy deals in abstractions. It is concerned with highly general categories, such as mind, matter, consciousness, causation, time, values, and so on. The limit of abstraction is reached with categories that apply equally to everything. The paradigm is existence, which applies to everything, of whichever kind, that exists. Truth, by contrast, characterizes only some of the things we might say or believe, for to every truth about how things are, there corresponds the falsehood asserting that they are otherwise. Suppose we call the things we might say or believe, propositions (there are some choices about that, but for the moment we ignore them). Then truth is similarly abstract in that it can apply to propositions of any kind, on any subject matter. We can talk of mind, matter, numbers, time, or of what was, or will be, or might have been, and we can talk of mundane things like snow and penguins. And on all these matters, we can say things that are true, or, of course, things that are not true. So what is truth, if propositions from any sphere of interest can equally share it? What do all true propositions share, that is lacked by all false ones?

It might seem easy enough to give an answer. Aristotle said 'To say of what is that it is, or of what is not that it is not, is true.'[1] This is perhaps the first expression of the *correspondence theory* of truth: True propositions tell it like it is, or in other words for a proposition to be true is for it to correspond with the facts. It is important to realize that this is a platitude that nobody denies. But the difficulties start when we try to flesh out the notions involved. What *kind* of 'thing' is a fact: for example, are there general facts, negative facts, hypothetical facts and if so, what are they made of? Then, what *kind* of correspondence is in question? If we think, for instance, of the correspondence between a portrait and a subject we have to imagine that true propositions correctly 'picture' the world. This

[1] *Metaphysics*, Γ. 7.27, trans. Christopher Kirwan (Oxford, 1993).

is not easy to understand, except metaphorically. And for that matter what kind of thing is a proposition? Some have taken propositions to be creatures of the mind, for only thinkers think things that are true or false. But what then is this complex in the mind that represents facts outside it? Others take propositions to be abstract structures, but then we would need to know both how the structure corresponds with facts, and also how the mind gets into a judgemental relationship to the complex. Still others hope to dispense with propositions in favour of sentences, and that will occupy us later.

Many of the philosophers represented in this collection are pessimistic about our ability to answer these questions. They think that the answers traditionally given generate insuperable problems. Some think that people trying to describe a correspondence relation make a category mistake, by turning facts into complexes of things, which they are not. We describe this issue in more detail later. Some think that the theory requires a separation between the mind, as the domain of propositions and judgements, and the world, as the domain of facts. And they think this separation generates an intolerable gulf, eventually leading to scepticism about our ability to know true things about the world. Again, we say a little about this later. Such philosophers turn their pessimism in one of two directions. Either they try to find something else than correspondence with the facts to discover what truth is. This was the direction taken by the earliest philosophers represented here, who suggest notions such as membership in some favoured coherent set of propositions (Bradley, Joachim, giving rise to the *coherence theory* of truth) or even utility (James, giving rise to the *pragmatic theory* of truth). Or, they reject the question, denying that there is in fact any real project of discovering what truth is. This is a far more popular move among the later opponents of correspondence theory. We start by saying a little about the second *deflationary* approach.

We talked of truth along with existence as reaching the heights of abstraction. When we approach these heights, the air becomes very thin indeed. Perhaps it becomes too thin to support philosophical reflection at all. If we asked 'what is existence, in general?' many philosophers might suppose that we have gone too far, so that while we might reasonably address the question of what the world must be like for stones or minds or penguins to exist, no entirely general question about 'what it is to exist' can be posed or addressed. At best, we might say something about the utility of an entirely general word, 'exists', ready to combine with particular noun phrases and perhaps other terms, so that we can frame intelligible thoughts about particular propositions: tame tigers exist, Santa Claus does not exist. And if this seems the right way to go here, it might also commend itself in the case of truth. Perhaps there is nothing in general to say about truth in general, although there will be things to say about particular truths, such as that they are important, or trivial, or interesting, or boring, or that some are more basic than others, or that they do or do not depend upon particular features of the world.

This deflationary view denies that there is an issue of 'the nature of truth in general'. After that, the rejection of any entirely abstract questions about the nature of truth can be phrased in different ways. It has been expressed by saying that truth is not a 'real' property, or a 'robust' or metaphysically interesting property, or even that 'is true' is not a predicate at all.[2] At their most flamboyant, deflationists have maintained that the concept of truth is 'redundant', or that talk in terms of truth is purely 'formal', so that the forms of words in which we say that something is true merely represent 'devices' with various logical purposes. The details of how to formulate a general deflationism matter, and some of the papers collected here take issue with others over just such details. But all such views agree that a general inquiry into the nature of truth as an abstract property is wrongheaded.

This collection is designed to take the reader into an appreciation of the problem of truth by looking mainly at the strengths, and weaknesses, of deflationism. The issue is amongst the most baffling and the most important in contemporary philosophy. For deflationism is both disconcerting and surprising. It is disconcerting, because if truth disappears as a general topic, then too much else may seem to disappear with it. Our awareness of the world is at least largely an awareness *that* various things are true: that we are in a room of some shape and size, surrounded by people like ourselves and so on. An awareness of our situation is just an awareness that various things are so, and that others are not. It is in these judgements of what is true that our minds meet the world. So if there is nothing to say about truth in general, this may seem to imply that there is nothing to say about the relationship between mind and world in general. And if that topic is denied to us, then much of philosophy seems to disappear with it. Can we really hope to say nothing about how it is that we represent the world to ourselves, or how it was that we became creatures capable of judgement and belief? Conversely, if these topics are indeed vivid and real, why should they not be described as inquiries that, by throwing light on

---

[2] 'Truth, to coin a phrase, isn't a real predicate': D. Grover, J. Camp, and N. Belnap, 'A Prosentential Theory of Truth', *Philosophical Studies*, 27 (1975), 97. See also the papers collected in D. Grover, *A Prosentential Theory of Truth* (Princeton, 1992). We return to prosententialism briefly below, p. 276.

the nature of our representation of reality, thereby throw light on the nature of truth?

2. LOSING THE ISSUES

The disconcerting effects of deflationism can also be illustrated if we consider what might at first sight look like an ascending ladder of things to say about a statement. Suppose we take a mathematical or moral judgement p, that virtually everyone will wish to assert, for example, that two plus two equals four, or that genocide is always wicked. The ladder takes us from p, to 'it is true that p', to 'it is a fact that it is true that p', to 'it is really a fact that it is true that p', and, if we like, to such flourishes as 'it corresponds to the eternal mathematical (or normative) order governing the universe that p'. Deflationism is then the claim that the view from the top of this ladder, or from any point on it, is just the same as the view from the bottom. The substantive content of what is said remains just the same: p (a deflationist can admit that rhetorical force is added or subtracted as we go up and down the ladder, but that is all). Other people may be inclined to ascend this ladder believing that by the end they are making substantial claims *about* the original proposition. The last, for instance, might be thought to be a deep, philosophical, Platonic, remark about the status of the original claim. But for the deflationist it is at best a flowery way of asserting that two plus two equals four, or that genocide is always wicked, which is where we started.[3] So we lose the *metatheoretical* standpoint, or place from which debates about the status of the original assertion might have been conducted. This is certainly surprising, and it may be regarded as a fatal loss. Or, instead it may be taken as a desirable liberation from old ghosts and metaphors. In this way the issue of deflationism is intimately connected with the question of whether we can achieve a standpoint from which to mount substantive metatheoretical claims. Indeed, in Chapter XVIII, Rorty argues that by dismantling any substantive conception of truth we enable ourselves to transcend almost the entire western philosophical tradition. If we become pessimistic about our chances of achieving such a standpoint, perhaps thinking of them as step-

---

[3] Blackburn calls this 'Ramsey's ladder', and registers warnings about philosophies that take advantage of the horizontal nature of Ramsey's ladder to climb it, but then announce a better view from the top. One way in which the theory of truth makes contact with more general, 'postmodernist', scepticism about 'truth' in the humanities in general is visible here: scepticism whether we get anywhere by climbing Ramsey's ladder can easily turn itself into scepticism about truth in general. See S. Blackburn, *Ruling Passions* (Oxford, 1998), 78.

ping outside our own skins, or standing on our own shoulders, then a deflationist approach to truth will be a natural ally.

Philosophically, it is an extremely powerful ally. Rorty is certainly correct that many debates in different areas are typically framed in terms of truth. Consider the example of ethics. People ask whether ethical commitments are capable of truth, or really true, or literally true, or true in the same sense as other commitments. These questions seem important. They are motivated by the sense that ethical 'facts' are especially elusive, or difficult to place in the order of nature. Some philosophers want to deny that there are such facts at all, preferring to see ethics as having a non-descriptive, non-representational function. Deflationism may threaten to undermine such positions, since they seem to require a substantial, robust, conception of truth in some areas by contrast with which ethics is supposed to be different.[4]

Again, people ask whether to accept a scientific theory and to assert its theses falls short of accepting or asserting them as true.[5] Some philosophers think scientists accept theories only as instruments for prediction, not as literal truths about the contents or structures of nature. But if we cannot defend a robust or substantive notion of truth, this contrast as well begins to disappear. There would be little or no contrast between putting forward a theory, and putting it forward as true. So the space for instrumentalism seems to become squeezed out. If the deflationist thinks there remains an issue here, then he will need to frame it in some quite different way.

Given deflationism, then, there is no question, for instance, whether ethical commitments are strictly or literally true, or true in the same sense as empirical judgements. The word 'true' has the same, deflated, use in every area, so ethical commitments will be true in just the same sense as any others. Similarly in the scientific case there seems to remain no gap between asserting p and asserting p to be true.

Another metaphysical inquiry that is threatened is that of looking for the 'truth-makers' for different categories of proposition. The idea is that there must be *something* in virtue of which various propositions are true, and the metaphysician can search for what it is. Some of this may survive deflationism, but the theory strongly suggests a trivial answer: the

---

[4] The debates about the correct way to frame 'expressivist' approaches to ethics are pursued in A. Gibbard, *Wise Choices, Apt Feelings: A Theory of Normative Judgment* (Cambridge, Mass., 1990); S. Blackburn, *Essays In Quasi-Realism* (New York, 1993); and M. Smith, 'Why Expressivists about Value should love Minimalism about Truth', *Analysis*, 54 (1994) 1–12.

[5] See B. C. Van Fraassen, *The Scientific Image* (Oxford, 1980) for the best-known recent suggestion that in science acceptance does and should fall short of belief in the truth of what is accepted.

truth-maker for the judgement that *p* is, trivially, that *p*. According to the deflationist, it will be characteristic of bad old correspondence views to want a more substantial answer than that, dissecting the fact that *p* into 'components', for example. The point is that if we want philosophical debates, we can no longer look to truth to help us to frame them.

Deflationism also threatens to rub the bloom off another flower. Truth is a grand notion, an ideal. It is important. It is the target or aim of our investigations. It forms a 'norm' for assertion and belief, as is argued by Wright in Chapter XIII.[6] Deflationism seems to sweep all that away. That can be alarming. Does it leave us with no conception of a difference between truth and falsehood at all? This sounds like postmodernism, or scepticism about whether there is any real distinction between the true and the false. But here, at least, deflationists can defend themselves. They do not have to be sceptics or postmodernists, for they can and should give their own account of what it is to think of truth as a goal, target, or norm. To say that truth is an ideal or a norm merely means this: you tell me about some claim in question, *p*, and I will tell you under what circumstances it would be right to believe it or assert it. It will be right to believe or assert *p* if, and only if, *p*. The point here is that this is a 'schema' which will fill out differently for different propositions. It is good or right to believe that cows fly if and only if cows fly; good to believe that cows swim if and only if cows swim. So, says the deflationist, there is no *single* norm or ideal in play. There is just a piecemeal construction of when it is right to assert or believe the individual things, one by one, that we might be interested in (this kind of deflationist reasoning is resisted by Wright in Chapter XIII).

But why sympathize with deflationism in the first place? It might seem to be quite easy to say substantive, interesting things about truth in general. Although the air is thin, we can just about breathe in it. True propositions correspond with the facts. As we have said, everyone will agree to this. And it *sounds* to be a robust proposal, enabling us to see truth as a relational property. Truth takes its place amongst other such two-term relations: the correspondence of the image in the mirror with the scene in front of the mirror, or the correspondence between a map and a landscape. The correspondence theory associates truth in belief or assertion with such things as a true likeness. Common sense surely applauds such a proposal, so what can be wrong with it?

---

[6] Another norm is that our assertions and beliefs should be *justified*, and that is different from being true. But we aim at truth, by obeying constraints of justification. An assertion is justified, in this sense, when it is reasonably supposed to be true. An act of assertion may be subject to still more norms, such as those of being appropriate or polite, but these are not our concern.

3. THE FLIGHT FROM ROBUST THEORIES

Everyone can agree that a statement is true if it corresponds with the facts. For 'corresponds with the facts' may be just an elaborate synonym for true. The question is whether it unpacks the notion, giving us a genuine account of it as a relation between elements of two different categories: propositions on the one hand, facts on the other. We have already met one reason for doubt. Thinking this way, it may appear, involves thinking of two distinct standpoints. There is the standpoint we occupy when we judge that *p*. Then in addition there is the standpoint we occupy when we step back, and judge that the judgement that *p* indeed bears the right relation to the fact that *p*. But then it is reasonable to urge that there are not two distinct standpoints here, but only one (see, especially, Frege in Chapter V). There are indeed mental processes that we can call 'standing back': becoming cautious about *p*, checking one more time whether *p*, and so on. But these are all processes of reflecting and checking whether *p*. None of them introduce a separate topic, and yet the correspondence theory seems to demand that there is both a separate topic and a separate standpoint from which it can be judged. It is here that we see the illusory nature of the idea that we can step outside our own skins or stand on our own shoulders. Another way of putting the point is that in examples like the mirror and the map we have access both to the original and the image, so there can be a genuine empirical investigation of their correspondence or fit. In the case of judgement, we apparently do not. To 'come upon the facts' is already to judge that things are thus-and-so.

It may seem natural to retort that nothing very extraordinary is called for here. Surely there is the everyday process of taking a judgement, say, that there are cows in the garden, and checking whether it corresponds with the facts—that is, verifying it. Indeed there is, but, insists the deflationist, this is just the process of verifying whether there are cows in the garden, best done by looking round the garden for cows. There is again only one standpoint, that of the investigator of the garden. There is not a *distinct* standpoint of having both the judgement and the fact before one, and essaying a comparison of them. Apprehending a fact is just the same things as judging that something is so. Facts are not *things* (not even bunches of things such as aggregates or structures) that can be seen to be present even if we do not know what to make of them. In the present volume this is stressed in different ways by Bradley, Ramsey, Strawson, and Wright. A good way to see this is to think of logically complex facts. It may be a fact that if you had touched the plug you would have got a shock, or a fact that Bishop Stubbs did not die on the scaffold, or a fact that either there were more than eighteen or fewer than seven people in the room. Facts have logical complexity: not surprisingly, they have exactly as much complexity as the propositions we choose to assert. And the real world—the world of dated, particular, events and things in specific spatial and temporal orderings—just does not seem able to contain anything of this kind of complexity: negative, or disjunctive, or counterfactual situations, for example.[7]

The difficulty, then, lies not in just saying that a judgement is true if it corresponds with the facts, for that is harmless. It consists in trying to pump the platitude up into a substantial theory involving a real two-place relation between judgements and facts. To many philosophers this is a hopeless enterprise, requiring that we treat both propositions and facts as 'things', which they are not.

Dissatisfaction with the correspondence view became orthodox both amongst philosophers influenced by Kant and Hegel, and by American pragmatists, around the beginning of the twentieth century. But their dissatisfaction typically took the form of offering different substantial theories, rather than deflationism. We start the collection with selections from this period, in which substantive alternative proposals about truth are made, by Joachim, Bradley, and James, and we include an example of a rebuttal of one such proposal (that of James), by Russell.

Russell rightly notices that James intertwines what is supposed to be a relatively pure proposal about the nature of truth, with rather more diffuse, but attractive, remarks about scientific method, empiricism, and so on. And one highly significant feature of this literature is the way in which the theory of truth is entangled with the theory of the *proposition*, or the theory of judgement, or in other words, of what it is to have a belief in the first place. So, in Chapter I, H. H. Joachim illustrates one way in which the idea of judgement has itself been thought problematical. Joachim was what later became known as a holist. He believed that individual propositions or judgements are logicians' abstractions from a much larger organized 'significant whole'. So to approach the problem of truth by

---

[7] Conversely, if a place for facts can be found in the world, then they cannot be as complex as propositions. But this compromises the correspondence relation: how do fine-grained propositions correspond to coarse-grained facts? For recent work on the correspondence theory that bears on the present issue, see D. M. Armstrong, *A World of States of Affairs* (Cambridge, 1997); J. Barwise and J. Perry, *Situations and Attitudes* (Cambridge, Mass., 1983); B. Taylor, 'States of Affairs', in G. Evans and J. McDowell, (eds.), *Truth and Meaning: Essays in Semantics* (Oxford, 1976), 263–84, also *Modes of Occurrence* (Oxford, 1985), ch. 2; M. Pendlebury, 'Facts as Truthmakers', *Monist*, 69 (1986), 177–88; and G. Forbes, 'Truth, Correspondence and Redundancy', in G. McDonald and C. Wright (eds.), *Fact, Science and Morality: Essays on A.-J. Ayer's* Language, Truth and Logic (Oxford, 1986), 27–54.

concentrating upon the individual judgement is to begin in the wrong place. The 'proposition' is already a heavily theoretical notion. Joachim insists that there is no such thing as understanding or knowing one proposition in isolation from others. Rather, we have to start with a systematic structure, a science, or what Joachim calls a system 'not of *truths* but of truth'.

Joachim's idea anticipates a later doctrine of Quine, who wrote that 'the unit of empirical significance is the whole of science'.[8] It can be appreciated if we reflect that there could be no state of understanding and knowing just one proposition of natural science (say 'electrons have negative charge') or one proposition from history ('Napoleon was an emperor'). To come to understand these things requires an education in a great deal of physics or a great deal of history. It requires coming to appreciate the inferences that would support them, and the consequences that they have (this is at least one of the things Bradley means by saying that 'much of given fact is inferential').[9] It requires coming to see the world in different terms. Such an education is not the brick-by-brick accumulation of individual self-standing pieces of knowledge, a thing which Joachim calls 'a mutilated shred torn from the living whole in which alone it possessed its significance'.[10] In such increases of understanding, as Wittgenstein put it, 'light dawns gradually over the whole'.[11]

What has this to do with truth? It suggests that the virtue of an individual proposition, of being true, cannot be understood except deriv-atively, from the virtue of a whole system or organized body of knowledge. For Joachim, as for the later Wittgenstein, it also suggests that it is wrong to consider even the whole system outside the context of the changing human practices that issue in its expression. But what is the virtue of whole systems, if it is not to consist in their containing numbers of individual truths? This is one problem facing the main historical competitor to the correspondence theory, namely the 'coherence' theory of truth. According to this a statement is true if it is a member of some suitable coherent set of statements. But the question is, which set?[12] Joachim, like Bradley, is far from clear. He talks of a 'self-fulfilling' process, as if there were some kind of internal motor ensuring that our increasingly coherent sets of beliefs are somehow on a progressive curve. This suggests uncomfortable overtones of Absolute Idealism, in which Thought progresses in accordance

[8] 'Two Dogmas of Empiricism', *Philosophical Review*, 60 (1951), 20–43, repr. in *From a Logical Point of View* (Cambridge, Mass., 1953), 42.
[9] p. 32 in this vol.   [10] p. 48 in this vol.
[11] *On Certainty* (Oxford, 1969), §141.
[12] See Wright, Ch. XIII in this vol.; see also R. Walker, *The Coherence Theory of Truth: Realism, Anti-Realism, Idealism* (London: Routledge, 1989).

with a complex score underwritten by Reason, and few philosophers can sympathize much with that.

Bradley indeed writes as if he thinks that an ideal system does not so much cohere together, as somehow become identical with the world.[13] The idea is this. The correspondence view gives us a picture of propositions or judgements on the one hand and facts on the other, entering into some mysterious relationship. Truth is 'seriously dyadic'.[14] But this implies an impassable gulf between mind, the domain of propositions, and the world, the domain of facts. The way to avoid this gulf, for Bradley, is to see the mind as itself *containing* facts. There is not a question of bringing mental entities into some favoured relation with worldly entities, and then comparing them. To avoid this we must make the mind and the world literally identical. Again, it is very unclear what this identity theory can mean, although some recent philosophers express sympathy with it.[15]

The writings of this period remind us that it is living, active, subjects that have thoughts and beliefs and are capable of judgement at all. To present the issue by starting with static mind contemplating static propositions, abstracted away from all the context of surrounding practices and judgements necessary to give them any sense in the first place, is certainly to court the danger of missing the main course. So these thoughts of Joachim and Bradley are designed to make us uneasy with a simplistic conception of 'the proposition' and 'the fact' as two elements that, as of right, exist— and that then may or may not correspond with each other. Each writer suggests that some highly complex abstraction is responsible for us being happy with talk of 'the proposition (judgement, etc.) that *p*'. And it is the very abstraction that is responsible for us being happy with correlated talk of the fact that *p*. The correspondence theory seems inevitable only because, in Strawson's words, 'What could fit more perfectly the fact that it is raining than the statement that it is raining? Of course statements and facts fit. They were made for each other'.[16] Bradley and Joachim could have said the same, only using it to motivate either coherence or identity theories, not deflationism, as Strawson intends.

For Russell as well the major problem with truth was first understanding the nature of judgement. Russell, at the time he was writing the essay collected here (1908), thought that the principal problem was one of saying what the mind was related to, when it made a judgement. We cannot simply

[13] For a convincing case that Bradley, at least, identified truth and the world, see S. Candlish, 'The Truth about F. H Bradley', *Mind*, 98 (1989), 331–48.

[14] The phrase is Crispin Wright's, *Truth and Objectivity* (Cambridge, Mass., 1992), 83.

[15] It is present in J. McDowell, *Mind and World* (Cambridge, Mass., 1994) and J. Hornsby, 'Truth: the Identity Theory', *Proceedings of the Aristotelian Society*, 97 (1997), 1–24.

[16] p. 168 in this vol.

say that the mind is related to a fact, for then we would have no theory of false judgement, where there is no fact in question (this remains a problem for modern versions of an identity theory). Russell instead related us to a complex of ingredients together making up whichever proposition we believe. These ingredients would include the things about which we make judgements, and the relations or properties attributed to them. But he was unable to explain how the ingredients united to make a distinctive judgement. Famously, unless there is some principle uniting them, we would be unable to distinguish between two subjects, each related to the complex ⟨John, loves, Mary⟩ but one of whom judges that John loves Mary, and the other of whom judges that Mary loves John.[17]

The problem of understanding judgement continues. In Chapter XVII, one of the most recent papers collected here, Davidson suggests that there is a family of connected concepts, including belief, desire, cause, action, and truth, which illuminate one another—but that it is folly to expect a definition of any one of them. It is a significant feature of Davidson's chapter that we are led back to the idea that deflationism itself is to be rejected principally because it gives us no wider philosophy of judgement and belief. This is also the concern aired in Chapter XV by Dummett, and it is approached from a different direction by Wright.

4. SENTENCES TO THE RESCUE?

By contrast, there has been a persistent tradition in the philosophy of language that turned its back on any problem about the nature of belief or judgement, and satisfied itself with the sentence or sometimes the utterance, as the bearer of truth. Compared with judgements or propositions, sentences and utterances might seem to be reassuringly solid: concrete, datable, manageable empirical items. For writers starting here, at least one side of the equation is under control, and then attention switches to the other side—the facts or situations or states of affairs that serve to make sentences true (or, if we are deflationists, attention switches to explaining why we need not worry about the other side). It will be for the reader to judge whether this is an improvement or a retrogression. It is, for example,

---

[17] This problem is not avoided by reminding ourselves that the sequence is an *ordered* triple. For there is no guarantee that anyone contemplating the ordered triple takes the first element to be the subject that does the loving. There are other ways of mapping elements of the triple onto a judgement or a fact. This echoes the difficulty of seeing facts as combinations of things. Frege had earlier made a contribution to this problem by comparing predicates to functions, introducing 'unsaturated' elements into the proposition.

a major part of Strawson's objection to Austin that the latter had simply mistaken the grammar of ascriptions of truth, by attaching them to utterances rather than statements.

The preference for sentences is, however, reinforced by at least two developments in recent philosophy. One is Tarski's influential work on truth. Tarski sought 'a materially adequate and formally correct definition of the term "true sentence"'.[18] We say more about Tarski's definition later. From the outset, Tarski described his project in terms of sentences. The definition that Tarski constructed was limited to the sentences of formalized languages—in Tarski's view, if we bring formal methods to bear on natural languages, contradictions associated with the Liar paradox inevitably arise. Nevertheless philosophers have applied Tarski's methods and ideas to natural languages, preserving for sentences the role of truth-bearer. The other development is the general mistrust of any notion of a proposition or judgement, most famously voiced by Quine.

If propositions are deemed disreputable, and good work seems mostly to proceed by embracing sentences, then concerns about the nature of judgement may seem to drop away. Dispensing with propositions Quine championed 'disquotationalism', a prominent contemporary form of deflationism that takes sentences to be the primary truth-bearers. According to Quine, saying

> 'snow is white' is true

is just an indirect way of saying something about the world—namely, that snow is white. So why employ 'true' at all, if instead we can talk directly about the world? The disquotationalist answer is that we do not always attach 'true' to a quote-name of a sentence. We may, for example, combine 'true' with a definite description ('What Claire said yesterday was true'), or a quantifier ('Every sentence of the form "p or not p" is true'). In the first case, our use of 'true' allows us to affirm something Claire said even if we cannot supply a quote-name of her utterance. What we say is equivalent to an infinite disjunction:

---

[18] Tarski, 'The Concept of Truth in a Formalized Language', in *Logic, Semantics, Metamathematics* (2nd edn.), trans. J. H. Woodger, ed. J. Corcoran (Indianapolis, 1983), 152. There is disagreement about Tarski's motivations: e.g. according to some, Tarski was after a physicalistic reduction of semantic concepts (see e.g. H. Field, 'Tarski's Theory of Truth', *Journal of Philosophy*, 69 (1972)), while according to others, Tarski was after an eliminative definition that would guarantee that a language for which 'true' could be defined was not subject to paradox and contradiction (see J. Etchemendy, 'Tarski on Truth and Logical Consequence', *Journal of Symbolic Logic*, 53 (1988); support for this reading can be found in Tarski (Ch. IX in this volume, 127).

What Claire said='aardvarks amble' and aardvarks amble
or what Claire said = 'antelopes graze' and antelopes graze
or . . . .

In the second case, by predicating 'true' of all sentences of a certain form, we affirm an infinite conjunction:

Tom is mortal or Tom is not mortal,
and snow is white or snow is not white,
and . . . .

So it is not just that the truth predicate is 'a device of disquotation';[19] it is also a device for expressing infinite conjunctions and disjunctions.[20] And these infinite conjunctions and disjunctions are about the world— about aardvarks, antelopes, Tom, and snow, among other things. Whether we mention sentences via quote-names, definite descriptions, or quantification, the truth predicate serves 'to point through the sentences to the reality'.[21]

If an important logical role of 'true' is to express infinite disjunctions and conjunctions, then the following disquotational definition of truth appears natural:

DisquT: x is true iff $(x = \text{'}s_1\text{'} \ \& \ s_1)$ or $(x = \text{'}s_2\text{'} \ \& \ s_2)$ or . . . ,

where $\text{'}s_1\text{'}$, $\text{'}s_2\text{'}$, . . . abbreviate sentences.[22] We may notice that Tarski's T-sentences

$\text{'}s_1\text{'}$ is true iff s_1
$\text{'}s_2\text{'}$ is true iff s_2
$\vdots$

---

[19] W. V. O. Quine, *Philosophy of Logic* (Englewood Cliffs, 1970), 12.

[20] See S. Leeds, 'Theories of Reference and Truth', *Erkenntnis*, 13 (1978), 111–29; H. Field, 'The Deflationary Conception of Truth', in MacDonald and Wright (eds.), *Fact, Science and Morality*, 85–117; Field, Ch. XIX in this vol.; Gupta, Ch. XVI in this vol.

[21] Quine, *Philosophy of Logic*, 11.

[22] Suppose that for x we put 'What Claire said yesterday'. Then among the infinitely many quote names $\text{'}s_1\text{'}$, $\text{'}s_2\text{'}$, . . . that occur in the definiens, there will be one, and only one, that is the quote name of what Claire said. Suppose this quote name is $\text{'}s_k\text{'}$. Then the disjunct 'what Claire said yesterday=$\text{'}s_k\text{'}$ & s_k' is the only true disjunct in the definiens—all the others will contain false identity statements. If we drop these false disjuncts, we obtain:

What Claire said yesterday is true iff what Claire said yesterday = $\text{'}s_k\text{'}$ & s_k.

So the truth of what Claire said is just a matter of the disquotation of its quote name. This is just the result we would expect from a disquotational definition of truth. Such a definition is suggested by remarks in Leeds, 'Theories of Reference and Truth', 121–1 and n. 10; and versions of it are presented explicitly in Field, 'Deflationary Conception of Truth', 58; M. Resnik, 'Immanent Truth', *Mind*, 99 (1990), 412; and M. David, *Correspondence and Disquotation* (Oxford: 1994), ch. 4 and p. 107.

are easy logical consequences of DisquT, given a suitable infinitary logic.[23] So, given such a logic, the definition satisfies Tarski's condition of material adequacy on a definition of truth.[24] Here is one way to present disquotationalism, in terms of a disquotational definition of truth. Alternatively, we might present disquotationalism as an axiomatic theory, where the axioms are the T-sentences. Either way, disquotationalism is an infinitary account of truth: it is expressed either in terms of an infinitary definition or in terms of infinitely many axioms. And this may give us pause.

We might instead turn to this finitely stated schematic definition:

x is a true sentence iff $\exists p(x = 'p' \ \& \ p)$.[25]

Obvious problems arise if we interpret the quantifier objectually.[26] But the alternative move to a substitutional reading has its difficulties, because there is a threat of circularity. Substitutional quantification is typically characterized in terms of truth (more specifically, in terms of true substitution instances).[27] A disquotationalist might abandon a direct definition of truth in favour of a recursive account, according to which 'true' is defined Tarski-style in terms of the more basic notions of reference and satisfaction. Given a language with a finite stock of names and predicates,

---

[23] e.g. put 'snow is white' for x. We will obtain just one true disjunct on the right. If we eliminate the false disjuncts, the definition yields:

'snow is white' is true iff 'snow is white' = 'snow is white' and snow is white.

(Compare the reasoning in n. 22, above.) Dropping the trivial identity conjunct on the right-hand side, we obtain the T-sentence:

'snow is white' is true iff snow is white.

For a discussion that bears on DisquT and infinitary logic, see David, *Correspondence and Disquotation*, 100–4.

[24] This condition, that all the T-sentences follow from the definition, is stated on p. 120 of this vol. Elsewhere Tarski endorses a definition of truth just like DisquT, but limited to languages that contain only a *finite* number of sentences that can be enumerated. See A. Tarski, 'The Concept of Truth in Formalized Languages', in *Logic, Semantics, Metamathematics* (2nd edn.) trans. and ed. John Corcoran (Indianapolis, 1983), 152–278, esp. 188). Even in the general case, where a language may contain infinitely many sentences, Tarski considers each T-sentence to be a 'partial definition of truth', and goes on to say: 'The general definition has to be, in a certain sense, a logical conjunction of all these partial definitions' (p. 120 in this vol.). As he immediately notes, since the number of partial definitions may be infinite, we will have to explain what is meant by a 'logical conjunction of infinitely many sentences'. Tarski himself deals with the complication by adopting the recursive method (see below).

[25] Following Tarski, 'Concept of Truth in Formalized Languages', 159.

[26] There is the problem of quantification into quotes. And the string '$x = "p"$ & p' is grammatically ill-formed, since the variable 'p', taken as an objectual variable, cannot serve as a conjunct.

[27] See David, *Correspondence and Disquotation*, 78–93; P. Horwich, *Truth* (Oxford, 1990, 26–8); Davidson, Ch. XVII. In this vol., 317–18. Field has suggested that we explain substitutional quantification in terms of infinite conjunctions and disjunctions, leading us back to the infinitary DisquT (see Field, 'The Deflationary Conception of Truth', 57–9, and David, *Correspondence and Disquotation*, 98 ff.).

reference may be disquotationally defined by a finite list of sentences of the form '"a" refers to a', and satisfaction by a finite list of sentences of the form 'x satisfies "F" iff x is F'. In this way, reference and satisfaction are finitely defined—and so truth is finitely defined too. But such a recursive disquotationalist is restricted to languages whose sentences have the appropriate kind of logical form. And there is an array of truths that are notoriously hard to fit into the Tarskian mould: belief attributions, counterfactuals, modal assertions, statements of probability, and so on.[28]

In short, there is a question about the very statement of the disquotational theory. There is also a question about its scope. According to the disquotational definition of truth, the sentence 'Penguins waddle' is true, given that penguins waddle. And on the axiomatic presentation, given the T-sentence '"Penguins waddle" is true iff penguins waddle' and given that penguins do waddle, we may infer that the sentence 'Penguins waddle' is true. But 'Penguins waddle' may be a *false* sentence of some language other than English. This is one reason for supposing that the disquotational theory must be restricted in scope, restricted perhaps to the sentences of a single language. And there is reason to think that even this restriction is not enough. The sentences within the scope of the definition are used (as well as mentioned) in the definiens; and in the axiomatic T-sentences, every sentence to which 'true' applies is used (as well as mentioned). If we are to understand the definiens, or understand all of the axiomatic T-sentences, we must understand each of these sentences. And even if the sentences are restricted to a single language, say English, such an understanding would require 'massive conceptual resources', to use Gupta's phrase (Chapter XVI, 297). If the scope of the definition goes beyond the English sentences that we understand, then our understanding of the definiens and the T-sentences, and hence our understanding of 'true', appears to be compromised.

Some disquotationalists favour a restriction to the idiolect of the speaker.[29] For example, according to Field's characterization of 'pure disquotational truth', a person can meaningfully apply 'true' only to utterances she understands. Field suggests, as a heuristic, that when I say a sentence is true (in the pure disquotational sense) I am saying that it is true-as-I-understand-it. And Field goes on to characterize pure disquotational truth in terms of a strong equivalence: my claim that utterance u is true (that is, true-as-I-understand-it) is cognitively equivalent to u (as I understand it). So the T-sentence:

[28] See Field, Ch. XIX in this vol., 374; Horwich, Ch. XIV in this vol., 253–4; David, *Correspondence and Disquotation*, 117–19.
[29] See Field, Ch. XIV in this vol.; Resnik, 'Immanent Truth'.

(T) 'Aardvarks amble' is true iff aardvarks amble

expresses a cognitive equivalence—according to Field, a T-sentence holds 'of conceptual necessity', and enjoys an 'axiomatic status' (Chapter XIX, 362, 372). In general, we should expect the disquotationalist to confer some kind of necessity on the T-sentences, given that the T-sentences are either the axioms of the theory or logical consequences of a definition along the lines of DisquT.

But we may feel a strong pull in the other direction: surely the T-sentences are contingent, not necessary. At first sight, rather than serve as an axiom or a partial definition of truth, (T) serves to say something contingent about a particular English inscription or type of inscription. It is, after all, a contingent matter that 'aardvarks amble' means what it does, or is used the way in which we use it. Consider a possible world w in which aardvarks amble, and the sentence 'aardvarks amble' is used to mean what we mean by 'pigs fly'. (T) is false in w: the left-hand side is false because in world w the sentence 'aardvarks amble' is not true, but the right-hand side of (T) is true, because aardvarks amble in w. So while (T) is true in the actual world, it is only contingently true. Or to put it another way: the sentence 'aardvarks amble' might not have had the truth conditions that aardvarks amble; it might have had the truth conditions that pigs fly.

At what point should the disquotationalist resist this reasoning? Note that while the used sentence on the right side of (T) is taken to be a sentence of actual English (which truly describes how things are in w), the mentioned sentence on the left is taken to have the meaning it has in w, and is evaluated according to this meaning and how things are in w. In reasoning to the contingency of (T), we apply 'true' to an interpreted sentence that does not belong to our idiolect. So it is here, presumably, that Field for one will balk: pure disquotational truth cannot be applied in this way. When I say that a sentence is true (in the pure disquotational sense), I am saying that it is true-as-I-actually-understand-it, not true-as-I-might-have-understood-it. The mentioned sentence on the left of (T) must be the same sentence as the used sentence on the right—the same sentence of my idiolect.

It is sometimes claimed[30] that disquotationalists can guarantee the necessity of the T-sentences by the restriction to idiolect only if the sentences in my idiolect are *necessarily* in my idiolect. The argument runs as follows. Let 'true-in-M' abbreviate 'true in my idiolect'. Consider the T-sentence:

---

[30] See e.g. David, *Correspondence and Disquotation*, 134–5.

(T′) 'Aardvarks amble' is true-in-M iff aardvarks amble.

Suppose there's a possible world in which aardvarks amble and in which I speak the same idiolect M, but 'aardvarks amble' is not in M. Then (T′) is false in this possible world. And so the disquotationalist cannot allow a sentence to belong only contingently to my idiolect. As a consequence there can be no changes within my idiolect: if I learn a new sentence or forget an old one, I speak a new idiolect. To most philosophers this would be a counter-intuitive result.

This may be a powerful argument against some forms of disquotationalism, but against Field's version it seems to have little force. In the possible world we envisaged, it is false that 'aardvarks amble' is true-in-M. So it is assumed that the predicate 'true-in-M' can fail to apply to a sentence which is actually a true sentence of my idiolect (supposing of course that aardvarks amble). But then the predicate 'true-in-M' cannot capture 'true' in Field's pure disquotational sense. For, on our understanding of this sense of 'true', to say of a sentence that it is true is to say that it is true-as-I-actually-understand-it. There is no possible world in which 'true' fails to apply to a sentence which is actually in my idiolect and is actually true. Compare this remark of Field's:

> 'So even if 'snow is white' had been used in English pretty much the way that 'grass is red' is actually used, 'snow is white' would still have been true in the purely disquotational sense.'[31]

'True' in the purely disquotational sense cannot apply to true sentences outside my idiolect—but it also cannot fail to apply to sentences actually within my idiolect, even if those sentences belong only contingently to my idiolect.

These restrictions on pure disquotational truth are very strong. They secure my understanding of the definiens of DisquT and the axiomatic T-sentences; and they secure a strong necessity for the T-sentences. But one may feel that we are a long way from our commonsensical notion of truth. After all, we do want to say that we might have used our words in such a way that 'snow is white' would not have been true. And we do apply 'true' to sentences beyond those of our actual idiolect. We do this when we express our modal intuition that 'aardvarks amble' might have had the truth conditions that pigs fly. We do it when we say 'Most of what Socrates said was true', even though we have little or no understanding of ancient Greek. And we are perfectly willing to admit that there are true sentences of our language (English) that we do not understand.

---

[31] p. 381 in this vol.

18   SIMON BLACKBURN AND KEITH SIMMONS

The broad concern here is that disquotationalism makes a subject's conception of *truth* too much dependent upon the question of which language she understands, and how much of a language she understands. A speaker ignorant of aardvarks will not know what would make the sentence 'aardvarks amble' true. This is what her lack of zoological knowledge consists in. But it seems strange to think that her notion of truth is itself impoverished. Similarly, if I expand my understanding, bringing new sentences into my repertoire, it is strange to say that I thereby expand my conception of truth. And if two people speak entirely distinct languages, then nothing will be in common between the list of T-sentences we construct for one and that which we construct for the other, yet we would not want to infer that their conceptions of truth are therefore entirely distinct.

5. BACK TO PROPOSITIONS?

According to Field, we should be *methodological deflationists* (Chapter XIX, 367–8), taking pure disquotational truth to be the fundamental truth concept as long as this adequately serves our practical and theoretical purposes. The present worry is that pure disquotational truth is just too restricted to serve these purposes. Perhaps, then, we would do better to abandon sentences, and return once more to the idea that judgements, beliefs, or propositions are the fundamental truth-bearers. Instead of working in terms of (T), we work in terms of

(P) The proposition that aardvarks amble is true if and only if aardvarks amble.

According to Horwich, the basic truth concept is propositional-truth, not utterance-truth or sentence-truth. And in its application to propositions, the truth predicate is unrestricted: 'true' applies to all propositions. To accommodate propositions that are not yet expressible, Horwich supposes that every proposition is expressed by a sentence in some *possible* language. He also assumes that whatever can be expressed in some possible language can be said in some possible extension of English. So in order to encompass all propositions we need only consider possible extensions of English.[32] The axioms of Horwich's minimal theory are all the instances of the schema:

The proposition that p is true iff p,

[32] Horwich, *Truth*, 20 n. 4.

and there is an axiom for each proposition, whether or not that proposition is actually expressible. Acceptable substituends for the occurrences of 'p' are sentences of English, actual and possible. So Horwich's minimal theory is composed of infinitely many axioms, infinitely many of which we cannot formulate or understand. We could hardly be further removed from speakers' idiolects.

Clearly, understanding 'true' cannot be a matter of understanding all the axioms of the minimal theory. According to Horwich, our understanding of 'true'—our knowledge of its meaning—consists in our disposition to accept a priori those axioms that we *can* formulate.[33] This disposition provides the best explanation of our overall use of the term 'true'. So, by appeal to the view that meaning is given by use, Horwich maintains that the meaning of 'true' is constituted by this disposition. This provides the truth predicate with a fixed meaning, even when it is applied to propositions that we cannot formulate or understand.

We can now see how Horwich will address the issues that confronted the disquotationalist. For Horwich, understanding 'true' is not a matter of understanding all the axioms of the truth theory, and so an understanding of 'true' does not require massive conceptual resources. Foreign languages present no special problem, because 'true' applies to all propositions, and in particular to all those expressed in foreign languages. And there seems less room for controversy about the modal status of:

(P) The proposition that aardvarks amble is true iff aardvarks amble.

(P) makes no reference to any apparently contingent fact about English, and it is interlinguistic rather than intralinguistic. We can maintain that (P) is a priori, for everyone is in a position to know that (P), whether they speak English or not—just as the speakers of a foreign language know that $2+2=4$, even if they don't recognize this sentence as an expression of what they know. So (P) cannot be criticized as presenting a contingent fact about English as part of the definition of truth.

The problem instead is whether the notion of a proposition is as innocent of involvement with truth as deflationism requires. Let us take a closer look at Horwich's minimalist schema:

(M) The proposition that p is true iff p.

Instances of this schematic generalization are obtained by replacing the two occurrences of 'p' by tokens of an English sentence. For example, putting a token of 'aardvarks amble' for each occurrence of 'p', we get (P).

---

[33] Horwich, Ch. XIV in this vol., and *Truth*, 36.

We may feel some discomfort here: the tokens of 'aardvarks amble' are placed in two quite different contexts. The first token forms part of a referring term, the term 'the proposition that p'. The second constitutes the right-hand side of the biconditional. With Davidson, we may wonder how these two appearances of 'aardvarks amble' are connected (Chapter XVII, 318). At any rate, it is clear that certain conditions must be placed on such an instantiation. We can list four (see Horwich, Chapter XIV, 244–5):

(i) each 'p' is replaced with tokens of an (actual or possible) English sentence,

(ii) these tokens are given the same interpretation,

(iii) under that interpretation they express a proposition, and

(iv) the terms 'that' and 'proposition' are given their English meanings.

So the very statement of Horwich's minimal theory is shot through with semantical concepts and talk of sentences. This may raise two concerns. First, since talk of sentence-tokens is unavoidable anyway, might it not be advisable to work with sentences (or token utterances) all along? Why not be more economical and adopt the schema

'p' is true iff p,

constrained by conditions (i) and (ii)? This avoids the overt appeal to propositions, which will come as a relief to anyone, like Quine, who finds them suspect or mysterious. The thought is encouraged by Horwich's own claim that the minimal theory of truth for propositions is easily inter-derivable with a minimal theory of truth for utterances.[34]

The second concern is prompted by the observation that when we specify the axioms of the minimal theory we must employ a number of semantical concepts: the notion of a *language* (specifically, English), the notion of an *interpretation*, the relation of *expressing*, and, of course, the notion of a *proposition*. Since the minimal theory of truth itself depends on these notions, the concept of truth cannot be used to explain them. So for the minimalist, the challenge is this: explain these fundamental semantical concepts, but do not appeal to the notion of truth anywhere in your explanations. Indeed both Horwich and Field suggest that deflationism about truth goes hand in hand with deflationism about reference, and if this is right there can be no appeal to reference either.[35]

---

[34] Horwich, *Truth*, 103–8.

[35] See Horwich, Ch. XIV, 248, and Field, Ch. XIX, 365. It is not entirely clear that a deflationist theory of truth implies a deflationist theory of reference. Philosophers such as Strawson deny the substantiality of 'facts' without denying the existence of robust word to world reference links. Elements of a sentence can pick out elements of the world, without the sentence as a whole corresponding to anything such as a 'complex' of such elements.

According to Horwich, a *use* theory of meaning will do the job.[36] (For example, Horwich assumes that a use-theoretic account can be given of 'u and v express the same proposition'.)[37] So a use theory of meaning does a lot of work for the minimalist, supplying a meaning for 'true' and for the semantical terms needed to state the minimal theory. And it does all this in terms that make no reference to truth. Many philosophers would doubt whether this can be done, and this is the central issue between Davidson and Horwich in the Chapters XVII and XIV respectively. Strawson anticipated the difficulty: 'And it is, indeed, very strange that people have so often proceeded by saying "Well, we're pretty clear what a statement is, aren't we? Now let us settle *the further question*, namely what it is for a statement to be true" '.[38]

Strawson's point is also visible in Ramsey's paper (Chapter VI). Having made deflationary noises about the concept of truth, Ramsey immediately goes on to raise worries about the notion of *belief.* So, for example, Ramsey would dismiss any problem about what it is for a judgement to be *true.* Just make the judgement, as either (T) or (P) instructs. But he thinks there is a big question over what is involved in making any judgement in the first place. His own approach is, in effect, behaviouristic. In particular cases, he thinks belief can indeed be identified without any reference to truth, or to situations or states of affairs, or to the worldly side of things. He thinks a belief in, say, the probability of a horse winning a race can be identified by means of the use such judgements have, for instance in voicing commitments to particular betting rates on events, at least under idealized conditions. Ramsey's work therefore provides an instance of the *kind* of thing Horwich thinks we must be able to do in general, which is to provide an account of meaning in terms that are entirely free of semantic notions such as reference and truth. Another hopeful example would be an expressive theory of ethical judgement, which explains what we are doing entirely without reference to ethical facts or situations.

But when it comes to generalizing such cases it must, we think, be doubted if the project could possibly succeed. On the face of it, there is a serious dilemma in front of the deflationist. Imagine a satisfactory account of how we use a simple sentence like 'this is a cat'. Suppose first that this account proceeds by saying things like: 'This' is an indexical that refers to an associated object on occasions of use; 'cat' is a predicate true of all and only cats. Then the deflationist promise evaporates, for the semantic terms reference and truth are presupposed by the account of meaning. But

---

[36] Field also advocates a 'truth-free' account, but one in which conceptual role is one ingredient of meaning and 'indication relations' are another. See Ch. XIX, 356–9.

[37] p. 249 in this vol.   [38] p. 171 in this vol.

suppose on the other hand that the account does not make these overt appeals to reference and truth. So for instance, suppose it proceeds using notions like causal links to the brain, or the fixation of attention on things, as key notions in understanding the use of demonstratives. And it might try similarly to talk of causal chains and the conceptual or inferential role of the term 'cat', thereby giving the use and thence the meaning of that term. To be successful, we might argue, it would have to fill in these notions enough so that we see how causal links, or attention-fixing or conceptual role together give a reasonable approximation to reference and truth. For instance, if, when we announce of some animal that it is a cat, for all the theory tells us we might be saying 'this is a rabbit' or 'that (other thing) is a cat', then the theory is inadequate. Indeed, we might think that the account of meaning in terms of use can only be satisfactory if it enables us to *infer* a corresponding T-sentence. But in that case, what could have been intended by denying that reference and truth are substantial or robust notions? They seem to have proved their robustness via the robust, non-deflationary story that started out trying to do without them, but ended up constructing them.[39]

6. THE LIAR

Sooner or later, any truth theorist—deflationist or not—must confront the notorious Liar paradox. It is perhaps surprising how little deflationists have to say about the Liar. Field and Horwich recognize that certain restrictions and exceptions must be made because of the semantic paradoxes,[40] but there the matter is allowed to rest. According to Horwich,

> There is no reason to suppose that the minimalist answers that are advanced in this essay could be undermined by any particular constructive solution to the paradoxes—so we can temporarily set those problems aside.[41]

But it remains to be seen whether deflationism is compatible with positive attempts to resolve the liar.

Consider a Liar sentence like

    (1) (1) is false

or

    (2) (2) is not true.

---

[39] Field for one is aware of this danger. There is always the possibility that when the deflationist's explanations are done 'he will have reconstructed the inflationist's relation "S has the truth conditions *p*", in fact if not in name' (p. 367 in this vol.; see also p. 356).

[40] See e.g. Field, Ch. XIX in this vol., 353, n. 1; Horwich, Ch. XIV in this vol., and *Truth*, 41–2.

[41] *Truth*, 42.

If we instantiate the disquotational definition DisquT to (1) or (2), a contradiction is easily reached, assuming classical logic and semantics. And since the T-sentences for (1) and (2) are contradictory, they cannot serve as axioms of a consistent disquotational theory. Principled restrictions are needed.

One way to avoid liars and truth-tellers is to define truth for a language in which 'true' does not appear. But this restriction is surely too severe. Deflationists are after an account of truth for natural languages or for speakers' idiolects, and 'true' is certainly a term of English and a term of my idiolect. And a perfectly ordinary utterance involving 'true' can turn out to be paradoxical. Suppose I write on the board:

(3) The sentence written on the board in room 101 is not true.

If a false sentence is written on the board in room 101, (3) is straightforwardly true. If I am in room 101, and I don't realize that I am, then I have unwittingly produced a Liar sentence. In this case, (3) is paradoxical not in virtue of its intrinsic syntactic or semantic form, but in virtue of the empirical facts.[42] If the disquotationalist throws out paradoxical utterances on the grounds that they belong to a language beyond the scope of the theory, then she will also need to throw out utterances of the same type that are within the intended scope of the theory. The deflationist must find some other approach to semantic paradox.

A familiar approach to the liar adopts a non-classical semantics that allows truth-value gaps. On such an approach, Liar sentences are neither true nor false. Now the correspondence account seems to have a natural enough way with gaps. If we characterize the correspondence theory as follows:

A sentence is true iff it corresponds to a state of affairs that obtains,

we can say that a sentence is false if it corresponds to a state of affairs that does not obtain, and neither true nor false if it fails to correspond to any state of affairs. Truth-value gaps do not seem to compromise the correspondence intuition.

Are gaps available to the disquotationalist? It is far from clear that they are. The natural disquotational definition of falsity is this:

DisquF: x is false iff $(x = \text{'}s_1\text{'} \ \& \ {\sim}s_1)$ or $(x = \text{'}s_2\text{'} \ \& \ {\sim}s_2)$ or . . . ,

where 's_1', 's_2', abbreviate sentences. Suppose we assume that some sentence 's_k' is neither true nor false. Then, using an infinitary logic which is

---

[42] As Kripke has pointed out, there is a riskiness to our ordinary uses of 'true': under suitably unfavourable circumstances, virtually any use of 'true', however innocent it may look, leads to paradox. See S. Kripke, 'Outline of a Theory of Truth', *Journal of Philosophy*, 72 (1975), 690–716.

otherwise classical, we obtain a contradiction: $\sim s_k$ follows from DisquT and $\sim\sim s_k$ follows from DisquF.[43]

In the face of this reasoning, the disquotationalist might place gappy sentences beyond the scope of the disquotational account. Or she might try to block the reasoning by adopting a non-classical logic (to be articulated in terms that cannot include truth, falsity, or gaps). Either way, the disquotationalist must supply a positive account of gaps if they are to play an explanatory role, and it is not obvious how that is to be done.

But suppose for a moment that a disquotational account of gaps is forthcoming. Then the disquotationalist might hope to avoid restrictions on DisquT and the T-schema. Consider for example the T-sentence associated with (1):

'(1) is false' is true iff (1) is false.

It might be proposed that this biconditional is true, because both sides are gappy. In general, suppose that 'p' is a Liar sentence. The idea is that

'p' is true iff p

may be counted true if both sides are gappy. So no contradiction follows if we instantiate DisquT to 'p', or take the T-sentence for 'p' as an axiom. Instead 'true' and 'false' will be ineliminable terms—DisquT will be a circular definition, and some T-sentences will contain ineliminable uses of 'true' and 'false' on their right-hand sides. In the spirit of the 'revision'

---

[43] Here is a derivation of the contradiction. Replacing x in DisquT by 's_k', we obtain:

's_k' is true iff ('s_k'='s_1' & s_1) or ('s_k'='s_2' & s_2) or ... ('s_k'='s_k' & s_k) or ....

Only one of the disjuncts on the right-hand side is true (all the others contain false identity statements). Eliminating the false disjuncts, we obtain:

(a) 's_k' is true iff 's_k'='s_k' & s_k.

Eliminating the trivial identity conjunct on the right-hand side, we arrive at the T-sentence for 's_k':

(b) 's_k' is true iff 's_k'

Since 's_k' is neither true nor false, 's_k' is not true, and so, given (b), we obtain

(c) $\sim s_k$.

Next replace 'x' in DisquF by 's_k'. We obtain

's_k' is false iff ('s_k'='s_1' & $\sim s_1$) or ('s_k'='s_2' & $\sim s_2$) or ... ('s_k'='s_k' & $\sim s_k$) or ....

Eliminating the false disjuncts on the right-hand side we obtain

(d) 's_k' is false iff 's_k'='s_k' & $\sim s_k$.

Eliminating the true conjunct on the right-hand side, we obtain

(e) 's_k' is false iff $\sim s_k$.

Since 's_k' is neither true nor false, 's_k' is not false, and so, given (e), we obtain

(f) $\sim\sim s_k$.

And we have a contradiction at lines (c) and (f).

theory of truth, we might accept each T-biconditional as a partial definition of truth for all sentences—liars included—and accept the consequence that truth is a circular notion.[44] Such an approach may well tempt the disquotationalist: even the truth of Liar sentences is a matter of disquotation.

However, it seems that the disquotationalist cannot take this tack. Consider again the T-sentence for the Liarlike sentence 'p'. We are taking 'p' to be gappy. So the right-hand side of the T-sentence is gappy. But the left-hand side is false: it is false that 'p' is true.[45] So the T-sentence is not true. This is an instance of a more general problem: given a gappy sentence (whether a Liar sentence or not), the corresponding T-sentence appears to be untrue. In order to maintain the truth of such a T-sentence, we might introduce a *weak* notion of truth,[46] where ' "p" is true' always has the same semantic status as 'p' (In particular, if 'p' is gappy, so is ' "p" is true'.) The revision theory is a theory of this weak notion.[47] But it would seem that the disquotationalist cannot ignore the *strong* notion of truth, where if we say of a gappy sentence that it is true, we have said something false. Presumably the deflationist wants to deflate all truth, weak and strong.

---

[44] We should emphasize that the revision theory itself does not appeal to gaps. The revision theory of truth was first developed in A. Gupta, 'Truth and Paradox', *Journal of Philosophical Logic*, 11 (1982) as a response to the Liar paradox. See also A. Gupta and N. Belnap, *The Revision Theory of Truth* (Cambridge, Mass., 1993). At the heart of the revision theory is the idea that all the instances of the T-schema together give a complete and correct definition of the concept of truth. Since no restriction is placed on the T-schema, there will be instantiations to sentences that essentially refer to truth (e.g. Liar sentences). Consequently, this definition is circular.

According to Gupta and Belnap, the revision theory of truth 'is a consequence of combining a general theory of definitions and Tarski's suggestion that the biconditionals be viewed as partial definitions. Tarski's suggestion brings out clearly the circularity in the notion of truth ...' (*Revision Theory of Truth*, 142).

The circularity in the concept of truth gives rise to a revision process—for certain sentences, their truth or falsity is not a stable feature. (Consider for example the Liar sentence 'This sentence is false'. If we ascribe truth to it, we must revise that ascription, declaring it false, and then in turn revise that ascription, and so on indefinitely.) According to the revision theory: '... the objects of the world are not neatly divided into those that have the property of truth and those that lack it, but rather they stand in a hypothetical relation to this property: if an object were to have (or lack) the property of truth, would it maintain that status?' (A. Yaqub, *The Liar speaks the Truth: A Defense of the Revision Theory of Truth* (Oxford, 1993) 5.

[45] Compare an argument of Dummett's (see M. Dummett, 'Truth', *Proceedings of the Aristotelian Society*, 59 (1959), 141–62) which arises in the course of examining Frege's claim that 'It is true that p' has the same sense as p: 'Suppose that p contains a singular term which has a sense but no reference: then, according to Frege, p expresses a proposition which has no truth value. This proposition is therefore not true, and hence the statement "It is true that p" will be *false*. p will therefore not have the same sense as "It is true that p", since the latter is false while the former is not.' (p. 145).

[46] Gupta and Belnap present this distinction in *Revision Theory of Truth*, 22, citing S. Yablo, 'Truth and Reflection', *Journal of Philosophical Logic*, 14 (1985), 297–349.

[47] See Gupta, and Belnap, *Revision Theory of Truth*, 22, 29 and n. 52.

The strong notion of truth is related to strengthened reasoning about the Liar. Versions of strengthened reasoning have provided the primary motivation for contextual views of truth.[48] For example, given the Liar sentence:

(L) (L) is not true,

we may go on to declare (L) gappy. But then it follows that

(P) (L) is not true.

But given (P) and given what (L) says, it seems that we may infer

(R) (L) is true.

On a contextual analysis, the reasoning is valid. (L) is *pathological* in its context of utterance. But then we can stand back from its context of utterance, and assess (L) on the basis both of its pathologicality and what it says. Since it is pathological and so not true, and since it says it isn't true, (L) can be assessed as true in the subsequent, reflective context of (R). On some but not all contextual views, the shift from the context of (L) to the reflective context of (P) and (R) is a shift in a Tarskian hierarchy from a lower to a higher level of language.[49]

It is not easy to square such contextual accounts with disquotationalism. If (L) really is semantically pathological, then it is so because it attributes lack of truth to itself: 'true' in (L) is ineliminable, and cannot be disquoted away. And if (L) really is true (when assessed from a reflective context, or from a higher level of language) then the disquotationalist must admit truths from which 'true' cannot be disquoted. And this compromises the disquotational conception of truth.

Strengthened reasoning also presents problems for the prosentential theory of truth. According to the prosentential theory, 'true' is used in forming prosentences. In the discourse:

Mary: Chicago is large
John: If that is true, it probably has a large airport

the expression 'that is true' is a prosentence, which shares its content with its antecedent, namely 'Chicago is large'. In a parallel fashion, the Liar

---

[48] See C. Parsons, 'The Liar Paradox', *Journal of Philosophical Logic*, 3 (1974), 381–412; T. Burge, 'Semantical Paradox', *Journal of Philosophy*, 76 (1979), 169–98; J. Barwise and J. Etchemendy, *The Liar* (Oxford, 1987); H. Gaifman, 'Pointers to Truth', *Journal of Philosophy*, 89 (1992), 223–61 and K. Simmons, *Universality and The Liar: An Essay on Truth and the Diagonal Argument* (Cambridge, 1993).
[49] See Burge, 'Semantical Paradox' and Barwise and Etchemendy, *The Liar* for contextual accounts that are hierarchical; the contextual account in Simmons, *Universality and the Liar*, rejects the hierarchy in favour of a 'singularity' account.

sentence 'this is false' relies on its antecedent for its content, but, in the words of Grover, 'it is, unfortunately, its own antecedent and, as such, fails as an antecedent supplier of content'.[50] According to the prosential account, Liar sentences fail to have content.

Consider, however, the strengthened reasoning, and (P) in particular. In a discussion of strengthened reasoning Grover remarks that 'if "true" is prosential' then (P) 'fails to express a proposition'.[51] The conditional does seem true: according to the prosential treatment (P) relies for its content on that of its antecedent (L)—but (L) has no content. Yet it is surely highly counter-intuitive that (P) is without content. Further, if we accept reflective evaluations like (R), then the prosential account is closed off to us. If Liar sentences are true or false (on reflection), then they cannot be without content.

In contrast, the correspondence intuition remains intact, or so it might be argued. According to the correspondence conception, (L) is true if and only if it corresponds to a state of affairs that obtains. And (L) does. The state of affairs here is a semantic state, that of (L)'s being untrue in its context of utterance. And this state obtains, because (L) is semantically pathological in its context of utterance. According to the correspondence conception, (L) is indeed true. On this correspondence line, (L)'s truth is grounded in a semantic state of affairs, and not a non-semantic state of the world. We cannot represent this fact or state of affairs in non-semantic terms. Perhaps—the correspondence theorist might conclude—this is why the disquotationalist finds strengthened reasoning so intractable.

It seems, then, that the disquotationalist will find little comfort in any of the resolutions of the Liar we have mentioned, whether gap approaches, the revision theory, contextual accounts, or certain hierarchical views. And the difficulties seem not to be confined to the disquotationalist—it is not clear that Horwich's minimalist is any better off. As Horwich himself notes, the move to propositions seems to close off any appeal to gaps.[52] And there is a further issue for the minimalist.

Consider again the Liar sentence

(L) (L) is not true.

Consider the associated instance of the minimalist truth schema (M):

(m) The proposition that (L) is not true is true iff (L) is not true.

What should we make of (m)? What is the proposition referred to on the left-hand side? If, for example, we adopt a contextual theory, then

---

[50] *Prosentential Theory of Truth*, 124.   [51] Ibid. 203.   [52] *Truth*, 80.

we might say that (L) expresses a true proposition. And if we take the right-hand side to be true as well, (m) is true. So (m) is not contradictory at all. We are in danger of losing sight of the Liar. To avoid that, we must bear in mind that (m)'s truth was established by a *prior* contextual theory of truth. Another theory may identify another proposition, or none, as the subject of the left-hand side, and a different truth-value for (m). The problem lies with the schematic expression 'the proposition that p'.[53] Given a Liar sentence, it is a highly non-trivial question as to what proposition, if any, it expresses. It takes a positive account of semantic paradox to determine the reference of 'the proposition that p' when we put a liar sentence for 'p'. We can make sense of (m) only if we're already in possession of a theory of truth. But then it seems that we cannot in general regard instances of Horwich's schema as *axioms* of a theory of truth, for there may be instances whose truth is established by a prior theory.[54]

7. CONCLUSION

These last reflections on the Liar paradox lend support to the contention that we cannot take the phrase 'the proposition that p' for granted, when we reflect upon truth. Deflationists pride themselves on avoiding any engagement with the disputed notion of a fact. But it is much harder for them to avoid engagement with the notion of a proposition, or that of a judgement or idiolect or language, at least while retaining any title to doing philosophy at all. And these notions seem to prove as difficult—and, if we may say so, as robust—as that of truth itself. Gaining an understanding of the nature of the truth-bearers is a common problem faced by deflationists as much as by philosophers on the robust side, and for that matter by contemporary writers just as much as by the older tradition.

Such considerations suggest that the prospects for robust semantic notions, truth included, are by no means as poor as some writers suppose. Perhaps indeed the idea that truth is seriously dyadic is too natural for it ever to disappear from the philosophical scene. It seems that in this area, at least, and in spite of a century of formidable achievements, philosophy is in little danger of talking itself out of a job.

[53] This is also a general concern of Davidson, Ch. XVII in this vol., 318.
[54] For more on deflationism and the liar, see K. Simmons, 'Deflationary Truth and the Liar', *Journal of Philosophical Logic* (forthcoming).

PART I

BACKGROUND 'ROBUST' THEORIES

I

ON TRUTH AND COPYING

F. H. BRADLEY

Mr Joachim in his interesting work on *The Nature of Truth* did, I think, well to discuss once more that view for which truth consists in copying reality. It is a view which, for myself, I have been accustomed to treat as exploded, but it is a natural way of taking things, and, I suppose, can never cease to be popular. And, since from time to time a discussion of this topic is likely to be useful, I will venture to offer some remarks on it here.

The idea that truth consists in mere copying is suggested from many sides. A man through language and ideas has to convey fact to other men, and how can he do this unless his ideas copy fact so far as the purpose requires? And, in dealing practically with the present or the future situation, unless I have mirrored in my mind the main features of that situation, how can I hope to succeed? And in recalling the past we are bound above all things not to alter it, and how can we avoid this unless in some way, however indirect, we produce a copy? Finally truth implies agreement amongst the ideas of separate individuals. And, since this agreement is not made by one or another individual, and so not by all of them, it therefore seems due to all of them following one original fact. But unless they mentally repeat this fact, how, it will be asked, can they follow it?

The above view is natural, but, even as it stands, seems hardly consistent with itself, for how the past or future can be copied is at least not evident. And it is soon in trouble, as is well known, with regard to the sensible properties of things. But, not to dwell on this, the whole theory goes to wreck in principle and at once on a fatal objection. Truth has to copy facts, but on the other side the facts to be copied show already in their nature the work of truth-making. The merely given facts are, in other words, the

From F. H. Bradley, 'On Truth and Copying', in *Essays on Truth and Reality* (Oxford: Clarendon Press, 1914), 107–26. This originally appeared in *Mind*, 16 (1907).

imaginary creatures of false theory. They are manufactured by a mind which abstracts one aspect of the concrete known whole, and sets this abstracted aspect out by itself as a real thing. If, on the other hand, we exaggerate when we maintain that all facts are inferences, yet undeniably much of given fact is inferential. And if we cannot demonstrate that every possible piece of fact is modified by apperception, the outstanding residue may at least perhaps be called insignificant.[1] Or (to put it from the other side) if there really is any datum, outward or inward, which, if you remove the work of the mind, would in its nature remain the same, yet there seems no way of our getting certainly to know of this. And, if truth is to copy fact, then truth at least seems to be in fact unattainable.

If the above objection cannot be met (and I do not know how it can be met) the theory in principle is ruined. In the end truth is not copying; but it is possible, while admitting this, to attempt to save the theory in a modified form. We may draw a distinction between perceptional and reflective thinking. As to what is perceived we may allow that we cannot argue that this is copied, but in any case, we may go on to urge, our ideas must copy our perceptions. And thus, after all, our secondary and reflective truth must seek to mirror reality. But the position taken here, though founded on a distinction, which in itself is important, for the purpose in hand seems wholly ineffectual. And, apart from such difficulties as might once more be raised as to given facts which are past and future, we have only to apply this view in order to find it break down in our hands.

Disjunctive, negative, and hypothetical judgements cannot be taken as all false, and yet cannot fairly be made to conform to our one type of truth. And in general the moment we leave perceived facts and seek explanation—which after all is implied in the desire for truth—we find that we are moving away from the given. Universal and abstract truths are not given facts, nor do they merely reproduce the given, nor are they even confined to the limits of actual perception. And in the end, when we come to general truth about the Universe, it seems impossible to regard this as transcribed from the given Universe. Our truths in short can all of them in some sense be verified in fact, but, if you ask if they all are copied from fact, the answer must be different. And we are driven to admit that, at least when we pass from individual truths, our truth no longer represents fact but merely 'holds' or 'is valid'. And, asking what these phrases mean, we are forced to perceive that both truth and reality go beyond the perceived

---

[1] I am not assuming here that we have no feelings so elementary as to be unmodified by apperception. But any assumption on the other side seems hazardous and could at any rate not extend far. Cf. Bradley, *Essays on Truth and Reality*, 204.

facts. The given facts in other words are not the whole of reality, while truth cannot be understood except in reference to this whole.[2]

We saw in the first place that given facts are even themselves not merely given, but already even in themselves contain truth. And secondly we have seen that, even if the perceived facts were given, truth cannot merely transcribe them. And, since truth goes beyond the given, it is impossible to understand how truth can copy reality. For, before the reality has been reached, there is no original to copy, and, when the reality has been attained, that attainment already is truth, and you cannot gain truth by transcribing it.

I will now break off the consideration of that view for which truth consists in copying fact, and will endeavour briefly to indicate a better way of resolving the problem. But I must begin by pointing out the main error which, if left unremoved, makes the problem insoluble. This error consists in the division of truth from knowledge and of knowledge from reality. The moment that truth, knowledge, and reality are taken as separate, there is no way in which consistently they can come or be forced together. And since on the other hand truth implies that they are somehow united, we have forthwith on our hands a contradiction in principle. And according to the side from which the subject is approached, this contradiction works itself out into a fatal dilemma.

This defect in principle has been illustrated by the view we have been examining, and it may repay us to notice in a different case the result of the self-same error. An attempt is sometimes made to escape from difficulty by insisting that truth is merely what 'holds', or is what merely 'serves' or merely 'works'. But since these phrases are relative and, I presume, relative to something which is known, we have at once a division of truth from knowledge. On the one side is known reality, and on the other side is mere truth, and in short we have repeated the error of that view which took truth as a copy. And the fatal result of our proceeding soon becomes manifest.[3] Truth is merely to be that which subserves something else, and I am to know that this is so, and that this is so is true. But such a truth about truth seems itself to go beyond truth, and our theory is dissolved in self-contradiction.

Let us consider this more in detail. We are, it seems, to take an end, such say as the abstraction of practical success or of felt pleasure, and we are

[2] This is the main conclusion which was urged in Bradley, *Principles of Logic* (London, 1922). It did not occur to me that I should be taken there or anywhere else to be advocating the copy-theory of truth.

[3] Cf. the Note at the end of the chapter.

to understand truth as a means, an external means, to this end. And what, we may hear, can be more plain and intelligible than this? It is, I agree, almost as clear as the former view for which truth merely copied things, and perhaps this suggestion may be an omen. But first let us ask as to our end, is this known or unknown? If it is unknown, how do we know that it is an end served by means? And, if it is known, then what are we going to say of *this* knowledge? Is it true? Can we discuss it? Have we got a truth about our end, and, if so, does 'about' mean no more than merely subserving? I do not myself know how these particular questions should be answered, but in general I cannot see how to defend truth which is external to knowledge or knowledge which is external to reality, and with this I must pass to another difficulty which attaches to the present view. Truth has been taken as being *merely* the means to an end, and we naturally understand this to say that truth is *really* the means. But here at once arises a well-known puzzle. The end, we all agree, in a sense dictates the means, but on the other hand the end, we are accustomed to think, must choose those means which are really possible. We are hence, given the end, in the habit of discussing the means. We have to consider, in short, about suggested means whether they are means really and in truth. But, with this, we seem to have knowledge and truth and reality, certainly all in relation with the one real end, but on the other side all external to it and apparently more or less independent of it. We started in other words by saying 'Truth is nothing beyond that which subserves', and we have ended in explaining that 'Truth is that which in fact and in truth subserves'. And when in a given case a question is raised as to this fact and truth, it is answered apparently by appealing to something other than the end. Any such appeal obviously is inadmissible; but, when we reject it, we seem now to have excluded all truth about our means, just as before we seemed to have no knowledge nor any truth about our end.[4]

And a prescribed remedy, if I rightly understand, is to throw overboard all preconceived ideas as to truth and reality. Truth is merely the ideas which are felt in a certain way, and are felt to dominate in a mind or in a set of minds, and any further question as to their truth is senseless.[5] You may indeed ask psychologically, if you please, how they have come to dominate, but, however they have come to dominate, their truth is the

---

[4] One is, I presume, naturally led to avoid this difficulty by maintaining that our knowledge in the end is intuitive. We have, that is to say, an experience in which reality, truth, and knowledge are one. But, with this, there is an end at once and in principle of the view that truth is an external means to something else. And on our new ground the problem of Error, the question how we can hold for true what is false, obviously threatens to become pressing.

[5] For some further discussion on this point the reader is referred to Bradley, *Essays on Truth and Reality*, ch. XI.

same. If you and I disagree we both so far have truth, and if you argue with me and persuade me, that is one way of agreement. But, if you prefer to knock me on the head, that, so far as truth goes, is the same thing, except that now there is truth not in two heads but one. And as to there being any other truth *about* all this state of things, or in short any truth at all beyond mere prevalence, the whole notion is ridiculous. And, if you deny this, you do but confirm it, since your denial (though of course true) must also be false, since it is true only because in fact it has prevailed. And if you want further proof, you can perhaps demonstrate all this by a downward deduction. For either this or the copy-theory must be the truth about truth, and as the copy-theory will not work, this by inevitable consequence remains as true. But there is no one, I think, who is ready apart from some reserve to accept wholly the above result.

It would be easy, passing on, to point out how the same main error, appearing in other forms, works itself out from other sides into conflicting dilemmas. But the limits of this chapter compel me to proceed. The division of reality from knowledge and of knowledge from truth must in any form be abandoned. And the only way of exit from the maze is to accept the remaining alternative. Our one hope lies in taking courage to embrace the result that reality is not outside truth. The identity of truth knowledge and reality, whatever difficulty that may bring, must be taken as necessary and fundamental. Or at least we have been driven to choose between this and nothing.

Any such conclusion, I know, will on many sides be rejected as monstrous. The last thing to which truth pretends, I shall hear, is actually to be, or even bodily to possess, the real. But though this question, I know, might well be argued at length, the issue in my judgement can be raised and can be settled briefly. Truth, it is contended, is not to be the same as reality. Well, if so, I presume that there is a difference between them. And this difference, I understand, is not to be contained in the truth. But, if this is so, then clearly to my mind the truth must so far be defective. How, I ask, is the truth about reality to be less or more than reality without so far ceasing to be the truth? The only answer, so far as I see, is this, that reality has something which is not a possible content of truth. But here arises forthwith the dilemma which ruined us before. If such an outstanding element is known, then so far we have knowledge and truth, while, if it is not known, then I do not know of it, and to me it is nothing. On the one hand to divide truth from knowledge seems impossible, and on the other hand to go beyond knowledge seems meaningless.

And, if we are to advance, we must accept once for all the identification of truth with reality. I do not say that we are to conclude that there is to be in no sense any difference between them. But we must, without raising doubts and without looking backwards, follow the guidance of our new principle. We must, that is, accept the claim of truth not to be judged from the outside. We must unhesitatingly assert that truth, if it were satisfied itself, and if for itself it were perfect, would be itself in the fullest sense the entire and absolute Universe. And agreeing to the uttermost with this claim made by truth, we must attempt, truth and ourselves together, to judge truth from its own standard.

I will endeavour first to point out briefly in what this standard consists. The end of truth is to be and to possess reality in an ideal form. This means first that truth must include without residue the entirety of what is in any sense given, and it means next that truth is bound to include this intelligibly. Truth is not satisfied until we have all the facts, and until we understand perfectly what we have. And we do not understand perfectly the given material until we have it all together harmoniously, in such a way, that is, that we are not impelled to strive for another and a better way of holding it together. Truth is not satisfied, in other words, until it is all-containing and one. We are not obliged here, I think, to inquire further how these aspects of the idea of system are related, and whether, and in what sense, they have their root in a single principle. It is sufficient here to insist that both aspects[6] are essential to truth, and that any theory which ends in dividing them is certainly false.

But, when we judge truth by its own standard, truth evidently fails. And it fails in two ways, the connexion between which I will not here discuss.[7] (i) In the first place its contents cannot be made intelligible throughout and entirely. A doubt may indeed be raised whether even in any part they are able wholly to satisfy, but this again is a question on which here it is unnecessary to enter. For in any case obviously a large mass of the facts remains in the end inexplicable. You have perpetually to repeat that things are so, though you do not fully understand how or why, and when on the other hand you cannot perceive that no how or why is wanted. You are left in short with brute conjunctions where you seek for connexions, and where this need for connexions seems part of your nature.[8] (ii) And, failing

---

[6] We may use a variety of phrases here. We may speak, for instance, of homogeneity and specification, or again of integration and differentiation. The main point is this, that truth must leave nothing outside, and, with regard to what it contains, must not have to ask for further explanation as to how one part stands to another part.

[7] The reader is referred on this and other points to the later chapters of Bradley, *Essays on Truth and Reality*.

[8] You want in other words to answer the question 'What' by and from the object itself, and not by and from something *else*.

thus, truth fails again to include all the given facts, and any such complete inclusion seems even to be in principle unattainable. (*a*) On the one hand the moment's felt immediacy remains for ever outstanding, and, if we feel this nowhere else, we realize at each moment the difference between the knower and his truth. (*b*) And on the other hand the facts before us in space and time remain always incomplete. How is it possible for truth to embrace the whole sensible past and future? Truth might understand them (do you say?) and so include them *ideally*. Well but, if truth could do as much as this, which I myself think not possible, truth after all would not include these facts *bodily*. The ideal fact after all and the sensible fact will still differ, and this difference left outside condemns truth even as ideal. And in short we are entangled once more in our old dilemma. We have an element given which in no way we can get inside the truth, while on the other side, if we leave it out, truth becomes defective. For there seems really no sense in endeavouring to maintain that what remains outside is irrelevant.

With this at first sight we have ended in bankruptcy, but perhaps we may find that the case is otherwise and that our failure has carried us to success. For we were looking for the connexion between truth and reality, and we discovered first that no external connexion is possible. We then resolved to take truth as being the same with reality, and we found that, taken so, truth came short of its end. But in this very point of failure, after all, lies the way to success. Truth came short because, and so far as, it could not become that which it desired to be and made sure that it was. Truth claimed identity with an individual and all-inclusive whole. But such a whole, when we examine it, we find itself to be the Universe and all reality. And when we had to see how truth fails, as truth, in attaining its own end, we were being shown the very features of difference between truth and reality. And in passing over into reality and in thus ceasing to be mere truth, truth does not pass beyond its own end nor does it fail to realize itself. Hence, being the same as reality, and at the same time different from reality, truth is thus able itself to apprehend its identity and difference. But, if this is so, we seem to have reached the solution of our problem.[9]

[9] On the whole question see Bradley, *Appearance*. From this basis we can deal with the difficulty as to truth's being able consistently to pronounce itself imperfect. The dilemma that arises here was noticed by me (p. 513) and solved by a distinction (pp. 544–7). On this a sceptical critic (in *Mind*, 11 (1902), 336), seizing his opportunity, urged against me this dilemma which I had noticed, forgetting to mention that I had noticed it, and omitting the fact that, having noticed it, I had offered a solution. This opportunity for criticism I confess that I had not observed, but in the second edition of my book, desiring always, so far as I can, to be of use to all the world, I called attention to this opening, more or less by way, if I may say so, of

Truth is the whole Universe realizing itself in one aspect. This way of realization is one-sided, and it is a way not in the end satisfying even its own demands but felt itself to be incomplete. On the other hand the completion of truth itself is seen to lead to an all-inclusive reality, which reality is not outside truth. For it is the whole Universe which, immanent throughout, realizes and seeks itself in truth. This is the end to which truth leads and points and without which it is not satisfied. And those aspects in which truth for itself is defective, are precisely those which make the difference between truth and reality. Here, I would urge, is the one road of exit from disastrous circles and from interminable dilemmas. For on the one side we have a difference between truth and reality, while on the other side this difference only carries out truth. It consists in no more than that which truth seeks itself internally to be and to possess.

Truth, we thus can say, at once is and is not reality, and we have found that the difference is not external to truth. For truth would be satisfied in its own self-sought completion, and that completion would be reality. And if you ask how truth after all stands to reality, and whether after all truth is not a copy, the answer is obvious. Apart from its aspect of truth the reality would not be the reality, and there surely is no meaning in a copy which makes its original. In truth and in other aspects of the Universe we find one-sidedness and defect, and we may go on to see that everywhere the remedy for defect lies in the inclusion of other aspects more or less left out. But as for comparing the Universe, as it is apart from one aspect, with the Universe as complete, such a comparison is out of our power. And it is even, when we reflect, ridiculous to seek to discover by thinking what the Universe would be like without thought. You cannot take reality to pieces and then see how once more it can be combined to make reality. And thus, if we are asked for the relation of truth to reality, we must reply that in the end there is no relation, since in the end there are no separate terms. All that we can say is that, in order for truth complete itself into reality, such and such defects in truth itself would have to be rectified.

That there are difficulties in the way of this solution I readily admit,[10]

---

invitation (p. 620). And this standing invitation, I was going to add, has been accepted by Captain Knox, in *Mind*, 14 (1905), 210. But in view of this writer's extensive ignorance of the work which he came forward to criticize, I can hardly suppose that such an assertion would be justified. Still, if I cannot credit myself here with a successful invitation, I think that at least I may lay claim to a true prophecy.

[10] On this whole matter see Bradley, *Appearance*. One difficulty, on which stress has been rightly laid, is that we have no direct experience of any total experience which comprises in itself finite centres (cf. Bradley, *Essays on Truth and Reality*, ch. xv). I do not however myself see that this is more than a difficulty.

but difficulties and impossibilities, I urge, are not the same thing. And any other exit from our maze is, I submit, closed impassably. On the one hand we must not use words that have no positive sense, and, with this, all reality that falls outside experience and knowledge is, to my mind, excluded. On the other hand we cannot rest in that which, when we try to think it, conflicts with itself internally, and is dissolved in dilemmas. But, in order to know that the Universe is a whole with such and such a general nature, it is not necessary to perceive and to understand how such a Universe is possible, and how its various aspects are held apart and together. We desire to know this, I agree, but I fail myself to see how we can, and I think that with less than this we can gain positive knowledge enough to save us from mere scepticism.[11]

If we now return to that view for which truth is a mere copy of things, we have seen that in the end no such doctrine is admissible. But from a lower point of view it may be conventient to speak of truth as corresponding with reality and as even reproducing facts. In the first place the individual in truth-seeking must subject himself. He must (I cannot attempt to explain this here) suppress ideas, wishes and fancies, and anything else in his nature which is irrelevant to and interferes with the process of truth-seeking. And hence in a sense the individuals can have something in common, correspondence to which is essential for truth. Secondly, in truth-seeking the individual (once again I cannot try to explain this) must follow the object. Our understanding has to co-operate in the ideal development of reality, and it has not, like will, to turn ideas into existences. And thus following the object the ideas of the individual in a sense must conform to it.[12] In the third place reflection, as we have seen, must take up sensible

[11] By scepticism I of course do not mean any positive view as to knowledge in general, and still less any kind of conclusion supported by proof. I mean by it denial or doubt with regard to the existence *de facto* for me of that which satisfies intellectually. This denial or doubt rests certainly on a positive basis, but, so long as the basis is not made explicit and the denial remains particular, the basis itself is not denied, and the position remains consistent. On the other hand the scepticism which itself poses as a doctrine, which deals in general truth, and in a word claims to be *de jure*, to my mind does not understand itself. No consistent scepticism can, in my opinion, offer a reasoned proof of itself, nor can a consistent scepticism maintain any general positive doctrine, or indeed any universal thesis of any kind whatever.

[12] So far as concerns 'the suppression of the subjective', as it is sometimes called, that of course belongs alike to everything serious in life. In this general respect there is no difference between the pursuits of truth beauty and moral goodness. When, in order to create a work of art, a man has to keep down (so far as is necessary) what is merely particular to himself, that does not mean either that the work of art makes itself without him, or that it is not different because he in particular has made it. So also in the process of the will for good. When that is called 'objective', the meaning is not that the individual's will makes no difference. The meaning is that whatever in him is irrelevant to the issue, is suppressed as *merely* 'subjective'. So again in truth-seeking. The ideal development of the object itself, which I follow, does not make itself. In the first place apart from individual minds there is no object anywhere. In the second

qualities as given matter, and it must accept also more or less brute conjunctions of fact. Intelligence of itself does not recreate the given past nor
does it procreate entirely the given present or future. And it may be said
to wait on and to follow a course of events which it is powerless to make.
And, finally, to some extent language and truth must seek even to copy
perceived facts, and, as we saw, to convey them faithfully, though of course
in a partial manner. In the above senses truth may be spoken of as corresponding to facts, and it is right and proper as against one-sided theories
to insist on this correspondence.[13] But, as we have seen, such a way of
speaking is not permissible in the end.

I will ask, in conclusion, how what we may call the copy-theory of truth
is affected by the connexion between thought and volition. That in some
sense thought depends on desire and will is even obvious, and it is a doctrine in which most of us perhaps have, we may say, been brought up. But
it is a doctrine on the other hand which can be interpreted in various ways.
If in the first place truth is made wholly to depend in its essence on the
individual's desire, then in this case, naturally, since truth itself goes, the
copy-theory of truth goes also, together with every other sane theory of
truth. But otherwise, if you simply take truth to be copying, the desire for
truth will be a desire for copying, and by laying emphasis on the aspect of
desire I do not see that you add anything.

Further, if you adopt a one-sided intellectual view, and maintain that
reality is an original system of thought which you try to rethink, or a world
of ideal essences whose presence you desire—it seems useless in such a
case to speak about copying, since copying is excluded. There may be an
original here, but, whatever else you are doing, you do not copy that orig-

place, so far as I in particular am concerned, the process of truth demands my personal self-
realization. If you took that away, the objective process would not exist in me at all, and, more
than that, its nature would to some extent be modified by my personal failure. On the other side
the 'objective' development cannot possibly take up into itself then and there everything that
is at the moment psychically present in myself when I seek truth. It calls therefore for the suppression, so far as is required, of whatever in me falls outside of and is irrelevant to this special
development.

Any reader who wishes not to criticize but to understand, must try to bear in mind two
things. (i) The suppression of 'the subjective' takes place in regard to truth beauty and goodness alike, and not more in regard to one than the others. (ii) The merely 'subjective' does *not*
mean what is personal. It means that which for the special purpose in hand is irrelevant and
in this sense is *merely* personal (see Bradley, *Appearance*, 237). On the other hand the reader
who wishes simply to criticize will, I think, find no difficulty so long as the above points are
ignored.

[13] This I myself did in *Mind*, 13 (1904). I did not refer here to the fact that I had written elsewhere on the nature of truth, but I took care to warn the reader (p. 311, now p. 75 of Bradley,
Essays on Truth and Reality) that I could not in that article attempt to point out the meaning
of truth and falsehood. Notwithstanding this my article has literally been taken as a statement
of my view as to the ultimate nature of truth.

inal, since obviously you have no original before you to copy. The realization in detail of a general end is clearly in itself not repetition, and on the other side, as clearly, repetition and reproduction cannot all be called copying. Hence to ask here why we should desire to copy, is obviously irrelevant. The rational question to ask is about our desire for reproduction and repetition or for the presence in or to our minds of a self-existent reality.

But, if we adopt a more concrete view, all such questions become idle. On such a view my desire and my will to have truth is the will and the desire of the world to become truth in me. Truth is a mode of the self-realization of myself and of the Universe in one. And if you ask why the full reality cares to spill itself into gratuitous vessels, or whence and why to me comes this mania for turning myself into a superfluous receptacle or instance—the answer is ready. Such inquiries are based on and betray a most stupendous misconception. The Universe is nowhere apart from the lives of the individuals, and, whether as truth or otherwise, the Universe realizes itself not at all except through their differences. On the other side the individuals, if they are to realize themselves personally, must specialize this common life of which truth is one aspect. And to suppose that the individuals can seek their end and their reality somehow apart (say in the abstraction of mere practice or of private pleasure) is in the end really meaningless. Thus truth, the same in all, is from the other side not wholly the same, since difference to it is vital and it gains difference in each. The personal diversity of the individuals is hence not superfluous but essential.[14] For viewed from one side this diversity brings with it fresh quality, and from the other side, even so far as truth is common to the individuals, it must be taken none the less as modified in each case by its fresh context. But I must hasten here to add that no such general doctrine can be verified in detail.

The process of knowledge is, on any view like this, not something apart and by itself. It is one aspect of the life of the undivided Universe, outside of which life there is no truth or reality. And to speak here of copying as in a mirror, we may once more repeat, is absurd. If you like to add that the absurdity is heightened when we remember that life in general, and knowledge in particular, imply will and desire, to this naturally I make no objection. But for myself I have always been contented to know that the whole suggestion of copying is here ridiculously irrelevant. Still, as according to some critics my destiny is to illustrate what they call 'intellectualism', this

---

[14] See further in Bradley, *Essays on Truth and Reality*, ch. XI.

chapter, if I could understand it, is doubtless a blind flutter against the limits of my cage.

Note to page 110. [p. 33 of this volume]—Compare here *Mind*, NS, 51: 323,[15] and again Höffding, *Problems of Philosophy*, 79 ff. (Eng. trans.), a passage the force of which, it seems to me, Prof. James fails to appreciate. I may perhaps use this opportunity to say something with regard to points really or apparently at issue between Prof. James and myself. I cannot undertake to criticize Prof. James's ultimate view as to truth knowledge and reality, because that is accessible nowhere, I believe, except in more or less occasional and fragmentary articles, and I do not think that justice can be done to it until it is put out in a more complete and systematic form. But it has been a relief to me to see that, as I understand him, Prof. James rejects the idea that the essence of truth consists in nothing but its mere practical results.[16] In accepting the standard of clearness and inclusiveness and self-consistency (*Mind*, NS, 52), Prof. James apparently adopts the view in which I at least was brought up, a view for which of course the notion of any external standard of truth was an exploded fallacy. This explanation on the part of Prof. James seems to me to have removed wholly one supposed point of disagreement.

Next as to 'working', I of course agree that in proportion as a truth is idle it is less true, and I again agree that in the end no truth can be wholly idle. A truth that makes no difference to truth is to my mind an impossibility. But I cannot agree that, wherever we fail to see this further difference, it is non-existent, and the alleged truth therefore not true at all. It is one thing to say that, so far as we perceive, such or such a truth has no importance, and to act accordingly, and it is surely another thing to insist that such a truth has no truth whatever. And I seem in passing to remember that Hegel, rightly or wrongly, incurred censure for an attitude more or less of this kind towards some facts or truths of natural science. Next I agree that in the end all truth has practical and again aesthetic consequences. I believe in a word in the implication of all aspects of reality with one another. But once more I cannot believe that we can see this implication in detail, so as everywhere to use the consequence (whatever consequence it is) as a criterion. And to my mind it would be senseless to allege that the several aspects of the whole are each nothing but their consequences. Further I have no objection to identifying reality with goodness or satisfaction, so long as it is clear that this does not mean mere practical

---

[15] 'On truth and Practice', *Mind*, 13 (1904), repr. in *Essays on Truth and Reality*, ch. IV.
[16] But on this and other points see the appendices to ch. V of Bradley, *Essays on Truth and Reality*.

or any other one-sided satisfaction. Again I agree that any idea which in any way 'works', has in some sense truth. Only to my mind it has not on this account ultimate truth. It need not be a way of expression which gives a theoretical satisfaction in which we can rest. In the sciences we use working ideas and convenient mythology, and, while not admitting that these have ultimate truth, I should think it absurd to deny to them truth altogether. And surely so it may be again with morality and religion. The ideas that are really here required, most certainly, I should say, must be true. But to conclude from this that they have ultimate truth for metaphysics is to my mind irrational. And if you ask what I am to say then when these truths are contradicted by metaphysics, I reply that in my opinion they are not so contradicted, though certainly in my opinion metaphysics must understand them otherwise. If however any one believes in this contradiction, he should in my judgement on no account sacrifice or subordinate his practical truths, though as certainly he should not offer them as the sole and final truth about the Universe. But nothing, I fear, that I can say is likely to shake the pernicious prejudice that what is wanted for working purposes is the last theoretical truth about things (see my *Appearance*, 451 and elsewhere). This prejudice tends everywhere to result in one-sided attempts at consistency. In our moral practice, for instance, there evidently in fact is involved some element of uncertainty as to the issue. Hence on this point the Christian religion, clinging to the concrete whole, on one side maintains this element of moral struggle, but on the other side completes it (inconsistently no doubt) by an assurance of final victory. And here from both sides comes a protest, and a one-sided cry for clearness and consequence. Unless really, and as an ultimate fact, there is an uncertain future, morality, we hear, is destroyed. God therefore, to save morality, must be made sufficiently ignorant and sufficiently weak for the future really to be doubtful. And apparently it is not seen that, with this, there is an end logically of all that is meant (and much is meant) by 'the peace of God'. Again, on the same principle but from the other side, some fanatic from time to time insists on the utter supremacy of Good. And hence he concludes in the older style that morality is irrelevant and worthless, or today in a newer mode that the individual, as such, is perfect, and that there is no toothache but ignorance. But for practical purposes surely there is something higher than theoretical consistency, even if such consistency in practice were actually attainable. Hence, unless ultimate theoretical truth itself may be inconsistent, it is better for practice surely not to identify our working ideas with ultimate truth. For practice you want ideas which keep hold of all sides of the main substance, and to sacrifice any part of that substance to theoretical consistency is practical error. But on the other hand the reader must be warned that to agree with us here is to incur the peril, whatever that is, of being called an 'Intellectualist'.

To come now to that which Prof. James would call 'humanism', I am reminded forthwith that an accusation of mere humanism was one of the charges long ago brought against German Idealism. And since (if I may speak for myself) I do not believe in any reality outside of and apart from the totality of finite mind,[17] and since there is certainly nothing original in my disbeliefs or beliefs, once more here I fail to perceive the chasm which separates the new 'humanism' from what went before. And I am again relieved to find that on the whole Prof. James himself takes this view, and regrets an attitude of hostile criticism on our side as due largely to mistake. Prof. James doubtless here does not remember that on our side nothing was said until we found ourselves judged and sentenced. The philosophic world, ostensibly in Prof. James's behalf, was divided into sheep and goats, and the trumpet was blown, and Plato and Aristotle summoned from the dead to witness the triumph of the one philosopher and the confusion of the sophists.[18] But for my part I have no wish to recall such extravagances, if Prof. James will not forget that it was his fortune, however ill-merited, to inspire them. And if I can do anything to remove or to throw light on any issue between Prof. James and those who cannot follow him, it will be a pleasure to me to attempt this.

(1) In the first place as to 'pragmatism', we want to hear definitely from Prof. James whether the practical side of our nature is to be made supreme, or whether there is anything else which has value and rights of its own. Even now I ask myself in what sense, or whether at all, mutilation is advocated. I still do not know if I am called on to enter into life halt and maimed, to say nothing of being blind of one eye. And a reassuring statement in general terms is, I think, not sufficient. But if Prof. James would explain to us how in the end he understands the human Good, and how its elements are related to one another, this point perhaps would become clear. We might at last know whether we all should or should not call ourselves Pragmatists. (2) Next as to 'humanism', surely we should be informed, first, whether 'finite mind' is to stand merely for some of the inhabitants of a single planet, or is to have a far wider meaning, and, if the latter, we should be told what that meaning is. This is not a new question (it might even be called an old and familiar one), and in some aspects the

difference here between various views may be really enormous. It seems, to myself at least, imperative that such a point should not be left in darkness. And (3) in the process of Humanity (however Humanity is understood) we have to inquire how the individuals stand to the whole. Have both sides of the process equal reality, or, if this is not so, what is the alternative? If the individuals are the final realities, what in the end are we to say of the 'together' and of the whole process? These are well-known problems, and they surely call for systematic treatment. (4) Then, to say nothing of questions about knowledge—a subject with which Prof. James has in some degree dealt—what in the end is the meaning of and the truth about Progress? Endless progress as an ideal is itself hardly above criticism, but is there in the end any meaning in progress at all? Is mere prevalence and survival to be the same as progress, and, if not that, then what else is progress to mean? And is the temporal process of the Universe (which process is apparently the one reality) to be taken as a progress, and if so, on what grounds? We have once more here an old problem which calls for solution. (5) Finally I need perhaps say nothing as to the difficulty with regard to 'a condition' outside of finite minds, except to point out that any obscurity on this head must naturally affect the entire view.

The above questions, and others, can hardly be answered satisfactorily unless they are dealt with all together and as connected parts of one inquiry. Prof. James's answer to them, when it comes, will not altogether, I imagine, meet all our difficulties, but most assuredly it will be welcome. Even at Oxford we have not yet been so deafened by periodical manifestoes and by prophetic outcries as to be incapable of hearing. And there, as indeed everywhere else, Prof. James may count upon willing and respectful attention.

II

THE NATURE OF TRUTH

H. H. JOACHIM

§24. (i) When Descartes laid it down as a principle for the seeker after truth 'to affirm nothing as true except that which he could clearly and distinctly perceive', he was in reality presupposing a very definite theory of knowledge and a correspondingly determinate metaphysics.[1] If we wish to pass a true judgement, we must affirm or deny only that content which we clearly and distinctly apprehend. Inner affirmation, or denial, which is the characteristic of judgement, is an act in which we exhibit our free choice or will.[2] But this act is exercised upon a material in the acceptance of which we are passive. The intellect—a passive recipient—apprehends a content, which the will—an active faculty—may affirm or deny. And if this affirmation is to constitute a true judgement, the content affirmed must force itself upon our intellect as a self-evident *datum*, which we immediately recognize as indubitable. Thus the immediate apprehension of indubitable truth, an 'intuition', is the necessary precondition of truth of judgement.[3] The content of such an 'intuition', namely that which we

From H. H. Joachim, *The Nature of Truth* (Oxford: Clarendon Press, 1906), 72–9. Reprinted by permission of Oxford University Press.

[1] Descartes's full meaning is best seen by comparing his *Regulae ad directionem ingenii* with the corresponding passages in the *Discours de la Méthode*, the *Meditationes*, and the *Principia Philosophiae*. On the whole subject cf. Adamson, *The Development of Modern Philosophy* (Edinburgh, 1908), vol. i, ch. i, and Broder Christiansen, *Das Urteil bei Descartes*.

[2] In certain cases we exhibit our freedom by neither affirming nor denying, but by suspending our will. But this is a detail of the theory which we can here disregard.—The affirmation (or negation) involved in judgement is *internal*; cf. e.g. Descartes's answer to Hobbes: 'Per se notum est . . . aliud esse videre hominem currentem, quam sibi ipsi affirmare se illum videre, quod fit sine voce.' (*Obi. et Resp. tertiae*, answer to objection vi).

[3] This double and ambiguous use of 'truth'—truth of judgement and truth of apprehension—exposes Descartes's theory of knowledge to serious criticism. But I cannot enter into the matter here. Neither is this the place to discuss the ambiguity in Descartes's statements concerning the 'Intellect' and 'Ideas'. At times 'ideas' are simply modes, phases, determinate states of the intellect; but at other times the intellect is said to 'attend to' ideas, which it 'finds' in itself. Cf. and contrast *Notae in progr. quodd.* (pp. 158 and 163 in the edn. of 1692), Letter of 1644 (*Œuvres de Descartes*, ed. C. Adam and P. Tannery (Paris, 1897–1910), iv. 113) and *Regulae* i, xii, *Medit.* vi. On the whole subject, cf. Norman Smith, *Studies in the Cartesian Philosophy* (London, 1902), 52, 90 ff.

apprehend intuitively as self-evident, is a 'simple idea', or rather (as Descartes sometimes[4] more clearly expresses it) a 'simple proposition'. Its 'simplicity' does not exclude inner distinction; for it is the immediate, but necessary, cohesion of two elements or two constituent ideas. In other words, the self-evident *datum*, which Descartes calls a 'simple idea' or a 'simple proposition', is a hypothetical judgement so formulated that the antecedent immediately necessitates the consequent, though the consequent need not reciprocally involve the antecedent.[5]

The elements in the content of an 'intuition' cohere by the immediate necessity which binds consequent to antecedent in a hypothetical judgement of the kind explained. But the content *as a whole* is grasped intuitively, or immediately, as an indubitable self-evident *datum*. Such self-evident indubitable truths constitute the foundation on which the structure of scientific and philosophical knowledge is built. They are the principles, from which the whole system of demonstrated and demonstrable truth must be derived.[6] And this system is, so to say, a network of chains of propositions. The links in each chain form an uninterrupted sequence from its first link. They follow with unbroken logical coherence from a self-evident *datum*, a 'simple proposition' apprehended intuitively. Each derivative link is grasped by the intellect as the necessary consequent of a link

[4] Particularly in the *Regulae*; cf. e.g. *Reg.* iii, xi, xii.

[5] Cf. Descartes's own instances: 'cogito ergo sum', i.e. 'if self-consciousness, then existence', but not necessarily also 'if existence, then self-consciousness'. So '2+2=4', i.e. 'if 2 be added to 2, there must be 4'; but there may be 4 without this mode of addition, as is evident from '3 + 1 = 4', which Descartes quotes as another instance of 'Intuition'. Cf. *Regulae*, iii; and, on the whole subject, see Adamson, *Development of Modern Philosophy*, i. 10 n. 3; and Christiansen, *Urteil bei Descartes*, 28ff.

[6] The mediate truths are reached from the immediate self-evidents by a process which Descartes calls 'deduction'. The logical character of this process is *not* syllogistic (cf. e.g. *Regulae*, x). It is a pure illation of the mind, which, in the simplest cases, is hardly distinguishable from the immediate intuition of a necessary nexus within a content. Thus e.g. we intuite that 2+2=4, and again that 3+1=4; we *deduce* that 3+1=2+2. But the latter (mediate) truth, when the movement of the mind is over, is itself grasped immediately, i.e. becomes an 'intuition' (cf. e.g. *Regulae*, iii, xi). In such cases, the term 'deduction' marks the movement of illation in distinction from the concentrated grasp of the articulated content in which that movement culminates and rests. In more complex cases, the inference presupposes an ordered grouping of the many self-evidents, from which the grasp of the mediate truth is ultimately to emerge. To this preparatory grouping Descartes gives the name of *induction* or *enumeration*; and he occasionally extends these titles to the inference as a whole (cf. *Regulae*, vii, xi, xii). But even here the logical character of the inference remains the same. The 'deduction', 'induction', or 'enumeration', is always the illative movement from a content or contents intuitively apprehended to another content which follows by direct logical necessity from the first. And it is a mere accident, due e.g. to the limitations of our memory, that the movement does not always issue in an 'intuition'. I cannot enter into further details here, though I am aware that *inductio* (or *enumeratio*) is usually interpreted as a distinct method of proof, differing in logical character from *deductio*. But I believe that a careful study of the *Regulae* will convince the reader that my interpretation is essentially correct, however paradoxical it may appear.

or links intuited as indubitable truths, and *as thus grasped* itself is manifest as an indubitable truth.

Thus, the ideal of knowledge for Descartes is a coherent system of truths, where each truth is apprehended in its logical position: the immediate as the basis, and the mediate truths in their necessary dependence on the immediate. Each truth in this ideal system is a cohesion of different elements united by a logical nexus; and every truth is true *per se* absolutely and unalterably.

But the theory which I am trying to expound is committed, for good or for evil, to a radically different view of the systematization of knowledge. The image of a chain, admirably suited to illustrate the theory of Descartes, is a sheer distortion of the conception of 'coherence' or 'conceivability', which, on my view, characterizes truth. The ideal of knowledge for me is a system, not of *truths*, but of *truth*. 'Coherence' cannot be attached to propositions from the outside: it is not a property which they can acquire by colligation, whilst retaining unaltered the truth they possessed in isolation. And whereas for Descartes ideally certain knowledge (indubitable truth) is typified in the intuitive grasp of the immediately cohering elements of a 'simple proposition', such a content is for me so remote from the ideal as hardly to deserve the name of 'truth' at all. For it is the smallest and most abstracted fragment of knowledge, a mere mutilated shred torn from the living whole in which alone it possessed its significance. The typical embodiments of the ideal must be sought, not in such isolated intuitions, but rather in the organized whole of a science: for that possesses at least *relative* self-dependence, and its significance is at least *relatively* immanent and self-contained.

§25. (ii) The second view with which I propose to contrast the coherence-theory may be regarded as a corollary of the first.[7] For, if there are certain judgements indubitably true, then these are the *materials* of knowledge. And, in the progress of thought, a *form* is imposed upon these materials which arranges without altering them. Truth is linked to truth until the arrangement constitutes that network of chains of truths which is the system of ideally complete knowledge. The form under which the infinitely various materials are ordered, is the universal form of all thinking. It is the characteristic grey of formal consistency, which any and every thinking monotonously paints over all its materials to stamp them as its own. This arrangement under the form of thinking cannot *of itself* guarantee the truth of the result. For false materials, as well as true, may be painted with the royal colour. But the result cannot be true *without* this arrangement,

---

[7] I do not suggest that the two views were *historically* so related.

which is thus a *sine qua non* or a 'negative condition' of truth. We may christen the observance of this condition 'validity'; and we may then draw the conclusion that the completely true must also be valid, though the valid may be false. Or if we prefer the term 'consistency' we shall point out that consistent lying and consistent error are occasionally achieved, and that a man may be a consistent scoundrel; but that the truth requires for its apprehension and utterance the same consistency of thought and purpose, which must also be expressed in the actions of the morally good man. The consistent, in short, need be neither true nor good; but the good and the true must be consistent.

This distinction between the universal form and the particular materials of thought has, in various modifications, played a great part in the history of philosophy. I am here concerned with it in its barest and most extreme shape, as the fundamental assumption of the traditional 'formal' logic. Pressed beyond the limits of legitimate provisional abstraction until it has become a mere caricature, the antithesis between form and matter has in that 'science'[8] been worked out through the whole domain and through all the functions of thinking. Judgement e.g. is that function of thought whereby two conceptions are combined; and whatever the materials, the form of combination exhibits a character of its own, which is to be studied apart. Hence those classifications of 'formal' logic which we have all of us learnt, and learnt to unlearn again: those rigid groupings of Judgements as Universal, Individual, Particular; as Negative, Affirmative, Infinite; as Categorical, Hypothetical, Necessary, &c., &c. So, Syllogism is the function of thought whereby two judgements are combined to generate a third; and 'formal' logic gives you the rules of 'valid' combination irrespective of *what* is combined, and impotent therefore to determine the truth of the result.

Formal logic, in this sense of the term, might be called 'the analysis of low-grade thinking';[9] but all thinking, even at its lowest, is a living process, which the mechanical methods of such an analysis are too crude to grasp. Yet all thinking—the most complicated and profound, as well as the most shallow and rudimentary—exhibits a certain unity of character. And the formal logician has followed a sound instinct in emphasizing the necessity of analysing and grasping this unity, if thinking is to understand itself. But he has erred in looking for the unity as an abstract common feature, to be found in the actual processes of thinking by stripping them of their concrete differences. And it is the same error which has led him to conceive

[8] Or 'art': it does not matter which title we give to what is neither one nor the other.
[9] Cf. e.g. Bosanquet, *Knowledge and Reality*, 2nd issue, p. 193.

thinking as a dead and finished product instead of a living and moving process. In the end and in principle his error is the failure to conceive a universal except as one element along with others in the particular: a failure which is tantamount to the negation of all universals. Or it is the failure to conceive a whole except as the sum of its parts: a failure which is the denial of unity and individual character to that which develops and lives. Hence formal logic assumes that the essential nature of thought is to be found in an abstractly self-identical form; in a tautologous self-consistency, where the 'self' has no diversity of content in which a genuine consistency could be manifested, or where diversity of content is cast aside as mere irrelevant material. But the essential nature of thought is a concrete unity, a living individuality. Thought is a form, which moves and expands, and exhibits its consistent character precisely in those ordered articulations of its structure which formal logic impotently dismisses as *mere* materials.

The 'systematic coherence', therefore, in which we are looking for the nature of truth, must not be confused with the 'consistency' of formal logic. A piece of thinking might be free from self-contradiction, might be 'consistent' and 'valid' as the formal logician understands those terms, and yet it might fail to exhibit that systematic coherence which is truth.

§26. We may now proceed to formulate the coherence-theory afresh in the following terms. Truth in its essential nature is that systematic coherence which is the character of a significant whole. A 'significant whole' is an organized individual experience, self-fulfilling and self-fulfilled. Its organization *is* the process of its self-fulfilment, and the concrete manifestation of its individuality. But this process is no mere surface-play between static parts within the whole: nor *is* the individuality of the whole, except in the movement which is its manifestation. The whole *is* not, if 'is' implies that its nature is a finished product prior or posterior to the process, or in any sense apart from it. And the whole *has* no parts, if 'to have parts' means to consist of fixed and determinate constituents, from and to which the actions and interactions of its organic life proceed, much as a train may travel backwards and forwards between the terminal stations. Its 'parts' are through and through in the process and constituted by it. They are 'moments' in the self-fulfilling process which is the individuality of the whole. And the individuality of the whole is *both* the pre-supposition of the distinctive being of its 'moments' or parts *and* the resultant which emerges as their co-operation, or which they make and continuously sustain.

It is this process of self-fulfilment which is truth, and it is *this* which the theory means by 'systematic coherence'. The process is not a movement playing between static elements, but the very substance of the moving elements. And the coherence is no abstract form imposed upon the surface of materials, which retain in their depths a nature untouched by the imposition. The coherence—if we call it a 'form'—is a form which through and through interpenetrates its materials; and they—if we call them 'materials'—are materials, which retain no inner privacy for themselves in independence of the form. They hold their distinctive being in and through, and not in sheer defiance of, their identical form; and its identity is the concrete sameness of different materials. The materials *are* only as moments in the process which is the continuous emergence of the coherence. And the form *is* only as the sustained process of self-fulfilment, wherein just these materials reveal themselves as constitutive moments of the coherence.

In the above formulation I have endeavoured to express the coherence-notion so as to emphasize the *concreteness* of the coherence which is truth, as against the view which found truth in formal consistency;[10] and I have insisted upon the conception of truth as a living and moving whole, as against the Cartesian view of fixed truths on which the structure of knowledge is built.[11] But the result at present is a mere vague sketch, which cannot pretend to be satisfactory. Even the well-disposed reader will regard it as the description of a mystical ideal with no obvious application to the actual problems of human knowledge; whilst the hostile critic will view it as a dishonest evasion of the difficulties, as mere words in place of a solid discussion. I shall accordingly attempt to work out my sketch in detail, so as to show the precise bearing of this conception of truth on the truth in human judgement and inference, and so as to defend it against the charge of mysticism or evasion of the difficulties.

§27. If we are to develop our vague sketch into a definite theory, we must make it clear *what* truth we are professing to describe. Was our sketch intended as an exposition of truth as it is for human knowledge? or were we describing an ideal experience, which no finite mind can ever actually enjoy?

This manner of formulating the question seems to challenge a choice between two unambiguous alternatives, and thus to put a clear issue before us. But in reality it involves certain assumptions which are open to debate, and which—as I think, and hope to show—are false.[12] For it is assumed that finite experience is sundered by a gulf from ideal experience. It is implied that an ideal experience is as such debarred from actuality, and it is suggested that knowledge which is severed from ideal experience can

[10] Cf. above, §25. [11] Cf. above, §24. [12] Cf. Joachim, *Nature of Truth*, 82, 83.

yet be true. But, whilst refusing to commit myself to these implications, I should reply that my sketch was intended to describe the nature of truth as an ideal, as the character of an ideally complete experience. Truth, we said, was the systematic coherence which characterized a significant whole. And we proceeded to identify a significant whole with 'an organized individual experience, self-fulfilling and self-fulfilled'. Now there can be one *and only one* such experience: or *only one* significant whole, the significance of which is self-contained in the sense required. For it is *absolute* self-fulfilment, *absolutely* self-contained significance, that is postulated; and nothing short of *absolute* individuality—nothing short of *the* completely whole experience—can satisfy this postulate. And human knowledge—not merely *my* knowledge or *yours*, but the best and fullest knowledge in the world at any stage of its development—is clearly not a significant whole in this ideally complete sense. Hence the truth, which our sketch described, is—*from the point of view of the human intelligence*—an Ideal, and an Ideal which can never *as such*, or in its completeness, be actual as human experience.

III

PRAGMATISM'S CONCEPTION OF TRUTH

WILLIAM JAMES

When Clerk-Maxwell was a child it is written that he had a mania for having everything explained to him, and that when people put him off with vague verbal accounts of any phenomenon he would interrupt them impatiently by saying, 'Yes; but I want you to tell me the *particular go* of it!' Had his question been about truth, only a pragmatist could have told him the particular go of it. I believe that our contemporary pragmatists, especially Messrs. Schiller and Dewey, have given the only tenable account of this subject. It is a very ticklish subject, sending subtle rootlets into all kinds of crannies, and hard to treat in the sketchy way that alone befits a public lecture. But the Schiller–Dewey view of truth has been so ferociously attacked by rationalistic philosophers, and so abominably misunderstood, that here, if anywhere, is the point where a clear and simple statement should be made.

I fully expect to see the pragmatist view of truth run through the classic stages of a theory's career. First, you know, a new theory is attacked as absurd; then it is admitted to be true, but obvious and insignificant; finally it is seen to be so important that its adversaries claim that they themselves discovered it. Our doctrine of truth is at present in the first of these three stages, with symptoms of the second stage having begun in certain quarters. I wish that this lecture might help it beyond the first stage in the eyes of many of you.

Truth, as any dictionary will tell you, is a property of certain of our ideas. It means their 'agreement', as falsity means their disagreement, with 'reality'. Pragmatists and intellectualists both accept this definition as a matter of course. They begin to quarrel only after the question is raised as to what may precisely be meant by the term 'agreement', and what by the term 'reality', when reality is taken as something for our ideas to agree with.

From William James, 'Pragmatism's Conception of Truth', in *Pragmatism: A New Name for Some Old Ways of Thinking* (Longmans, 1907), 197–236.

In answering these questions the pragmatists are more analytic and painstaking, the intellectualists more offhand and irreflective. The popular notion is that a true idea must copy its reality. Like other popular views, this one follows the analogy of the most usual experience. Our true ideas of sensible things do indeed copy them. Shut your eyes and think of yonder clock on the wall, and you get just such a true picture or copy of its dial. But your idea of its 'works' (unless you are a clockmaker) is much less of a copy, yet it passes muster, for it in no way clashes with the reality. Even though it should shrink to the mere word 'works', that word still serves you truly; and when you speak of the 'time-keeping function' of the clock, or of its spring's 'elasticity', it is hard to see exactly what your ideas can copy.

You perceive that there is a problem here. Where our ideas cannot copy definitely their object, what does agreement with that object mean? Some idealists seem to say that they are true whenever they are what God means that we ought to think about that object. Others hold the copy-view all through, and speak as if our ideas possessed truth just in proportion as they approach to being copies of the Absolute's eternal way of thinking.

These views, you see, invite pragmatistic discussion. But the great assumption of the intellectualists is that truth means essentially an inert static relation. When you've got your true idea of anything, there's an end of the matter. You're in possession; you *know*; you have fulfilled your thinking destiny. You are where you ought to be mentally; you have obeyed your categorical imperative; and nothing more need follow on that climax of your rational destiny. Epistemologically you are in stable equilibrium.

Pragmatism, on the other hand, asks its usual question. 'Grant an idea or belief to be true,' it says, 'what concrete difference will its being true make in any one's actual life? How will the truth be realized? What experiences will be different from those which would obtain if the belief were false? What, in short, is the truth's cash-value in experiential terms?'

The moment pragmatism asks this question, it sees the answer: *True ideas are those that we can assimilate, validate, corroborate and verify. False ideas are those that we can not.* That is the practical difference it makes to us to have true ideas; that, therefore, is the meaning of truth, for it is all that truth is known-as.

This thesis is what I have to defend. The truth of an idea is not a stagnant property inherent in it. Truth *happens* to an idea. It *becomes* true, is *made* true by events. Its verity *is* in fact an event, a process: the process namely of its verifying itself, its veri-*fication*. Its validity is the process of its valid-*ation*.

But what do the words verification and validation themselves pragmatically mean? They again signify certain practical consequences of the verified and validated idea. It is hard to find any one phrase that characterizes these consequences better than the ordinary agreement-formula— just such consequences being what we have in mind whenever we say that our ideas 'agree' with reality. They lead us, namely, through the acts and other ideas which they instigate, into or up to, or towards, other parts of experience with which we feel all the while—such feeling being among our potentialities—that the original ideas remain in agreement. The connexions and transitions come to us from point to point as being progressive, harmonious, satisfactory. This function of agreeable leading is what we mean by an idea's verification. Such an account is vague and it sounds at first quite trivial, but it has results which it will take the rest of my hour to explain.

Let me begin by reminding you of the fact that the possession of true thoughts means everywhere the possession of invaluable instruments of action; and that our duty to gain truth, so far from being a blank command from out of the blue, or a 'stunt' self-imposed by our intellect, can account for itself by excellent practical reasons.

The importance to human life of having true beliefs about matters of fact is a thing too notorious. We live in a world of realities that can be infinitely useful or infinitely harmful. Ideas that tell us which of them to expect count as the true ideas in all this primary sphere of verification, and the pursuit of such ideas is a primary human duty. The possession of truth, so far from being here an end in itself, is only a preliminary means towards other vital satisfactions. If I am lost in the woods and starved, and find what looks like a cow-path, it is of the utmost importance that I should think of a human habitation at the end of it, for if I do so and follow it, I save myself. The true thought is useful here because the house which is its object is useful. The practical value of true ideas is thus primarily derived from the practical importance of their objects to us. Their objects are, indeed, not important at all times. I may on another occasion have no use for the house; and then my idea of it, however verifiable, will be practically irrelevant, and had better remain latent. Yet since almost any object may some day become temporarily important, the advantage of having a general stock of *extra* truths, of ideas that shall be true of merely possible situations, is obvious. We store such extra truths away in our memories, and with the overflow we fill our books of reference. Whenever such an extra truth becomes practically relevant to one of our emergencies, it passes from cold-storage to do work in the world and our belief in it grows active.

You can say of it then either that 'it is useful because it is true' or that 'it is true because it is useful'. Both these phrases mean exactly the same thing, namely that here is an idea that gets fulfilled and can be verified. True is the name for whatever idea starts the verification-process, useful is the name for its completed function in experience. True ideas would never have been singled out as such, would never have acquired a class-name, least of all a name suggesting value, unless they had been useful from the outset in this way.

From this simple cue pragmatism gets her general notion of truth as something essentially bound up with the way in which one moment in our experience may lead us towards other moments which it will be worth while to have been led to. Primarily, and on the common-sense level, the truth of a state of mind means this function of a *leading that is worth while*. When a moment in our experience, of any kind whatever, inspires us with a thought that is true, that means that sooner or later we dip by that thought's guidance into the particulars of experience again and make advantageous connexion with them. This is a vague enough statement, but I beg you to retain it, for it is essential.

Our experience meanwhile is all shot through with regularities. One bit of it can warn us to get ready for another bit, can 'intend' or be 'significant of' that remoter object. The object's advent is the significance's verification. Truth, in these cases, meaning nothing but eventual verification, is manifestly incompatible with waywardness on our part. Woe to him whose beliefs play fast and loose with the order which realities follow in his experience; they will lead him nowhere or else make false connexions.

By 'realities' or 'objects' here, we mean either things of common sense, sensibly present, or else common-sense relations, such as dates, places, distances, kinds, activities. Following our mental image of a house along the cow-path, we actually come to see the house; we get the image's full verification. *Such simply and fully verified leadings are certainly the originals and prototypes of the truth-process.* Experience offers indeed other forms of truth-process, but they are all conceivable as being primary verifications arrested, multiplied or substituted one for another.

Take, for instance, yonder object on the wall. You and I consider it to be a 'clock', although no one of us has seen the hidden works that make it one. We let our notion pass for true without attempting to verify. If truths mean verification-process essentially, ought we then to call such unverified truths as this abortive? No, for they form the overwhelmingly large number of the truths we live by. Indirect as well as direct verifications pass muster. Where circumstantial evidence is sufficient, we can go without eyewitnessing. Just as we here assume Japan to exist without ever having been there, because it *works* to do so, everything we know conspiring with the belief, and nothing interfering, so we assume that thing to be a clock. We *use* it as a clock, regulating the length of our lecture by it. The verification of the assumption here means its leading to no frustration or contradiction. Verifi*ability* of wheels and weights and pendulum is as good as verification. For one truth-process completed there are a million in our lives that function in this state of nascency. They turn us *towards* direct verification; lead us into the *surroundings* of the objects they envisage; and then, if everything runs on harmoniously, we are so sure that verification is possible that we omit it, and are usually justified by all that happens.

Truth lives, in fact, for the most part on a credit system. Our thoughts and beliefs 'pass', so long as nothing challenges them, just as banknotes pass so long as nobody refuses them. But this all points to direct face-to-face verifications somewhere, without which the fabric of truth collapses like a financial system with no cash-basis whatever. You accept my verification of one thing, I yours of another. We trade on each other's truth. But beliefs verified concretely by *somebody* are the posts of the whole superstructure.

Another great reason—beside economy of time—for waiving complete verification in the usual business of life is that all things exist in kinds and not singly. Our world is found once for all to have that peculiarity. So that when we have once directly verified our ideas about one specimen of a kind, we consider ourselves free to apply them to other specimens without verification. A mind that habitually discerns the kind of thing before it, and acts by the law of the kind immediately, without pausing to verify, will be a 'true' mind in ninety-nine out of a hundred emergencies, proved so by its conduct fitting everything it meets, and getting no refutation.

Indirectly or only potentially verifying processes may thus be true as well as full verification-processes. They work as true processes would work, give us the same advantages, and claim our recognition for the same reasons. All this on the common-sense level of matters of fact, which we are alone considering.

But matters of fact are not our only stock in trade. *Relations among purely mental ideas* form another sphere where true and false beliefs obtain, and here the beliefs are absolute, or unconditional. When they are true they bear the name either of definitions or of principles. It is either a principle or a definition that 1 and 1 make 2, that 2 and 1 make 3, and so on; that white differs less from grey than it does from black; that when the cause begins to act the effect also commences. Such propositions hold of all possible 'ones', of all conceivable 'whites' and 'greys' and 'causes'. The objects here are mental objects. Their relations are perceptually obvious at a glance, and no sense-verification is necessary. Moreover, once true, always true, of those same mental objects. Truth here has an 'eternal' character. If you can find a concrete thing anywhere that is 'one' or 'white' or 'grey' or an 'effect,' then your principles will everlastingly apply to it. It is but a case of ascertaining the kind, and then applying the law of its kind to the particular object. You are sure to get truth if you can but name the kind rightly, for your mental relations hold good of everything of that kind without exception. If you then, nevertheless, failed to get truth concretely, you would say that you had classed your real objects wrongly.

In this realm of mental relations, truth again is an affair of leading. We relate one abstract idea with another, framing in the end great systems of logical and mathematical truth, under the respective terms of which the sensible facts of experience eventually arrange themselves, so that our eternal truths hold good of realities also. This marriage of fact and theory is endlessly fertile. What we say is here already true in advance of special verification, *if we have subsumed our objects rightly*. Our ready-made ideal framework for all sorts of possible objects follows from the very structure of our thinking. We can no more play fast and loose with these abstract relations than we can do so with our sense-experiences. They coerce us; we must treat them consistently, whether or not we like the results. The rules of addition apply to our debts as rigorously as to our assets. The hundredth decimal of π, the ratio of the circumference to its diameter, is predetermined ideally now, though no one may have computed it. If we should ever need the figure in our dealings with an actual circle we should need to have it given rightly, calculated by the usual rules; for it is the same kind of truth that those rules elsewhere calculate.

Between the coercions of the sensible order and those of the ideal order, our mind is thus wedged tightly. Our ideas must agree with realities, be such realities concrete or abstract, be they facts or be they principles, under penalty of endless inconsistency and frustration.

So far, intellectualists can raise no protest. They can only say that we have barely touched the skin of the matter.

Realities mean, then, either concrete facts, or abstract kinds of thing and relations perceived intuitively between them. They furthermore and thirdly mean, as things that new ideas of ours must no less take account of, the whole body of other truths already in our possession. But what now does 'agreement' with such threefold realities mean?—to use again the definition that is current.

Here it is that pragmatism and intellectualism begin to part company. Primarily, no doubt, to agree means to copy, but we saw that the mere word 'clock' would do instead of a mental picture of its works, and that of many realities our ideas can only be symbols and not copies. 'Past time', 'power', 'spontaneity'—how can our mind copy such realities?

To 'agree' in the widest sense with a reality *can only mean to be guided either straight up to it or into its surroundings, or to be put into such working touch with it as to handle either it or something connected with it better than if we disagreed.* Better either intellectually or practically! And often agreement will only mean the negative fact that nothing contradictory from the quarter of that reality comes to interfere with the way in which our ideas guide us elsewhere. To copy a reality is, indeed, one very important way of agreeing with it, but it is far from being essential. The essential thing is the process of being guided. Any idea that helps us to *deal*, whether practically or intellectually, with either the reality or its belongings, that doesn't entangle our progress in frustrations, that *fits*, in fact, and adapts our life to the reality's whole setting, will agree sufficiently to meet the requirement. It will hold true of that reality.

Thus, *names* are just as 'true' or 'false' as definite mental pictures are. They set up similar verification-processes, and lead to fully equivalent practical results.

All human thinking gets discursified; we exchange ideas; we lend and borrow verifications, get them from one another by means of social intercourse. All truth thus gets verbally built out, stored up, and made available for every one. Hence, we must *talk* consistently just as we must *think* consistently: for both in talk and thought we deal with kinds. Names are arbitrary, but once understood they must be kept to. We mustn't now call Abel 'Cain' or Cain 'Abel'. If we do, we ungear ourselves from the whole book of Genesis, and from all its connexions with the universe of speech and fact down to the present time. We throw ourselves out of whatever truth that entire system of speech and fact may embody.

The overwhelming majority of our true ideas admit of no direct or face-to-face verification—those of past history, for example, as of Cain and Abel. The stream of time can be remounted only verbally, or verified indirectly by the present prolongations or effects of what the past harbored. Yet if they agree with these verbalities and effects, we can know that our ideas of the past are true. *As true as past time itself was*, so true was Julius Cæsar, so true were antediluvian monsters, all in their proper dates and settings. That past time itself was, is guaranteed by its coherence with everything that's present. True as the present *is*, the past *was* also.

Agreement thus turns out to be essentially an affair of leading—leading that is useful because it is into quarters that contain objects that are important. True ideas lead us into useful verbal and conceptual quarters as well as directly up to useful sensible termini. They lead to consistency, stability and flowing human intercourse. They lead away from eccentricity and isolation, from foiled and barren thinking. The untrammelled flowing of the leading-process, its general freedom from clash and contradiction, passes for its indirect verification; but all roads lead to Rome, and in the end and eventually, all true processes must lead to the face of directly verifying sensible experiences *somewhere*, which somebody's ideas have copied.

Such is the large loose way in which the pragmatist interprets the word agreement. He treats it altogether practically. He lets it cover any process of conduction from a present idea to a future terminus, provided only it run prosperously. It is only thus that 'scientific' ideas, flying as they do beyond common sense, can be said to agree with their realities. It is, as I have already said, *as if* reality were made of ether, atoms or electrons, but we mustn't think so literally. The term 'energy' doesn't even pretend to stand for anything 'objective'. It is only a way of measuring the surface of phenomena so as to string their changes on a simple formula.

Yet in the choice of these man-made formulas we can not be capricious with impunity any more than we can be capricious on the common-sense practical level. We must find a theory that will *work*; and that means something extremely difficult; for our theory must mediate between all previous truths and certain new experiences. It must derange common sense and previous belief as little as possible, and it must lead to some sensible terminus or other that can be verified exactly. To 'work' means both these things; and the squeeze is so tight that there is little loose play for any hypothesis. Our theories are wedged and controlled as nothing else is. Yet sometimes alternative theoretic formulas are equally compatible with all the truths we know, and then we choose between them for subjective reasons. We choose the kind of theory to which we are already partial; we follow 'elegance' or 'economy'. Clerk-Maxwell somewhere says it would be 'poor scientific taste' to choose the more complicated of two equally well-evidenced conceptions; and you will all agree with him. Truth in science is what gives us the maximum possible sum of satisfactions, taste included, but consistency both with previous truth and with novel fact is always the most imperious claimant.

I have led you through a very sandy desert. But now, if I may be allowed so vulgar an expression, we begin to taste the milk in the coconut. Our rationalist critics here discharge their batteries upon us, and to reply to them will take us out from all this dryness into full sight of a momentous philosophical alternative.

Our account of truth is an account of truths in the plural, of processes of leading, realized *in rebus*, and having only this quality in common, that they *pay*. They pay by guiding us into or towards some part of a system that dips at numerous points into sense-percepts, which we may copy mentally or not, but with which at any rate we are now in the kind of commerce vaguely designated as verification. Truth for us is simply a collective name for verification-processes, just as health, wealth, strength, etc., are names for other processes connected with life, and also pursued because it pays to pursue them. Truth is *made*, just as health, wealth, and strength are made, in the course of experience.

Here rationalism is instantaneously up in arms against us. I can imagine a rationalist to talk as follows:

'Truth is not made,' he will say; 'it absolutely obtains, being a unique relation that does not wait upon any process, but shoots straight over the head of experience, and hits its reality every time. Our belief that yon thing on the wall is a clock is true already, although no one in the whole history of the world should verify it. The bare quality of standing in that transcendent relation is what makes any thought true that possesses it, whether or not there be verification. You pragmatists put the cart before the horse in making truth's being reside in verification-processes. These are merely signs of its being, merely our lame ways of ascertaining after the fact, which of our ideas already has possessed the wondrous quality. The quality itself is timeless, like all essences and natures. Thoughts partake of it directly, as they partake of falsity or of irrelevancy. It can't be analysed away into pragmatic consequences.'

The whole plausibility of this rationalist tirade is due to the fact to which we have already paid so much attention. In our world, namely, abounding as it does in things of similar kinds and similarly associated, one verification serves for others of its kind, and one great use of knowing things is to be led not so much to them as to their associates, especially to human talk about them. The quality of truth, obtaining *ante rem*, pragmatically means, then, the fact that in such a world innumerable ideas work better by their indirect or possible than by their direct and actual verification. Truth *ante rem* means only verifiability, then; or else it is a case of the stock rationalist trick of treating the *name* of a concrete phenomenal reality as an independent prior entity, and placing it behind the reality as its explanation. Professor Mach quotes somewhere an epigram of Lessing's:

Sagt Hänschen Schlau zu Vetter Fritz,
'Wie kommt es, Vetter Fritzen,
Dass grad' die Reichsten in der Welt,
Das meiste Geld besitzen?'

Hänschen Schlau here treats the principle 'wealth' as something distinct from the facts denoted by the man's being rich. It antedates them; the facts become only a sort of secondary coincidence with the rich man's essential nature.

In the case of 'wealth' we all see the fallacy. We know that wealth is but a name for concrete processes that certain men's lives play a part in, and not a natural excellence found in Messrs. Rockefeller and Carnegie, but not in the rest of us.

Like wealth, health also lives *in rebus*. It is a name for processes, as digestion, circulation, sleep, etc., that go on happily, though in this instance we are more inclined to think of it as a principle and to say the man digests and sleeps so well *because* he is so healthy.

With 'strength' we are, I think, more rationalistic still, and decidedly inclined to treat it as an excellence pre-existing in the man and explanatory of the herculean performances of his muscles.

With 'truth' most people go over the border entirely, and treat the rationalistic account as self-evident. But really all these words in *th* are exactly similar. Truth exists *ante rem* just as much and as little as the other things do.

The scholastics, following Aristotle, made much of the distinction between habit and act. Health *in actu* means, among other things, good sleeping and digesting. But a healthy man need not always be sleeping, or always digesting, any more than a wealthy man need be always handling money, or a strong man always lifting weights. All such qualities sink to the status of 'habits' between their times of exercise; and similarly truth becomes a habit of certain of our ideas and beliefs in their intervals of rest from their verifying activities. But those activities are the root of the whole matter, and the condition of there being any habit to exist in the intervals.

'*The true*', to put it very briefly, is only the expedient in the way of our thinking, just as 'the right' is only the expedient in the way of our behaving. Expedient in almost any fashion; and expedient in the long run and on the whole of course; for what meets expediently all the experience in sight won't necessarily meet all farther experiences equally satisfactorily. Experience, as we know, has ways of *boiling over*, and making us correct our present formulas.

The 'absolutely' true, meaning what no further experience will ever alter, is that ideal vanishing-point towards which we imagine that all our temporary truths will some day converge. It runs on all fours with the perfectly wise man, and with the absolutely complete experience; and, if these ideals are ever realized, they will all be realized together. Meanwhile we have to live today by what truth we can get today, and be ready tomorrow to call it falsehood. Ptolemaic astronomy, Euclidean space, Aristotelian logic, scholastic metaphysics, were expedient for centuries, but human experience has boiled over those limits, and we now call these things only relatively true, or true within those borders of experience. 'Absolutely' they are false; for we know that those limits were casual, and might have been transcended by past theorists just as they are by present thinkers.

When new experiences lead to retrospective judgements, using the past tense, what these judgements utter *was* true, even though no past thinker had been led there. We live forwards, a Danish thinker has said, but we understand backwards. The present sheds a backward light on the world's previous processes. They may have been truth-processes for the actors in them. They are not so for one who knows the later revelations of the story.

This regulative notion of a potential better truth to be established later, possibly to be established some day absolutely, and having powers of retroactive legislation, turns its face, like all pragmatist notions, towards concreteness of fact, and towards the future. Like the half-truths, the absolute truth will have to be *made*, made as a relation incidental to the growth of a mass of verification-experience, to which the half-true ideas are all along contributing their quota.

I have already insisted on the fact that truth is made largely out of previous truths. Men's beliefs at any time are so much experience *funded*. But the beliefs are themselves parts of the sum total of the world's experience, and become matter, therefore, for the next day's funding operations. So far as reality means experienceable reality, both it and the truths men gain about it are everlastingly in process of mutation—mutation towards a definite goal, it may be—but still mutation.

Mathematicians can solve problems with two variables. On the Newtonian theory, for instance, acceleration varies with distance, but distance also varies with acceleration. In the realm of truth-processes facts come independently and determine our beliefs provisionally. But these beliefs make us act, and as fast as they do so, they bring into sight or into existence new facts which redetermine the beliefs accordingly. So the whole coil and ball of truth, as it rolls up, is the product of a double influence. Truths emerge from facts; but they dip forward into facts again and add to them; which facts again create or reveal new truth (the word is indifferent) and so on indefinitely. The 'facts' themselves meanwhile are not *true*. They simply *are*. Truth is the function of the beliefs that start and terminate among them.

The case is like a snowball's growth, due as it is to the distribution of the snow on the one hand, and to the successive pushes of the boys on the other, with these factors co-determining each other incessantly.

The most fateful point of difference between being a rationalist and being a pragmatist is now fully in sight. Experience is in mutation, and our psychological ascertainments of truth are in mutation—so much rationalism will allow; but never that either reality itself or truth itself is mutable. Reality stands complete and ready-made from all eternity, rationalism insists, and the agreement of our ideas with it is that unique unanalysable virtue in them of which she has already told us. As that intrinsic excellence, their truth has nothing to do with our experiences. It adds nothing to the content of experience. It makes no difference to reality itself; it is supervenient, inert, static, a reflexion merely. It doesn't *exist*, it *holds* or *obtains*, it belongs to another dimension from that of either facts or fact-relations, belongs, in short, to the epistemological dimension—and with that big word rationalism closes the discussion.

Thus, just as pragmatism faces forward to the future, so does rationalism here again face backward to a past eternity. True to her inveterate habit, rationalism reverts to 'principles', and thinks that when an abstraction once is named, we own an oracular solution.

The tremendous pregnancy in the way of consequences for life of this radical difference of outlook will only become apparent in my later lectures. I wish meanwhile to close this lecture by showing that rationalism's sublimity does not save it from inanity.

When, namely, you ask rationalists, instead of accusing pragmatism of desecrating the notion of truth, to define it themselves by saying exactly what *they* understand by it, the only positive attempts I can think of are these two:

1 'Truth is the system of propositions which have an unconditional claim to be recognized as valid.'[1]

2 Truth is a name for all those judgements which we find ourselves under obligation to make by a kind of imperative duty.[2]

The first thing that strikes one in such definitions is their unutterable triviality. They are absolutely true, of course, but absolutely insignificant

---

[1] A. E. Taylor, *Philosophical Review*, 14: 288.
[2] H. Rickert, *Der Gegenstand der Erkenntniss; Einfuhrung in die tranzendentale philosophie* (Tübingen, 1904), ch. on 'Die Urtheilsnothwendigkeit'.

until you handle them pragmatically. What do you mean by 'claim' here, and what do you mean by 'duty'? As summary names for the concrete reasons why thinking in true ways is overwhelmingly expedient and good for mortal men, it is all right to talk of claims on reality's part to be agreed with, and of obligations on our part to agree. We feel both the claims and the obligations, and we feel them for just those reasons.

But the rationalists who talk of claim and obligation *expressly say that they have nothing to do with our practical interests or personal reasons.* Our reasons for agreeing are psychological facts, they say, relative to each thinker, and to the accidents of his life. They are his evidence merely, they are no part of the life of truth itself. That life transacts itself in a purely logical or epistemological, as distinguished from a psychological, dimension, and its claims antedate and exceed all personal motivations whatsoever. Though neither man nor God should ever ascertain truth, the word would still have to be defined as that which *ought* to be ascertained and recognized.

There never was a more exquisite example of an idea abstracted from the concretes of experience and then used to oppose and negate what it was abstracted from.

Philosophy and common life abound in similar instances. The 'sentimentalist fallacy' is to shed tears over abstract justice and generosity, beauty, etc., and never to know these qualities when you meet them in the street, because the circumstances make them vulgar. Thus I read in the privately printed biography of an eminently rationalistic mind: 'It was strange that with such admiration for beauty in the abstract, my brother had no enthusiasm for fine architecture, for beautiful painting, or for flowers.' And in almost the last philosophic work I have read, I find such passages as the following: 'Justice is ideal, solely ideal. Reason conceives that it ought to exist, but experience shows that it can not. . . . Truth, which ought to be, can not be. . . . Reason is deformed by experience. As soon as reason enters experience it becomes contrary to reason.'

The rationalist's fallacy here is exactly like the sentimentalist's. Both extract a quality from the muddy particulars of experience, and find it so pure when extracted that they contrast it with each and all its muddy instances as an opposite and higher nature. All the while it is *their* nature. It is the nature of truths to be validated, verified. It pays for our ideas to be validated. Our obligation to seek truth is part of our general obligation to do what pays. They payments true ideas bring are the sole why of our duty to follow them. Identical whys exist in the case of wealth and health.

Truth makes no other kind of claim and imposes no other kind of

ought than health and wealth do. All these claims are conditional; the
concrete benefits we gain are what we mean by calling the pursuit a
duty. In the case of truth, untrue beliefs work as perniciously in the long
run as true beliefs work beneficially. Talking abstractly, the quality 'true'
may thus be said to grow absolutely precious and the quality 'untrue'
absolutely damnable: the one may be called good, the other bad, un-
conditionally. We ought to think the true, we ought to shun the false,
imperatively.

But if we treat all this abstraction literally and oppose it to its mother
soil in experience, see what a preposterous position we work ourselves
into.

We cannot then take a step forward in our actual thinking. When shall
I acknowledge this truth and when that? Shall the acknowledgment be
loud?—or silent? If sometimes loud, sometimes silent, which *now*? When
may a truth go into cold-storage in the encyclopedia? and when shall it
come out for battle? Must I constantly be repeating the truth 'twice two
are four' because of its eternal claim on recognition? or is it sometimes
irrelevant? Must my thoughts dwell night and day on my personal sins and
blemishes, because I truly have them?— or may I sink and ignore them in
order to be a decent social unit, and not a mass of morbid melancholy and
apology?

It is quite evident that our obligation to acknowledge truth, so far
from being unconditional, is tremendously conditioned. Truth with a
big T, and in the singular, claims abstractly to be recognized, of course; but
concrete truths in the plural need be recognized only when their recognition is expedient. A truth must always be preferred to a falsehood
when both relate to the situation; but when neither does, truth is as little
of a duty as falsehood. If you ask me what o'clock it is and I tell you that
I live at 95 Irving Street, my answer may indeed be true, but you don't
see why it is my duty to give it. A false address would be as much to the
purpose.

With this admission that there are conditions that limit the application
of the abstract imperative, *the pragmatistic treatment of truth sweeps back
upon us in its fulness*. Our duty to agree with reality is seen to be grounded
in a perfect jungle of concrete expediencies.

When Berkeley had explained what people meant by matter, people
thought that he denied matter's existence. When Messrs. Schiller and
Dewey now explain what people mean by truth, they are accused of
denying *its* existence. These pragmatists destroy all objective standards,
critics say, and put foolishness and wisdom on one level. A favourite
formula for describing Mr Schiller's doctrines and mine is that we are

persons who think that by saying whatever you find it pleasant to say and calling it truth you fulfil every pragmatistic requirement.

I leave it to you to judge whether this be not an impudent slander. Pent in, as the pragmatist more than anyone else sees himself to be, between the whole body of funded truths squeezed from the past and the coercions of the world of sense about him, who so well as he feels the immense pressure of objective control under which our minds perform their operations? If anyone imagines that this law is lax, let him keep its commandment one day, says Emerson. We have heard much of late of the uses of the imagination in science. It is high time to urge the use of a little imagination in philosophy. The unwillingness of some of our critics to read any but the silliest of possible meanings into our statements is as discreditable to their imaginations as anything I know in recent philosophic history. Schiller says the true is that which 'works'. Thereupon he is treated as one who limits verification to the lowest material utilities. Dewey says truth is what gives 'satisfaction'. He is treated as one who believes in calling everything true which, if it were true, would be pleasant.

Our critics certainly need more imagination of realities. I have honestly tried to stretch my own imagination and to read the best possible meaning into the rationalist conception, but I have to confess that it still completely baffles me. The notion of a reality calling on us to 'agree' with it, and that for no reasons, but simply because its claim is 'unconditional' or 'transcendent', is one that I can make neither head nor tail of. I try to imagine myself as the sole reality in the world, and then to imagine what more I would 'claim' if I were allowed to. If you suggest the possibility of my claiming that a mind should come into being from out of the void inane and stand and *copy* me, I can indeed imagine what the copying might mean, but I can conjure up no motive. What good it would do me to be copied, or what good it would do that mind to copy me, if further consequences are expressly and in principle ruled out as motives for the claim (as they are by our rationalist authorities) I can not fathom. When the Irishman's admirers ran him along to the place of banquet in a sedan chair with no bottom, he said, 'Faith, if it wasn't for the honour of the thing, I might as well have come on foot.' So here: but for the honour of the thing, I might as well have remained uncopied. Copying is one genuine mode of knowing (which for some strange reason our contemporary transcendentalists seem to be tumbling over each other to repudiate); but when we get beyond copying, and fall back on unnamed forms of agreeing that are expressly denied to be either copyings or leadings or fittings, or any other processes pragmatically definable, the *what* of the 'agreement' claimed becomes as unintelligible as the why of it. Neither content nor motive can be imagined for it. It is an absolutely meaningless abstraction.[3]

Surely in this field of truth it is the pragmatists and not the rationalists who are the more genuine defenders of the universe's rationality.

[3] I am not forgetting that Professor Rickert long ago gave up the whole notion of truth being founded on agreement with reality. Reality according to him, is whatever agrees with truth, and truth is founded solely on our primal duty. This fantastic flight, together with Mr Joachim's candid confession of failure in his book *The Nature of Truth* (Oxford, 1906), seems to me to mark the bankruptcy of rationalism when dealing with this subject. Rickert deals with part of the pragmatistic position under the head of what he calls 'Relativismus'. I cannot discuss his text here. Suffice it to say that his argumentation in that chapter is so feeble as to seem almost incredible in so generally able a writer.

IV

WILLIAM JAMES'S CONCEPTION OF TRUTH[1]

BERTRAND RUSSELL

'The history of philosophy', as William James observes, 'is to a great extent that of a certain clash of human temperaments.' In dealing with a temperament of such charm as his, it is not pleasant to think of a 'clash'; one does not willingly differ, or meet so much urbanity by churlish criticisms. Fortunately, a very large part of his book is concerned with the advocacy of positions which pragmatism shares with other forms of empiricism; with all this part of his book, I, as an empiricist, find myself, broadly speaking, in agreement. I might instance the lecture devoted to a problem which he considers 'the most central of all philosophic problems', namely, that of the One and the Many. In this lecture he declares himself on the whole a pluralist, after a discussion of the kinds and degrees of unity to be found in the world to which any empiricist may wholly assent. Throughout the book, the distinctive tenets of pragmatism only make their appearance now and again, after the ground has been carefully prepared. James speaks somewhere of Dr Schiller's 'butt-end foremost statement of the humanist position'. His own statement is the very reverse of 'butt-end foremost'; it is insinuating, gradual, imperceptible.

A good illustration of his insinuating method is afforded by his lecture on common sense. The categories of common sense, as he points out, and as we may all agree, embody discoveries of our remote ancestors; but these discoveries cannot be regarded as final, because science, and still more philosophy, finds common-sense notions inadequate in many ways. Common sense, science, and philosophy, we are told, are all insufficiently true in

From Bertrand Russell, 'William James's Conception of Truth', in *Philosophical Essays* (London: George Allen & Unwin, 1996), 112–30. Reprinted with permission of Routledge and the Bertrand Russell Peace Foundation.

[1] *Pragmatism: A New Name for Some Old Ways of Thinking*, Popular Lectures on Philosophy, by William James (New York: Longmans, Green, and Co., 1907). This chapter has been criticized by William James in *The Meaning of Truth* (New York: Longmans, 1909), in the article called 'Two English Critics'.

some respect; and to this again we may agree. But he adds: 'It is evident that the conflict of these so widely differing systems obliges us to overhaul the very idea of truth, for at present we have no definite notion of what the word may mean' (p. 192). Here, as I think, we have a mere non sequitur. A damson-tart, a plum-tart, and a gooseberry-tart may all be insufficiently sweet; but does that oblige us to overhaul the very notion of sweetness, or show that we have no definite notion of what the word 'sweetness' may mean? It seems to me, on the contrary, that if we perceive that they are insufficiently sweet, that shows that we do know what 'sweetness' is; and the same surely applies to truth. But this remark is merely by the way.

James, like most philosophers, represents his views as mediating between two opposing schools. He begins by distinguishing two philosophic types called respectively the 'tender-minded' and the 'tough-minded'. The 'tender-minded' are 'rationalistic, intellectualistic, idealistic, optimistic, religious, free-willist, monistic, dogmatical'. The 'tough-minded' are 'empiricist, sensationalistic, materialistic, pessimistic, irreligious, fatalistic, pluralistic, sceptical'. Traditionally, German philosophy was on the whole 'tender-minded', British philosophy was on the whole 'tough-minded'. It will clear the ground for me to confess at once that I belong, with some reserves, to the 'tough-minded' type. Pragmatism, William James avers, 'can satisfy both kinds of demand. It can remain religious like the rationalisms, but at the same time, like the empiricisms, it can preserve the richest intimacy with facts'. This reconciliation, to my mind, is illusory; I find myself agreeing with the 'tough-minded' half of pragmatism and totally disagreeing with the 'tender-minded' half. But the disentangling of the two halves must be postponed till we have seen how the reconciliation professes to be effected. Pragmatism represents, on the one hand, a method and habit of mind, on the other, a certain theory as to what constitutes truth. The latter is more nearly what Dr Schiller calls humanism; but this name is not adopted by James. We must, therefore, distinguish the pragmatic *method* and the pragmatic *theory of truth*. The former, up to a point, is involved in all induction, and is certainly largely commendable. The latter is the essential novelty and the point of real importance. But let us first consider the pragmatic method.

'Pragmatism', says James, 'represents a perfectly familiar attitude in philosophy, the empiricist attitude, but it represents it, as it seems to me, both in a more radical and in a less objectionable form than it has ever yet assumed. A pragmatist turns his back resolutely and once for all upon a lot of inveterate habits dear to professional philosophers. He turns away from abstraction and insufficiency, from verbal solutions, from bad *a priori* reasons, from fixed principles, closed systems, and pretended absolutes and origins. He turns towards concreteness and adequacy towards facts, towards action and towards power. That means the empiricist temper regnant and the rationalist temper sincerely given up. It means the open air and possibilities of nature, as against dogma, artificiality, and the pretence of finality in truth' (p. 51).

The temper of mind here described is one with which I, for my part, in the main cordially sympathize. But I think there is an impression in the mind of William James, as of some other pragmatists, that pragmatism involves a more open mind than its opposite. As regards scientific questions, or even the less important questions of philosophy, this is no doubt more or less the case. But as regards the fundamental questions of philosophy—especially as regards what I consider *the* fundamental question, namely, the nature of truth—pragmatism is absolutely dogmatic. The hypothesis that pragmatism is erroneous is not allowed to enter for the pragmatic competition; however well it may work, it is not to be entertained. To 'turn your back resolutely and once for all' upon the philosophy of others may be heroic or praiseworthy, but it is not undogmatic or open-minded. A modest shrinking from self-assertion, a sense that all our theories are provisional, a constant realization that after all the hypothesis of our opponents may be the right one—these characterize the truly empirical temper, but I do not observe that they invariably characterize the writings of pragmatists. Dogmatism in fundamentals is more or less unavoidable in philosophy, and I do not blame pragmatists for what could not be otherwise; but I demur to their claim to a greater open-mindedness than is or may be possessed by their critics.

William James, however, it must be admitted, is about as little pontifical as a philosopher well can be. And his complete absence of unction is most refreshing. 'In this real world of sweat and dirt', he says, 'it seems to me that when a view of things is "noble", that ought to count as a presumption against its truth and as a philosophic disqualification' (p. 72). Accordingly his contentions are never supported by 'fine writing'; he brings them into the market place, and is not afraid to be homely, untechnical, and slangy. All this makes his books refreshing to read, and shows that they contain what he really lives by, not merely what he holds in his professional capacity.

But it is time to return to the pragmatic method.

'The pragmatic method', we are told, 'is primarily a method of settling metaphysical disputes that otherwise might be interminable. Is the world one or many?—fated or free?—material or spiritual?—here are notions either of which may or may not hold good of the world; and disputes over such notions are unending. The pragmatic method in such cases is to try to interpret each notion by tracing its respective practical consequences.

What difference would it practically make to anyone if this notion rather than that notion were true? If no practical difference whatever can be traced, then the alternatives mean practically the same thing, and all dispute is idle. Whenever a dispute is serious, we ought to be able to show some practical difference that must follow from one side or the other's being right.' And again: 'To attain perfect clearness in our thoughts of an object, then, we need only consider what conceivable effects of a practical kind the object may involve—what sensations we are to expect from it, and what reactions we must prepare. Our conception of these effects, whether immediate or remote, is then for us the whole of our conception of the object, so far as that conception has positive significance at all' (pp. 45–7).

To this method, applied within limits and to suitable topics, there is no ground for objecting. On the contrary, it is wholesome to keep in touch with concrete facts, as far as possible, by remembering to bring our theories constantly into connection with them. The method, however, involves more than is stated in the extract which I quoted just now. It involves also the suggestion of the pragmatic criterion of truth: a belief is to be judged true in so far as the practical consequences of its adoption are good. Some pragmatists, for example, Le Roy (who has lately suffered papal condemnation), regard the pragmatic test as giving *only* a criterion;[2] others, notably Dr Schiller, regard it as giving the actual *meaning* of truth. William James agrees on this point with Dr Schiller, though, like him, he does not enter into the question of criterion *versus* meaning.

The pragmatic theory of truth is the central doctrine of pragmatism, and we must consider it at some length. William James states it in various ways, some of which I shall now quote. He says: 'Ideas (which themselves are but parts of our experience) become true just in so far as they help us to get into satisfactory relation with other parts of our experience' (p. 58). Again: 'Truth is *one species of good*, and not, as is usually supposed, a category distinct from good, and coordinate with it. *The true is the name of whatever proves itself to be good in the way of belief, and good, too, for definite, assignable reasons*' (p. 75). That truth means 'agreement with reality' may be said by a pragmatist as well as by anyone else, but the pragmatist differs from others as to what is meant by 'agreement', and also (it would seem) as to what is meant by 'reality'. William James gives the following definition of 'agreement': 'To "agree" in the widest sense with a reality *can only mean to be guided either straight up to it or into its surroundings, or to be put into such working touch with it as to handle either it or something connected with it better than if we disagreed'* (p. 212 [p. 59 in this volume]). This language is rather metaphorical, and a little puzzling; it is plain, however, that 'agreement' is regarded as practical, not as merely intellectual. This emphasis on practice is, of course, one of the leading features of pragmatism.

In order to understand the pragmatic notion of truth, we have to be clear as to the basis of *fact* upon which truths are supposed to rest. Immediate sensible experience, for example, does not come under the alternative of *true* and *false*. 'Day follows day', says James, 'and its contents are simply added. The new contents themselves are not true, they simply *come* and *are*. Truth is *what we say about* them' (p. 62). Thus when we are merely aware of sensible objects, we are not to be regarded as knowing any truth, although we have a certain kind of contact with reality. It is important to realize that the *facts* which thus lie outside the scope of truth and false-hood supply the material which is presupposed by the pragmatic theory. Our beliefs have to agree with matters of fact: it is an essential part of their 'satisfactoriness' that they should do so. James also mentions what he calls 'relations among purely mental ideas' as part of our stock-in-trade with which pragmatism starts. He mentions as instances '1 and 1 make 2', 'white differs less from grey than it does from black', and so on. All such propo-sitions as these, then, we are supposed to know for certain before we can get under way. As James puts it: 'Between the coercions of the sensible order and those of the ideal order, our mind is thus wedged tightly. Our ideas must agree with realities, be such realities concrete or abstract, be they facts or be they principles, under penalty of endless inconsistency and frustration' (p. 211 [p. 58 in this volume]). Thus it is only when we pass beyond plain matters of fact and a priori truisms that the pragmatic notion of truth comes in. It is, in short, the notion to be applied to doubtful cases, but it is not the notion to be applied to cases about which there can be no doubt. And that there are cases about which there can be no doubt is pre-supposed in the very statement of the pragmatist position. 'Our account of truth', James tells us, 'is an account . . . of processes of leading, realized *in rebus*, and having only this quality in common, that they *pay*' (p. 218 [p. 61 in this volume]). We may thus sum up the philosophy in the following definition: 'A truth is anything which it pays to believe.' Now, if this definition is to be useful, as pragmatism intends it to be, it must be possi-ble to know that it pays to believe something without knowing anything that pragmatism would call a truth. Hence the knowledge that a certain belief pays must be classed as knowledge of a sensible fact or of a 'rela-tion among purely mental ideas', or as some compound of the two, and must be so easy to discover as not to be worthy of having the pragmatic test applied to it. There is, however, some difficulty in this view. Let us consider for a moment what it means to say that a belief 'pays'. We must suppose that this means that the consequences of entertaining the belief are better than those of rejecting it. In order to know this, we must know what are the consequences of entertaining it, and what are the consequences of rejecting it; we must know also what consequences are good, what bad, what consequences are better, and what worse. Take, say, belief in the Roman Catholic Faith. This, we may agree, causes a certain amount of happiness at the expense of a certain amount of stupidity and priestly domination. Such a view is disputable and disputed, but we will let that pass. But then comes the question whether, admitting the effects to be such, they are to be classed as on the whole good or on the whole bad; and this question is one which is so difficult that our test of truth becomes practically useless. It is far easier, it seems to me, to settle the plain question of fact: 'Have Popes been always infallible?' than to settle the question whether the effects of thinking them infallible are on the whole good. Yet this question, of the truth of Roman Catholicism, is just the sort of question that pragmatists consider specially suitable to their method.

The notion that it is quite easy to know when the consequences of a belief are good, so easy, in fact, that a theory of knowledge need take no account of anything so simple—this notion, I must say, seems to me one of the strangest assumptions for a theory of knowledge to make. Let us take another illustration. Many of the men of the French Revolution were disciples of Rousseau, and their belief in his doctrines had far-reaching effects, which make Europe at this day a different place from what it would have been without that belief. If, on the whole, the effects of their belief have been good, we shall have to say that their belief was true; if bad, that it was false. But how are we to strike the balance? It is almost impossible to disentangle what the effects have been; and even if we could ascertain them, our judgment as to whether they have been good or bad would depend upon our political opinions. It is surely far easier to discover by direct investigation that the *Contrat social* is a myth than to decide whether belief in it has done harm or good on the whole.

Another difficulty which I feel in regard to the pragmatic meaning of 'truth' may be stated as follows: Suppose I accept the pragmatic criterion, and suppose you persuade me that a certain belief is useful. Suppose I thereupon conclude that the belief is true. Is it not obvious that there is a transition in my mind from seeing that the belief is useful to actually holding that the belief is true? Yet this could not be so if the pragmatic account of truth were valid. Take, say, the belief that other people exist. According to the pragmatists, to say 'it is true that other people exist' *means* 'it is useful to believe that other people exist'. But if so, then these two phrases are merely different words for the same proposition; therefore when I believe the one I believe the other. If this were so, there could be no transition from the one to the other, as plainly there is. This shows that the word 'true' represents for us a different idea from that represented by the phrase 'useful to believe', and that, therefore, the pragmatic definition of truth ignores, without destroying, the meaning commonly given to the word 'true', which meaning, in my opinion, is of fundamental importance, and can only be ignored at the cost of hopeless inadequacy.

This brings me to the difference between *criterion* and *meaning*—a point on which neither James nor Dr Schiller is very clear. I may best explain the difference, to begin with, by an instance. If you wish to know whether a certain book is in a library, you consult the catalogue: books mentioned in the catalogue are presumably in the library, books not mentioned in it are presumably not in the library. Thus the catalogue affords a *criterion* of whether a book is in the library or not. But even supposing the catalogue perfect, it is obvious that when you say the book is in the library you do not *mean* that it is mentioned in the catalogue. You mean that the actual book is to be found somewhere in the shelves. It therefore remains an intelligible hypothesis that there are books in the library which are not yet catalogued, or that there are books catalogued which have been lost and are no longer in the library. And it remains an inference from the discovery that a book is mentioned in the catalogue to the conclusion that the book is in the library. Speaking abstractly, we may say that a property A is a *criterion* of a property B when the same objects possess both; and A is a *useful* criterion of B if it is easier to discover whether an object possesses the property A than whether it possesses the property B. Thus being mentioned in the catalogue is a *useful* criterion of being in the library, because it is easier to consult the catalogue than to hunt through the shelves.

Now if pragmatists only affirmed that utility is a *criterion* of truth, there would be much less to be said against their view. For there certainly seem to be few cases, if any, in which it is clearly useful to believe what is false. The chief criticism one would then have to make on pragmatism would be to deny that utility is a *useful* criterion, because it is so often harder to determine whether a belief is useful than whether it is true. The arguments of pragmatists are almost wholly directed to proving that utility is a *criterion*; that utility is the *meaning* of truth is then supposed to follow. But, to return to our illustration of the library, suppose we had conceded that there are no mistakes in the British Museum catalogue: would it follow that the catalogue would do without the books? We can imagine some person long engaged in a comparative study of libraries, and having, in the process, naturally lost all taste for reading, declaring that the catalogue is the only important thing—as for the books, they are useless lumber; no one ever wants them, and the principle of economy should lead us to be content with the catalogue. Indeed, if you consider the matter with an open mind, you will see that the catalogue *is* the library, for it tells you everything you can possibly with to know about the library. Let us, then, save the taxpayers' money by destroying the books: allow free access to the catalogue, but condemn the desire to read as involving an exploded dogmatic realism.

This analogy of the library is not, to my mind, fantastic or unjust, but as close and exact an analogy as I have been able to think of. The point I am trying to make clear is concealed from pragmatists, I think, by the fact that their theories start very often from such things as the general hypotheses of science—ether, atoms, and the like. In such cases, we take little interest in the hypotheses themselves, which, as we well know, are liable to rapid change. What we care about are the inferences as to sensible phenomena which the hypotheses enable us to make. All we ask of the hypotheses is that they should 'work'—though it should be observed that what constitutes 'working' is not the general agreeableness of their results, but the conformity of these results with observed phenomena. But in the case of these general scientific hypotheses, no sensible man believes that they are true as they stand. They are believed to be true in part, and to work because of the part that is true; but it is expected that in time some element of falsehood will be discovered, and some truer theory will be substituted. Thus pragmatism would seem to derive its notion of what constitutes belief from cases in which, properly speaking, belief is absent, and in which—what is pragmatically important—there is but a slender interest in truth or falsehood as compared to the interest in what 'works'.

But when this method is extended to cases in which the proposition in question has an emotional interest on its own account, apart from its working, the pragmatic account becomes less satisfactory. This point has been well brought out by Professor Stout,[3] and what I have to say is mostly contained in his remarks. Take the question whether other people exist. It seems perfectly possible to suppose that the hypothesis that they exist will always work, even if they do not in fact exist. It is plain, also, that it makes for happiness to believe that they exist—for even the greatest misanthropist would not wish to be deprived of the objects of his hate. Hence the belief that other people exist is, pragmatically, a true belief. But if I am troubled by solipsism, the discovery that a belief in the existence of others

---

[3] In *Mind*, 16 (1907), 586–8. This criticism occurs in the course of a very sympathetic review of Dr Schiller's *Studies in Humanism*.

is 'true' in the pragmatist's sense is not enough to allay my sense of lone-liness: the perception that I should profit by rejecting solipsism is not alone sufficient to make me reject it. For what I desire is not that the belief in solipsism should be false in the pragmatic sense, but that other people should in fact exist. And with the pragmatist's meaning of truth, these two do not necessarily go together. The belief in solipsism might be false even if I were the only person or thing in the universe.

This paradoxical consequence would, I presume, not be admitted by pragmatists. Yet it is an inevitable outcome of the divorce which they make between *fact* and *truth*. Returning to our illustration, we may say that 'facts' are represented by the books, and 'truths' by the entries in the catalogue. So long as you do not wish to read the books, the 'truths' will do in place of the 'facts', and the imperfections of your library can be remedied by simply making new entries in the catalogue. But as soon as you actually wish to read a book, the 'truths' become inadequate, and the 'facts' become all-important. The pragmatic account of truth assumes, so it seems to me, that no one takes any interest in facts, and that the truth of the proposi-tion that your friend exists is an adequate substitute for the fact of his exis-tence. 'Facts', they tell us, are neither true nor false, therefore truth cannot be concerned with them. But the truth 'A exists', if it is a truth, is concerned with A, who in that case is a fact; and to say that 'A exists' may be true even if A does not exist is to give a meaning to 'truth' which robs it of all interest. Dr Schiller is fond of attacking the view that truth must corre-spond with reality; we may conciliate him by agreeing that *his* truth, at any rate, need not correspond with reality. But we shall have to add that reality is to us more interesting than such truth.

I am, of course, aware that pragmatists minimize the basis of 'fact', and speak of the 'making of reality' as proceeding *pari passu* with the 'making of truth'. It is easy to criticize the claim to 'make reality' except within obvious limits. But when such criticisms are met by pointing to the prag-matist's admission that, after all, there must be a basis of 'fact' for our cre-ative activity to work upon, then the opposite line of criticism comes into play. Dr Schiller, in his essay on 'the making of reality', minimizes the importance of the basis of 'fact', on the ground (it would seem) that 'facts' will not submit to pragmatic treatment, and that, if pragmatism is true, they are unknowable.[4] Hence, on pragmatistic principles, it is useless to think about facts. We therefore return to fictions with a sigh of relief, and soothe our scruples by calling them 'realities'. But it seems something of a *petitio principii* to condemn 'facts' because pragmatism, though it finds them

---

[4] Cf. *Studies in Humanism* (London, 1907), 434–6.

necessary, is unable to deal with them. And William James, it should be said, makes less attempt than Dr Schiller does to minimize facts. In this essay, therefore, I have considered the difficulties which pragmatism has to face if it admits 'facts' rather than those (no less serious) which it has to face if it denies them.

It is chiefly in regard to religion that the pragmatist use of 'truth' seems to me misleading. Pragmatists boast much of their ability to reconcile religion and science, and William James, as we saw, professes to have discovered a position combining the merits of tender-mindedness and tough-mindedness. The combination is really effected, if I am not mistaken, in a way of which pragmatists are not themselves thoroughly aware. For their position, if they fully realized it, would, I think, be this: 'We cannot know whether, in fact, there is a God or a future life, but we can know that the belief in God and a future life is true.' This position, it is to be feared, would not afford much comfort to the religious if it were understood, and I cannot but feel some sympathy with the Pope in his condemnation of it.

'On pragmatic principles', James says, 'we cannot reject any hypothesis if consequences useful to life flow from it' (p. 273). He proceeds to point out that consequences useful to life flow from the hypothesis of the Absolute, which is therefore so far a true hypothesis. But it should be observed that these useful consequences flow from the hypothesis that the Absolute is a fact, not from the hypothesis that useful consequences flow from belief in the Absolute. But we cannot believe the hypothesis that the Absolute is a fact merely because we perceive that useful consequences flow from this hypothesis. What we can believe on such grounds is that this hypothesis is what pragmatists call 'true', i.e. that it is useful; but it is not from this belief that the useful consequences flow, and the grounds alleged do not make us believe that the Absolute is a fact, which is the useful belief. In other words, the useful belief is that the Absolute is a fact, and prag-matism shows that this belief is what it calls 'true'. Thus pragmatism per-suades us that belief in the Absolute is 'true', but does not persuade us that the Absolute is a fact. The belief which it persuades us to adopt is there-fore not the one which is useful. In ordinary logic, if the belief in the Absolute is true, it follows that the Absolute is a fact. But with the prag-matist's meaning of 'true' this does not follow; hence the proposition which he proves is not, as the thinks, the one from which comforting conse-quences flow.

In another place James says: 'On pragmatistic principles, if the hypoth-esis of God works satisfactorily in the widest sense of the word, it is true' (p. 299). This proposition is, in reality, a mere tautology. For we have laid down the definition: 'The word "true" means "working satisfactorily in the widest sense of the word".' Hence the proposition stated by James is merely a verbal variant on the following: 'On pragmatistic principles, if the hypothesis of God works satisfactorily in the widest sense of the word, then it works satisfactorily in the widest sense of the word.' This would hold even on other than pragmatistic principles; presumably what is peculiar to pragmatism is the belief that this is an important contribution to the philosophy of religion. The advantage of the pragmatic method is that it decides the question of the truth of the existence of God by purely mundane arguments, namely, by the effects of belief in his existence upon our life in this world. But unfortunately this gives a merely mundane conclusion, namely, that belief in God is true, i.e. useful, whereas what religion desires is the conclusion that God exists, which pragmatism never even approaches. I infer, therefore, that the pragmatic philosophy of religion, like most philosophies whose conclusions are interesting, turns on an unconscious play upon words. A common word—in this case, the word 'true'—is taken at the outset in an uncommon sense, but as the argument proceeds, the usual sense of the word gradually slips back, and the conclusions arrived at seem, therefore, quite different from what they would be seen to be if the initial definition had been remembered.

The point is, of course, that, so soon as it is admitted that there are things that exist, it is impossible to avoid recognizing a distinction, to which we may give what name we please, between believing in the existence of something that exists and believing in the existence of something that does not exist. It is common to call the one belief true, the other false. But if, with the pragmatists, we prefer to give a different meaning to the words 'true' and 'false', that does not prevent the distinction commonly called the distinction of 'true' and 'false' from persisting. The pragmatist attempt to ignore this distinction fails, as it seems to me, because a basis of fact cannot be avoided by pragmatism, and this basis of fact demands the *usual* antithesis of 'true' and 'false'. It is hardly to be supposed that pragmatists will admit this conclusion. But it may be hoped that they will tell us in more detail how they propose to avoid it.

Pragmatism, if I have not misunderstood it, is largely a generalization from the procedure of the inductive sciences. In so far as it lays stress upon the importances of induction, I find myself in agreement with it; and as to the nature of induction also, I think it is far more nearly right than are most of the traditional accounts. But on fundamental questions of philosophy I find myself wholly opposed to it, and unable to see that inductive procedure gives any warrant for its conclusions. To make this clear, I will very briefly explain how I conceive the nature and scope of induction.

When we survey our beliefs, we find that we hold different beliefs with very different degrees of conviction. Some—such as the belief that I am sitting in a chair, or that $2+2=4$—can be doubted by few except those who have had a long training in philosophy. Such beliefs are held so firmly that non-philosophers who deny them are put into lunatic asylums. Other beliefs, such as the facts of history, are held rather less firmly, but still in the main without much doubt where they are well authenticated. Beliefs about the future, as that the sun will rise tomorrow and that the trains will run approximately as in Bradshaw, may be held with almost as great conviction as beliefs about the past. Scientific laws are generally believed less firmly, and there is a gradation among them from such as seem nearly certain to such as have only a slight probability in their favour. Philosophical beliefs, finally, will, with most people, take a still lower place, since the opposite beliefs of others can hardly fail to induce doubt. Belief, therefore, is a matter of degree. To speak of belief, disbelief, doubt, and suspense of judgment as the only possibilities is as if, from the writing on the thermometer, we were to suppose that blood heat, summer heat, temperate, and freezing were the only temperatures. There is a continuous gradation in belief, and the more firmly we believe anything, the less willing we are to abandon it in case of conflict.

Besides the degree of our belief, there is another important respect in which a belief may vary, namely, in the extent to which it is *spontaneous* or *derivative*. A belief obtained by inference may be called *derivative*; one not so obtained, *spontaneous*. When we do not need any outside evidence to make us entertain a belief, we may say that what we believe is *obvious*. Our belief in the existence of sensible objects is of this nature: 'seeing is believing', and we demand no further evidence. The same applies to certain logical principles, e.g. that whatever follows from a true proposition must be true. A proposition may be obvious in very varying degrees. For example, in matters of æsthetic taste we have to judge immediately whether a work of art is beautiful or not, but the degree of obviousness involved is probably small, so that we feel no very great confidence in our judgment. Thus our spontaneous beliefs are not necessarily stronger than derivative beliefs. Moreover, few beliefs, if any, are *wholly* spontaneous in an educated man. The more a man has organized his knowledge, the more his beliefs will be interdependent, and the more will obvious truths be reinforced by their connection with other obvious truths. In spite of this fact, however, obviousness remains always the ultimate source of our beliefs; for what is called verification or deduction consists always in being brought into relation with one or more obvious propositions. This process of verification is necessary even for propositions which seem obvious, since it appears on examination that two apparently obvious propositions may be inconsistent, and hence that apparent obviousness is not a sufficient guarantee of truth. We therefore have to subject our beliefs to a process of organization, making groups of such as are mutually consistent, and when two such groups are not consistent with each other, selecting that group which seems to us to contain the most evidence, account being taken both of the degree of obviousness of the propositions it contains and of the number of such propositions. It is as the result of such a process, for example, that we are led, if we are led, to conclude that colours are not objective properties of things. Induction, in a broad sense, may be described as the process of selecting hypotheses which will organize our spontaneous beliefs, preserving as many of them as possible, and interconnecting them by general propositions which, as is said, 'explain' them, i.e. give a ground from which they can be deduced. In this sense, all knowledge is inductive as soon as it is reflective and organized. In any science, there is a greater or less degree of obviousness about many of its propositions: those that are obvious are called *data*; other propositions are only accepted because of their connection with the data. This connection itself may be of two kinds, either that the propositions in question can be deduced from the data, or that the data can be deduced from the propositions in question, and we know of no way of deducing the data without assuming the propositions in question. The latter is the case of working hypotheses, which covers all the general laws of science and all the metaphysics both of common sense and of professed philosophy. It is, apparently, by generalizing the conception of 'working hypothesis' that pragmatism has arisen. But three points seem to me to have been overlooked in this generalization. First, working hypotheses are only a small part of our beliefs, not the whole, as pragmatism seems to think. Secondly, prudent people give only a low degree of belief to working hypotheses; it is therefore a curious procedure to select them as the very types of beliefs in general. Thirdly, pragmatism seems to confound two very different conceptions of 'working'. When *science* says that a hypothesis works, it means that from this hypothesis we can deduce a number of propositions which are verifiable, i.e. obvious under suitable circumstances, and that we cannot deduce any propositions of which the contradictories are verifiable. But when *pragmatism* says that a hypothesis works, it means that the effects of believing it are good, including among the effects not only the beliefs which we deduce from it, but also the emotions entailed by it or its perceived consequences, and the actions to which we are prompted by it or its perceived consequences. This is a totally different conception of 'working', and one for which the authority of scientific procedure cannot be invoked.

I infer, therefore, that induction, rightly analysed, does not lead us to pragmatism, and that the inductive results which pragmatism takes as the very type of truth are precisely those among our beliefs which should be held with most caution and least conviction.

To sum up: while agreeing with the empirical temper of pragmatism, with its readiness to treat all philosophical tenets as 'working hypotheses', we cannot agree that when we say a belief is true we mean that it is a hypothesis which 'works', especially if we mean by this to take account of the excellence of its effects, and not merely of the truth of its consequences. If, to avoid disputes about words, we agree to accept the pragmatic definition of the word 'truth', we find that the belief that A exists may be 'true' even when A does not exist. This shows that the conclusions arrived at by pragmatism in the sphere of religion do not have the meaning which they appear to have, and are incapable, when rightly understood, of yielding us the satisfaction which they promise. The attempt to get rid of 'fact' turns out to be a failure, and thus the old notion of truth reappears. And if the pragmatist states that utility is to be merely a *criterion* of truth, we shall reply first, that it is not a useful criterion, because it is usually harder to discover whether a belief is useful than whether it is true; secondly, that since no a priori reason is shown why truth and utility should always go together, utility can only be shown to be a criterion at all by showing inductively that it accompanies truth in all known instances, which requires that we should already know in many instances what things are true. Finally, therefore, the pragmatist theory of truth is to be condemned on the ground that it does not 'work'.

PART II

EARLY MINIMALIST THEORIES

THE THOUGHT: A LOGICAL INQUIRY

GOTTLOB FREGE
(translated by A. M. and Marcelle Quinton)

The word 'true' indicates the aim of logic as does 'beautiful' that of aes-
thetics or 'good' that of ethics. All sciences have truth as their goal; but
logic is also concerned with it in a quite different way from this. It has much
the same relation to truth as physics has to weight or heat. To discover
truths is the task of all sciences; it falls to logic to discern the laws of truth.
The word 'law' is used in two senses. When we speak of laws of morals or
the state we mean regulations which ought to be obeyed but with which
actual happenings are not always in conformity. Laws of nature are the
generalization of natural occurrences with which the occurrences are
always in accordance. It is rather in this sense that I speak of laws of truth.
This is, to be sure, not a matter of what happens so much as of what is.
Rules for asserting, thinking, judging, inferring, follow from the laws of
truth. And thus one can very well speak of laws of thought too. But there
is an imminent danger here of mixing different things up. Perhaps the
expression 'law of thought' is interpreted by analogy with 'law of nature'
and the generalization of thinking as a mental occurrence is meant by it.
A law of thought in this sense would be a psychological law. And so one
might come to believe that logic deals with the mental process of thinking
and the psychological laws in accordance with which it takes place. This
would be a misunderstanding of the task of logic, for truth has not been
given the place which is its due here. Error and superstition have causes
just as much as genuine knowledge. The assertion both of what is false and
of what is true takes place in accordance with psychological laws. A derivation from these and an explanation of a mental process that terminates in
an assertion can never take the place of a proof of what is asserted. Could
not logical laws also have played a part in this mental process? I do not
want to dispute this, but when it is a question of truth possibility is not

From Gottlob Frege, 'The Thought: A Logical Inquiry', *Mind*, 65 (1956), 289–311. Reprinted by
permission of Oxford University Press.

enough. For it is also possible that something not logical played a part in the process and deflected it from the truth. We can only decide this after we have discerned the laws of truth; but then we will probably be able to do without the derivation and explanation of the mental process if it is important to us to decide whether the assertion in which the process terminates is justified. In order to avoid this misunderstanding and to prevent the blurring of the boundary between psychology and logic, I assign to logic the task of discovering the laws of truth, not of assertion or thought. The meaning of the word 'true' is explained by the laws of truth.

But first I shall attempt to outline roughly what I want to call true in this connexion. In this way other uses of our word may be excluded. It is not to be used here in the sense of 'genuine' or 'veracious', nor, as it sometimes occurs in the treatment of questions of art, when, for example, truth in art is discussed, when truth is set up as the goal of art, when the truth of a work of art or true feeling is spoken of. The word 'true' is put in front of another word in order to show that this word is to be understood in its proper, unadulterated sense. This use too lies off the path followed here; that kind of truth is meant whose recognition is the goal of science.

Grammatically the word 'true' appears as an adjective. Hence the desire arises to delimit more closely the sphere in which truth can be affirmed, in which truth comes into the question at all. One finds truth affirmed of pictures, ideas, statements, and thoughts. It is striking that visible and audible things occur here alongside things which cannot be perceived with the sense. This hints that shifts of meaning have taken place. Indeed! Is a picture, then, as a mere visible and tangible thing, really true, and a stone, a leaf, not true? Obviously one would not call a picture true unless there were an intention behind it. A picture must represent something. Furthermore, an idea is not called true in itself but only with respect to an intention that it should correspond to something. It might be supposed from this that truth consists in the correspondence of a picture with what it depicts. Correspondence is a relation. This is contradicted, however, by the use of the word 'true', which is not a relation-word and contains no reference to anything else to which something must correspond. If I do not know that a picture is meant to represent Cologne Cathedral then I do not know with what to compare the picture to decide on its truth. A correspondence, moreover, can only be perfect if the corresponding things coincide and are, therefore, not distinct things at all. It is said to be possible to establish the authenticity of a banknote by comparing it stereoscopically with an authentic one. But it would be ridiculous to try to compare a gold piece with a twenty-mark note stereoscopically. It would only be possible to compare an idea with a thing if the thing were an idea too. And then, if the first did correspond perfectly with the second, they would coincide. But this is not at all what is wanted when truth is defined as the correspondence of an idea with something real. For it is absolutely essential that the reality be distinct from the idea. But then there can be no complete correspondence, no complete truth. So nothing at all would be true; for what is only half true is untrue. Truth cannot tolerate a more or less. But yet? Can it not be laid down that truth exists when there is correspondence in a certain respect? But in which? For what would we then have to do to decide whether something were true? We should have to inquire whether it were true that an idea and a reality, perhaps, corresponded in the laid-down respect. And then we should be confronted by a question of the same kind and the game could begin again. So the attempt to explain truth as correspondence collapses. And every other attempt to define truth collapses too. For in a definition certain characteristics would have to be stated. And in application to any particular case the question would always arise whether it were true that the characteristics were present. So one goes round in a circle. Consequently, it is probable that the content of the word 'true' is unique and indefinable.

When one ascribes truth to a picture one does not really want to ascribe a property which belongs to this picture altogether independently of other things, but one always has something quite different in mind and one wants to say that that picture corresponds in some way to this thing. 'My idea corresponds to Cologne Cathedral' is a sentence and the question now arises of the truth of this sentence. So what is improperly called the truth of pictures and ideas is reduced to the truth of sentences. What does one call a sentence? A series of sounds; but only when it has a sense, by which is not meant that every series of sounds that has sense is a sentence. And when we call a sentence true we really mean its sense is. From which it follows that it is for the sense of a sentence that the question of truth arises in general. Now is the sense of a sentence an idea? In any case being true does not consist in the correspondence of this sense with something else, for otherwise the question of truth would reiterate itself to infinity.

Without wishing to give a definition, I call a thought something for which the question of truth arises. So I ascribe what is false to a thought just as much as what is true.[1] So I can say: the thought is the sense of the sentence without wishing to say as well that the sense of every sentence is a thought.

---

[1] In a similar way it has perhaps been said 'a judgement is something which is either true or false'. In fact I use the word 'thought' in approximately the sense which 'judgement' has in the writings of logicians. I hope it will become clear in what follows why I choose 'thought'. Such an explanation has been objected to on the ground that in it a distinction is drawn between true and false judgements which of all possible distinctions among judgements has perhaps the least significance. I cannot see that it is a logical deficiency that a distinction is given with the explanation. As far as significance is concerned, it should not by any means be judged as trifling if, as I have said, the word 'true' indicates the aim of logic.

The thought, in itself immaterial, clothes itself in the material garment of a sentence and thereby becomes comprehensible to us. We say a sentence expresses a thought.

A thought is something immaterial and everything material and perceptible is excluded from this sphere of that for which the question of truth arises. Truth is not a quality that corresponds with a particular kind of sense-impression. So it is sharply distinguished from the qualities which we denote by the words 'red', 'bitter', 'lilac-smelling'. But do we not see that the sun has risen and do we not then also see that this is true? That the sun has risen is not an object which emits rays that reach my eyes, it is not a visible thing like the sun itself. That the sun has risen is seen to be true on the basis of sense-impressions. But being true is not a material, perceptible property. For being magnetic is also recognized on the basis of sense-impressions of something, though this property corresponds as little as truth with a particular kind of sense-impressions. So far these properties agree. However, we need sense-impressions in order to recognize a body as magnetic. On the other hand, when I find that it is true that I do not smell anything at this moment, I do not do so on the basis of sense-impressions.

It may nevertheless be thought that we cannot recognize a property of a thing without at the same time realizing the thought that this thing has this property to be true. So with every property of a thing is joined a property of a thought, namely, that of truth. It is also worthy of notice that the sentence 'I smell the scent of violets' has just the same content as the sentence 'it is true that I smell the scent of violets'. So it seems, then, that nothing is added to the thought by my ascribing to it the property of truth. And yet is it not a great result when the scientist after much hesitation and careful inquiry, can finally say 'what I supposed is true'? The meaning of the word 'true' seems to be altogether unique. May we not be dealing here with something which cannot, in the ordinary sense, be called a quality at all? In spite of this doubt I want first to express myself in accordance with ordinary usage, as if truth were a quality, until something more to the point is found.

In order to work out more precisely what I want to call thought, I shall distinguish various kinds of sentences.[2] One does not want to deny sense to an imperative sentence, but this sense is not such that the question of truth could arise for it. Therefore I shall not call the sense of an impera-

---

[2] I am not using the word 'sentence' here in a purely grammatical sense where it also includes subordinate clauses. An isolated subordinate clause does not always have a sense about which the question of truth can arise, whereas the complex sentence to which it belongs has such a sense.

tive sentence a thought. Sentences expressing desires or requests are ruled out in the same way. Only those sentences in which we communicate or state something come into the question. But I do not count among these exclamations in which one vents one's feelings, groaning, sighing, laughing, unless it has been decided by some agreement that they are to communicate something. But how about interrogative sentences? In a word-question we utter an incomplete sentence which only obtains a true sense through the completion for which we ask. Word-questions are accordingly left out of consideration here. Sentence-questions are a different matter. We expect to hear 'yes' or 'no'. The answer 'yes' means the same as an indicative sentence, for in it the thought that was already completely contained in the interrogative sentence is laid down as true. So a sentence-question can be formed from every indicative sentence. An exclamation cannot be regarded as a communication on this account, since no corresponding sentence-question can be formed. An interrogative sentence and an indicative one contain the same thought; but the indicative contains something else as well, namely, the assertion. The interrogative sentence contains something more too, namely a request. Therefore two things must be distinguished in an indicative sentence: the content, which it has in common with the corresponding sentence-question, and the assertion. The former is the thought, or at least contains the thought. So it is possible to express the thought without laying it down as true. Both are so closely joined in an indicative sentence that it is easy to overlook their separability. Consequently we may distinguish:

(1) the apprehension of a thought—thinking,
(2) the recognition of the truth of a thought—judgement,[3]
(3) the manifestation of this judgement—assertion.

We perform the first act when we form a sentence-question. An advance in science usually takes place in this way, first a thought is apprehended, such as can perhaps be expressed in a sentence-question, and, after appropriate investigations, this thought is finally recognized to be true. We declare the recognition of truth in the form of an indicative sentence. We do not have to use the word 'true' for this. And even when we do use it the real assertive force lies, not in it, but in the form of the indicative

---

[3] It seems to me that thought and judgement have not hitherto been adequately distinguished. Perhaps language is misleading. For we have no particular clause in the indicative sentence which corresponds to the assertion, that something is being asserted lies rather in the form of the indicative. We have the advantage in German that main and subordinate clauses are distinguished by the word-order. In this connexion it is noticeable that a subordinate clause can also contain an assertion and that often neither main nor subordinate clause express a complete thought by themselves but only the complex sentence does.

sentence and where this loses its assertive force the word 'true' cannot put it back again. This happens when we do not speak seriously. As stage thunder is only apparent thunder and a stage fight only an apparent fight, so stage assertion is only apparent assertion. It is only acting, only fancy. In his part the actor asserts nothing, nor does he lie, even if he says something of whose falsehood he is convinced. In poetry we have the case of thoughts being expressed without being actually put forward as true in spite of the form of the indicative sentence, although it may be suggested to the hearer to make an assenting judgement himself. Therefore it must still always be asked, about what is presented in the form of an indicative sentence, whether it really contains an assertion. And this question must be answered in the negative if the requisite seriousness is lacking. It is irrelevant whether the word 'true' is used here. This explains why it is that nothing seems to be added to a thought by attributing to it the property of truth.

An indicative sentence often contains, as well as a thought and the assertion, a third component over which the assertion does not extend. This is often said to act on the feelings, the mood of the hearer or to arouse his imagination. Words like 'alas' and 'thank God' belong here. Such constituents of sentences are more noticeably prominent in poetry, but are seldom wholly absent from prose. They occur more rarely in mathematical, physical, or chemical than in historical expositions. What are called the humanities are more closely connected with poetry and are therefore less scientific than the exact sciences which are drier the more exact they are, for exact science is directed toward truth and only the truth. Therefore all constituents of sentences to which the assertive force does not reach do not belong to scientific exposition but they are sometimes hard to avoid, even for one who sees the danger connected with them. Where the main thing is to approach what cannot be grasped in thought by means of guesswork these components have their justification. The more exactly scientific an exposition is the less will the nationality of its author be discernible and the easier will it be to translate. On the other hand, the constituents of language, to which I want to call attention here, make the translation of poetry very difficult, even make a complete translation almost always impossible, for it is in precisely that in which poetic value largely consists that languages differ most.

It makes no difference to the thought whether I use the word 'horse' or 'steed' or 'cart-horse' or 'mare'. The assertive force does not extend over that in which these words differ. What is called mood, fragrance, illumination in a poem, what is portrayed by cadence and rhythm, does not belong to the thought.

Much of language serves the purpose of aiding the hearer's understanding, for instance the stressing of part of a sentence by accentuation or word-order. One should remember words like 'still' and 'already' too. With the sentence 'Alfred has still not come' one really says 'Alfred has not come' and, at the same time, hints that his arrival is expected, but it is only hinted. It cannot be said that, since Alfred's arrival is not expected, the sense of the sentence is therefore false. The word 'but' differs from 'and' in that with it one intimates that what follows is in contrast with what would be expected from what preceded it. Such suggestions in speech make no difference to the thought. A sentence can be transformed by changing the verb from active to passive and making the object the subject at the same time. In the same way the dative may be changed into the nominative while 'give' is replaced by 'receive'. Naturally such transformations are not indifferent in every respect; but they do not touch the thought, they do not touch what is true or false. If the inadmissibility of such transformations were generally admitted then all deeper logical investigation would be hindered. It is just as important to neglect distinctions that do not touch the heart of the matter as to make distinctions which concern what is essential. But what is essential depends on one's purpose. To a mind concerned with what is beautiful in language what is indifferent to the logician can appear as just what is important.

Thus the contents of a sentence often go beyond the thoughts expressed by it. But the opposite often happens too, that the mere wording, which can be grasped by writing or the gramophone does not suffice for the expression of the thought. The present tense is used in two ways: first, in order to give a date, second, in order to eliminate any temporal restriction where timelessness or eternity is part of the thought. Think, for instance, of the laws of mathematics. Which of the two cases occurs is not expressed but must be guessed. If a time indication is needed by the present tense one must know when the sentence was uttered to apprehend the thought correctly. Therefore the time of utterance is part of the expression of the thought. If someone wants to say the same today as he expressed yesterday using the word 'today', he must replace this word with 'yesterday'. Although the thought is the same its verbal expression must be different so that the sense, which would otherwise be affected by the differing times of utterance, is readjusted. The case is the same with words like 'here' and 'there'. In all such cases the mere wording, as it is given in writing, is not the complete expression of the thought, but the knowledge of certain accompanying conditions of utterance, which are used as means of expressing the thought, are needed for its correct apprehension. The pointing of fingers, hand movements, glances may belong here too. The same utterance containing the word 'I' will express different thoughts in the mouths of different men, of which some may be true, others false.

The occurrence of the word 'I' in a sentence gives rise to some questions.

Consider the following case. Dr Gustav Lauben says, 'I have been wounded'. Leo Peter hears this and remarks some days later, 'Dr Gustav Lauben has been wounded'. Does this sentence express the same thought as the one Dr Lauben uttered himself? Suppose that Rudolph Lingens were present when Dr Lauben spoke and now hears what is related by Leo Peter. If the same thought is uttered by Dr Lauben and Leo Peter then Rudolph Lingens, who if fully master of the language and remembers what Dr Lauben has said in his presence, must now know at once from Leo Peter's report that the same thing is under discussion. But knowledge of the language is a separate thing when it is a matter of proper names. It may well be the case that only a few people associate a particular thought with the sentence 'Dr Lauben has been wounded'. In this case one needs for complete understanding a knowledge of the expression 'Dr Lauben'. Now if both Leo Peter and Rudolph Lingens understand by 'Dr Lauben' the doctor who lives as the only doctor in a house known to both of them, then they both understand the sentence 'Dr Gustav Lauben has been wounded' in the same way, they associate the same thought with it. But it is also possible that Rudolph Lingens does not know Dr Lauben person-ally and does not know that he is the very Dr Lauben who recently said 'I have been wounded.' In this case Rudolph Lingens cannot know that the same thing is in question. I say, therefore, in this case: the thought which Leo Peter expresses is not the same as that which Dr Lauben uttered.

Suppose further that Herbert Garner knows that Dr Gustav Lauben was born on 13 September 1875 in N.N. and this is not true of anyone else; against this, suppose that he does not know where Dr Lauben now lives nor indeed anything about him. On the other hand, suppose Leo Peter does not know that Dr Lauben was born on 13 September 1875, in N.N. Then as far as the proper name 'Dr Gustav Lauben' is concerned, Herbert Garner and Leo Peter do not speak the same language, since, although they do in fact refer to the same man with this name, they do not know that they do so. Therefore Herbert Garner does not associate the same thought with the sentence 'Dr Gustav Lauben has been wounded' as Leo Peter wants to express with it. To avoid the drawback of Herbert Garner's and Leo Peter's not speaking the same language, I am assuming that Leo Peter uses the proper name 'Dr Lauben' and Herbert Garner, on the other hand, uses the proper name 'Gustav Lauben'. Now it is possible that Herbert Garner takes the sense of the sentence 'Dr Lauben has been wounded' to be true while, misled by false information, taking the sense of the sentence 'Gustav Lauben has been wounded' to be false. Under the assumptions given these thoughts are therefore different.

Accordingly, with a proper name, it depends on how whatever it refers to is presented. This can happen in different ways and every such way corresponds with a particular sense of a sentence containing a proper name. The different thoughts which thus result from the same sentence correspond in their truth-value, of course; that is to say, if one is true then all are true, and if one is false then all are false. Nevertheless their distinctness must be recognized. So it must really be demanded that a single way in which whatever is referred to is presented be associated with every proper name. It is often unimportant that this demand should be fulfilled but not always.

Now everyone is presented to himself in a particular and primitive way, in which he is presented to no one else. So, when Dr Lauben thinks that he has been wounded, he will probably take as a basis this primitive way in which he is presented to himself. And only Dr Lauben himself can grasp thoughts determined in this way. But now he may want to communicate with others. He cannot communicate a thought which he alone can grasp. Therefore, if he now says 'I have been wounded', he must use the 'I' in a sense which can be grasped by others, perhaps in the sense of 'he who is speaking to you at this moment', by doing which he makes the associated conditions of his utterance serve for the expression of his thought.[4]

Yet there is a doubt. Is it at all the same thought which first that man expresses and now this one?

A person who is still untouched by philosophy knows first of all things which he can see and touch, in short, perceive with the senses, such as trees, stones and houses, and he is convinced that another person equally can see and touch the same tree and the same stone which he himself sees and touches. Obviously no thought belongs to these things. Now can he, nevertheless, stand in the same relation to a person as a tree?

Even an unphilosophical person soon finds it necessary to recognize an inner world distinct from the outer world, a world of sense-impressions, of creations of his imagination, of sensations, of feelings and moods, a world

---

[4] I am not in the happy position here of a mineralogist who shows his hearers a mountain crystal. I cannot put a thought in the hands of my readers with the request that they should minutely examine it from all sides. I have to content myself with presenting the reader with a thought, in itself immaterial, dressed in sensible linguistic form. The metaphorical aspect of language presents difficulties. The sensible always breaks in and makes expression metaphorical and so improper. So a battle with language takes place and I am compelled to occupy myself with language although it is not my proper concern here. I hope I have succeeded in making clear to my readers what I want to call a thought.

of inclinations, wishes and decisions. For brevity I want to collect all these, with the exception of decisions, under the word 'idea'.

Now do thoughts belong to this inner world? Are they ideas? They are obviously not decisions. How are ideas distinct from the things of the outer world?

First: ideas cannot be seen or touched, cannot be smelled, nor tasted, nor heard.

I go for a walk with a companion. I see a green field, I have a visual impression of the green as well. I have it but I do not see it.

Secondly: ideas are had. One has sensations, feelings, moods, inclinations, wishes. An idea which someone has belongs to the content of his consciousness.

The field and the frogs in it, the sun which shines on them are there no matter whether I look at them or not, but the sense-impression I have of green exists only because of me, I am its bearer. It seems absurd to us that a pain, a mood, a wish should rove about the world without a bearer, independently. An experience is impossible without an experient. The inner world presupposes the person whose inner world it is.

Thirdly: ideas need a bearer. Things of the outer world are however independent.

My companion and I are convinced that we both see the same field; but each of us has a particular sense-impression of green. I notice a strawberry among the green strawberry leaves. My companion does not notice it, he is colour-blind. The colour-impression, which he receives from the strawberry, is not noticeably different from the one he receives from the leaf. Now does my companion see the green leaf as red, or does he see the red berry as green, or does he see both as of one colour with which I am not acquainted at all? These are unanswerable, indeed really nonsensical, questions. For when the word 'red' does not state a property of things but is supposed to characterize sense-impressions belonging to my consciousness, it is only applicable within the sphere of my consciousness. For it is impossible to compare my sense-impression with that of someone else. For that it would be necessary to bring together in one consciousness a sense-impression, belonging to one consciousness, with a sense-impression belonging to another consciousness. Now even if it were possible to make an idea disappear from one consciousness and, at the same time, to make an idea appear in another consciousness, the question whether it were the same idea in both would still remain unanswerable. It is so much of the essence of each of my ideas to be the content of my consciousness, that every idea of another person is, just as such, distinct from mine. But might it not be possible that my ideas, the entire content of my consciousness might be at the same time the content of a more embracing, perhaps divine, consciousness? Only if I were myself part of the divine consciousness. But then would they really be my ideas, would I be their bearer? This over-steps the limits of human understanding to such an extent that one must leave its possibility out of account. In any case it is impossible for us as men to compare another person's ideas with our own. I pick the straw-berry, I hold it between my fingers. Now my companion sees it too, this very same strawberry; but each of us has his own idea. No other person has my idea but many people can see the same thing. No other person has my pain. Someone can have sympathy for me but still my pain always belongs to me and his sympathy to him. He does not have my pain and I do not have his sympathy.

Fourthly: every idea has only one bearer; no two men have the same idea.

For otherwise it would exist independently of this person and independently of that one. Is that lime-tree my idea? By using the expression 'that lime-tree' in this question I have really already anticipated the answer, for with this expression I want to refer to what I see and to what other people can also look at and touch. There are now two possibilities. If my intention is realized when I refer to something with the expression 'that lime-tree' then the thought expressed in the sentence 'that lime-tree is my idea' must obviously be negated. But if my intention is not realized, if I only think I see without really seeing, if on that account the designation 'that lime-tree' is empty, then I have gone astray into the sphere of fiction without knowing it or wanting to. In that case neither the content of the sentence 'that lime-tree is my idea' nor the content of the sentence 'that lime-tree is not my idea' is true, for in both cases I have a statement which lacks an object. So then one can only refuse to answer the question for the reason that the content of the sentence 'that lime-tree is my idea' is a piece of fiction. I have, naturally, got an idea then, but I am not referring to this with the words 'that lime-tree'. Now someone may really want to refer to one of his ideas with the words 'that lime-tree'. He would then be the bearer of that to which he wants to refer with those words, but then he would not see that lime-tree and no one else would see it or be its bearer.

I now return to the question: is a thought an idea? If the thought I express in the Pythagorean theorem can be recognized by others just as much as by me then it does not belong to the content of my consciousness, I am not its bearer; yet I can, nevertheless, recognize it to be true. However, if it is not the same thought at all which is taken to be the content of the Pythagorean theorem by me and by another person, one should not really say 'the Pythagorean theorem' but 'my Pythagorean theorem', 'his

Pythagorean theorem' and these would be different; for the sense belongs necessarily to the sentence. Then my thought can be the content of my consciousness and his thought the content of his. Could the sense of my Pythagorean theorem be true while that of his was false? I said that the word 'red' was applicable only in the sphere of my consciousness if it did not state a property of things but was supposed to characterize one of my sense-impressions. Therefore the words 'true' and 'false', as I understand them, could also be applicable only in the sphere of my consciousness, if they were not supposed to be concerned with something of which I was not the bearer, but were somehow appointed to characterize the content of my consciousness. Then truth would be restricted to the content of my consciousness and it would remain doubtful whether anything at all comparable occurred in the consciousness of others.

If every thought requires a bearer, to the contents of whose consciousness it belongs, then it would be a thought of this bearer only and there would be no science common to many, on which many could work. But I, perhaps, have my science, namely, a whole of thought whose bearer I am and another person has his. Each of us occupies himself with the contents of his own consciousness. No contradiction between the two sciences would then be possible and it would really be idle to dispute about truth, as idle, indeed almost ludicrous, as it would be for two people to dispute whether a hundred-mark note were genuine, where each meant the one he himself had in his pocket and understood the word 'genuine' in his own particular sense. If someone takes thoughts to be ideas, what he then recognizes to be true is, on his own view, the content of his consciousness and does not properly concern other people at all. If he were to hear from me the opinion that a thought is not an idea he could not dispute it, for, indeed, it would not now concern him.

So the result seems to be: thoughts are neither things of the outer world nor ideas.

A third realm must be recognized. What belongs to this corresponds with ideas, in that it cannot be perceived by the senses, but with things, in that it needs no bearer to the contents of whose consciousness to belong. Thus the thought, for example, which we expressed in the Pythagorean theorem is timelessly true, true independently of whether anyone takes it to be true. It needs no bearer. It is not true for the first time when it is discovered, but is like a planet which, already before anyone has seen it, has been in interaction with other planets.[5]

---

[5] One sees a thing, one has an idea, one apprehends or thinks a thought. When one apprehends or thinks a thought one does not create it but only comes to stand in a certain relation, which is different from seeing a thing or having an idea, to what already existed beforehand.

But I think I hear an unusual objection. I have assumed several times that the same thing that I see can also be observed by other people. But how could this be the case, if everything were only a dream? If I only dreamed I was walking in the company of another person, if I only dreamed that my companion saw the green field as I did, if it were all only a play performed on the stage of my consciousness, it would be doubtful whether there were things of the outer world at all. Perhaps the realm of things is empty and I see no things and no men, but have only ideas of which I myself am the bearer. An idea, being something which can as little exist independently of me as my feeling of fatigue, cannot be a man, cannot look at the same field together with me, cannot see the strawberry I am holding. It is quite incredible that I should really have only my inner world instead of the whole environment, in which I am supposed to move and to act. And yet it is an inevitable consequence of the thesis that only what is my idea can be the object of my awareness. What would follow from this thesis if it were true? Would there then be other men? It would certainly be possible but I should know nothing of it. For a man cannot be my idea, consequently, if our thesis were true, he also cannot be an object of my awareness. And so the ground would be removed from under any process of thought in which I might assume that something was an object for another person as for myself, for even if this were to happen I should know nothing of it. It would be impossible for me to distinguish that of which I was the bearer from that of which I was not. In judging something not to be my idea I would make it the object of my thinking and, therefore, my idea. On this view, is there a green field? Perhaps, but it would not be visible to me. For if a field is not my idea, it cannot, according to our thesis, be an object of my awareness. But if it is my idea it is invisible, for ideas are not visible. I can indeed have the idea of a green field, but this is not green for there are no green ideas. Does a shell weighing a hundred kilogrammes exist, according to this view? Perhaps, but I could know nothing of it. If a shell is not my idea then, according to our thesis, it cannot be an object of my awareness, of my thinking. But if a shell were my idea, it would have no weight. I can have an idea of a heavy shell. This then contains the idea of weight as a part-idea. But this part-idea is not a property of the whole idea any more than Germany is a property of Europe. So it follows:

Either the thesis that only what is my idea can be the object of my awareness is false, or all my knowledge and perception is limited to the range of my ideas, to the stage of my consciousness. In this case I should have only an inner world and I should know nothing of other people.

It is strange how, upon such reflections, the opposites collapse into each other. There is, let us suppose, a physiologist of the senses. As is proper for a scholarly scientist, he is, first of all, far from supposing the things he is convinced he sees and touches to be his ideas. On the contrary, he believes that in sense-impressions he has the surest proof of things which are wholly independent of his feeling, imagining, thinking, which have no need of his consciousness. So little does he consider nerve-fibres and ganglion-cells to be the content of his consciousness that he is, on the contrary, rather inclined to regard his consciousness as dependent on nerve-fibres and ganglion-cells. He establishes that light-rays, refracted in the eye, strike the visual nerve-endings and bring about a change, a stimulus, there. Some of it is transmitted through nerve-fibres and ganglion-cells. Further processes in the nervous system are perhaps involved, colour-impressions arise and these perhaps join themselves to what we call the idea of a tree. Physical, chemical, and physiological occurrences insert themselves between the tree and my idea. These are immediately connected with my consciousness but, so it seems, are only occurrences in my nervous system and every spectator of the tree has his particular occurrences in his particular nervous system. Now the light-rays, before they enter my eye, may be reflected by a mirror and be spread further as if they came from a place behind the mirror. The effects on the visual nerves and all that follows will now take place just as they would if the light-rays had come from a tree behind the mirror and had been transmitted undisturbed to the eye. So an idea of a tree will finally occur even though such a tree does not exist at all. An idea, to which nothing at all corresponds, can also arise through the bending of light, with the mediation of the eye and the nervous system. But the stimulation of the visual nerves need not even happen through light. If lightning strikes near us we believe we see flames, even though we cannot see the lightning itself. In this case the visual nerve is perhaps stimulated by electric currents which originate in our body in consequence of the flash of lightning. If the visual nerve is stimulated by this means, just as it would be stimulated by light-rays coming from flames, then we believe we see flames. It just depends on the stimulation of the visual nerve, it is indifferent how that itself comes about.

One can go a step further still. This stimulation of the visual nerve is not actually immediately given, but is only a hypothesis. We believe that a thing, independent of us, stimulates a nerve and by this means produces a sense-impression, but, strictly speaking, we experience only the end of this process which projects into our consciousness. Could not this sense-impression, this sensation, which we attribute to a nerve-stimulation, have other causes also, as the same nerve-stimulation can arise in different ways? If we call what happens in our consciousness idea, then we really experience only ideas but not their causes. And if the scientist wants to avoid all mere hypothesis, then only ideas are left for him, everything resolves into ideas, the light-rays, nerve-fibres, and ganglion-cells from which he started. So he finally undermines the foundations of his own construction. Is everything an idea? Does everything need a bearer, without which it could have no stability? I have considered myself as the bearer of my ideas, but am I not an idea myself? It seems to me as if I were lying in a deck-chair, as if I could see the toes of a pair of waxed boots, the front part of a pair of trousers, a waistcoat, buttons, part of a jacket, in particular sleeves, two hands, the hair of a beard, the blurred outline of a nose. Am I myself this entire association of visual impressions, this total idea? It also seems to me as if I see a chair over there. It is an idea. I am not actually much different from this myself, for am I not myself just an association of sense-impressions, an idea? But where then is the bearer of these ideas? How do I come to single out one of these ideas and set it up as the bearer of the rest? Why must it be the idea which I choose to call 'I'? Could I not just as well choose the one that I am tempted to call a chair? Why, after all, have a bearer for ideas at all? But this would always be something essentially different from merely borne ideas, something independent, needing no extraneous bearer. If everything is idea, then there is no bearer of ideas. And so now, once again, I experience a change into the opposite. If there is no bearer of ideas then there are also no ideas, for ideas need a bearer without which they cannot exist. If there is no ruler, there are also no subjects. The dependence, which I found myself induced to confer on the experience as opposed to the experient, is abolished if there is no more bearer. What I called ideas are then independent objects. Every reason is wanting for granting an exceptional position to that object which I call 'I'.

But is that possible? Can there be an experience without someone to experience it? What would this whole play be without an onlooker? Can there be a pain without someone who has it? Being experienced is necessarily connected with pain, and someone experiencing is necessarily connected with being experienced. But there is something which is not my idea and yet which can be the object of my awareness, of my thinking, I am myself of this nature. Or can I part of the content of my consciousness while another part is, perhaps, an idea of the moon? Does this perhaps take place when I judge that I am looking at the moon? Then this first part would have a consciousness and part of the content of this consciousness would be I myself once more. And so on. Yet it is surely inconceivable that I should be boxed into myself in this way to infinity, for then there would not be only one I but infinitely many. I am not my own idea and if I assert something about myself, e.g. that I do not feel any pain at this moment, then my judgement concerns something which is not a content of my consciousness, is not my idea, that is me myself. Therefore that about which I state something is not necessarily my idea. But, someone perhaps objects, if I think I have no pain at the moment, does not the word 'I' nevertheless correspond with something in the content of my consciousness and is that not an idea? That may be. A certain idea in my consciousness may be associated with the idea of the word 'I'. But then it is an idea among other ideas and I am its bearer as I am the bearer of the other ideas. I have an idea of myself but I am not identical with this idea. What is a content of my consciousness, my idea, should be sharply distinguished from what is an object of my thought. Therefore the thesis that only what belongs to the content of my consciousness can be the object of my awareness, of my thought, is false.

Now the way is clear for me to recognize another person as well as to be an independent bearer of ideas. I have an idea of him but I do not confuse it with him himself. And if I state something about my brother I do not state it about the idea that I have of my brother.

The invalid who has a pain is the bearer of this pain, but the doctor in attendance who reflects on the cause of this pain is not the bearer of the pain. He does not imagine he can relieve the pain by anaesthetizing himself. An idea in the doctor's mind may very well correspond to the pain of the invalid but that is not the pain and not what the doctor is trying to remove. The doctor might consult another doctor. Then one must distinguish: first, the pain whose bearer is the invalid, second, the first doctor's idea of this pain, third, the second doctor's idea of this pain. This idea does indeed belong to the content of the second doctor's consciousness, but it is not the object of his reflection, it is rather an aid to reflection, as a drawing can be such an aid perhaps. Both doctors have the invalid's pain, which they do not bear, as their common object of thought. It can be seen from this that not only a thing but also an idea can be the common object of thought of people who do not have the idea.

So, it seems to me, the matter becomes intelligible. If man could not think and could not take something of which he was not the bearer as the object of his thought he would have an inner world but no outer world. But may this not be based on a mistake? I am convinced that the idea I associate with the words 'my brother' corresponds to something that is not my idea and about which I can say something. But may I not be making a mistake about this? Such mistakes do happen. We then, against our will, lapse into fiction, Indeed! By the step with which I secure an environment for myself I expose myself to the risk of error. And here I come up against a further distinction between my inner and outer worlds. I cannot doubt that I have a visual impression of green but it is not so certain that I see a lime-leaf. So, contrary to widespread views, we find certainty in the inner world while doubt never altogether leaves us in our excursions into the outer world. It is difficult in many cases, nevertheless, to distinguish probability from certainty here, so we can presume to judge about things in the outer world. And we must presume this even at the risk of error if we do not want to succumb to far greater dangers.

In consequence of these last considerations I lay down the following: not everything that can be the object of my understanding is an idea. I, as a bearer of ideas, am not myself an idea. Nothing now stands in the way of recognizing other people to be bearers of ideas as I am myself. And, once given the possibility, the probability is very great, so great that it is in my opinion no longer distinguishable from certainty. Would there be a science of history otherwise? Would not every precept of duty, every law otherwise come to nothing? What would be left of religion? The natural sciences too could only be assessed as fables like astrology and alchemy. Thus the reflections I have carried on, assuming that there are other people besides myself who can take the same thing as the object of their consideration, of their thinking, remain essentially unimpaired in force.

Not everything is an idea. Thus I can also recognize the thought, which other people can grasp just as much as I, as being independent of me. I can recognize a science in which many people can be engaged in research. We are not bearers of thoughts as we are bearers of our ideas. We do not have a thought as we have, say, a sense-impression, but we also do not see a thought as we see, say, a star. So it is advisable to choose a special expression and the word 'apprehend' offers itself for the purpose. A particular mental capacity, the power of thought, must correspond to the apprehension[6] of thought. In thinking we do not produce thoughts but we apprehend them. For what I have called thought stands in the closest relation to truth. What I recognize as true I judge to be true quite independently of my recognition of its truth and of my thinking about it. That someone thinks it has nothing to do with the truth of a thought. 'Facts, facts, facts' cries the scientist if he wants to emphasize the necessity of a firm foundation for science. What is a fact? A fact is a thought that is true. But the scientist will surely not recognize something which depends on men's varying states of mind to be the firm foundation of science. The work of science

---

[6] The expression 'apprehend' is as metaphorical as 'content of consciousness'. The nature of language does not permit anything else. What I hold in my hand can certainly be regarded as the content of my hand but is all the same the content of my hand in quite a different way from the bones and muscles of which it is made and their tensions, and is much more extraneous to it than they are.

does not consist of creation but of the discovery of true thoughts. The astronomer can apply a mathematical truth in the investigation of long past events which took place when on earth at least no one had yet recognized that truth. He can do this because the truth of a thought is timeless. Therefore that truth cannot have come into existence with its discovery.

Not everything is an idea. Otherwise psychology would contain all the sciences within it or at least it would be the highest judge over all the sciences. Otherwise psychology would rule over logic and mathematics. But nothing would be a greater misunderstanding of mathematics than its subordination to psychology. Neither logic nor mathematics has the task of investigating minds and the contents of consciousness whose bearer is a single person. Perhaps their task could be represented rather as the investigation of the mind, of the mind not of minds.

The apprehension of a thought presupposes someone who apprehends it, who thinks. He is the bearer of the thinking but not of the thought. Although the thought does not belong to the contents of the thinker's consciousness yet something in his consciousness must be aimed at the thought. But this should not be confused with the thought itself. Similarly Algol itself is different from the idea someone has of Algol.

The thought belongs neither to my inner world as an idea nor yet to the outer world of material, perceptible things.

This consequence, however cogently it may follow from the exposition, will nevertheless not perhaps be accepted without opposition. It will, I think, seem impossible to some people to obtain information about something not belonging to the inner world except by sense-perception. Sense-perception indeed is often thought to be the most certain, even to be the sole, source of knowledge about everything that does not belong to the inner world. But with what right? For sense-impressions are necessary constituents of sense-perceptions and are a part of the inner world. In any case two men do not have the same, though they may have similar, sense-impressions. These alone do not disclose the outer world to us. Perhaps there is a being that has only sense-impressions without seeing or touching things. To have visual impressions is not to see things. How does it happen that I see the tree just there where I do see it? Obviously it depends on the visual impressions I have and on the particular type which occur because I see with two eyes. A particular image arises, physically speaking, on each of the two retinas. Another person sees the tree in the same place. He also has two retinal images but they differ from mine. We must assume that these retinal images correspond to our impressions. Consequently we have visual impressions, not only not the same, but markedly different from each other. And yet we move about in the same outer world. Having visual impressions is certainly necessary for seeing things but not sufficient. What must still be added is non-sensible. And yet this is just what opens up the outer world for us; for without this non-sensible something everyone would remain shut up in his inner world. So since the answer lies in the non-sensible, perhaps something non-sensible could also lead us out of the inner world and enable us to grasp thoughts where no sense-impressions were involved. Outside one's inner world one would have to distinguish the proper outer world of sensible, perceptible things from the realm of the non-sensibly perceptible. We should need something non-sensible for the recognition of both realms but for the sensible perception of things we should need sense-impressions as well and these belong entirely to the inner world. So that in which the distinction between the way in which a thing and a thought is given mainly consists is something which is attributable, not to both realms, but to the inner world. Thus I cannot find this distinction to be so great that on its account it would be impossible for a thought to be given that did not belong to the inner world.

The thought, admittedly, is not something which it is usual to call real. The world of the real is a world in which this acts on that, changes it and again experiences reactions itself and is changed by them. All this is a process in time. We will hardly recognize what is timeless and unchangeable as real. Now is the thought changeable or is it timeless? The thought we express by the Pythagorean theorem is surely timeless, eternal, unchangeable. But are there not thoughts which are true today but false in six months time? The thought, for example, that the tree there is covered with green leaves, will surely be false in six months time. No, for it is not the same thought at all. The words 'this tree is covered with green leaves' are not sufficient by themselves for the utterance, the time of utterance is involved as well. Without the time-indication this gives we have no complete thought, i.e. no thought at all. Only a sentence supplemented by a time-indication and complete in every respect expresses a thought. But this, if it is true, is true not only today or tomorrow but timelessly. Thus the present tense in 'is true' does not refer to the speaker's present but is, if the expression be permitted, a tense of timelessness. If we use the mere form of the indicative sentence, avoiding the word 'true', two things must be distinguished, the expression of the thought and the assertion. The time-indication that may be contained in the sentence belongs only to the expression of the thought, while the truth, whose recognition lies in the form of the indicative sentence, is timeless. Yet the same words, on account of the variability of language with time, take on another sense, express another thought; this change, however, concerns only the linguistic aspect of the matter.

And yet! What value could there be for us in the eternally unchangeable which could neither undergo effects nor have effect on us? Something entirely and in every respect inactive would be unreal and non-existent for us. Even the timeless, if it is to be anything for us, must somehow be implicated with the temporal. What would a thought be for me that was never apprehended by me? But by apprehending a thought I come into a relation to it and it to me. It is possible that the same thought that is thought by me today was not thought by me yesterday. In this way the strict timelessness is of course annulled. But one is inclined to distinguish between essential and inessential properties and to regard something as timeless if the changes it undergoes involve only its inessential properties. A property of a thought will be called inessential which consists in, or follows from the fact that, it is apprehended by a thinker.

How does a thought act? By being apprehended and taken to be true. This is a process in the inner world of a thinker which can have further consequences in this inner world and which, encroaching on the sphere of the will, can also make itself noticeable in the outer world. If, for example, I grasp the thought which we express by the theorem of Pythagoras, the consequence may be that I recognize it to be true and, further, that I apply it, making a decision which brings about the acceleration of masses. Thus our actions are usually prepared by thinking and judgement. And so thought can have an indirect influence on the motion of masses. The influence of one person on another is brought about for the most part by thoughts. One communicates a thought. How does this happen? One brings about changes in the common outside world which, perceived by another person, are supposed to induce him to apprehend a thought and take it to be true. Could the great events of world history have come about without the communication of thoughts? And yet we are inclined to regard thoughts as unreal because they appear to be without influence on events, while thinking, judging, stating, understanding and the like are facts of human life. How much more real a hammer appears compared with a thought. How different the process of handing over a hammer is from the communication of a thought. The hammer passes from one control to another, it is gripped, it undergoes pressure and on account of this its density, the disposition of its parts, is changed in places. There is nothing of all this with a thought. It does not leave the control of the communicator by being communicated, for after all a person has no control over it. When a thought is apprehended, it at first only brings about changes in the inner world of the apprehended, yet it remains untouched in its true essence, since the changes it undergoes involve only inessential properties. There is lacking here something we observe throughout the order of nature: reciprocal action. Thoughts are by no means unreal but their reality is of quite a different kind from that of things. And their effect is brought about by an act of the thinker without which they would be ineffective, at least as far as we can see. And yet the thinker does not create them but must take them as they are. They can be true without being apprehended by a thinker and are not wholly unreal even then, at least if they could be apprehended and by this means be brought into operation.

VI

ON FACTS AND PROPOSITIONS

F. P. RAMSEY

But before we proceed further with the analysis of judgement, it is necessary to say something about truth and falsehood, in order to show that there is really no separate problem of truth but merely a linguistic muddle. Truth and falsity are ascribed primarily to propositions. The proposition to which they are ascribed may be either explicitly given or described. Suppose first that it is explicitly given; then it is evident that 'It is true that Caesar was murdered' means no more than that Caesar was murdered, and 'It is false that Caesar was murdered' means that Caesar was not murdered. They are phrases which we sometimes use for emphasis or for stylistic reasons, or to indicate the position occupied by the statement in our argument. So also we can say 'It is a fact that he was murdered' or 'That he was murdered is contrary to fact'.

In the second case in which the proposition is described and not given explicitly we have perhaps more of a problem, for we get statements from which we cannot in ordinary language eliminate the words 'true' and 'false'. Thus if I say 'He is always right', I mean that the propositions he asserts are always true, and there does not seem to be any way of expressing this without using the word 'true'. But suppose we put it thus 'For all p, if he asserts p, p is true', then we see that the propositional function p is true is simply the same as p, as e.g. its value 'Caesar was murdered is true' is the same as 'Caesar was murdered'. We have in English to add 'is true' to give the sentence a verb, forgetting that 'p' already contains a (variable) verb. This may perhaps be made clearer by supposing for a moment that only one form of proposition is in question, say the relational form aRb; then 'He is always right' could be expressed by 'For all a, R, b, if he asserts aRb, then aRb', to which 'is true' would be an obviously superfluous

From F. P. Ramsey, 'On Facts and Propositions', in D. H. Mellor (ed.), *Prospects for Pragmatism: Essays in Memory of F. P. Ramsey*, ed. D. H. Mellor (Cambridge: Cambridge University Press, 1980). Originally published in *The Foundations of Mathematics* ed. R. B. Braithwaite (Routledge & Kegan Paul, 1931), reprinted by permission of Routledge.

addition. When all forms of proposition are included the analysis is more complicated but not essentially different; and it is clear that the problem is not as to the nature of truth and falsehood, but as to the nature of judgement or assertion, for what is difficult to analyse in the above formulation is 'He asserts aRb'.

It is, perhaps, also immediately obvious that if we have analysed judgement we have solved the problem of truth; for taking the mental factor in a judgement (which is often itself called a judgement), the truth or falsity of this depends only on what proposition it is that is judged, and what we have to explain is the meaning of saying that the judgement is a judgement that a has R to b, i.e. is true if aRb, false if not. We can, if we like, say that it is true if there exists a corresponding fact that a has R to b, but this is essentially not an analysis but a periphrasis, for 'The fact that a has R to b exists' is no different from 'a has R to b'.

In order to proceed further, we must now consider the mental factors in a belief. Their nature will depend on the sense in which we are using the ambiguous term belief: it is, for instance, possible to say that a chicken believes a certain sort of caterpillar to be poisonous, and mean by that merely that it abstains from eating such caterpillars on account of unpleasant experiences connected with them. The mental factors in such a belief would be parts of the chicken's behaviour, which are somehow related to the objective factors, viz. the kind of caterpillar and poisonousness. An exact analysis of this relation would be very difficult, but it might well be held that in regard to this kind of belief the pragmatist view was correct, i.e. that the relation between the chicken's behaviour and the objective factors was that the actions were such as to be useful if, and only if, the caterpillars were actually poisonous. Thus any set of actions for whose utility p is a necessary and sufficient condition might be called a belief that p, and so would be true if p, i.e. if they are useful.[1]

But without wishing to depreciate the importance of this kind of belief, it is not what I wish to discuss here. I prefer to deal with those beliefs which are expressed in words, or possibly images or other symbols, consciously asserted or denied; for these beliefs, in my view, are the most proper subject for logical criticism.

---

[1] It is useful to believe aRb would mean that it is useful to do things which are useful if, and only if, aRb; which is evidently equivalent to aRb.

VII

PHILOSOPHICAL EXTRACTS

LUDWIG WITTGENSTEIN

PHILOSOPHICAL REMARKS

The use of the words 'fact' and 'act'.—'That was a noble act.'—'But, that never happened.'—

It is natural to want to use the word 'act' so that it only corresponds to a *true* proposition. So that we then don't talk of an act which was never performed. But the proposition 'That was a noble act' must still have a sense even if I am mistaken in thinking that what I call an act occurred. And that of itself contains all that matters, and I can only make the stipulation that I will only use the words 'fact', 'act' (perhaps also 'event') in a proposition which, when complete, asserts that this fact obtains.

It would be better to drop the restriction on the use of these words, since it only leads to confusion, and say quite happily: 'This act was never performed', 'This fact does not obtain', 'This event did not occur'.

Complex is not like fact. For I can, e.g., say of a complex that it moves from one place to another, but not of a fact.

But that this complex is now situated here is a fact.

'This complex of buildings is coming down' is tantamount to: 'The buildings thus grouped together are coming down'.

I call a flower, a house, a constellation, complexes: moreover, complexes of petals, bricks, stars, etc.

Extracts from Ludwig Wittgenstein, *Philosophical Remarks*, ed. Rush Rhees, trans. Raymond Hargreaves and Roger White (Blackwell, 1975); *Culture and Value*, ed. G. H. von Wright in collaboration with Heikki Hyman, trans. Peter Winch (Blackwell, 1980); *Philosophical Grammar*, ed. Rush Rhees, trans. Anthony Kenny (Blackwell, 1974); *Remarks on the Foundations of Mathematics*, ed. G. H. von Wright, R. Rhees, G. E. M. Anscombe, trans. G. E. M. Anscombe (Blackwell, 1956); *Philosophical Investigations*, trans. G. E. M. Anscombe (Blackwell, 1958); *On Certainty*, ed. G. E. M. Anscombe and G. H. von Wright, trans. Denis Paul and G. E. M. Anscombe (Blackwell, 1969). All extracts reprinted with permission.

That this constellation is located here, can of course be described by a proposition in which only its stars are mentioned and neither the word 'constellation' nor its name occurs.

But that is all there is to say about the relation between complex and fact. And a complex is a spatial object, composed of spatial objects. (The concept 'spatial' admitting of a certain extension.)

A complex is composed of its parts, the things of a kind which go to make it up. (This is of course a grammatical proposition concerning the words 'complex', 'part', and 'compose'.)

To say that a red circle is *composed* of redness and circularity, or is a complex with these component parts, is a misuse of these words and is misleading. (Frege was aware of this and told me.)

It is just as misleading to say the fact that this circle is red (that I am tired) is a complex whose component parts are a circle and redness (myself and tiredness).

Neither is a house a complex of bricks and their spatial relations; i.e. that too goes against the correct use of the word.

Now, you can of course point at a constellation and say: this constellation is composed entirely of objects with which I am already acquainted; but you can't 'point at a fact' and say this.

'To describe a fact', or 'the description of a fact', is also a misleading expression for the assertion stating that the fact obtains, since it sounds like: 'describing the animal that I saw'.

Of course we also say: 'to point out a fact', but that always means; 'to point out the fact that . . .'. Whereas 'to point at (or point out) a flower' doesn't mean to point out that this blossom is on this stalk; for we needn't be talking about this blossom and this stalk at all.

It's just as impossible for it to mean: to point out the fact that this flower is situated there.

To point out a fact means to assert something, to state something. 'To point out a flower' doesn't mean this.

A chain, too, is composed of its links, not of these and their spatial relations.

The fact that these links are so concatenated, isn't '*composed*' of anything at all.

The root of this muddle is the confusing use of the word 'object'.

The part is smaller than the whole: applied to fact and component part (constituent), that would yield an absurdity.

CULTURE AND VALUE

The limit of language is shown by its being impossible to describe the fact which corresponds to (is the translation of) a sentence, without simply repeating the sentence.

(This has to do with the Kantian solution of the problem of philosophy.)

PHILOSOPHICAL GRAMMAR

79 The definition 'A proposition is whatever can be true or false' fixes the concept of proposition in a particular language system as what in that system can be an argument of a truth-function.

And if we speak of what makes a proposition a proposition, we are inclined to mean the truth-functions.

'A proposition is whatever can be true or false' means the same as 'a proposition is whatever can be denied'.

> 'p' is true $= p$
> 'p' is false $= \sim p$
> What he says is true = Things are as he says.

One might say: the words 'true' and 'false' are only items in a particular notation for truth-functions.

So is it correct to write ' "p" is true', ' "p" is false'; mustn't it be 'p is true' (or false)? The ink mark is after all not *true*; in the way in which it's black and curved.

Does ' "p" is true' state anything about the sign 'p' then? 'Yes, it says that "p" agrees with reality.' Instead of a sentence of our word language consider a drawing that can be compared with reality according to exact projection-rules. This surely must show as clearly as possible what ' "p" is true' states about the picture 'p'. The proposition ' "p" is true' can thus be compared with the proposition 'this object is as long as this metre rule' and 'p' to the proposition 'this object is one metre long'. But the comparison is incorrect, because 'this metre rule' is a description, whereas 'metre rule' is the determination of a concept. On the other hand in ' "p" is true' the ruler enters immediately into the proposition. 'p' represents here simply the length and not the metre rule. For the representing drawing is also not 'true' except in accordance with a particular method of projection which makes the ruler a purely geometrical appendage of the measured line.

It can also be put thus: The proposition ' "p" is true' can only be understood if one understands the grammar of the sign 'p' as a propositional sign; not if '*p*' is simply the name of the shape of a particular ink mark. In the end one can say that the quotation marks in the sentence ' "*p*" is true' are simply superfluous.

REMARKS ON THE FOUNDATIONS OF MATHEMATICS

Appendix III

1. It is easy to think of a language in which there is not a form for questions, or commands, but question and command are expressed in the form of statements, e.g. in forms corresponding to our: 'I should like to know if . . .' and 'My wish is that . . .'.

No one would say of a question (e.g. whether it is raining outside) that it was true or false. Of course it is English to say so of such a sentence as 'I want to know whether . . .'. But suppose this form were always used instead of the question?—

2. The great majority of sentences that we speak, write and read, are statement sentences.

And—you say—these sentences are true or false. Or, as I might also say, the game of truth-functions is played with them. For assertion is not something that gets added to the proposition, but an essential feature of the game we play with it. Comparable, say, to that characteristic of chess by which there is winning and losing in it, the winner being the one who takes the other's king. Of course, there could be a game in a certain sense very near akin to chess, consisting in making the chess moves, but without there being any winning and losing in it; or with different conditions for winning.

3. Imagine it were said: A command consists of a proposal ('assumption') and the commanding of the thing proposed.

4. Might we not do arithmetic without having the idea of uttering arithmetical *propositions*, and without ever having been struck by the similarity between a multiplication and a proposition?

Should we not shake our heads, though, when someone showed us a multiplication done wrong, as we do when someone tells us it is raining, if it is not raining?—Yes; and here is a point of connexion. But we also make gestures to stop our dog, e.g. when he behaves as we do not wish.

We are used to saying '2 times 2 is 4', and the verb 'is' makes this into a proposition, and apparently establishes a close kinship with everything that we call a 'proposition'. Whereas it is a matter only of a very superficial relationship.

5. Are there true propositions in Russell's system, which cannot be proved in his system?—What is called a true proposition in Russell's system, then?

6. For what does a proposition's *being true* mean? '*p*' *is true* = *p*. (That is the answer.)

So we want to ask something like: under what circumstances do we assert a proposition? Or: how is the assertion of the proposition used in the language-game? And the 'assertion of the proposition' is here contrasted with the utterance of the sentence e.g. as practice in elocution,— or as *part* of another proposition, and so on.

If, then, we ask in this sense: 'Under what circumstances is a proposition asserted in Russell's game?' the answer is: at the end of one of his proofs, or as a 'fundamental law' (Pp.). There is no other way in this system of employing asserted propositions in Russell's symbolism.

PHILOSOPHICAL INVESTIGATIONS

134. Let us examine the proposition: 'This is how things are.'—How can I say that this is the general form of propositions?—It is first and foremost *itself* a proposition, an English sentence, for it has a subject and a predicate. But how is this sentence applied—that is, in our everyday language? For I got it from there and nowhere else.

We may say, e.g.: 'He explained his position to me, said that this was how things were, and that therefore he needed an advance'. So far, then, one can say that that sentence stands for any statement. It is employed as a propositional *schema*, but *only* because it has the construction of an English sentence. It would be possible to say instead 'such and such is the case', 'this is the situation', and so on. It would also be possible here simply to use a letter, a variable, as in symbolic logic. But no one is going to call the letter '*p*' the general form of propositions. To repeat: 'This is how things are' had that position only because it is itself what one calls an English sentence. But though it is a proposition, still it gets employed as a propositional variable. To say that this proposition agrees (or does not agree) with reality would be obvious nonsense. Thus it illustrates the fact that *one* feature of our concept of a proposition is, *sounding like a proposition*.

135. But haven't we got a concept of what a proposition is, of what we take 'proposition' to mean?—Yes; just as we also have a concept of what

we mean by 'game'. Asked what a proposition is—whether it is another person or ourselves that we have to answer—we shall give examples and these will include what one may call inductively defined series of propositions. *This* is the kind of way in which we have such a concept as 'proposition'. (Compare the concept of a proposition with the concept of number.)

136. At bottom, giving 'This is how things are' as the general form of propositions is the same as giving the definition: a proposition is whatever can be true or false. For instead of 'This is how things are' I could have said 'This is true'. (Or again 'This is false'.) But we have

'*p*' is true=*p*

'*p*' is false=not-*p*.

And to say that a proposition is whatever can be true or false amounts to saying: we call something a proposition when *in our language* we apply the calculus of truth functions to it.

Now it looks as if the definition—a proposition is whatever can be true or false—determined what a proposition was, by saying: what fits the concept 'true', or what the concept 'true' fits, is a proposition. So it is as if we had a concept of true and false, which we could use to determine what is and what is not a proposition. What *engages* with the concept of truth (as with a cogwheel), is a proposition.

But this is a bad picture. It is as if one were to say 'The king in chess is *the* piece that one can check.' But this can mean no more than that in our game of chess we only check the king. Just as the proposition that only a *proposition* can be true or false can say no more than that we only predicate 'true' and 'false' of what we call a proposition. And what a proposition is is in one sense determined by the rules of sentence formation (in English for example), and in another sense by the use of the sign in the language-game. And the use of the words 'true' and 'false' may be among the constituent parts of this game; and if so it *belongs* to our concept 'proposition' but does not '*fit*' it. As we might also say, check *belongs* to our concept of the king in chess (as so to speak a constituent part of it). To say that check did not *fit* our concept of the pawns, would mean that a game in which pawns were checked, in which, say, the players who lost their pawns lost, would be uninteresting or stupid or too complicated or something of the kind.

137. What about learning to determine the subject of a sentence by means of the question 'Who or what. . . . ?'—Here, surely, there is such a thing as the subject's 'fitting' this question; for otherwise how should we find out what the subject was by means of the question? We find it out

much as we find out which letter of the alphabet comes after 'K' by saying the alphabet up to 'K' to ourselves. Now in what sense does 'L' fit on to this series of letters?—In *that* sense 'true' and 'false' could be said to fit propositions; and a child might be taught to distinguish between propositions and other expressions by being told 'Ask yourself if you can say "is true" after it. If these words fit, it's a proposition.' (And in the same way one might have said: Ask yourself if you can put the words '*This* is how things are:' in front of it.)

ON CERTAINTY

196. Sure evidence is what we *accept* as sure, it is evidence that we go by in *acting* surely, acting without any doubt.

What we call 'a mistake' plays a quite special part in our language games, and so too does what we regard as certain evidence.

197. It would be nonsense to say that we regard something as sure evidence because it is certainly true.

198. Rather, we must first determine the role of deciding for or against a proposition.

199. The reason why the use of the expression 'true or false' has something misleading about it is that it is like saying 'it tallies with the facts or it doesn't', and the very thing that is in question is what 'tallying' is here.

200. Really 'The proposition is either true or false' only means that it must be possible to decide for or against it. But this does not say what the ground for such a decision is like.

VIII

THE SEMANTIC CONCEPTION OF TRUTH AND THE FOUNDATIONS OF SEMANTICS

ALFRED TARSKI

This chapter consists of two parts; the first has an expository character, and the second is rather polemical.

In the first part I want to summarize in an informal way the main results of my investigations concerning the definition of truth and the more general problem of the foundations of semantics. These results have been embodied in a work which appeared in print several years ago.[1] Although my investigations concern concepts dealt with in classical philosophy, they happen to be comparatively little known in philosophical circles, perhaps because of their strictly technical character. For this reason I hope I shall be excused for taking up the matter once again.[2]

Since my work was published, various objections, of unequal value, have

From A. Tarski, 'The Semantic Conception of Truth', *Philosophy and Phenomenological Research*, 4 (1944). Reprinted with permission.

[1] Compare A. Tarski, 'Der Wahrheitsbegriff in den formalisierten Sprachen', *Studia philosophica*, 1 (1935), 261–405. This work may be consulted for a more detailed and formal presentation of the subject of this chapter, especially of the material included in Sects. 6 and 9–13. It contains also references to my earlier publications on the problems of semantics (a communication in Polish, 1930; the article 'Sur les ensembles définissables de nombres réels. I', *Fundamenta mathematicae*, 17 (1931), 210–39; a communication in German, 1932; and a book in Polish, 1933). The expository part of the present chapter is related in its character to Tarski, 'Grundlegung der wissenschaftlichen Semantik', *Actes du congrès international de philosophie scientifique*, iii (Paris, 1936), 1–8. My investigations on the notion of truth and on theoretical semantics have been reviewed or discussed in A. Hofstadter, 'On Semantic Problems', *Journal of Philosophy*, 35 (1938), 225–32; B. von Juhos, 'The Truth of Empirical Statements', *Analysis*, 4 (1937), 65–70; M. Kokoszyńska, 'Über den absoluten Wahrheitsbegriff und einige andere semantische Begriffe', *Erkenntnis*, 6 ((1936), 143–65, and 'Syntax, Semantik, unde Wissenschaftslogik', *Actes du congres international de philosophie scientifique*, iii (Paris, 1936), 9–14; T. Kotarbiński, 'W sprawie pojęcia prawdy' (Polish) ('Concerning the Concept of Truth'), *Przegląd filozoficzny*, 37: 85–91; H. Scholz, Review of *Studia Philosophica*, vol. i, *Deutsche Literatur zeitung*, 58 (1937), 1914–17; J. Weinberg, Review of *Studia Philosophica*, vol. i, *Philosophical Review*, 47 (1938), 70–7, etc.

[2] It may be hoped that the interest in theoretical semantics will now increase, as a result of the recent publication of the important work in R. Carnap, *Introduction to Semantics* (Cambridge, 1942).

been raised to my investigations; some of these appeared in print, and others were made in public and private discussions in which I took part.[3] In the second part of the chapter I should like to express my views regarding these objections. I hope that the remarks which will be made in this context will not be considered as purely polemical in character, but will be found to contain some constructive contributions to the subject.

In the second part of the paper I have made extensive use of material graciously put at my disposal by Dr Marja Kokoszyńska (University of Lvov). I am especially indebted and grateful to Professors Ernest Nagel (Columbia University) and David Rynin (University of California, Berkeley) for their help in preparing the final text and for various critical remarks.

1. EXPOSITION

1. The Main Problem—A Satisfactory Definition of Truth. Our discussion will be centred around the notion[4] of *truth.* The main problem is that of giving a *satisfactory definition* of this notion, i.e., a definition which is *materially adequate* and *formally correct.* But such a formulation of the problem, because of its generality, cannot be considered unequivocal, and requires some further comments.

In order to avoid any ambiguity, we must first specify the conditions under which the definition of truth will be considered adequate from the material point of view. The desired definition does not aim to specify the meaning of a familiar word used to denote a novel notion; on the contrary, it aims to catch hold of the actual meaning of an old notion. We must then characterize this notion precisely enough to enable anyone to determine whether the definition actually fulfils its task.

Secondly, we must determine on what the formal correctness of the definition depends. Thus, we must specify the words or concepts which we wish to use in defining the notion of truth; and we must also give the formal

---

[3] This applies in particular to public discussions during the I. International Congress for the Unity of Science (Paris, 1935) and the Conference of International Congresses for the Unity of Science (Paris, 1937); cf. e.g. O. Neurath, 'Ersten Internationaler Kongress fur Einheit der Wissenschaft in Paris 1935', *Erkenntnis,* 5 (1935), 377–406, and F. Gonseth, 'Le Congrès Descartes: Questions de philosophie scientifique', *Revue thomiste,* 44 (1938), 183–93.

[4] The words 'notion' and 'concept' are used in this chapter with all of the vagueness and ambiguity with which they occur in philosophical literature. Thus, sometimes they refer simply to a term, sometimes to what is meant by a term, and in other cases to what is denoted by a term. Sometimes it is irrelevant which of these interpretations is meant; and in certain cases perhaps none of them applies adequately. While on principle I share the tendency to avoid these words in any exact discussion, I did not consider it necessary to do so in this informal presentation.

rules to which the definition should conform. Speaking more generally, we must describe the formal structure of the language in which the definition will be given.

The discussion of these points will occupy a considerable portion of the first part of the chapter.

2. *The Extension of the Term 'True'.* We begin with some remarks regarding the extension of the concept of truth which we have in mind here.

The predicate '*true*' is sometimes used to refer to psychological phenomena such as judgements or beliefs, sometimes to certain physical objects, namely, linguistic expressions and specifically sentences, and sometimes to certain ideal entities called 'propositions'. By 'sentence' we understand here what is usually meant in grammar by 'declarative sentence'; as regards the term 'proposition', its meaning is notoriously a subject of lengthy disputations by various philosophers and logicians, and it seems never to have been made quite clear and unambiguous. For several reasons it appears most convenient to *apply the term 'true' to sentences*, and we shall follow this course.[5]

Consequently, we must always relate the notion of truth, like that of a sentence, to a specific language; for it is obvious that the same expression which is a true sentence in one language can be false or meaningless in another.

Of course, the fact that we are interested here primarily in the notion of truth for sentences does not exclude the possibility of a subsequent extension of this notion to other kinds of objects.

3. *The Meaning of the Term 'True'.* Much more serious difficulties are connected with the problem of the meaning (or the intension) of the concept of truth.

The word '*true*', like other words from our everyday language, is certainly not unambiguous. And it does not seem to me that the philosophers who have discussed this concept have helped to diminish its ambiguity. In works and discussions of philosophers we meet many different conceptions of truth and falsity, and we must indicate which conception will be the basis of our discussion.

We should like our definition to do justice to the intuitions which adhere to the *classical Aristotelian conception of truth*—intuitions which find their expression in the well-known words of Aristotle's *Metaphysics*:

---

[5] For our present purposes it is somewhat more convenient to understand by 'expressions', 'sentences', etc., not individual inscriptions, but classes of inscriptions of similar form (thus, not individual physical things, but classes of such things).

> *To say of what is that it is not, or of what is not that it is, is false, while to say of what is that it is, or of what is not that it is not, is true.*

If we wished to adapt ourselves to modern philosophical terminology, we could perhaps express this conception by means of the familiar formula:

> *The truth of a sentence consists in its agreement with (or correspondence to) reality.*

(For a theory of truth which is to be based upon the latter formulation the term 'correspondence theory' has been suggested.)

If, on the other hand, we should decide to extend the popular usage of the term '*designate*' by applying it not only to names, but also to sentences, and if we agreed to speak of the designata of sentences as 'states of affairs', we could possibly use for the same purpose the following phrase:

> *A sentence is true if it designates an existing state of affairs.*[6]

However, all these formulations can lead to various misunderstandings, for none of them is sufficiently precise and clear (though this applies much less to the original Aristotelian formulation than to either of the others); at any rate, none of them can be considered a satisfactory definition of truth. It is up to us to look for a more precise expression of our intuitions.

4. A Criterion for the Material Adequacy of the Definition.[7] Let us start with a concrete example. Consider the sentence '*snow is white*'. We ask the question under what conditions this sentence is true or false. It seems clear that if we base ourselves on the classical conception of truth, we shall say that the sentence is true if snow is white, and that it is false if snow is not white. Thus, if the definition of truth is to conform to our conception, it must imply the following equivalence:

---

[6] For the Aristotelian formulation see Aristotle, *Metaphysics* Γ, 7, 27. The other two formulations are very common in the literature, but I do not know with whom they originate. A critical discussion of various conceptions of truth can be found e.g. in T. Kotarbiński *Elementy teorji poznania, logiki formalnej i metodologji nauk* (Elements of Epistemology, formal Logic, and the Methodology of Sciences) (LVOV, 1929) (so far available only in Polish), 123 ff., and B. Russell, *An Inquiry into Meaning and Truth* (New York, 1940), 362 ff.

[7] For most of the remarks contained in Sects. 4 and 8, I am indebted to the late S. Leśniewski who developed them in his unpublished lectures in the University of Warsaw (in 1919 and later). However, Leśniewski did not anticipate the possibility of a rigorous development of the theory of truth, and still less of a definition of this notion; hence, while indicating equivalences of the form (T) as premisses in the antinomy of the liar, he did not conceive them as any sufficient conditions for an adequate usage (or definition) of the notion of truth. Also the remarks in Sect. 8 regarding the occurrence of an empirical premiss in the antinomy of the liar, and the possibility of eliminating this premiss, do not originate with him.

The sentence 'snow is white' is true if, and only if, snow is white.

Let me point out that the phrase '*snow is white*' occurs on the left side of this equivalence in quotation marks, and on the right without quotation marks. On the right side we have the sentence itself, and on the left the name of the sentence. Employing the medieval logical terminology we could also say that on the right side the words '*snow is white*' occur in *suppositio formalis*, and on the left in *suppositio materialis*. It is hardly necessary to explain why we must have the name of the sentence, and not the sentence itself, on the left side of the equivalence. For, in the first place, from the point of view of the grammar of our language, an expression of the form '*X is true*' will not become a meaningful sentence if we replace in it '*X*' by a sentence or by anything other than a name—since the subject of a sentence may be only a noun or an expression functioning like a noun. And, in the second place, the fundamental conventions regarding the use of any language require that in any utterance we make about an object it is the name of the object which must be employed, and not the object itself. In consequence, if we wish to say something about a sentence, for example, that it is true, we must use the name of this sentence, and not the sentence itself.[8]

It may be added that enclosing a sentence in quotation marks is by no means the only way of forming its name. For instance, by assuming the usual order of letters in our alphabet, we can use the following expression as the name (the description) of the sentence '*snow is white*':

> *the sentence constituted by three words, the first of which consists of the 19th, 14th, 15th, and 23rd letters, the second of the 9th and 19th letters, and the third of the 23rd, 8th, 9th, 20th, and 5th letters of the English alphabet.*

We shall now generalize the procedure which we have applied above. Let us consider an arbitrary sentence; we shall replace it by the letter '*p*'. We form the name of this sentence and we replace it by another letter, say '*X*'. We ask now what is the logical relation between the two sentences '*X is true*' and '*p*'. It is clear that from the point of view of our basic conception of truth these sentences are equivalent. In other words, the following equivalence holds:

(T) *X is true if, and only if, p.*

---

[8] In connection with various logical and methodological problems involved in this paper the reader may consult Tarski, *Introduction to Logic* (New York, 1941).

We shall call any such equivalence (with '*p*' replaced by any sentence of the language to which the word '*true*' refers, and 'X' replaced by a name of this sentence) an '*equivalence of the form* (T)'.

Now at last we are able to put into a precise form the conditions under which we will consider the usage and the definition of the term '*true*' as adequate from the material point of view: we wish to use the term '*true*' in such a way that all equivalences of the form (T) can be asserted, and *we shall call a definition of truth 'adequate' if all these equivalences follow from it.*

It should be emphasized that neither the expression (T) itself (which is not a sentence, but only a schema of a sentence) nor any particular instance of the form (T) can be regarded as a definition of truth. We can only say that every equivalence of the form (T) obtained by replacing '*p*' by a particular sentence, and 'X' by a name of this sentence, may be considered a partial definition of truth, which explains wherein the truth of this one individual sentence consists. The general definition has to be, in a certain sense, a logical conjunction of all these partial definitions.

(The last remark calls for some comments. A language may admit the construction of infinitely many sentences; and thus the number of partial definitions of truth referring to sentences of such a language will also be infinite. Hence to give our remark a precise sense we should have to explain what is meant by a 'logical conjunction of infinitely many sentences'; but this would lead us too far into technical problems of modern logic.)

5. *Truth as a Semantic Concept.* I should like to propose the name '*the semantic conception of truth*' for the conception of truth which has just been discussed.

Semantics is a discipline which, speaking loosely, *deals with certain relations between expressions of a language and the objects* (or 'states of affairs') '*referred to*' *by those expressions.* As typical examples of semantic concepts we may mention the concepts of *designation, satisfaction,* and *definition* as these occur in the following examples:

> the expression '*the father of his country*' designates (denotes) George Washington;
> snow satisfies the sentential function (the condition) '*x is white*';
> the equation '2·x=1' defines (*uniquely determines*) the number 1/2.

While the words '*designates*', '*satisfies*', and '*defines*' express relations (between certain expressions and the objects 'referred to' by these expressions), the word '*true*' is of a different logical nature: it expresses a property (or denotes a class) of certain expressions, namely of sentences.

However, it is easily seen that all the formulations which were given earlier and which aimed to explain the meaning of this word (cf. Sections 3 and 4) referred not only to sentences themselves, but also to objects 'talked about' by these sentences, or possibly to 'states of affairs' described by them. And, moreover, it turns out that the simplest and the most natural way of obtaining an exact definition of truth is one which involves the use of other semantic notions, e.g., the notion of satisfaction. It is for these reasons that we count the concept of truth which is discussed here among the concepts of semantics, and the problem of defining truth proves to be closely related to the more general problem of setting up the foundations of theoretical semantics.

It is perhaps worth while saying that semantics as it is conceived in this chapter (and in former papers of the author) is a sober and modest discipline which has no pretentions of being a universal patent-medicine for all the ills and diseases of mankind, whether imaginary or real. You will not find in semantics any remedy for decayed teeth or illusions of grandeur or class conflicts. Nor is semantics a device for establishing that everyone except the speaker and his friends is speaking nonsense.

From antiquity to the present day the concepts of semantics have played an important role in the discussions of philosophers, logicians, and philologists. Nevertheless, these concepts have been treated for a long time with a certain amount of suspicion. From a historical standpoint, this suspicion is to be regarded as completely justified. For although the meaning of semantic concepts as they are used in everyday language seems to be rather clear and understandable, still all attempts to characterize this meaning in a general and exact way miscarried. And what is worse, various arguments in which these concepts were involved, and which seemed otherwise quite correct and based upon apparently obvious premises, led frequently to paradoxes and antinomies. It is sufficient to mention here the *antinomy of the liar*, Richard's *antinomy of definability* (by means of a finite number of words), and Grelling–Nelson's *antinomy of heterological terms*.[9]

I believe that the method which is outlined in this chapter helps to overcome these difficulties and assures the possibility of a consistent use of semantic concepts.

6. Languages with a Specified Structure. Because of the possible

---

[9] The antinomy of the liar (ascribed to Eubulides or Epimenides) is discussed here in Sects. 7 and 8. For the antinomy of definability (due to J. Richard) see e.g. D. Hilbert and P. Bernays, *Grundlagen der Mathematik*, 2 vols. (Berlin, 1934–9), ii, 263 ff.; for the antinomy of heterological terms see K. Grelling and L. Nelson, 'Bemerkungen zu den Paradoxien von Russell und Burali-forli', Abhandlungen der Fries'schen Schule, NS 2 (1908), 307.

occurrence of antinomies, the problem of specifying the formal structure and the vocabulary of a language in which definitions of semantic concepts are to be given becomes especially acute; and we turn now to this problem.

There are certain general conditions under which the structure of a language is regarded as *exactly specified*. Thus, to specify the structure of a language, we must characterize unambiguously the class of those words and expressions which are to be considered *meaningful*. In particular, we must indicate all words which we decide to use without defining them, and which are called '*undefined* (or *primitive*) *terms*'; and we must give the so-called *rules of definition* for introducing new or *defined terms*. Furthermore, we must set up criteria for distinguishing within the class of expressions those which we call '*sentences*'. Finally, we must formulate the conditions under which a sentence of the language can be *asserted*. In particular, we must indicate all *axioms* (or *primitive sentences*), i.e., those sentences which we decide to assert without proof; and we must give the so-called *rules of inference* (or *rules of proof*) by means of which we can deduce new asserted sentences from other sentences which have been previously asserted. Axioms, as well as sentences deduced from them by means of rules of inference, are referred to as '*theorems*' or '*provable sentences*'.

If in specifying the structure of a language we refer exclusively to the form of the expressions involved, the language is said to be *formalized*. In such a language theorems are the only sentences which can be asserted.

At the present time the only languages with a specified structure are the formalized languages of various systems of deductive logic, possibly enriched by the introduction of certain non-logical terms. However, the field of application of these languages is rather comprehensive; we are able, theoretically, to develop in them various branches of science, for instance, mathematics and theoretical physics.

(On the other hand, we can imagine the construction of languages which have an exactly specified structure without being formalized. In such a language the assertability of sentences, for instance, may depend not always on their form, but sometimes on other, non-linguistic factors. It would be interesting and important actually to construct a language of this type, and specifically one which would prove to be sufficient for the development of a comprehensive branch of empirical science; for this would justify the hope that languages with specified structure could finally replace everyday language in scientific discourse.)

The problem of the definition of truth obtains a precise meaning and can be solved in a rigorous way only for those languages whose structure has been exactly specified. For other languages—thus, for all natural, 'spoken' languages—the meaning of the problem is more or less vague, and its solution can have only an approximate character. Roughly speaking, the approximation consists in replacing a natural language (or a portion of it in which we are interested) by one whose structure is exactly specified, and which diverges from the given language 'as little as possible'.

7. *The Antinomy of the Liar.* In order to discover some of the more specific conditions which must be satisfied by languages in which (or for which) the definition of truth is to be given, it will be advisable to begin with a discussion of that antinomy which directly involves the notion of truth, namely, the antinomy of the liar.

To obtain this antinomy in a perspicuous form,[10] consider the following sentence:

> *The sentence printed in this chapter on* p. 123 l. 15–16 *of this volume, is not true.*

For brevity we shall replace the sentence just stated by the letter '*s*'.

According to our convention concerning the adequate usage of the term '*true*', we assert the following equivalence of the form (T):

> (1) '*s*' *is true if, and only if, the sentence printed in this chapter on* p. 123 l. 15–16 *of this volume, is not true.*

On the other hand, keeping in mind the meaning of the symbol '*s*', we establish empirically the following fact:

> (2) '*s*' *is identical with the sentence printed in this chapter on* p. 123 l. 15–16 *of this volume.*

Now, by a familiar law from the theory of identity (Leibniz's law), it follows from (2) that we may replace in (1) the expression '*the sentence printed in this chapter on* p. 123 l. 15–16 *of this volume* by the symbol '*s*'. We thus obtain what follows:

> (3) '*s*' *is true if, and only if, '*s*' is not true.*

In this way we have arrived at an obvious contradiction.

In my judgement, it would be quite wrong and dangerous from the standpoint of scientific progress to depreciate the importance of this and other antinomies, and to treat them as jokes or sophistries. It is a fact that we are here in the presence of an absurdity, that we have been compelled to assert a false sentence (since (3), as an equivalence between two contradictory sentences, is necessarily false). If we take our work

---

[10] Due to Professor J. Łukasiewicz (University of Warsaw).

seriously, we cannot be reconciled with this fact. We must discover its cause, that is to say, we must analyse premisses upon which the antinomy is based; we must then reject at least one of these premisses, and we must investigate the consequences which this has for the whole domain of our research.

It should be emphasized that antinomies have played a pre-eminent role in establishing the foundations of modern deductive sciences. And just as class-theoretical antinomies, and in particular Russell's antinomy (of the class of all classes that are not members of themselves), were the starting point for the successful attempts at a consistent formalization of logic and mathematics, so the antinomy of the liar and other semantic antinomies give rise to the construction of theoretical semantics.

8. *The Inconsistency of Semantically Closed Languages.*[7] If we now analyse the assumptions which lead to the antinomy of the liar, we notice the following:

(I) We have implicitly assumed that the language in which the antinomy is constructed contains, in addition to its expressions, also the names of these expressions, as well as semantic terms such as the term *'true'* referring to sentences of this language; we have also assumed that all sentences which determine the adequate usage of this term can be asserted in the language. A language with these properties will be called *'semantically closed'*.

(II) We have assumed that in this language the ordinary laws of logic hold.

(III) We have assumed that we can formulate and assert in our language an empirical premiss such as the statement (2) which has occurred in our argument.

It turns out that the assumption (III) is not essential, for it is possible to reconstruct the antinomy of the liar without its help.[11] But the assumptions (I) and (II) prove essential. Since every language which satisfies both of these assumptions is inconsistent, we must reject at least one of them.

----

[11] This can roughly be done in the following way. Let S be any sentence beginning with the words *'Every sentence'*. We correlate with S a new sentence $S*$ by subjecting S to the following two modifications: we replace in S the first word, *'Every'*, by *'The'*; and we insert after the second word, *'sentence'*, the whole sentence S enclosed in quotation marks. Let us agree to call the sentence S '(self-)applicable' or 'non-(self-)applicable' dependent on whether the correlated sentence $S*$ is true or false. Now consider the following sentence:

Every sentence is non-applicable.

It can easily be shown that the sentence just stated must be both applicable and non-applicable; hence a contradiction. It may not be quite clear in what sense this formulation of the antinomy does not involve an empirical premiss; however, I shall not elaborate on this point.

It would be superfluous to stress here the consequences of rejecting the assumption (II), that is, of changing our logic (supposing this were posible) even in its more elementary and fundamental parts. We thus consider only the possibility of rejecting the assumption (I). Accordingly, we decide *not to use any language which is semantically closed* in the sense given.

This restriction would of course be unacceptable for those who, for reasons which are not clear to me, believe that there is only one 'genuine' language (or, at least, that all 'genuine' languages are mutually translatable). However, this restriction does not affect the needs or interests of science in any essential way. The languages (either the formalized languages or—what is more frequently the case—the portions of everyday language) which are used in scientific discourse do not have to be semantically closed. This is obvious in case linguistic phenomena and, in particular, semantic notions do not enter in any way into the subject matter of a science; for in such a case the language of this science does not have to be provided with any semantic terms at all. However, we shall see in the next section how semantically closed languages can be dispensed with even in those scientific discussions in which semantic notions are essentially involved.

The problem arises as to the position of everyday language with regard to this point. At first blush it would seem that this language satisfies both assumptions (I) and (II), and that therefore it must be inconsistent. But actually the case is not so simple. Our everyday language is certainly not one with an exactly specified structure. We do not know precisely which expressions are sentences, and we know even to a smaller degree which sentences are to be taken as assertible. Thus the problem of consistency has no exact meaning with respect to this language. We may at best only risk the guess that a language whose structure has been exactly specified and which resembles our everyday language as closely as possible would be inconsistent.

9. Object-Language and Metalanguage. Since we have agreed not to employ semantically closed languages, we have to use two different languages in discussing the problem of the definition of truth and, more generally, any problems in the field of semantics. The first of these languages is the language which is 'talked about' and which is the subject matter of the whole discussion; the definition of truth which we are seeking applies to the sentences of this language. The second is the language in which we 'talk about' the first language, and in terms of which we wish, in particular, to construct the definition of truth for the first language. We shall refer to the first language as '*the object-language*', and to the second as '*the metalanguage*'.

It should be noticed that these terms 'object-language' and 'metalanguage' have only a relative sense. If, for instance, we become interested in the notion of truth applying to sentences, not of our original object-language, but of its metalanguage, the latter becomes automatically the object-language of our discussion; and in order to define truth for this language, we have to go to a new metalanguage—so to speak, to a metalanguage of a higher level. In this way we arrive at a whole hierarchy of languages.

The vocabulary of the metalanguage is to a large extent determined by previously stated conditions under which a definition of truth will be considered materially adequate. This definition, as we recall, has to imply all equivalences of the form (T):

(T) *X is true if, and only if, p.*

The definition itself and all the equivalences implied by it are to be formulated in the metalanguage. On the other hand, the symbol '*p*' in (T) stands for an arbitrary sentence of our object-language. Hence it follows that every sentence which occurs in the object-language must also occur in the metalanguage; in other words, the metalanguage must contain the object-language as a part. This is at any rate necessary for the proof of the adequacy of the definition—even though the definition itself can sometimes be formulated in a less comprehensive metalanguage which does not satisfy this requirement.

(The requirement in question can be somewhat modified, for it suffices to assume that the object-language can be translated into the metalanguage; this necessitates a certain change in the interpretation of the symbol '*p*' in (T). In all that follows we shall ignore the possibility of this modification.)

Furthermore, the symbol '*X*' in (T) represents the name of the sentence which '*p*' stands for. We see therefore that the metalanguage must be rich enough to provide possibilities of constructing a name for every sentence of the object-language.

In addition, the metalanguage must obviously contain terms of a general logical character, such as the expression 'if, and only if'.[12]

It is desirable for the metalanguage not to contain any undefined terms except such as are involved explicitly or implicitly in the remarks above,

---

[12] The terms 'logic' and 'logical' are used in this chapter in a broad sense, which has become almost traditional in the last decades; logic is assumed here to comprehend the whole theory of classes and relations (i.e., the mathematical theory of sets). For many different reasons I am personally inclined to use the term 'logic' in a much narrower sense, so as to apply it only to what is sometimes called 'elementary logic', i.e., to the sentential calculus and the (restricted) predicate calculus.

i.e.: terms of the object-language; terms referring to the form of the expressions of the object-language, and used in building names for these expressions; and terms of logic. In particular, we desire *semantic terms* (referring to the object-language) *to be introduced into the metalanguage only by definition*. For, if this postulate is satisfied, the definition of truth, or of any other semantic concept, will fulfil what we intuitively expect from every definition; that is, it will explain the meaning of the term being defined in terms whose meaning appears to be completely clear and unequivocal. And, moreover, we have then a kind of guarantee that the use of semantic concepts will not involve us in any contradictions.

We have no further requirements as to the formal structure of the object-language and the metalanguage; we assume that it is similar to that of other formalized languages known at the present time. In particular, we assume that the usual formal rules of definition are observed in the metalanguage.

10. Conditions for a Positive Solution of the Main Problem. Now, we have already a clear idea both of the conditions of material adequacy to which the definition of truth is subjected, and of the formal structure of the language in which this definition is to be constructed. Under these circumstances the problem of the definition of truth acquires the character of a definite problem of a purely deductive nature.

The solution of the problem, however, is by no means obvious, and I would not attempt to give it in detail without using the whole machinery of contemporary logic. Here I shall confine myself to a rough outline of the solution and to the discussion of certain points of a more general interest which are involved in it.

The solution turns out to be sometimes positive, sometimes negative. This depends upon some formal relations between the object-language and its metalanguage; or, more specifically, upon the fact whether the metalanguage in its logical part is '*essentially richer*' than the object-language or not. It is not easy to give a general and precise definition of this notion of 'essential richness'. If we restrict ourselves to languages based on the logical theory of types, the condition for the metalanguage to be 'essentially richer' than the object-language is that it contain variables of a higher logical type than those of the object-language.

If the condition of 'essential richness' is not satisfied, it can usually be shown that an interpretation of the metalanguage in the object-language is possible; that is to say, with any given term of the metalanguage a well-determined term of the object-language can be correlated in such a way that the assertible sentences of the one language turn out to be correlated with assertible sentences of the other. As a result of this interpretation, the hypothesis that a satisfactory definition of truth has been formulated in the metalanguage turns out to imply the possibility of reconstructing in that language the antinomy of the liar; and this in turn forces us to reject the hypothesis in question.

(The fact that the metalanguage, in its non-logical part, is ordinarily more comprehensive than the object-language does not affect the possibility of interpreting the former in the latter. For example, the names of expressions of the object-language occur in the metalanguage, though for the most part they do not occur in the object-language itself; but, nevertheless, it may be possible to interpret these names in terms of the object-language.)

Thus we see that the condition of 'essential richness' is necessary for the possibility of a satisfactory definition of truth in the metalanguage. If we want to develop the theory of truth in a metalanguage which does not satisfy this condition, we must give up the idea of defining truth with the exclusive help of those terms which were indicated above (in Section 8). We have then to include the term '*true*', or some other semantic term, in the list of undefined terms of the metalanguage, and to express fundamental properties of the notion of truth in a series of axioms. There is nothing essentially wrong in such an axiomatic procedure, and it may prove useful for various purposes.[13]

It turns out, however, that this procedure can be avoided. For *the condition of the 'essential richness' of the metalanguage proves to be, not only necessary, but also sufficient for the construction of a satisfactory definition of truth*; i.e., if the meta-language satisfies this condition, the notion of truth can be defined in it. We shall now indicate in general terms how this construction can be carried through.

11. The Construction (in Outline) of the Definition.[14] A definition of truth can be obtained in a very simple way from that of another semantic notion, namely, of the notion of *satisfaction*.

Satisfaction is a relation between arbitrary objects and certain expressions called '*sentential functions*'. These are expressions like '*x is white*', '*x is greater than y*', etc. Their formal structure is analogous to that of sentences; however, they may contain the so-called free variables (like '*x*' and '*y*' in '*x is greater than y*'), which cannot occur in sentences.

In defining the notion of a sentential function in formalized languages, we usually apply what is called a 'recursive procedure'; i.e., we first describe

---

[13] Cf. here, however, Tarski, 'Grundlegung', 5–6.
[14] The method of construction we are going to outline can be applied—with appropriate changes—to all formalized languages that are known at the present time; although it does not follow that a language could not be constructed to which this method would not apply.

sentential functions of the simplest structure (which ordinarily presents no difficulty), and then we indicate the operations by means of which compound functions can be constructed from simpler ones. Such an operation may consist, for instance, in forming the logical disjunction or conjunction of two given functions, i.e., by combining them by the word '*or*' or '*and*'. A sentence can now be defined simply as a sentential function which contains no free variables.

As regards the notion of satisfaction, we might try to define it by saying that given objects satisfy a given function if the latter becomes a true sentence when we replace in it free variables by names of given objects. In this sense, for example, snow satisfies the sentential function '*x is white*' since the sentence '*snow is white*' is true. However, apart from other difficulties, this method is not available to us, for we want to use the notion of satisfaction in defining truth.

To obtain a definition of satisfaction we have rather to apply again a recursive procedure. We indicate which objects satisfy the simplest sentential functions; and then we state the conditions under which given objects satisfy a compound function—assuming that we know which objects satisfy the simpler functions from which the compound one has been constructed. Thus, for instance, we say that given numbers satisfy the logical disjunction '*x is greater than y or x is equal to y*' if they satisfy at least one of the functions '*x is greater than y*' or '*x is equal to y*'.

Once the general definition of satisfaction is obtained, we notice that it applies automatically also to those special sentential functions which contain no free variables, i.e., to sentences. It turns out that for a sentence only two cases are possible: a sentence is either satisfied by all objects, or by no objects. Hence we arrive at a definition of truth and falsehood simply by saying that *a sentence is true if it is satisfied by all objects, and false otherwise*.[15]

---

[15] In carrying through this idea a certain technical difficulty arises. A sentential function may contain an arbitrary number of free variables; and the logical nature of the notion of satisfaction varies with this number. Thus, the notion in question when applied to functions with one variable is a binary relation between these functions and single objects; when applied to functions with two variables it becomes a ternary relation between functions and couples of objects; and so on. Hence, strictly speaking, we are confronted, not with one notion of satisfaction, but with infinitely many notions; and it turns out that these notions cannot be defined independently of each other, but must all be introduced simultaneously.

To overcome this difficulty, we employ the mathematical notion of an infinite sequence (or, possibly, of a finite sequence with an arbitrary number of terms). We agree to regard satisfaction, not as a many-termed relation between sentential functions and an indefinite number of objects, but as a binary relation between functions and sequences of objects. Under this assumption the formulation of a general and precise definition of satisfaction no longer presents any difficulty; and a true sentence can now be defined as one which is satisfied by every sequence.

(It may seem strange that we have chosen a roundabout way of defining the truth of a sentence, instead of trying to apply, for instance, a direct recursive procedure. The reason is that compound sentences are constructed from simpler sentential functions, but not always from simpler sentences; hence no general recursive method is known which applies specifically to sentences.)

From this rough outline it is not clear where and how the assumption of the 'essential richness' of the metalanguage is involved in the discussion; this becomes clear only when the construction is carried through in a detailed and formal way.[16]

12. Consequences of the Definition. The definition of truth which was outlined above has many interesting consequences.

In the first place, the definition proves to be not only formally correct, but also materially adequate (in the sense established in Section 4); in other words, it implies all equivalences of the form (T). In this connection it is important to notice that the conditions for the material adequacy of the definition determine uniquely the extenstion of the term '*true*'. Therefore, every definition of truth which is materially adequate would necessarily be equivalent to that actually constructed. The semantic conception of truth gives us, so to speak, no possibility of choice between various non-equivalent definitions of this notion.

Moreover, we can deduce from our definition various laws of a general nature. In particular, we can prove with its help the *laws of contradiction and of excluded middle*, which are so characteristic of the Aristotelian conception of truth; i.e., we can show that one and only one of any two contradictory sentences is true. These semantic laws should not be identified with the related logical laws of contradiction and excluded middle; the latter belong to the sentential calculus, i.e., to the most elementary part of logic, and do not involve the term '*true*' at all.

Further important results can be obtained by applying the theory of truth to formalized languages of a certain very comprehensive class of mathematical disciplines; only disciplines of an elementary character and

---

[16] To define recursively the notion of satisfaction, we have to apply a certain form of recursive definition which is not admitted in the object-language. Hence the 'essential richness' of the metalanguage may simply consist in admitting this type of definition. On the other hand, a general method is known which makes it possible to eliminate all recursive definitions and to replace them by normal, explicit ones. If we try to apply this method to the definition of satisfaction, we see that we have either to introduce into the metalanguage variables of a higher logical type than those which occur in the object-language; or else to assume axiomatically in the metalanguage the existence of classes that are more comprehensive than all those whose existence can be established in the object-language. See here Tarski, 'Wahrheitsbegriff', 393 ff., and Tarski, 'On Undecidable Statements in Enlarged Systems of Logic and the Concept of Truth', *Journal of Symbolic Logic*, 4 (1939), 110.

a very elementary logical structure are excluded from this class. It turns out that for a discipline of this class *the notion of truth never coincides with that of provability*; for all provable sentences are true, but there are true sentences which are not provable.[17] Hence it follows further that every such discipline is consistent, but incomplete; that is to say, of any two contradictory sentences at most one is provable, and—what is more—there exists a pair of contradictory sentences neither of which is provable.[18]

13. *Extension of the Results to Other Semantic Notions.* Most of the results at which we arrived in the preceding sections in discussing the notion of truth can be extended with appropriate changes to other semantic notions, for instance, to the notion of satisfaction (involved in our previous discussion), and to those of *designation* and *definition*.

Each of these notions can be analysed along the lines followed in the analysis of truth. Thus, criteria for an adequate usage of these notions can be established; it can be shown that each of these notions, when used in a semantically closed language according to those criteria, leads necessarily

---

[17] Due to the development of modern logic, the notion of mathematical proof has undergone a far-reaching simplification. A sentence of a given formalized discipline is provable if it can be obtained from the axioms of this discipline by applying certain simple and purely formal rules of inference, such as those of detachment and substitution. Hence to show that all provable sentences are true, it suffices to prove that all the sentences accepted as axioms are true, and that the rules of inference when applied to true sentences yield new true sentences; and this usually presents no difficulty.

On the other hand, in view of the elementary nature of the notion of provability, a precise definition of this notion requires only rather simple logical devices. In most cases, those logical devices which are available in the formalized discipline itself (to which the notion of provability is related) are more than sufficient for this purpose. We know, however, that as regards the definition of truth just the opposite holds. Hence, as a rule, the notions of truth and provability cannot coincide; and since every provable sentence is true, there must be true sentences which are not provable.

[18] Thus the theory of truth provides us with a general method for consistency proofs for formalized mathematical disciplines. It can be easily realized, however, that a consistency proof obtained by this method may possess some intuitive value—i.e., may convince us, or strengthen our belief, that the discipline under consideration is actually consistent—only in case we succeed in defining truth in terms of a metalanguage which does not contain the object-language as a part (cf. here a remark in Sect. 9). For only in this case the deductive assumptions of the metalanguage may be intuitively simpler and more obvious than those of the object-language—even though the condition of 'essential richness' will be formally satisfied. Cf. here also Tarski, 'Grundlegung', 7. The incompleteness of a comprehensive class of formalized disciplines constitutes the essential content of a fundamental theorem of K. Gödel; cf. Gödel 'Über formal unentscheidbare Sätze der *Principia Mathematica* und verwandter systeme, I', *Monatshefte für Mathematik und Physik*, 38 (1931), 187 ff. The explanation of the fact that the theory of truth leads so directly to Gödel's theorem is rather simple. In deriving Gödel's result from the theory of truth we make an essential use of the fact that the definition of truth cannot be given in a metalanguage which is only as 'rich' as the object-language (cf. n. 17, above); however, in establishing this fact, a method of reasoning has been applied which is very closely related to that used (for the first time) by Gödel. It may be added that Gödel was clearly guided in his proof by certain intuitive considerations regarding the notion of truth, although this notion does not occur in the proof explicitly; cf. Gödel, 'Über formal unentscheidbare Sätze', 174–5.

to a contradiction;[19] a distinction between the object-language and the metalanguage becomes again indispensable; and the 'essential richness' of the metalanguage proves in each case to be a necessary and sufficient condition for a satisfactory definition of the notion involved. Hence the results obtained in discussing one particular semantic notion apply to the general problem of the foundations of theoretical semantics.

Within theoretical semantics we can define and study some further notions, whose intuitive content is more involved and whose semantic origin is less obvious; we have in mind, for instance, the important notions of *consequence*, *synonymity*, and *meaning*.[20]

We have concerned ourselves here with the theory of semantic notions related to an individual object-language (although no specific properties of this language have been involved in our arguments). However, we could also consider the problem of developing *general semantics* which applies to a comprehensive class of object-languages. A considerable part of our previous remarks can be extended to this general problem; however, certain new difficulties arise in this connection, which will not be discussed here. I shall merely observe that the axiomatic method (mentioned in Section 10) may prove the most appropriate for the treatment of the problem.[21]

II. POLEMICAL REMARKS

14. Is the Semantic Conception of Truth the 'Right' One? I should like to begin the polemical part of the chapter with some general remarks.

I hope nothing which is said here will be interpreted as a claim that the semantic conception of truth is the 'right' or indeed the 'only possible' one. I do not have the slightest intention to contribute in any way to those

---

[19] The notions of designation and definition lead respectively to the antinomies of Grelling and Nelson, and Richard (cf. n. 9, above). To obtain an antinomy for the notion of satisfaction, we construct the following expression:

The sentential function X does not satisfy X.

A contradiction arises when we consider the question whether this expression, which is clearly a sentential function, satisfies itself or not.

[20] All notions mentioned in this section can be defined in terms of satisfaction. We can say e.g. that a given term designates a given object if this object satisfies the sentential function 'x *is identical with T*' where '*T*' stands for the given term. Similarly, a sentential function is said to define a given object if the latter is the only object which satisfies this function. For a definition of consequence see A. Tarski, 'Über den Begriff der logischen folgerung', *Actes du congrès internationale de philosophie scientifique*, vii (Paris, 1937), 1–11 and for that of synonymity R. Carnap, *Introduction to Semantics* (Cambridge, 1942).

[21] General semantics is the subject of Carnap, *Introduction*. Cf. here also remarks in Tarski, 'Wahrheitsbegriff', 388–9.

endless, often violent discussions on the subject 'What is the right conception of truth?'[22] I must confess I do not understand what is at stake in such
disputes; for the problem itself is so vague that no definite solution is possible. In fact, it seems to me that the sense in which the phrase 'the right
conception' is used has never been made clear. In most cases one gets the
impression that the phrase is used in an almost mystical sense based upon
the belief that every word has only one 'real' meaning (a kind of Platonic
or Aristotelian idea), and that all the competing conceptions really attempt
to catch hold of this one meaning; since, however, they contradict each
other, only one attempt can be successful, and hence only one conception
is the 'right' one.

Disputes of this type are by no means restricted to the notion of truth.
They occur in all domains where—instead of an exact, scientific terminology—common language with its vagueness and ambiguity is used; and they
are always meaningless, and therefore in vain.

It seems to me obvious that the only rational approach to such problems would be the following: We should reconcile ourselves with the fact
that we are confronted, not with one concept, but with several different
concepts which are denoted by one word; we should try to make these concepts as clear as possible (by means of definition, or of an axiomatic procedure, or in some other way); to avoid further confusions, we should agree
to use different terms for different concepts; and then we may proceed to
a quiet and systematic study of all concepts involved, which will exhibit
their main properties and mutual relations.

Referring specifically to the notion of truth, it is undoubtedly the case
that in philosophical discussions—and perhaps also in everyday usage—
some incipient conceptions of this notion can be found that differ essentially from the classical one (of which the semantic conception is but
a modernized form). In fact, various conceptions of this sort have been
discussed in the literature, for instance, the pragmatic conception, the
coherence theory, etc.[6]

It seems to me that none of these conceptions have been put so far in
an intelligible and unequivocal form. This may change, however; a time
may come when we find ourselves confronted with several incompatible,
but equally clear and precise, conceptions of truth. It will then become necessary to abandon the ambiguous usage of the word '*true*', and to introduce several terms instead, each to denote a different notion. Personally,
I should not feel hurt if a future world congress of the 'theoreticians of

[22] Cf. various quotations in A. Ness, ' "Truth" as conceived by those who are not Professional
Philosophers', *Skrifter utgitt av Det Norske Videnskaps-Akademi i Oslo, II. Hist.-Filos. Klasse*, iv
(Oslo, 1938), 13–14.

truth' should decide—by a majority of votes—to reserve the word '*true*' for one of the non-classical conceptions, and should suggest another word, say, '*frue*', for the conception considered here. But I cannot imagine that anybody could present cogent arguments to the effect that the semantic conception is 'wrong' and should be entirely abandoned.

15. *Formal Correctness of the Suggested Definition of Truth.* The specific objections which have been raised to my investigations can be divided into several groups; each of these will be discussed separately.

I think that practically all these objections apply, not to the special definition I have given, but to the semantic conception of truth in general. Even those which were levelled against the definition actually constructed could be related to any other definition which conforms to this conception.

This holds, in particular, for those objections which concern the formal correctness of the definition. I have heard a few objections of this kind; however, I doubt very much whether any one of them can be treated seriously.

As a typical example let me quote in substance such an objection.[23] In formulating the definition we use necessarily sentential connectives, i.e., expressions like '*if* . . . , *then*', '*or*', etc. They occur in the definiens; and one of them, namely, the phrase '*if, and only if*' is usually employed to combine the definiendum with the definiens. However, it is well known that the meaning of sentential connectives is explained in logic with the help of the words '*true*' and '*false*'; for instance, we say that an equivalence, i.e., a sentence of the form '*p if, and only if, q*', is true if either both of its members, i.e. the sentences represented by '*p*' and '*q*', are true or both are false. Hence the definition of truth involves a vicious circle.

If this objection were valid, no formally correct definition of truth would be possible; for we are unable to formulate any compound sentence without using sentential connectives, or other logical terms defined with their help. Fortunately, the situation is not so bad.

It is undoubtedly the case that a strictly deductive development of logic is often preceded by certain statements explaining the conditions under which sentences of the form '*if p, then q*', etc., are considered true or false. (Such explanations are often given schematically, by means of the so-called truth-tables.) However, these statements are outside of the system of logic, and should not be regarded as definitions of the terms involved. They are not formulated in the language of the system, but constitute rather special

---

[23] The names of persons who have raised objections will not be quoted here, unless their objections have appeared in print.

consequences of the definition of truth given in the metalanguage. Moreover, these statements do not influence the deductive development of logic in any way. For in such a development we do not discuss the question whether a given sentence is true, we are only interested in the problem whether it is provable.[24]

On the other hand, the moment we find ourselves within the deductive system of logic—or of any discipline based upon logic, e.g. of semantics— we either treat sentential connectives as undefined terms, or else we define them by means of other sentential connectives, but never by means of semantic terms like '*true*' or '*false*'. For instance, if we agree to regard the expressions '*not*' and '*if. . ., then*' (and possibly also '*if, and only if*') as undefined terms, we can define the term '*or*' by stating that a sentence of the form '*p or q*' is equivalent to the corresponding sentence of the form '*if not p, then q*'. The definition can be formulated, e.g. in the following way:

   (p or q) if, and only if, (if not p, then q).

This definition obviously contains no semantic terms.

However, a vicious circle in definition arises only when the definiens contains either the term to be defined itself, or other terms defined with its help. Thus we clearly see that the use of sentential connectives in defining the semantic term '*true*' does not involve any circle.

I should like to mention a further objection which I have found in the literature and which seems also to concern the formal correctness, if not of the definition of truth itself, then at least of the arguments which lead to this definition.[25]

The author of this objection mistakenly regards scheme (T) (from Section 4) as a definition of truth. He charges this alleged definition with 'inadmissible brevity, i.e. incompleteness', which 'does not give us the means of deciding whether by "equivalence" is meant a logical-formal, or

---

[24] It should be emphasized, however, that as regards the question of an alleged vicious circle the situation would not change even if we took a different point of view, represented e.g. in Carnap, *Introduction*; i.e., if we regarded the specification of conditions under which sentences of a language are true as an essential part of the description of this language. On the other hand, it may be noticed that the point of view represented in the text does not exclude the possibility of using truth-tables in a deductive development of logic. However, these tables are to be regarded then merely as a formal instrument for checking the provability of certain sentences; and the symbols 'T' and 'F' which occur in them and which are usually considered abbreviations of '*true*' and '*false*' should not be interpreted in any intuitive way.

[25] Cf. Juhos, 'Truth'. I must admit that I do not clearly understand von Juhos's objections and do not know how to classify them; therefore, I confine myself here to certain points of a formal character. Von Juhos does not seem to know my definition of truth; he refers only to an informal presentation in Tarski, 'Grundlegung', where the definition has not been given at all. If he knew the actual definition, he would have to change his argument. However, I have no doubt that he would discover in this definition some 'defects' as well. For he believes he has proved that 'on ground of principle it is impossible to give such a definition at all'.

a non-logical and also structurally non-describable relation'. To remove this 'defect' he suggests supplementing (T) in one of the two following ways:

    (T′) *X is true if, and only if, p is true,*

or

    (T″) *X is true if, and only if, p is the case (i.e., if what p states is the case).*

Then he discusses these two new 'definitions', which are supposedly free from the old, formal 'defect', but which turn out to be unsatisfactory for other, non-formal reasons.

This new objection seems to arise from a misunderstanding concerning the nature of sentential connectives (and thus to be somehow related to that previously discussed). The author of the objection does not seem to realize that the phrase '*if, and only if*' (in opposition to such phrases as '*are equivalent*' or '*is equivalent to*') expresses no relation between sentences at all since it does not combine names of sentences.

In general, the whole argument is based upon an obvious confusion between sentences and their names. It suffices to point out that—in contradistinction to (T)—schemata (T′) and (T″) do not give any meaningful expressions if we replace in them '*p*' by a sentence; for the phrases '*p is true*' and '*p is the case*' (i.e., '*what p states is the case*') become meaningless if '*p*' is replaced by a sentence, and not by the name of a sentence (cf. Section 4).[26]

While the author of the objection considers schema (T) 'inadmissibly brief', I am inclined, on my part, to regard schemata (T′) and (T″) as 'inadmissibly long'. And I think even that I can rigorously prove this statement on the basis of the following definition: An expression is said to be 'inadmissibly long' if (i) it is meaningless, and (ii) it has been obtained from a meaningful expression by inserting superfluous words.

16. Redundancy of Semantic Terms—Their Possible Elimination. The objection I am going to discuss now no longer concerns the formal correctness of the definition, but is still concerned with certain formal features of the semantic conception of truth.

---

[26] The phrases '*p is true*' and '*p is the case*' (or better '*it is true that p*' and '*it is the case that p*') are sometimes used in informal discussions, mainly for stylistic reasons; but they are considered then as synonymous with the sentence represented by '*p*'. On the other hand, as far as I understand the situation, the phrases in question cannot be used by von Juhos synonymously with '*p*'; for otherwise the replacement of (T) by (T′) or (T″) would not constitute any 'improvement'.

We have seen that this conception essentially consists in regarding the sentence '*X is true*' as equivalent to the sentence denoted by '*X*' (where '*X*' stands for a name of a sentence of the object-language). Consequently, the term '*true*' when occurring in a simple sentence of the form '*X is true*' can easily be eliminated, and the sentence itself, which belongs to the meta-language, can be replaced by an equivalent sentence of the object-language; and the same applies to compound sentences provided the term '*true*' occurs in them exclusively as a part of the expressions of the form '*X is true*'.

Some people have therefore urged that the term '*true*' in the semantic sense can always be eliminated, and that for this reason the semantic conception of truth is altogether sterile and useless. And since the same considerations apply to other semantic notions, the conclusion has been drawn that semantics as a whole is a purely verbal game and at best only a harmless hobby.

But the matter is not quite so simple.[27] The sort of elimination here discussed cannot always be made. It cannot be done in the case of universal statements which express the fact that all sentences of a certain type are true, or that all true sentences have a certain property. For instance, we can prove in the theory of truth the following statement:

> *All consequences of true sentences are true.*

However, we cannot get rid here of the word '*true*' in the simple manner contemplated.

Again, even in the case of particular sentences having the form '*X is true*' such a simple elimination cannot always be made. In fact, the elimination is possible only in those cases in which the name of the sentence which is said to be true occurs in a form that enables us to reconstruct the sentence itself. For example, our present historical knowledge does not give us any possibility of eliminating the word '*true*' from the following sentence:

> *The first sentence written by Plato is true.*

Of course, since we have a definition for truth and since every definition enables us to replace the definiendum by its definiens, an elimination of the term '*true*' in its semantic sense is always theoretically possible. But this would not be the kind of simple elimination discussed above, and it would not result in the replacement of a sentence in the metalanguage by a sentence in the object-language.

---

[27] Cf. the discussion of this problem in Kokoszyńska, 'Absoluten Wahrheitsbegriff', 161 ff.

If, however, anyone continues to urge that—because of the theoretical possibility of eliminating the word '*true*' on the basis of its definition—the concept of truth is sterile, he must accept the further conclusion that all defined notions are sterile. But this outcome is so absurd and so unsound historically that any comment on it is unnecessary. In fact, I am rather inclined to agree with those who maintain that the moments of greatest creative advancement in science frequently coincide with the introduction of new notions by means of definition.

17. Conformity of the Semantic Conception of Truth with Philosophical and Common-sense Usage. The question has been raised whether the semantic conception of truth can indeed be regarded as a precise form of the old, classical conception of this notion.

Various formulations of the classical conception were quoted in the early part of this chapter (Section 3). I must repeat that in my judgement none of them is quite precise and clear. Accordingly, the only sure way of settling the question would be to confront the authors of those statements with our new formulation, and to ask them whether it agrees with their intentions. Unfortunately, this method is impractical since they died quite some time ago.

As far as my own opinion is concerned, I do not have any doubts that our formulation does conform to the intuitive content of that of Aristotle. I am less certain regarding the later formulations of the classical conception, for they are very vague indeed.[28]

Furthermore, some doubts have been expressed whether the semantic conception does reflect the notion of truth in its common-sense and everyday usage. I clearly realize (as I already indicated) that the common meaning of the word '*true*'—as that of any other word of everyday language—is to some extent vague, and that its usage more or less fluctuates. Hence the problem of assigning to this word a fixed and exact meaning is relatively unspecified, and every solution of this problem implies necessarily a certain deviation from the practice of everyday language.

In spite of all this, I happen to believe that the semantic conception does conform to a very considerable extent with the common-sense usage—although I readily admit I may be mistaken. What is more to the point, however, I believe that the issue raised can be settled scientifically, though of course not by a deductive procedure, but with the help of the statistical questionnaire method. As a matter of fact, such research has been carried

---

[28] Most authors who have discussed my work on the notion of truth are of the opinion that my definition does conform with the classical conception of this notion; see e.g. Kotarbiński, 'Syntax' and Scholz, 'Review'.

on, and some of the results have been reported at congresses and in part published.[29]

I should like to emphasize that in my opinion such investigations must be conducted with the utmost care. Thus, if we ask a high-school boy, or even an adult intelligent man having no special philosophical training, whether he regards a sentence to be true if it agrees with reality, or if it designates an existing state of affairs, it may simply turn out that he does not understand the question; in consequence his response, whatever it may be, will be of no value for us. But his answer to the question whether he would admit that the sentence 'it is snowing' could be true although it is not snowing, or could be false although it is snowing, would naturally be very significant for our problem.

Therefore, I was by no means surprised to learn (in a discussion devoted to these problems) that in a group of people who were questioned only 15 per cent agreed that 'true' means for them 'agreeing with reality', while 90 per cent agreed that a sentence such as 'it is snowing' is true if, and only if, it is snowing. Thus, a great majority of these people seemed to reject the classical conception of truth in its 'philosophical' formulation, while accepting the same conception when formulated in plain words (waiving the question whether the use of the phrase 'the same conception' is here justified).

18. The Definition in its Relation to 'The Philosophical Problem of Truth' and to Various Epistemological Trends. I have heard it remarked that the formal definition of truth has nothing to do with 'the philosophical problem of truth'.[30] However, nobody has ever pointed out to me in an intelligible way just what this problem is. I have been informed in this connection that my definition, though it states necessary and sufficient conditions for a sentence to be true, does not really grasp the 'essence' of this concept. Since I have never been able to understand what the 'essence' of a concept is, I must be excused from discussing this point any longer.

In general, I do not believe that there is such a thing as 'the philosophical problem of truth'. I do believe that there are various intelligible and interesting (but not necessarily philosophical) problems concerning the notion of truth, but I also believe that they can be exactly formulated and possibly solved only on the basis of a precise conception of this notion.

---

[29] Cf. Ness, 'Truth'. Unfortunately, the results of that part of Ness's research which is especially relevant for our problem are not discussed in his book; compare p. 148 n. 1.

[30] Though I have heard this opinion several times, I have seen it in print only once and, curiously enough, in a work which does not have a philosophical character—in fact, in Hilbert and Bernays, *Grundlagen*, ii, 269 (where, by the way, it is not expressed as any kind of objection). On the other hand, I have not found any remark to this effect in discussions of my work by professional philosophers (cf. note 1).

While on the one hand the definition of truth has been blamed for not being philosophical enough, on the other a series of objections have been raised charging this definition with serious philosophical implications, always of a very undesirable nature. I shall discuss now one special objection of this type; another group of such objections will be dealt with in the next section.

It has been claimed that—due to the fact that a sentence like 'snow is white' is taken to be semantically true if snow is *in fact* white (italics by the critic)—logic finds itself involved in a most uncritical realism.[31]

If there were an opportunity to discuss the objection with its author, I should raise two points. First, I should ask him to drop the words '*in fact*', which do not occur in the original formulation and which are misleading, even if they do not affect the content. For these words convey the impression that the semantic conception of truth is intended to establish the conditions under which we are warranted in asserting any given sentence, and in particular any empirical sentence. However, a moment's reflection shows that this impression is merely an illusion; and I think that the author of the objection falls victim to the illusion which he himself created.

In fact, the semantic definition of truth implies nothing regarding the conditions under which a sentence like (1):

(1) *snow is white*

can be asserted. It implies only that, whenever we assert or reject this sentence, we must be ready to assert or reject the correlated sentence (2):

(2) *the sentence 'snow is white' is true.*

Thus, we may accept the semantic conception of truth without giving up any epistemological attitude we may have had; we may remain naive realists, critical realists or idealists, empiricists or metaphysicians—whatever we were before. The semantic conception is completely neutral toward all these issues.

In the second place, I should try to get some information regarding the conception of truth which (in the opinion of the author of the objection) does not involve logic in a most naive realism. I would gather that this conception must be incompatible with the semantic one. Thus, there must be sentences which are true in one of these conceptions without being true in the other. Assume, e.g., the sentence (1) to be of this kind. The truth of this sentence in the semantic conception is determined by an equivalence of the form (T):

---

[31] Cf. Gonseth, 'Congrès Descartes', 187–8.

The sentence 'snow is white' is true if, and only if, snow is white.

Hence in the new conception we must reject this equivalence, and consequently we must assume its denial:

The sentence 'snow is white' is true if, and only if, snow is not white (or perhaps: *snow, in fact, is not white*).

This sounds somewhat paradoxical. I do not regard such a consequence of the new conception as absurd; but I am a little fearful that someone in the future may charge this conception with involving logic in a 'most sophisticated kind of irrealism'. At any rate, it seems to me important to realize that every conception of truth which is incompatible with the semantic one carries with it consequences of this type.

I have dwelt a little on this whole question, not because the objection discussed seems to me very significant, but because certain points which have arisen in the discussion should be taken into account by all those who for various epistemological reasons are inclined to reject the semantic conception of truth.

19. Alleged Metaphysical Elements in Semantics. The semantic conception of truth has been charged several times with involving certain metaphysical elements. Objections of this sort have been made to apply not only to the theory of truth, but to the whole domain of theoretical semantics.[32]

I do not intend to discuss the general problem whether the introduction of a metaphysical element into a science is at all objectionable. The only point which will interest me here is whether and in what sense metaphysics is involved in the subject of our present discussion.

The whole question obviously depends upon what one understands by 'metaphysics'. Unfortunately, this notion is extremely vague and equivocal. When listening to discussions in this subject, sometimes one gets the impression that the term 'metaphysical' has lost any objective meaning, and is merely used as a kind of professional philosophical invective.

For some people metaphysics is a general theory of objects (ontology)—a discipline which is to be developed in a purely empirical way, and which differs from other empirical sciences only by its generality. I do not know whether such a discipline actually exists (some cynics claim that it is customary in philosophy to baptize unborn children); but I think that in any

---

[32] See E. Nagel, Review of Hofstader, 'On Semantic Problems', *Journal of Symbolic Logic*, 3 (1938), 90, and Review of Carnap, *Introduction to Semantics, Journal of Philosophy*, 39 (1942), 471–2. A remark which goes, perhaps, in the same direction, is also to be found in Weinberg, Review, 77; cf., however, his earlier remarks, pp. 75–6.

case metaphysics in this conception is not objectionable to anybody, and has hardly any connections with semantics.

For the most part, however, the term 'metaphysical' is used as directly opposed—in one sense or another—to the term 'empirical'; at any rate, it is used in this way by those people who are distressed by the thought that any metaphysical elements might have managed to creep into science. This general conception of metaphysics assumes several more specific forms.

Thus, some people take it to be symptomatic of a metaphysical element in a science when methods of inquiry are employed which are neither deductive nor empirical. However, no trace of this symptom can be found in the development of semantics (unless some metaphysical elements are involved in the object-language to which the semantic notions refer). In particular, the semantics of formalized languages is constructed in a purely deductive way.

Others maintain that the metaphysical character of a science depends mainly on its vocabulary and, more specifically, on its primitive terms. Thus, a term is said to be metaphysical if it is neither logical nor mathematical, and if it is not associated with an empirical procedure which enables us to decide whether a thing is denoted by this term or not. With respect to such a view of metaphysics it is sufficient to recall that a metalanguage includes only three kinds of undefined terms: (i) terms taken from logic, (ii) terms of the corresponding object-language, and (iii) names of expressions in the object-language. It is thus obvious that no metaphysical undefined terms occur in the metalanguage (again, unless such terms appear in the object-language itself).

There are, however, some who believe that, even if no metaphysical terms occur among the primitive terms of a language, they may be introduced by definitions; namely, by those definitions which fail to provide us with general criteria for deciding whether an object falls under the defined concept. It is argued that the term '*true*' is of this kind, since no universal criterion of truth follows immediately from the definition of this term, and since it is generally believed (and in a certain sense can even be proved) that such a criterion will never be found. This comment on the actual character of the notion of truth seems to be perfectly just. However, it should be noticed that the notion of truth does not differ in this respect from many notions in logic, mathematics, and theoretical parts of various empirical sciences, e.g., in theoretical physics.

In general, it must be said that if the term 'metaphysical' is employed in so wide a sense as to embrace certain notions (or methods) of logic, mathematics, or empirical sciences, it will apply *a fortiori* to those of semantics. In fact, as we know from part I of the chapter, in developing the semantics of a language we use all the notions of this language, and we apply even a stronger logical apparatus than that which is used in the language itself. On the other hand, however, I can summarize the arguments given above by stating that in no interpretation of the term 'metaphysical' which is familiar and more or less intelligible to me does semantics involve any metaphysical elements peculiar to itself.

I should like to make one final remark in connection with this group of objections. The history of science shows many instances of concepts which were judged metaphysical (in a loose, but in any case derogatory sense of this term) before their meaning was made precise; however, once they received a rigorous, formal definition, the distrust in them evaporated. As typical examples we may mention the concepts of negative and imaginary numbers in mathematics. I hope a similar fate awaits the concept of truth and other semantic concepts; and it seems to me, therefore, that those who have distrusted them because of their alleged metaphysical implications should welcome the fact that precise definitions of these concepts are now available. If in consequence semantic concepts lose philosophical interest, they will only share the fate of many other concepts of science, and this need give rise to no regret.

IX

PHILOSOPHY OF LOGIC

W. V. QUINE

TRUTH AND SEMANTIC ACCENT

Philosophers who favour propositions have said that propositions are needed because truth is intelligible only of propositions, not of sentences. An unsympathetic answer is that we can explain truth of sentences to the propositionalist in his own terms: sentences are true whose meanings are true propositions. Any failure of intelligibility here is already his own fault.

But there is a deeper and vaguer reason for his feeling that truth is intelligible primarily for propositions. It is that truth should hinge on reality, not language; sentences are language. His way of producing a reality for truth to hinge on is shabby, certainly: an imaginary projection from sentences. But he is right that truth should hinge on reality, and it does. No sentence is true but reality makes it so. The sentence 'Snow is white' is true, as Tarski has taught us, if and only if real snow is really white. The same can be said of the sentence 'Der Schnee ist weiss'; language is not the point. In speaking of the truth of a given sentence there is only indirection; we do better simply to say the sentence and so speak not about language but about the world. So long as we are speaking only of the truth of singly given sentences, the perfect theory of truth is what Wilfrid Sellars has called the disappearance theory of truth.

Truth hinges on reality; but to object, on this score, to calling sentences true, is a confusion. Where the truth predicate has its utility is in just those places where, though still concerned with reality, we are impelled by certain technical complications to mention sentences. Here the truth predicate serves, as it were, to point through the sentence to the reality; it serves as a reminder that though sentences are mentioned, reality is still the whole point.

From W. V. Quine, *Philosophy of Logic* (Englewood Cliffs.: Prentice Hall, 1970), 10–13. Reprinted by permission of the author.

What, then, are the places where, though still concerned with unlinguistic reality, we are moved to proceed indirectly and talk of sentences? The important places of this kind are places where we are seeking generality, and seeking it along certain oblique planes that we cannot sweep out by generalizing over objects.

We can generalize on 'Tom is mortal', 'Dick is mortal', and so on, without talking of truth or of sentences; we can say 'All men are mortal'. We can generalize similarly on 'Tom is Tom', 'Dick is Dick', '0 is 0', and so on, saying 'Everything is itself'. When on the other hand we want to generalize on 'Tom is mortal or Tom is not mortal', 'Snow is white or snow is not white', and so on, we ascend to talk of truth and of sentences, saying 'Every sentence of the form "p or not p" is true', or 'Every alternation of a sentence with its negation is true'. What prompts this semantic ascent is not that 'Tom is mortal or Tom is not mortal' is somehow about sentences while 'Tom is mortal' and 'Tom is Tom' are about Tom. All three are about Tom. We ascend only because of the oblique way in which the instances over which we are generalizing are related to one another.

We were able to phrase our generalization 'Everything is itself' without such ascent just because the changes that were rung in passing from instance to instance—'Tom is Tom', 'Dick is Dick', '0 is 0'—were changes in names. Similarly for 'All men are mortal'. This generalization may be read 'x is mortal for all *men* x'—all things x of the sort that 'Tom' is a name of. But what would be a parallel reading of the generalization of 'Tom is mortal or Tom is not mortal'? It would read 'p or not p for all things p of the sort that sentences are names of'. But sentences are not names, and this reading is simply incoherent; it uses 'p' both in positions that call for sentence clauses and in a position that calls for a noun substantive. So, to gain our desired generality, we go up one step and talk about sentences: 'Every *sentence* of the *form* "p or not p" is *true*'.

The incoherent alternative reading might of course be expressly accorded meaning, if there were anything to gain by so doing. One could cause sentences to double as names, by specifying what they were to be names of. One might declare them to be names of propositions. In earlier pages,[1] when propositions were still under advisement, I represented propositions as the meanings of sentences rather than as things named by sentences; still one could declare them to be named by sentences, and some there are who have done so. Until such a line is adopted, the letter 'p' is no variable ranging over objects; it is only a schematic letter for sentences, only a dummy to mark a position appropriate to a component sentence in

[1] [*Editors' note*: pp. 2–5, not reproduced in this vol.].

some logical form or grammatical construction. Once the sentences are taken as names of propositions, on the other hand, the letter 'p' comes to double as a variable ranging over objects which are propositions. Thereafter we can coherently say 'p or not p for all propositions p'.

However, this move has the drawback of reinstating propositions, which we saw reason not to welcome. Moreover, the move brings no visible benefit; for we already saw how to express generalizations of the desired sort without appeal to propositions, by just going up a step and attributing truth to sentences. This ascent to a linguistic plane of reference is only a momentary retreat from the world, for the utility of the truth predicate is precisely the cancellation of linguistic reference. The truth predicate is a reminder that, despite a technical ascent to talk of sentences, our eye is on the world. This cancellatory force of the truth predicate is explicit in Tarski's paradigm:

'Snow is white' is true if and only if snow is white.

Quotation marks make all the difference between talking about words and talking about snow. The quotation is a name of a sentence that contains a name, namely 'snow', of snow. By calling the sentence true, we call snow white. The truth predicate is a device of disquotation. We may affirm the single sentence by just uttering it, unaided by quotation or by the truth predicate; but if we want to affirm some infinite lot of sentences that we can demarcate only by talking about the sentences, then the truth predicate has its use. We need it to restore the effect of objective reference when for the sake of some generalization we have resorted to semantic ascent.

Tarski's paradigm cannot be generalized to read:

'p' is true if and only if p,

since quoting the schematic sentence letter 'p' produces a name only of the sixteenth letter of the alphabet, and no generality over sentences. The truth predicate in its general use, attachable to a quantifiable variable in the fashion 'x is true', is eliminable by no facile paradigm. It can be defined, Tarski shows, in a devious way, but only if some powerful apparatus is available.

PART III

THE EARLY MODERN DEBATE

X

TRUTH

J. L. AUSTIN

1. 'What is truth?' said jesting Pilate, and would not stay for an answer. Pilate was in advance of his time. For 'truth' itself is an abstract noun, a camel, that is, of a logical construction, which cannot get past the eye even of a grammarian. We approach it cap and categories in hand: we ask ourselves whether Truth is a substance (the Truth, the Body of Knowledge), or a quality (something like the colour red, inhering in truths), or a relation ('correspondence').[1] But philosophers should take something more nearly their own size to strain at. What needs discussing rather is the use, or certain uses, of the word 'true'. *In vino*, possibly, '*veritas*', but in a sober symposium '*verum*'.

2. What is it that we say is true or is false? Or, how does the phrase 'is true' occur in English sentences? The answers appear at first multifarious. We say (or are said to say) that beliefs are true, that descriptions or accounts are true, that propositions or assertions or statements are true, and that words or sentences are true: and this is to mention only a selection of the more obvious candidates. Again, we say (or are said to say) 'It is true that the cat is on the mat', or 'It is true to say that the cat is on the mat', or ' "The cat is on the mat" is true'. We also remark on occasion, when someone else has said something, 'Very true' or 'That's true' or 'True enough'.

Most (though not all) of these expressions, and others besides, certainly do occur naturally enough. But it seems reasonable to ask whether there is not some use of 'is true' that is primary, or some generic name for that which at bottom we are always saying 'is true'. Which, if any, of these expressions is to be taken *au pied de la lettre*? To answer this will not take

From J. L. Austin, 'Truth', *Aristotelian Society*, suppl. *vol.* 24 (1950), 111–29. Reprinted by permission of the Editor of the Aristotelian Society. © 1950.

[1] It is sufficiently obvious that 'truth' is a substantive, 'true' an adjective, and 'of' in 'true of' a preposition.

us long, nor, perhaps, far: but in philosophy the foot of the letter is the foot of the ladder.

I suggest that the following are the primary forms of expression:

It is true (to say) that the cat is on the mat.
That statement (of his, &c.) is true.
The statement that the cat is on the mat is true.

But first for the rival candidates.

(*a*) Some say that 'truth is primarily a property of beliefs'. But it may be doubted whether the expression 'a true belief' is at all common outside philosophy and theology: and it seems clear that a man is said to hold a true belief when and in the sense that he believes (in) *something which* is true, or believes that *something which* is true is true. Moreover if, as some also say, a belief is 'of the nature of a picture', then it is of the nature of what cannot be true, though it may be, for example, faithful.[2]

(*b*) True descriptions and true accounts are simply varieties of true statements or of collections of true statements, as are true answers and the like. The same applies to propositions too, in so far as they are genuinely said to be true (and not, as more commonly, sound, tenable and so on).[3] A proposition in law or in geometry is something portentous, usually a generalization, that we are invited to accept and that has to be recommended by argument: it cannot be a direct report on current observation—if you look and inform me that the cat is on the mat, that is not a proposition though it is a statement. In philosophy, indeed, 'proposition' is sometimes used in a special way for 'the meaning or sense of a sentence or family of sentences': but whether we think a lot or little of this usage, a proposition in this sense cannot, at any rate, be what we say is true or false. For we never say 'The meaning (or sense) of this sentence (or of these words) is true': what we do say is what the judge or jury says, namely that '*The words* taken in this sense, or if we assign to them such and such a meaning, or so interpreted or understood, *are true*'.

(*c*) Words and sentences are indeed said to be true, the former often, the latter rarely. But only in certain senses. Words as discussed by philologists, or by lexicographers, grammarians, linguists, phoneticians, printers, critics (stylistic or textual) and so on, are not true or false: they are wrongly formed, or ambiguous or defective or untranslatable or unpronounceable

---

[2] A likeness is true *to* life, but not true *of* it. A *word* picture can be true, just because it is *not* a picture.
[3] Predicates applicable also to 'arguments', which we likewise do not say are true, but, for example, valid.

or misspelled or archaistic or corrupt or what not.[4] Sentences in similar contexts are elliptic or involved or alliterative or ungrammatical. We may, however, genuinely say 'His closing words were very true' or 'The third sentence on page 5 of his speech is quite false': but here 'words' and 'sentence' refer, as is shown by the demonstratives (possessive pronouns, temporal verbs, definite descriptions, &c.), which in this usage consistently accompany them, to the words or sentence *as used by a certain person on a certain occasion*. That is, they refer (as does 'Many a true word spoken in jest') to *statements*.

A statement is made and its making is a historic event, the utterance by a certain speaker or writer of certain words (a sentence) to an audience with reference to a historic situation, event or what not.[5]

A sentence is made *up of* words, a statement is made *in* words. A sentence is not English or not good English, a statement is not in English or not in good English. Statements are made, words or sentences are used. We talk of *my* statement, but of *the English* sentence (if a sentence is mine, I coined it, but I do not coin statements). The *same* sentence is used in making *different* statements (I say 'It is mine', you say 'It is mine'): it may also be used on two occasions or by two persons in making the *same* statement, but for this the utterance must be made with reference to the same situation or event.[6] We speak of 'the statement that S', but of 'the sentence "S"', not of 'the sentence that S'.[7]

When I say that a statement is what is true, I have no wish to become wedded to one word. 'Assertion', for example, will in most contexts do just

---

[4] Peirce made a beginning by pointing out that there are two (or three) different senses of the word 'word', and adumbrated a technique ('counting' words) for deciding what is a 'different sense'. But his two senses are not well defined, and there are many more—the 'vocable' sense, the philologist's sense in which 'grammar' is the same word as 'glamour', the textual critic's sense in which the 'the' in l. 254 has been written twice, and so on. With all his 66 divisions of signs, Peirce does not, I believe, distinguish between a sentence and a statement.

[5] 'Historic' does not, of course, mean that we cannot speak of future or possible statements. A 'certain' speaker need not be any definite speaker. 'Utterance' need not be public utterance—the audience may be the speaker himself.

[6] 'The same' does not always mean the same. In fact it has no meaning in the way that an 'ordinary' word like 'red' or 'horse' has a meaning: it is a (the typical) device for establishing and distinguishing the meanings of ordinary words. Like 'real', it is part of our apparatus *in* words for fixing and adjusting the semantics *of* words.

[7] Inverted commas show that the words, though uttered (in writing), are not to be taken as a statement by the utterer. This covers two possible cases, (i) where what is to be discussed is the sentence, (ii) where what is to be discussed is a statement made elsewhere in the words 'quoted'. Only in case (i) is it correct to say simply that the token is doing duty for the type (and even here it is quite incorrect to say that 'The cat is on the mat' is the *name* of an English sentence—though possibly *The Cat is on the Mat* might be the title of a novel, or a bull might be known as *Catta est in matta*). Only in case (ii) is there something true or false, namely (not the quotation but) the statement made in the words quoted.

as well, though perhaps it is slightly wider. Both words share the weakness of being rather solemn (much more so than the more general 'what you said' or 'your words')—though perhaps we are generally being a little solemn when we discuss the truth of anything. Both have the merit of clearly referring to the historic use of a sentence by an utterer, and of being therefore precisely not equivalent to 'sentence'. For it is a fashionable mistake to take as primary '(The sentence) "S" is true (in the English language)'. Here the addition of the words 'in the English language' serves to emphasize that 'sentence' is not being used as equivalent to 'statement' so that it precisely is not what can be true or false (and moreover, 'true in the English language' is a solecism, mismodelled presumably, and with deplorable effect, on expressions like 'true in geometry').

3. When is a statement true? The temptation is to answer (at least if we confine ourselves to 'straightforward' statements): 'When it corresponds to the facts'. And as a piece of standard English this can hardly be wrong. Indeed, I must confess I do not really think it is wrong at all: the theory of truth is a series of truisms. Still, it can at least be misleading.

If there is to be communication of the sort that we achieve by language at all, there must be a stock of symbols of some kind which a communicator ('the speaker') can produce 'at will' and which a communicatee ('the audience') can observe: these may be called the 'words', though, of course, they need not be anything very like what we should normally call words— they might be signal flags, &c. There must also be something other than the words, which the words are to be used to communicate about: this may be called the 'world'. There is no reason why the world should not include the words, in every sense except the sense of the actual statement itself which on any particular occasion is being made about the world. Further, the world must exhibit (we must observe) similarities and dissimilarities (there could not be the one without the other): if everything were either absolutely indistinguishable from anything else or completely unlike anything else, there would be nothing to say. And finally (for present purposes—of course there are other conditions to be satisfied too) there must be two sets of conventions:

Descriptive conventions correlating the words (= sentences) with the *types* of situation, thing, event, &c., to be found in the world.

Demonstrative conventions correlating the words (= statements) with the *historic* situations, &c., to be found in the world.[8]

A statement is said to be true when the historic state of affairs to which it is correlated by the demonstrative conventions (the one to which it

---

[8] Both sets of conventions may be included together under 'semantics'. But they differ greatly.

'refers') is of a type[9] with which the sentence used in making it is correlated by the descriptive conventions.[10]

3a. Troubles arise from the use of the word 'facts' for the historic situations, events, &c., and in general, for the world. For 'fact' is regularly used in conjunction with 'that' in the sentences 'The fact is that S' or 'It is a fact that S' and in the expression 'the fact that S', all of which imply that it would be true to say that S.[11]

This may lead us to suppose that

  (i) 'fact' is only an alternative expression for 'true statement'. We note that when a detective says 'Let's look at the facts' he does not crawl round the carpet, but proceeds to utter a string of statements: we even talk of 'stating the facts';

  (ii) for every true statement there exists 'one' and its own precisely corresponding fact—for every cap the head it fits.

It is (i) which leads to some of the mistakes in 'coherence' or formalist theories; (ii) to some of those in 'correspondence' theories. Either we

---

[9] 'Is of a type with which' means 'is sufficiently like those standard states of affairs with which'. Thus, for a statement to be true one state of affairs must be *like* certain others, which is a natural relation, but also *sufficiently* like to merit the same 'description', which is no longer a purely natural relation. To say 'This is red' is not the same as to say 'This is like those', nor even as to say 'This is like those which were called red'. That things are *similar*, or even 'exactly' similar, I may literally see, but that they are the *same* I cannot literally see—in calling them the same colour a convention is involved additional to the conventional choice of the name to be given to the colour which they are said to be.

[10] The trouble is that sentences contain words or verbal devices to serve both descriptive and demonstrative purposes (not to mention other purposes), often both at once. In philosophy, we mistake the descriptive for the demonstrative (theory of universals) or the demonstrative for the descriptive (theory of monads). A sentence as normally distinguished from a mere word or phrase is characterized by its containing a minimum of verbal demonstrative devices (Aristotle's 'reference to time'); but many demonstrative conventions are non-verbal (pointing, &c.), and using these we can make a statement in a single word which is not a 'sentence'. Thus, 'languages' like that of (traffic, &c.) *signs* use quite distinct media for their descriptive and demonstrative elements (the sign on the post, the site of the post). And however many verbal demonstrative devices we use as auxiliaries, there must *always* be a non-verbal *origin* for these co-ordinates, which is the point of utterance of the statement.

[11] I use the following *abbreviations*:

  S for the cat is on the mat.
  ST for it is true that the cat is on the mat.
  tst for the statement that.

I take tstS as my example throughout and not, say, tst Julius Caesar was bald or tst all mules are sterile, because these latter are apt in their different ways to make us overlook the distinction between sentence and statement: we have, apparently, in the one case a sentence capable of being used to refer to only one historic situation, in the other a statement without reference to at least (or to any particular) one.

If space permitted other types of statement (existential, general, hypothetical, &c.) should be dealt with: these raise problems rather of meaning than of truth, though I feel uneasiness about hypotheticals.

suppose that there is nothing there but the true statement itself, nothing to which it corresponds, or else we populate the world with linguistic doppelgänger (and grossly overpopulate it—every nugget of 'positive' fact overlaid by a massive concentration of 'negative' facts, every tiny detailed fact larded with generous general facts, and so on).

When a statement is true, there is, *of course*, a state of affairs which makes it true and which is *toto mundo* distinct from the true statement about it: but equally of course, we can only *describe* that state of affairs *in words* (either the same or, with luck, others). I can only describe the situation in which it is true to say that I am feeling sick by saying that it is one in which I am feeling sick (or experiencing sensations of nausea):[12] yet between stating, however truly, that I am feeling sick and feeling sick there is a great gulf fixed.[13]

'Fact that' is a phrase designed for use in situations where the distinction between a true statement and the state of affairs about which it is a truth is neglected; as it often is with advantage in ordinary life, though seldom in philosophy—above all in discussing truth, where it is precisely our business to prise the words off the world and keep them off it. To ask 'Is the fact that S the true statement that S or that which it is true of?' may beget absurd answers. To take an analogy: although we may sensibly ask 'Do we *ride* the word "elephant" or the animal?' and equally sensibly 'Do we *write* the word or the animal?' it is nonsense to ask 'Do we *define* the word or the animal?' For defining an elephant (supposing we ever do this) is a compendious description of an operation involving both word and animal (do we focus the image or the battleship?); and so speaking about 'the fact that' is a compendious way of speaking about a situation involving both words and world.[14]

3b. 'Corresponds' also gives trouble, because it is commonly given too restricted or too colourful a meaning, or one which in this context it cannot bear. The only essential point is this: that the correlation between the words (= sentences) and the type of situation, event, &c., which is to be such that when a statement in those words is made with reference to a historic situation of that type the statement is then true, is *absolutely and purely* conventional. We are absolutely free to appoint *any* symbol

---

[12] If this is what was meant by ' "It is raining" is true if and only if it is raining', so far so good.

[13] It takes two to make a truth. Hence (obviously) there can be no criterion of truth in the sense of some feature detectable in the statement itself which will reveal whether it is true or false. Hence, too, a statement cannot without absurdity refer to itself.

[14] 'It is true that S' and 'It is a fact that S' are applicable in the same circumstances; the cap fits when there is a head it fits. Other words can fill the same role as 'fact': we say, e.g. 'The situation is that S'.

to describe *any* type of situation, so far as merely being true goes. In a small one-spade language tst nuts might be true in exactly the same circumstances as the statement in English that the National Liberals are the people's choice.[15] There is no need whatsoever for the words used in making a true statement to 'mirror' in any way, however indirect, any feature whatsoever of the situation or event; a statement no more needs, in order to be true, to reproduce the 'multiplicity,' say, or the 'structure' or 'form' of the reality, than a word needs to be echoic or writing pictographic. To suppose that it does, is to fall once again into the error of reading back into the world the features of language.

The more rudimentary a language, the more, very often, it will tend to have a 'single' word for a highly 'complex' type of situation: this has such disadvantages as that the language becomes elaborate to learn and is incapable of dealing with situations which are non-standard, unforeseen, for which there may just be no word. When we go abroad equipped only with a phrase book, we may spend long hours learning by heart—

A[1]-moest-fa'nd-[e]tschâ[r] woum[e]n,
Ma'hwîl-iz-wau[r]pt (bènt),

and so on and so on, yet faced with the situation where we have the pen of our aunt, find ourselves quite unable to say so. The characteristics of a more developed language (articulation, morphology, syntax, abstractions, &c.), do not make statements in it any more capable of being true or capable of being any more true, they make it more adaptable, more learnable, more comprehensive, more precise, and so on; and *these* aims may no doubt be furthered by making the language (allowance made for the nature of the medium) 'mirror' in conventional ways features descried in the world.

Yet even when a language does 'mirror' such features very closely (and does it ever?) the truth of statements remains still a matter, as it was with the most rudimentary languages, of the words used being the ones *conventionally appointed* for situations of the type to which that referred to belongs. A picture, a copy, a replica, a photograph—these are *never* true in so far as they are reproductions, produced by natural or mechanical means: a reproduction can be accurate or lifelike (true *to* the original), as a gramophone recording or a transcription may be, but not true (*of*) as a record of proceedings can be. In the same way a (natural) sign *of* something can

[15] We could use 'nuts' even now as a code-word: but a code, as a transformation of a language, is distinguished from a language, and a code-word dispatched is not (called) 'true'.

be infallible or unreliable but only an (artificial) sign *for* something can be right or wrong.[16]

There are many intermediate cases between a true account and a faithful picture, as here somewhat forcibly contrasted, and it is from the study of these (a lengthy matter) that we can get the clearest insight into the contrast. For example, maps: these may be called pictures, yet they are highly conventionalized pictures. If a map can be clear or accurate or misleading, like a statement, why can it not be true or exaggerated? How do the 'symbols' used in map-making differ from those used in statement-making? On the other hand, if an air-mosaic is not a map, why is it not? And when does a map become a diagram? These are the really illuminating questions.

4. Some have said that—

> To say that an assertion is true is not to make any further assertion at all.
>
> In all sentences of the form 'p is true' the phrase 'is true' is logically superfluous.
>
> To say that a proposition is true is just to assert it, and to say that it is false is just to assert its contradictory.

But wrongly. TstS (except in paradoxical cases of forced and dubious manufacture) refers to the world or any part of it exclusive of tstS, i.e. of itself.[17] TstST refers to the world or any part of it *inclusive* of tstS, though once again exclusive of itself, i.e. of tstST. That is, tstST refers to something to which tstS cannot refer. TstST does not, certainly, include any statement referring to the world exclusive of tstS which is not included already in tstS—more, it seems doubtful whether it does include that statement about the world exclusive of tstS which is made when we state that S. (If I state that tstS is true, should we really agree that I have stated that S? Only 'by implication'.)[18] But all this does not go any way to show that tstST is not a statement different from tstS. If Mr Q writes on a noticeboard 'Mr W is a burglar', then a trial is held to decide whether Mr Q's published statement that Mr W is a burglar is a libel: finding 'Mr Q's statement was true (in substance and in fact)'. Thereupon a second trial is held, to decide

---

[16] Berkeley confuses these two. There will not be books in the running brooks until the dawn of hydro-semantics.

[17] A statement may refer to 'itself' in the sense, for example, of the sentence used or the utterance uttered in making it ('statement' is not exempt from all ambiguity). But paradox does result if a statement purports to refer to itself in a more full-blooded sense, purports, that is, to state that it itself is true, or to state what it itself refers to ('This statement is about Cato').

[18] And 'by implication' tstST asserts something about the making of a statement which tstS certainly does not assert.

whether Mr W is a burglar, in which Mr Q's statement is no longer under consideration: verdict 'Mr W is a burglar'. It is an arduous business to hold a second trial: why is it done if the verdict is the same as the previous finding?[19]

What is felt is that the evidence considered in arriving at the one verdict is the same as that considered in arriving at the other. This is not strictly correct. It is more nearly correct that whenever tstS is true then tstST is also true and conversely, and that whenever tstS is false tstST is also false and conversely.[20] And it is argued that the words 'is true' are logically superfluous because it is believed that generally if any two statements are always true together and always false together then they must mean the same. Now whether this is in general a sound view may be doubted: but even if it is, why should it not break down in the case of so obviously 'peculiar' a phrase as 'is true'? Mistakes in philosophy notoriously arise through thinking that what holds of 'ordinary' words like 'red' or 'growls' must also hold of extraordinary words like 'real' or 'exists'. But that 'true' is just such another extraordinary word is obvious.[21]

There is something peculiar about the 'fact' which is described by tstST, something which may make us hesitate to call it a 'fact' at all; namely, that the relation between tstS and the world which tstST asserts to obtain is a *purely conventional* relation (one which 'thinking makes so'). For we are aware that this relation is one which we could alter at will, whereas we like to restrict the word 'fact' to *hard* facts, facts which are natural and unalterable, or anyhow not alterable at will. Thus, to take an analogous case, we may not like calling it a fact that the word elephant means what it does, though we can be induced to call it a (soft) fact—and though, of course, we have no hesitation in calling it a fact that contemporary English speakers use the word as they do.

An important point about this view is that it confuses falsity with negation: for according to it, it is the same thing to say 'He is not at home' as to say 'It is false that he is at home'. (But what if no one has said that he *is* at home? What if he is lying upstairs dead?) Too many philosophers maintain, when anxious to explain away negation, that a negation is just a second order affirmation (to the effect that a certain first order affirmation is false), yet, when anxious to explain away falsity, maintain that to assert that a statement is false is just to assert its negation (contradictory). It is

---

[19] This is not quite fair: there are many legal and personal reasons for holding two trials—which, however, do not affect the point that the issue being tried is not the same.

[20] Not *quite* correct, because tstST is only in place at all when tstS is envisaged as made and has been verified.

[21] *Unum, verum, bonum*—the old favourites deserve their celebrity. There is something odd about each of them. Theoretical theology is a form of onomatolatry.

impossible to deal with so fundamental a matter here.[22] Let me assert the following merely. Affirmation and negation are exactly on a level, in this sense, that no language can exist which does not contain conventions for both and that both refer to the world equally directly, not to statements about the world: whereas a language can quite well exist without any device to do the work of 'true' and 'false'. Any satisfactory theory of truth must be able to cope equally with falsity:[23] but 'is false' can only be maintained to be logically superfluous by making this fundamental confusion.

5. There is another way of coming to see that the phrase 'is true' is not logically superfluous, and to appreciate what sort of a statement it is to say that a certain statement is true. There are numerous other adjectives which are in the same class as 'true' and 'false', which are concerned, that is, with the relations between the words (as uttered with reference to a historic situation) and the world, and which nevertheless no one would dismiss as logically superfluous. We say, for example, that a certain statement is exaggerated or vague or bald, a description somewhat rough or misleading or not very good, an account rather general or too concise. In cases like these it is pointless to insist on deciding in simple terms whether the statement is 'true or false'. Is it true or false that Belfast is north of London? That the galaxy is the shape of a fried egg? That Beethoven was a drunkard? That Wellington won the battle of Waterloo? There are various *degrees and dimensions* of success in making statements: the statements fit the facts

---

[22] The following two sets of logical axioms are, as Aristotle (though not his successors) makes them, quite distinct:

   (a) No statement can be both true and false.
       No statement can be neither true nor false.
   (b) Of two contradictory statements—
       Both cannot be true.
       Both cannot be false.

The second set demands a definition of contradictories, and is usually joined with an unconscious postulate that for every statement there is one and only one other statement such that the pair are contradictories. It is doubtful how far any language does or must contain contradictories, however defined, such as to satisfy both this postulate and the set of axioms (b).

Those of the so-called 'logical paradoxes' (hardly a genuine class) which concern 'true' and 'false' are *not* to be reduced to cases of self-contradiction, any more than 'S but I do not believe it' is. A statement to the effect that it is itself true is every bit as absurd as one to the effect that it is itself false. There are *other* types of sentence which offend against the fundamental conditions of all communication in ways *distinct from* the way in which 'This is red and is not red' offends—e.g. 'This does (I do) not exist', or equally absurd 'This exists (I exist)'. There are more deadly sins than one; nor does the way to salvation lie through any hierarchy.

[23] To be false is (not, of course, to correspond to a non-fact, but) to miscorrespond with a fact. Some have not seen how, then, since the statement which is false does not describe the fact with which it miscorresponds (but misdescribes it), we know which fact to compare it with: this was because they thought of all linguistic conventions as descriptive—but it is the demonstrative conventions which fix which situation it is to which the statement refers. No statement can state what it itself refers to.

always more or less loosely, in different ways on different occasions for different intents and purposes. What may score full marks in a general knowledge test may in other circumstances get a gamma. And even the most adroit of languages may fail to 'work' in an abnormal situation or to cope, or cope reasonably simply, with novel discoveries: is it true or false that the dog goes round the cow?[24] What, moreover, of the large class of cases where a statement is not so much false (or true) as out of place, *inept* ('All the signs of bread' said when the bread is before us)?

We become obsessed with 'truth' when discussing statements, just as we become obsessed with 'freedom' when discussing conduct. So long as we think that what has always and alone to be decided is whether a certain action was done freely or was not, we get nowhere: but so soon as we turn instead to the numerous other adverbs used in the same connexion ('accidentally', 'unwillingly', 'inadvertently', &c.), things become easier, and we come to see that no concluding inference of the form 'Ergo, it was done freely (or not freely)' is required. Like freedom, truth is a bare minimum or an illusory ideal (the truth, the whole truth and nothing but the truth about, say, the battle of Waterloo or the *Primavera*).

6. Not merely is it jejune to suppose that all a statement aims to be is 'true', but it may further be questioned whether every 'statement' does aim to be true at all. The principle of Logic, that 'Every proposition must be true or false', has too long operated as the simplest, most persuasive and most pervasive form of the descriptive fallacy. Philosophers under its influence have forcibly interpreted all 'propositions' on the model of the statement that a certain thing is red, as made when the thing concerned is currently under observation.

Recently, it has come to be realized that many utterances which have been taken to be statements (merely because they are not, on grounds of grammatical form, to be classed as commands, questions, &c.) are not in fact descriptive, nor susceptible of being true or false. When is a statement not a statement? When it is a formula in a calculus: when it is a performatory utterance: when it is a value judgement: when it is a definition: when it is part of a work of fiction—there are many such suggested answers. It is simply not the business of such utterances to 'correspond to

[24] Here there is much sense in 'coherence' (and pragmatist) theories of truth, despite their failure to appreciate the trite but central point that truth is a matter of the relation between words and world, and despite their wrong-headed *Gleichschaltung* of all varieties of statemental failure under the lone head of 'partly true' (thereafter wrongly equated with 'part of the truth'). 'Correspondence' theorists too often talk as one would who held that every map is either accurate or inaccurate; that accuracy is a single and the sole virtue of a map; that every country can have but one accurate map; that a map on a larger scale or showing different features must be a map of a different country; and so on.

the facts' (and even genuine statements have other businesses besides that of so corresponding).

It is a matter for decision how far we should continue to call such masqueraders 'statements' at all, and how widely we should be prepared to extend the uses of 'true' and 'false' in 'different senses'. My own feeling is that it is better, when once a masquerader has been unmasked, *not* to call it a statement and *not* to say it is true or false. In ordinary life we should not call most of them statements at all, though philosophers and grammarians may have come to do so (or rather, have lumped them all together under the term of art 'proposition'). We make a difference between 'You said you promised' and 'You stated that you promised': the former can mean that you said 'I promise', whereas the latter must mean that you said 'I promised': the latter, which we say you 'stated', is something which is true or false, whereas for the former, which is not true or false, we use the wider verb to 'say'. Similarly, there is a difference between 'You say this is (call this) a good picture' and 'You state that this is a good picture'. Moreover, it was only so long as the real nature of arithmetical formulae, say, or of geometrical axioms remained unrecognized, and they were thought to record information about the world, that it was reasonable to call them 'true' (and perhaps even 'statements'—though were they ever so called?): but, once their nature has been recognized, we no longer feel tempted to call them 'true' or to dispute about their truth or falsity.

In the cases so far considered the model 'This is red' breaks down because the 'statements' assimilated to it are not of a nature to correspond to facts at all—the words are not descriptive words, and so on. But there is also another type of case where the words *are* descriptive words and the 'proposition' does in a way have to correspond to facts, but precisely not in the way that 'This is red' and similar statements setting up to be true have to do.

In the human predicament, for use in which our language is designed, we may wish to speak about states of affairs which have not been observed or are not currently under observation (the future, for example). And although we *can* state anything 'as a fact' (which statement will then be true or false[25]) we need not do so: we need only say 'The cat *may be* on the mat'. This utterance is quite different from tstS—it is not a statement at all (it is not true or false; it is compatible with 'The cat may *not* be on the mat'). In the same way, the situation in which we discuss whether and state that tstS is *true* is different from the situation in which we discuss whether it is *probable* that S. Tst it is probable that S is out of place, inept,

---

[25] Though it is not yet in place to call it either. For the same reason, one cannot lie or tell the truth about the future.

in the situation where we can make tstST, and, I think, conversely. It is not our business here to discuss probability: but is worth observing that the phrases 'It is true that' and 'It is probable that' are in the same line of business,[26] and in so far incompatibles.

7. In a recent article in *Analysis* Mr Strawson has propounded a view of truth which it will be clear I do not accept. He rejects the 'semantic' account of truth on the perfectly correct ground that the phrase 'is true' is not used in talking about *sentences*, supporting this with an ingenious hypothesis as to how meaning may have come to be confused with truth: but this will not suffice to show what he wants—that 'is true' is not used in talking about (or that 'truth is not a property of') *anything*. For it *is* used in talking about *statements* (which in his article he does not distinguish clearly from sentences). Further, he supports the 'logical superfluity' view to this extent, that he agrees that to say that ST is not to make any further assertion at all, beyond the assertion that S: but he disagrees with it in so far as he thinks that to say that ST *is* to *do* something more than just to assert that S—it is namely to *confirm* or to *grant* (or something of that kind) the assertion, made or taken as made already, that S. It will be clear that and why I do not accept the first part of this: but what of the second part? I agree that to say that ST 'is' very often, and according to the all-important linguistic occasion, to confirm tstS or to grant it or what not; but this cannot show that to say that ST is not also and at the same time to make an assertion about tstS. To say that I believe you 'is' on occasion to accept your statement; but it is also to make an assertion, which is not made by the strictly performatory utterance 'I accept your statement'. It is common for quite ordinary statements to have a performatory 'aspect': to say that you are a cuckold may be to insult you, but it is also and at the same time to make a statement which is true or false. Mr Strawson, moreover, seems to confine himself to the case where I *say* 'Your statement is true' or something similar—but what of the case where you state that S and I *say* nothing but '*look and see*' that your statement is true? I do not see how this critical case, to which nothing analogous occurs with strictly performatory utterances, could be made to respond to Mr Strawson's treatment.

One final point: if it is admitted (*if*) that the rather boring yet satisfactory relation between words and world which has here been discussed does genuinely occur, why should the phrase 'is true' not be our way of describing it? And if it is not, what else is?

---

[26] Compare the odd behaviours of 'was' and 'will be' when attached to 'true' and to 'probable'.

XI

TRUTH

P. F. STRAWSON

Mr Austin offers us a purified version of the correspondence theory of truth. On the one hand he disclaims the semanticists' error of supposing that 'true' is a predicate of sentences; on the other, the error of supposing that the relation of correspondence is other than purely conventional, the error which models the word on the world or the world on the word. His own theory is, roughly, that to say that a statement is true is to say that a certain speech-episode is related in a certain conventional way to something in the world exclusive of itself. But neither Mr Austin's account of the two terms of the truth-conferring relation, nor his account of the relation itself, seems to me satisfactory. The correspondence theory requires, not purification, but elimination.

1. *Statements.*—It is, of course, indisputable that we use various substantival expressions as grammatical subjects of 'true'. These are, commonly, noun-phrases like 'What he said' or 'His statement'; or pronouns or noun-phrases, with a 'that'-clause in apposition, e.g., 'It . . . that *p*' and 'The statement that *p*'. Austin proposes that we should use 'statement' to do general duty for such expressions as these. I have no objection. This will enable us to say, in a philosophically non-committal way, that, in using 'true', we are talking about statements. By 'saying this in a non-committal way', I mean saying it in a way which does not commit us to any view about the nature of statements so talked about; which does not commit us, for example, to the view that statements so talked about are historic events.

The words 'assertion' and 'statement' have a parallel and convenient duplicity of sense. 'My statement' may be either what I say or my saying it. My saying something is certainly an episode. What I say is not. It is the latter, not the former, we declare to be true. (Speaking the truth is not a manner of speaking: it is saying something true.) When we say 'His

From P. F. Strawson, 'Truth', *Aristotelian Society*, suppl. vol. 24 (1950), 129–56. Reprinted by permission of the Editor of the Aristotelian Society and the author. © 1950.

statement was received with thunderous applause' or 'His vehement assertion was followed by a startled silence', we are certainly referring to, characterizing, a historic event, and placing it in the context of others. If I say that the same statement was first whispered by John and then bellowed by Peter, uttered first in French and repeated in English, I am plainly still making historical remarks about utterance-occasions; but the word 'statement' has detached itself from reference to any particular speech-episode. The episodes I am talking about are the whisperings, bellowings, utterings, and repetitions. The statement is not something that figures in all these episodes. Nor, when I say that the statement is true, as opposed to saying that it was, in these various ways, made, am I talking indirectly about these episodes or any episodes at all. (Saying of a statement that it is true is not related to saying of a speech-episode that it was true as saying of a statement that it was whispered is related to saying of a speech-episode that it was a whisper.) It is futile to ask what thing or event I *am* talking about (over and above the subject matter of the statement) in declaring a statement to be true; for there is no such thing or event. The word 'statement' and the phrase 'What he said', like the conjunction 'that' followed by a noun clause, are convenient, grammatically substantival, devices, which we employ, on certain occasions, for certain purposes, notably (but not only) the occasions on which we use the word 'true'. What these occasions are I shall try later to elucidate. To suppose that, whenever we use a singular substantive, we are, or ought to be, using it to refer to something, is an ancient, but no longer a respectable, error.

More plausible than the thesis that in declaring a statement to be true I am talking about a speech-episode is the thesis that in order for me to declare a statement true, there must have occurred, within my knowledge, at least one episode which was a making of that statement. This is largely, but (as Austin sees) not entirely, correct. The occasion of my declaring a statement to be true may be not that someone has made the statement, but that I am envisaging the possibility of someone's making it. For instance, in discussing the merits of the Welfare State, I might say: 'It is true that the general health of the community has improved (that p), but this is due only to the advance in medical science.' It is not necessary that anyone should have said that p, in order for this to be a perfectly proper observation. In making it, I am not talking *about* an actual or possible speech-episode. I am myself asserting that p, in a certain way, with a certain purpose. I am anticipatorily conceding, in order to neutralize, a possible objection. I forestall someone's making the statement that p by making it myself, with additions. It is of prime importance to distinguish the fact that the use of 'true' always glances backwards or forwards to the actual or envisaged making of a statement by someone, from the theory that it is used to characterize such (actual or possible) episodes.

It is not easy to explain the non-episodic and non-committal sense of 'statement' in which 'statement' = 'what is said to be true or false'. But, at the risk of being tedious, I shall pursue the subject. For if Austin is right in the suggestion that it is basically of speech-episodes that we predicate 'true', it should be possible to 'reduce' assertions in which we say of a statement in the non-episodic sense that it is true to assertions in which we are predicating truth of episodes. Austin points out that the same sentence may be used to make different statements. He would no doubt agree that different sentences may be used to make the same statement. I am not thinking only of different languages or synonymous expressions in the same language; but also of such occasions as that on which you say of Jones 'He is ill', I say *to* Jones 'You are ill', and Jones says 'I am ill'. Using, not only different sentences, but sentences with different meanings, we all make 'the same statement'; and this is the sense of 'statement' we need to discuss, since it is, prima facie, of statements in this sense that we say that they are true or false (e.g. 'What they all said, namely, that Jones was ill, was quite true.'). We could say: people make the same statement when the words they use in the situations in which they use them are such that they must (logically) either all be making a true statement or all be making a false statement. But this is to use 'true' in the elucidation of 'same statement'. Or we could say, of the present case: Jones, you and I all make the same statement because, using the words we used in the situation in which we used them, we were all applying the same description to the same person at a certain moment in his history; anyone applying that description to that person (etc.), would be making that statement. Mr Austin might then wish to analyse (A) 'The statement that Jones was ill is true' in some such way as the following: 'If anyone has uttered, or were to utter, words such that in the situation in which they are uttered, he is applying to a person the same description as I apply to that person when I now utter the words "Jones was ill", then the resulting speech-episode was, or would be, true.' It seems plain, however, that nothing but the desire to find a metaphysically irreproachable first term for the correspondence relation could induce anyone to accept this analysis of (A) as an elaborate general hypothetical. It would be a plausible suggestion only if the grammatical subjects of 'true' were *commonly* expressions referring to particular, uniquely datable, speech-episodes. But the simple and obvious fact is that the expressions occurring as such grammatical subjects ('What they said', 'It . . . that *p*', and so on) never do, in these contexts, stand for such episodes.[1] *What they said* has no date, though their several sayings of it are datable. *The statement that p* is not an event, though it had to be made for the first time and made within my knowledge if I am to talk of its truth or falsity. If I endorse Plato's view, wrongly attributing it to Lord Russell ('Russell's view that *p* is quite true'), and am corrected, I have not discovered that I was talking of an event separated by centuries from the one I imagined I was talking of. (Corrected, I may say: 'Well it's true, whoever said it.') My *implied* historical judgement is false; that is all.

2. *Facts.*—What of the second term of the correspondence relation? For this Mr Austin uses the following words or phrases: 'thing', 'event', 'situation', 'state of affairs', 'feature', and 'fact'. All these are words which should be handled with care. I think that through failing to discriminate sufficiently between them, Mr Austin (1) encourages the assimilation of facts to things, or (what is approximately the same thing) of stating to referring; (2) misrepresents the use of 'true'; and (3) obscures another and more fundamental problem.

In section 3 of his paper [pp. 152–6 of this volume], Mr Austin says, or suggests, that all stating involves both referring ('demonstration') and characterizing ('description'). It is questionable whether all statements do involve both,[2] though it is certain that some do. The following sentences, for example, could all be used to make such statements; i.e., statements in the making of which both the referring and describing functions are performed, the performance of the two functions being approximately (though not exclusively) assignable to different parts of the sentences as uttered:

> The cat has the mange.
> That parrot talks a lot.
> Her escort was a man of medium build, clean-shaven, well-dressed and with a North Country accent.

In using such sentences to make statements, we refer to a thing or person (object) in order to go on to characterize it: (we demonstrate in order to describe). *A reference* can be correct or incorrect. A *description* can fit, or fail to fit, the thing or person to which it is applied.[3] When we refer

---

[1] And the cases where such phrases might most plausibly be exhibited as having an episode-referring role are precisely those which yield most readily to another treatment; namely, those in which one speaker corroborates, confirms or grants what another has just said (*see* Sect. 4, below).

[2] *See* Sect. 5, below. The thesis that all statements involve both demonstration and description is, roughly, the thesis that all statements are, or involve, subject-predicate statements (not excluding relational statements).

[3] Cf. the phrase 'He is described as ...'. What fills the gap is not a sentence (expression which could normally be used to make a statement), but a phrase which could occur as a part of an expression so used.

correctly, there certainly is a conventionally established relation between the words, so used, and the thing to which we refer. When we describe correctly, there certainly is a conventionally established relation between the words we use in describing and the type of thing or person we describe. These relations, as Mr Austin emphasizes, are different. An expression used referringly has a different logical role from an expression used describingly. They are differently related to the object. And *stating* is different from referring, and different from describing; for it is (in such cases) both these at once. Statement (*some* statement) is reference-cum-description. To avoid cumbersome phrasing, I shall speak henceforward of *parts* of statements (the referring part and the describing part); though parts of statements are no more to be equated with parts of sentences (or parts of speech-episodes) than statements are to be equated with sentences (or speech-episodes).

That (person, thing, etc.) to which the referring part of the statement refers, and which the describing part of the statement fits or fails to fit, is that which the statement is *about*. It is evident that there is nothing else in the world for the statement itself to be related to either in some further way of its own or in either of the different ways in which these different parts of the statement are related to what the statement is about. And it is evident that the demand that there should be such a relatum is logically absurd: a logically fundamental type-mistake. But the demand for something in the world *which makes the statement true* (Mr Austin's phrase), or *to which the statement corresponds when it is true*, is just this demand. And the answering theory that to say that a statement is true is to say that a speech-episode is conventionally related in a certain way to such a relatum reproduces the type-error embodied in this demand. For while we certainly say that a statement corresponds to (fits, is borne out by, agrees with) the facts, as a variant on saying that it is true, we *never* say that a statement corresponds to the thing, person, etc., it is about. What 'makes the statement' that the cat has mange 'true', is not the cat, but the *condition* of the cat, i.e., the fact that the cat has mange. The only plausible candidate for the position of what (in the world) makes the statement true is the fact it states; but the fact it states is not something in the world.[4] It is not an object; not even (as some have supposed) a complex object consisting of

---

[4] This is not, of course, to deny that there is that in the world which a statement of this kind is about (true or false *of*), which is *referred to* and *described* and which the description fits (if the statement is true) or fails to fit (if it is false). This truism is an inadequate introduction to the task of elucidating, not our use of 'true', but a certain general way of using language, a certain type of discourse, namely the fact-stating type of discourse. What confuses the issue about the use of the word 'true' is precisely its entanglement with this much more fundamental and difficult problem. (*See* (ii) of this section.)

one or more particular elements (constituents, parts) and a universal element (constituent, part). I can (perhaps) hand you, or draw a circle round, or time with a stop-watch the things or incidents that are referred to when a statement is made. Statements are about such objects; but they state facts. Mr Austin seems to ignore the complete difference of type between, e.g., 'fact' and 'thing', to talk as if 'fact' were just a very general word (with, unfortunately, some misleading features) for 'event', 'thing', etc., instead of being (as it is) both wholly different from these, and yet the only possible candidate for the desired non-linguistic correlate of 'statement'. Roughly: the thing, person, etc., referred to is the material correlate of the referring part of the statement; the quality or property the referent is said to 'possess' is the *pseudo*-material correlate of its describing part; and the fact to which the statement 'corresponds' is the *pseudo*-material correlate of the statement as a whole.

These points are, of course, reflected in the behaviour of the word 'fact' in ordinary language; behaviour which Mr Austin notes, but by which he is insufficiently warned. 'Fact', like 'true', 'states', and 'statement' is wedded to 'that'-clauses; and there is nothing unholy about this union. Facts are known, stated, learnt, forgotten, overlooked, commented on, communicated, or noticed. (Each of these verbs may be followed by a 'that'-clause or a 'the fact that'-clause.) Facts are what statements (when true) state; they are not what statements are about. They are not, like things or happenings on the face of the globe, witnessed or heard or seen, broken or overturned, interrupted or prolonged, kicked, destroyed, mended, or noisy. Mr Austin notes the expression 'fact that', warns us that it may tempt us to identify facts with true statements and explains its existence by saying that for certain purposes in ordinary life we neglect, or take as irrelevant, the distinction between saying something true and the thing or episode of which we are talking. It would indeed be wrong—but not for Mr Austin's reasons—to identify 'fact' and 'true statement'; for these expressions have different roles in our language, as can be seen by the experiment of trying to interchange them in context. Nevertheless their roles—or those of related expressions—overlap. There is no nuance, except of style, between 'That's true' and 'That's a fact'; nor between 'Is it true that . . . ?' and 'Is it a fact that . . . ?'[5] But Mr Austin's reasons for objecting to the identification

---

[5] I think in general the difference between them is that while the use of 'true', as already acknowledged, glances backwards or forwards at an actual or envisaged making of a statement, the use of 'fact' does not generally do this though it may do it sometimes. It certainly does not do it in, e.g., the phrase 'The fact is that . . .' which serves rather to prepare us for the unexpected and unwelcome.

seem mistaken, as does his explanation of the usage which (he says) tempts us to make it. Because he thinks of a statement as something in the world (a speech-episode) and a fact as something else in the world (what the statement either 'corresponds to' or 'is about'), he conceives the distinction as of overriding importance in philosophy, though (surprisingly) sometimes negligible for ordinary purposes. But I can conceive of no occasion on which I could possibly be held to be 'neglecting or taking as irrelevant' the distinction between, say, my wife's bearing me twins (at midnight) and my saying (ten minutes later) that my wife had borne me twins. On Mr Austin's thesis, however, my announcing 'The fact is that my wife has borne me twins' would be just such an occasion.

Elsewhere in his paper, Mr Austin expresses the fact that there is no theoretical limit to what could truly be said about things in the world, while there are very definite practical limits to what human beings actually can and do say about them, by the remark that statements 'always fit the facts more or less loosely, in different ways for different purposes'. But what could fit more perfectly the fact that it is raining than the statement that it is raining? Of course, statements and facts fit. They were made for each other. If you prise the statements off the world you prise the facts off it too; but the world would be none the poorer. (You don't also prise off the world what the statements are about—for this you would need a different kind of lever.)

A symptom of Mr Austin's uneasiness about facts is his preference for the expressions 'situation' and 'state of affairs'; expressions of which the character and function are a little less transparent than those of 'fact'. They are more plausible candidates for inclusion in the world. For while it is true that situations and state of affairs are not seen or heard (any more than facts are), but are rather *summed up* or *taken in at a glance* (phrases which stress the connection with statement and 'that'-clause respectively), it is also true that there is a sense of 'about' in which we do talk about, do describe, situations and states of affairs. We say, for example, 'The international situation is serious' or 'This state of affairs lasted from the death of the King till the dissolution of Parliament.' In the same sense of 'about', we talk about facts; as when we say 'I am alarmed by the fact that kitchen expenditure has risen by 50 per cent, in the last year.' But whereas 'fact' in such usages is lined with a 'that'-clause (or connected no less obviously with 'statement', as when we 'take down the facts' or hand someone the facts on a sheet of paper), 'situation' and 'state of affairs' stand by themselves, states of affairs are said to have a beginning and an end, and so on. Nevertheless, situations and states of affairs so talked of are (like facts so talked of), abstractions that a logician, if not a grammarian, should be able to see through. Being alarmed by a fact is not like being frightened by a shadow. It is being alarmed because. . . . One of the most economical and pervasive devices of language is the use of substantival expressions to abbreviate, summarize and connect. Having made a series of descriptive statements, I can comprehensively connect with these the remainder of my discourse by the use of such expressions as 'this situation' or 'this state of affairs'; just as, having produced what I regard as a set of reasons for a certain conclusion I allow myself to draw breath by saying 'Since *these things* are so, then . . . ', instead of prefacing the entire story by the conjunction. A situation or state of affairs is, roughly, a set of facts not a set of things.

A point which it is important to notice in view of Mr Austin's use of these expressions (in sections 3a and 3b of his paper) is that when we *do* 'talk about' situations (as opposed to things and persons) the situation we talk about is not, as he seems to think it is, correctly identified with the fact we state (with 'what makes the statement true'). If a situation is the 'subject' of our statement, then what 'makes the statement true' is not the situation, but the fact that the situation has the character it is asserted to have. I think much of the persuasiveness of the phrase 'talking about situations' derives from that use of the word on which I have just commented. But if a situation is treated as the 'subject' of a statement, then it will not serve as the non-linguistic term, for which Mr Austin is seeking, of the 'relation of correspondence'; and if it is treated as the non-linguistic term of this relation, it will not serve as the subject of the statement.

Someone might now say: 'No doubt "situation", "state of affairs", "facts" are related in this way to "that"-clauses and assertive sentences; can serve, in certain ways and for certain purposes, as indefinite stand-ins for specific expressions of these various types. So also is "thing" related to some nouns; "event" to some verbs, nouns, and sentences; "quality" to some adjectives; "relation" to some nouns, verbs, and adjectives. Why manifest this prejudice in favour of things and events as alone being parts of the world or its history? Why not situations and facts as well?' The answer to this (implicit in what has gone before) is twofold.

(i) The first part of the answer[6] is that the whole charm of talking of situations, states of affairs or facts as included in, or parts of, the world, consists in thinking of them as things, and groups of things; that the temptation to talk of situations, etc., in the idiom appropriate to talking of things and events is, once this first step is taken, overwhelming. Mr Austin does

---

[6] Which could be more shortly expressed by saying that if we read 'world' (a sadly corrupted word) as 'heavens and earth', talk of facts, situations, and states of affairs, as 'included in' or 'parts of' the world is, obviously, metaphorical. The world is the totality of things, not of facts.

not withstand it. He significantly slips in the word 'feature' (noses and hills are *features*, of faces and landscapes) as a substitute for 'facts'. He says that the reason why photographs and maps are not 'true' in the way that statements are true is that the relation of a map or a photograph to what it is a map or a photograph of is not wholly (in the first case) and not at all (in the second) a conventional relation. But this is not the only, or the fundamental, reason. (The relation between the Prime Minister of England and the phrase 'the Prime Minister of England' *is* conventional; but it doesn't make sense to say that someone uttering the phrase out of context is saying something true or false.) The (for present purposes) fundamental reason is that 'being a map of' or 'being a photograph of' *are* relations, of which the non-photographic, non-cartographical, relata are, say, personal or geographical *entities*. The trouble with correspondence theories of truth is not primarily the tendency to substitute non-conventional relations for what is really a wholly conventional relation. It is the misrepresentation of 'correspondence between statement and fact' *as a relation, of any kind, between events or things or groups of things* that is the trouble. Correspondence theorists think of a statement as 'describing that which makes it true' (fact, situation, state of affairs) in the way a descriptive predicate may be used to describe, or a referring expression to refer to, a thing.[7]

(ii) The second objection to Mr Austin's treatment of facts, situations, states of affairs as 'parts of the world' which we declare to stand in a certain relation to a statement when we declare that statement true, goes deeper than the preceding one but is, in a sense, its point. Mr Austin rightly says or implies (section 3) that for some of the purposes for which we use language, there must be conventions correlating the words of our language

---

[7] Suppose the pieces set on a chessboard, a game in progress. And suppose someone gives, in words, an exhaustive statement of the position of the pieces. Mr Austin's objection (or one of his objections) to earlier correspondence theories is that they would represent the relation between the description and the board with the pieces on it as like, say, the relation between a newspaper diagram of a chess-problem and a board with the pieces correspondingly arranged. He says, rather, that the relation is a purely conventional one. My objection goes farther. It is that there is no thing or event called 'a statement' (though there is the making of the statement) and there is no thing or event called 'a fact' or 'situation' (though there is the chessboard with the pieces on it) which stand to one another in any, even a purely conventional, relation as the newspaper diagram stands to the board-and-pieces. The facts (situation, state of affairs) cannot, like the chessboard-and-pieces, have coffee spilt on them or be upset by a careless hand. It is because Mr Austin needs such events and things for his theory that he takes the making of the statement as the statement, and that which the statement is about as the fact which it states.

Events can be dated and things can be located. But the facts which statements (when true) state can be neither dated nor located. (Nor can the statements, though the making of them can be.) Are they included in the world?

with what is to be found in the world. Not all the linguistic purposes for which this necessity holds, however, are identical. Orders, as well as information, are conventionally communicated. Suppose 'orange' always meant what we mean by 'Bring me an orange' and 'that orange' always meant what we mean by 'Bring me that orange', and, in general, our language contained only sentences in some such way imperative. There would be no less need for a conventional correlation between the word and the world. Nor would there be any less to be found in the world. But those pseudo-entities which *make statements true* would not figure among the non-linguistic correlates. They would no more be found; (they never were found, and never did figure among the non-linguistic correlates). The point is that the word 'fact' (and the 'set-of-facts' words like 'situation' 'state of affairs') have, like the words 'statement' and 'true' themselves, a certain type of word-world-relating discourse (the informative) *built in* to them. The occurrence in ordinary discourse of the words 'fact' 'statement' 'true' signalizes the occurrence of this type of discourse; just as the occurrence of the words' order' 'obeyed' signalizes the occurrence of another kind of conventional communication (the imperative). If our task were to elucidate the nature of the first type of discourse, it would be futile to attempt to do it in terms of the words 'fact', 'statement', 'true', for these words contain the problem, not its solution. It would, for the same reason, be equally futile to attempt to elucidate any one of these words (in so far as the elucidation of *that* word would be the elucidation of *this* problem) in terms of the others. And it is, indeed, very strange that people have so often proceeded by saying 'Well, we're pretty clear what a statement is, aren't we? Now let us settle *the further question*, namely, what it is for a statement to be true.' This is like 'Well, we're clear about what a command is: now what is it for a command to be obeyed?' As if one could divorce statements and commands from the point of making or giving them!

Suppose we had in our language the word 'execution' meaning 'action which is the carrying out of a command'. And suppose someone asked the philosophical question: What is *obedience*? What is it for a command to be *obeyed*? A philosopher might produce the answer: 'Obedience is a conventional relation between a command and an execution. A command is obeyed when it corresponds to an execution.'

This is the correspondence theory of obedience. It has, perhaps, a little less value as an attempt to elucidate the nature of one type of communication than the correspondence theory of truth has as an attempt to elucidate that of another. In both cases, the words occurring in the solution incorporate the problem. And, of course, this intimate relation between 'statement' and 'fact' (which is understood when it is seen that they both incorporate this problem) explains why it is that when we seek to explain *truth* on the model of naming or classifying or any other kind of conventional or non-conventional relation between one thing and another, we always find ourselves landed with 'fact', 'situation', 'state of affairs' as the non-linguistic terms of the relation.

But why should the problem of Truth (the problem about our use of 'true') be seen as this problem of elucidating the fact-stating type of discourse? The answer is that it shouldn't be; but that the correspondence theory can only be fully seen through when it is seen as a barren attempt on this second problem. Of course, a philosopher concerned with the second problem, concerned to elucidate a certain general type of discourse, must stand back from language and talk about the different ways in which utterances are related to the world (though he must get beyond 'correspondence of statement and fact' if his talk is to be fruitful). But—to recur to something I said earlier—the occurrence *in ordinary discourse* of the words 'true', 'fact', etc., signalizes, without commenting on, the occurrence of a certain way of using language. When we use these words in ordinary life, we are talking within, and not about, a certain frame of discourse; we are precisely not talking about the way in which utterances are, or may be, conventionally related to the world. We are talking about persons and things, but in a way in which we could not talk about them if conditions of certain kinds were not fulfilled. The problem about the use of 'true' is to see how this word fits into that frame of discourse. The surest route to the wrong answer is to confuse this problem with the question: What type of discourse is this?[8]

3. *Conventional Correspondence.*—It will be clear from the previous paragraph what I think wrong with Mr Austin's account of the relation itself, as opposed to its terms. In section 4 of his paper [pp. 156–8 of this volume] he says that, when we declare a statement to be true, the relation between the statement and the world which our declaration 'asserts to obtain' is 'a purely conventional relation' and 'one which we could alter at will'. This remark reveals the fundamental confusion of which Mr Austin is guilty between:

(*a*) the semantic conditions which must be satisfied for the statement that a certain statement is true to be itself true; and

(*b*) what is asserted when a certain statement is stated to be true.

---

[8] A parallel mistake would be to think that in our ordinary use (as opposed to a philosopher's use) of the word 'quality', we were talking about people's uses of words; on the ground (correct in itself) that this word would have no use but for the occurrence of a certain general way of using words.

Suppose A makes a statement, and B declares A's statement to be true. Then for B's statement to be true, it is, *of course*, necessary that the words used by A in making the statement should stand in a certain conventional (semantical) relationship with the world; and that the 'linguistic rules' underlying this relationship should be rules 'observed' by both A and B. It should be remarked that these conditions (with the exception of the condition about B's observance of linguistic rules) are equally necessary conditions of A's having made a true statement in using the words he used. *It is no more and no less absurd to suggest that B, in making his statement, asserts that these semantic conditions are fulfilled than it is to suggest that A, in making his statement, asserts that these semantic conditions are fulfilled* (i.e., that we can never use words without mentioning them). *If* Mr Austin is right in suggesting that to say that a statement is true is to say that 'the historic state of affairs to which it [i.e., for Mr Austin, the episode of making it] is correlated by the demonstrative conventions (the one it "refers to") is of a type with which the sentence used in making the statement is correlated by the descriptive conventions', *then* (and this is shown quite clearly by his saying that the relation we assert to obtain is a 'purely conventional one' which 'could be altered at will') in declaring a statement to be true, we are either:

(*a*) talking about the meanings of the words used by the speaker whose making of the statement is the occasion for our use of 'true' (i.e., profiting by the occasion to give semantic rules); or

(*b*) saying that the speaker has used correctly the words he did use.

It is *patently* false that we are doing either of these things. Certainly, we use the word 'true' when the semantic conditions described by Austin[9] are fulfilled; but we do not, in using the word, *state* that they are fulfilled. (And this, incidentally, is the answer to the question with which Mr Austin

---

[9] In what, owing to his use of the words 'statement' 'fact' 'situation', etc., is a misleading form. The quoted account of the conditions of truthful statement is more nearly appropriate as an account of the conditions of correct descriptive reference. Suppose, in a room with a bird in a cage, I say 'That parrot is very talkative'. Then my use of the referring expression ('That parrot') with which my sentence begins is correct when the token-object (bird) with which my token-expression (event) is correlated by the conventions of demonstration is of a kind with which the type-expression is correlated by the conventions of description. Here we do have an event and a thing and a (type-mediated) conventional relation between them. If someone corrects me, saying 'That's not a parrot; it's a cockatoo,' he may be correcting either a linguistic or a factual error on my part. (The question of which he is doing is the question of whether I would have stuck to my story on a closer examination of the bird.) Only in the former case is he declaring a certain semantic condition to be unfulfilled. In the latter case, he is talking about the bird. He asserts that it is a cockatoo and not a parrot. This he could have done whether I had spoken or not. He also *corrects* me, which he could not have done if I had not spoken.

concludes his paper [see p. 161 of this volume].) The damage is done (the two problems distinguished at the end of the previous section confused) by asking the question: *When* do we use the word 'true'? instead of the question: *How* do we use the word 'true'?

Someone says: 'It's true that French Governments rarely last more than a few months, but the electoral system is responsible for that.' Is the fact he states in the first part of his sentence alterable by changing the conventions of language? It is not.

4. *Uses of 'that'-clauses; and of 'statement', 'true', 'fact', 'exaggerated', etc.*—(*a*) There are many ways of making an assertion about a thing, X, besides the bare use of the sentence-pattern 'X is Y'. Many of these involve the use of 'that'-clauses. For example:

> How often shall I have to tell you
> Today I learnt
> It is surprising
> The fact is
> I have just been reminded of the fact } that X is Y.
> It is indisputable
> It is true
> It is established beyond question

These are all ways of asserting, in very different context and circumstances, that X is Y.[10] Some of them involve autobiographical assertions as well; others do not. In the grammatical sense already conceded, all of them are 'about' facts or statements. In no other sense is any of them about either, though some of them carry *implications* about the *making* of statements.

(*b*) There are many different circumstances in which the simple sentence-pattern 'X is Y' may be used to do things which are not merely stating (though they all involve stating) that X is Y. In uttering words of this simple pattern we may be encouraging, reproving, or warning someone; reminding someone; answering, or replying to, someone; denying what someone has said; confirming, granting, corroborating, agreeing with, admitting what someone has said. Which of these, if any, we are doing depends on the circumstances in which, using this simple sentence-pattern, we assert that X is Y.

(*c*) In many of the cases in which we are doing something besides

---

[10] One might prefer to say that in some of these cases one was asserting only *by implication* that X is Y; though it seems to me more probable that in all these cases we should say, of the speaker, not 'What he said implied that X is Y', but 'He *said* that X was Y'.

merely stating that X is Y, we have available, for use in suitable contexts, certain abbreviatory devices which enable us to state that X is Y (to make our denial, answer, admission or whatnot) *without* using the sentence-pattern 'X is Y'. Thus, if someone asks us 'Is X Y?', we may state (in the way of reply) that X is Y by saying 'Yes'. If someone says 'X is Y', we may state (in the way of denial) that X is not Y, by saying 'It is not' or by saying 'That's not true'; or we may state (in the way of corroboration, agreement, granting, etc.) that X is Y by saying 'It is indeed' or 'That is true'. In all these cases (of reply, denial and agreement) the context of our utterance, as well as the words we use, must be taken into account if it is to be clear what we are asserting, namely that X is (or is not) Y. It seems to me plain that in these cases 'true' and 'not true' (we rarely use 'false') are functioning as abbreviatory statement-devices of the same general kind as the others quoted. And it seems also plain that the *only* difference between these devices which might tempt us, while saying of some ('Yes', 'It is indeed', 'It is not') that, in using them, we were talking about X, to say of others ('That's true', 'That's not true') that, in using them, we were talking about something quite different, namely the utterance which was the occasion for our use of these devices, is their difference in grammatical structure, i.e., the fact that 'true' occurs as a grammatical predicate.[11] (It is obviously not a predicate of X.) If Mr Austin's thesis, that in using the word 'true' we make an assertion about a statement, were no more than the thesis that the word 'true' occurs as a grammatical predicate, with, as grammatical subjects, such words and phrases as 'That', 'What he said', 'His statement', etc., then, of course, it would be indisputable. It is plain, however, that he means more than this, and I have already produced my objections to the more that he means.

(*d*) It will be clear that, in common with Mr Austin, I reject the thesis that the phrase 'is true' is logically superfluous, together with the thesis that to say that a proposition is true is *just* to assert it and to say that it is false is *just* to assert its contradictory. 'True' and 'not true' have jobs of their own to do, *some*, but by no means all, of which I have characterized above. In using them, we are not *just* asserting that X is Y or that X is not Y. We are asserting this in a way in which we could not assert it unless certain conditions were fulfilled; we may also be granting, denying,

[11] Compare also the English habit of making a statement followed by an interrogative appeal for agreement in such forms as 'isn't it?', 'doesn't he?' etc., with the corresponding German and Italian idioms, 'Nicht wahr?', 'non è vero?'. There is surely no significant difference between the phrases which do not employ the word for 'true' and those which do: they all appeal for agreement in the same way.

confirming, etc. It will be clear also that the rejection of these two theses does not entail acceptance of Mr Austin's thesis that in using 'true' we are making an assertion about a statement. Nor does it entail the rejection of the thesis which Mr Austin (in section 4 of his paper) couples with these two, namely the thesis that to say that an assertion is true is not to make any further *assertion* at all. This thesis holds for many uses, but requires modification for others.

(*e*) The occasions for using 'true' mentioned so far in this section are evidently not the only occasions of its use. There is, for example, the generally concessive employment of 'It is true that *p* . . .', which it is difficult to see how Mr Austin could accommodate. All these occasions have, however, a certain contextual immediacy which is obviously absent when we utter such sentences as 'What John said yesterday is quite true' and 'What La Rochefoucauld said about friendship is true'. Here the context of our utterance does not identify for us the statement we are talking about (in the philosophically non-committal sense in which we *are* 'talking about statements' when we use the word 'true'), and so we use a descriptive phrase to do the job. But the descriptive phrase does not identify an event; though the statement we make carries the implication (in some sense of 'implication') that there occurred an event which was John's making yesterday (or Rochefoucauld's making sometime) the statement that *p* (i.e., the statement we declare to be true). We are certainly not telling our audience that the event occurred, e.g. that John made the statement that *p*, for (i) we do not state, either by way of quotation or otherwise, what it was that John said yesterday, and (ii) our utterance achieves its main purpose (that of making, by way of confirmation or endorsement, the statement that *p*) only if our audience already knows that John yesterday made the statement that *p*. The abbreviatory function of 'true' in cases such as these becomes clearer if we compare them with what we say in the case where (i) we want to assert that *p*; (ii) we want to indicate (or display our knowledge that) an event occurred which was John's making yesterday the statement that *p*; (iii) we believe our audience ignorant or forgetful of the fact that John said yesterday that *p*. We then use the formula 'As John said yesterday, *p*' or 'It is true, as John said yesterday, that *p*,' or 'What John said yesterday, namely that *p*, is true.' (Of course the words represented by the letter *p*, which we use, may be—sometimes, if we are to make the same statement, must be—different from the words which John used.) Sometimes, to embarrass, or test, our audience, we use, in cases where the third of these conditions is fulfilled, the formula appropriate to its non-fulfilment, namely 'What John said yesterday is true.'

(*f*) In criticism of my view of truth put forward in *Analysis*,[12] and presumably in support of his own thesis that 'true' is used to assert that a certain relation obtains between a speech-episode and something in the world exclusive of that episode, Mr Austin makes, in section 7 of his paper, the following point. He says: 'Mr Strawson seems to confine himself to the case when I say "Your statement is true" or something similar—but what of the case when you state that S and I say nothing, but *look and see* that your statement is true?' The point of the objection is, I suppose, that since I *say* nothing, I cannot be making any performatory use of 'true'; yet I can see *that* your statement is true. The example, however, seems to have a force precisely contrary to what Mr Austin intended. Of course, 'true' has a different role in 'X sees that Y's statement is true' from its role in 'Y's statement is true'. What is this role? Austin says in my hearing 'There is a cat on the mat' and I look and see a cat on the mat. Someone (Z) reports: 'Strawson saw that Austin's statement was true.' What is he reporting? He is reporting that I have seen a cat on the mat; but he is reporting this in a way in which he could not report it except in certain circumstances, namely, in the circumstances of Austin's having said in my hearing that there was a cat on the mat. Z's remark also carries the implication that Austin made a statement, but cannot be regarded as *reporting* this by implication since it fulfils its main purpose only if the audience already knows that Austin made a statement and what statement he made; and the implication (which *can* be regarded as an implied report) that I heard and understood what Austin said.[13] The man who looks and sees that the statement that there is a cat on the mat is true, sees no more and no less than the man who looks and sees that there is a cat on the mat, or the man who looks and sees that there is *indeed* a cat on the mat. But the *settings* of the first and third cases may be different from that of the second.

This example has value, however. It emphasizes the importance of the concept of the 'occasion' on which we may make use of the assertive device which is the subject of this symposium (the word 'true'); and minimizes (what I was inclined to overemphasize) the performatory character of our uses of it.

(*g*) Mr Austin stresses the differences between negation and falsity; rightly, in so far as to do so is to stress the difference (of occasion and context) between asserting that X is not Y and denying the assertion that X is Y. He also exaggerates the difference; for, if I have taken the point of

---

[12] 9/6 (June 1949).

[13] If *I* report: 'I see that Austin's statement is true', this is simply a first-hand corroborative report that there is a cat on the mat, made in a way in which it could not be made except in these circumstances.

his example, he suggests that there are cases in which 'X is not Y' is inappropriate to a situation in which, if anyone stated that X was Y, it would be correct to say that the statement that X was Y was false. These are cases where the question of whether X is or is not Y does not arise (where the conditions of its arising are not fulfilled). They are equally, it seems to me, cases when the question of the truth or falsity of the statement that X is Y does not arise.

(*h*) A qualification of my general thesis, that in using 'true' and 'untrue' we are not talking about a speech-episode, is required to allow for those cases where our interest is not primarily in what the speaker asserts, but in the speaker's asserting it, in, say, the fact of his having *told the truth* rather than in the fact which he reported in doing so. (We may, of course, be interested in both; or our interest in a man's evident truthfulness on one occasion may be due to our concern with the degree of his reliability on others.)

But this case calls for no special analysis and presents no handle to any theorist of truth; for to use 'true' in this way is simply to characterize a certain *event* as *the making*, by someone, of a true statement. The problem of analysis remains.

(*i*) Mr Austin says that we shall find it easier to be clear about 'true' if we consider other adjectives 'in the same class', such as 'exaggerated', 'vague', 'rough', 'misleading', 'general', 'too concise'. I do not think these words *are* in quite the same class as 'true' and 'false'. In any language in which statements can be made at all, it must be possible to make true and false statements. But statements can suffer from the further defects Mr Austin mentions only when language has attained a certain richness. Imagine one of Mr Austin's rudimentary languages with 'single words' for 'complex situations' of totally different kinds. One could make true or false statements; but not statements which were exaggerated, overconcise, too general, or rather rough. And even given a language as rich as you please, whereas all statements made in it could be true or false, not all statements could be exaggerated. When can we say that the statement that p is exaggerated? *One* of the conditions is this: that, if the sentence S_1 is used to make the statement that p, there should be some sentence S_2 (which could be used to make the statement that q) such that S_1 and S_2 are related somewhat as 'There were 200 people there' is related to 'There were 100 people there'. (To the remark 'We got married yesterday', you cannot, except as a joke, reply: 'You're exaggerating'.)

Mr Austin's belief, then, that the word 'exaggerated' stands for a relation between a statement and something in the world exclusive of the statement, would at least be an oversimplification, even if it were not objectionable in other ways. But it is objectionable in other ways. The difficulties about statement and fact recur; and the difficulties about the relation. Mr Austin would not want to say that the relation between an exaggerated statement and the world was like that between a glove and a hand too small for it. He would say that the relation was a conventional one. But the fact that the statement that p is exaggerated is not in any sense a conventional fact. (It is, perhaps, the fact that there were 1,200 people there and not 2,000.) If a man says: 'There were at least 2,000 people there,' you may reply (A) 'No, there were not so many (far more),' or you may reply (B) 'That's an exaggeration (understatement)'. (A) and (B) say the same thing. Look at the situation more closely. In saying (A), you are not merely asserting that there were fewer than 2,000 people there: you are also correcting the first speaker, and correcting him in a certain general way, which you could not have done if he had not spoken as he did, though you could merely have asserted that there were fewer than 2,000 there without his having spoken. Notice also that what is being asserted by the use of (A)—that there were fewer than 2,000 there—cannot be understood without taking into account the original remark which was the occasion for (A). (A) has both contextually-assertive and performatory features. (B) has the same features, and does the same job as (A), but more concisely and with greater contextual reliance.

Not all the words taken by Austin as likely to help us to be clear about 'true' are in the same class as one another. 'Exaggerated' is, of those he mentions, the one most relevant to his thesis; but has been seen to yield to my treatment. Being 'overconcise' and 'too general' are not ways of being 'not quite true'. These obviously relate to the specific purposes of specific makings of statements; to the unsatisfied wishes of specific audiences. No alteration in things in the world, nor any magical replaying of the course of events, could bring statements so condemned into line, in the way that an 'exaggerated assessment' of the height of a building could be brought into line by inorganic growth. Whether the statement (that p) is true or false is a matter of the way things are (of whether p); whether a statement is exaggerated (if the question arises—which depends on the type of statement and the possibilities of the language) is a matter of the way things are (e.g. of whether or not there were fewer than 2,000 there). But whether a statement is overconcise[14] or too general depends on what the hearer

---

[14] 'Concise' is perhaps less often used of what a man says than of the way he says it (e.g. 'concisely put', 'concisely expressed', 'a concise formulation'). A may take 500 words to say what B says in 200. Then I shall say that B's formulation was more concise than A's, meaning simply that he used fewer words.

wants to know. The world does not demand to be described with one
degree of detail rather than another.

5. *The scope of 'statement', 'true', 'false' and 'fact'*.—Commands and
questions, obviously do not claim to be statements of fact: they are not true
or false. In section 6 of his paper [pp. 159–61 of this volume], Mr Austin
reminds us that there are many expressions neither interrogative nor
imperative in form which we use for other purposes than that of reportage
or forecast. From our employment of these expressions he recommends
that we withhold (suspects that we do, in practice, largely withhold) the
appellation 'stating facts', the words 'true' and 'false'. Philosphers, even in
the sphere of language are not legislators; but I have no wish to challenge
the restriction, in some philosophical contexts, of the words 'statement',
'true', 'false', to what I have myself earlier called the 'fact-stating' type of
discourse.

What troubles me more is Mr Austin's own incipient analysis of this type
of discourse. It seems to me such as to force him to carry the restriction
further than he wishes or intends. And here there are two points which,
though connected, need to be distinguished. First, there are difficulties
besetting the relational theory of truth as such; second, there is the persistence of these difficulties in a different form when this 'theory of truth'
is revealed as, rather, an incipient analysis of the statement-making use of
language.

First then, facts of the cat-on-the-mat-type are the favoured species for
adherents of Mr Austin's type of view. For here we have one thing (one
chunk of reality) sitting on another: we can (if we are prepared to commit
the errors commented on in Section (2) above) regard the two together as
forming a single chunk, if we like, and call it a fact or state of affairs. The
view may then seem relatively plausible that to say that the statement
(made by me to you) that the cat is on the mat is true is to say that the
three-dimensional state of affairs with which the episode of my making the
statement is correlated by the demonstrative conventions is of a type with
which the sentence I use is correlated by the descriptive conventions.
Other species of fact, however, have long been known to present more
difficulty: the fact that the cat is not on the mat, for example, or the fact
that there are white cats, or that cats persecute mice, or that if you give my
cat an egg, it will smash it and eat the contents. Consider the simplest of
these cases, that involving negation. With what type of state-of-affairs
(chunk of reality) is the sentence 'The cat is not on the mat' correlated by
conventions of description? With a mat *simpliciter*? With a dog on a mat?
With a cat up a tree? The amendment of Mr Austin's view to which one
might be tempted for negative statements (i.e. 'S is true'='The state of

affairs to which S is correlated by the demonstrative conventions is *not* of a type with which *the affirmative form of* S is correlated by the descriptive conventions') destroys the simplicity of the story by creating the need for a different sense of 'true' when we discuss negative statements. And worse is to follow. Not all statements employ conventions of demonstration. Existential statements don't, nor do statements of (even relatively) unrestricted generality. Are we to deny that these are statements, or create a further sense of 'true'? And what has become of the non-linguistic correlate, the chunk of reality? Is this, in the case of existential or general statements, the entire world? Or, in the case of negatively existential statements, a ubiquitous non-presence?

As objections to a correspondence theory of truth, these are familiar points; though to advance them as such is to concede too much to the theory. What makes them of interest is their power to reveal how such a theory, in addition to its intrinsic defects, embodies too narrow a conception of the fact-stating use of language. Mr Austin's description of the conditions under which a statement is true, regarded as an analysis of the fact-stating use, applies only to affirmative subject-predicate statements, i.e., to statements in making which we refer to some one or more localized thing or group of things, event or set of events, and characterize it or them in some positive way (identify the object or objects and affix the label). It does not apply to negative, general and existential statements nor, straightforwardly, to hypothetical and disjunctive statements. I agree that any language capable of the fact-stating use must have some devices for performing the function to which Mr Austin exclusively directs his attention, and that other types of statements of fact can be understood only in relation to this type. But the other types *are* other types. For example, the word 'not' can usefully be regarded as a kind of crystallizing-out of something *implicit* in all use of descriptive language (since no predicate would have any descriptive force if it were compatible with everything). But from this it does not follow that negation (i.e. the *explicit* exclusion of some characteristic) is a kind of affirmation, that negative statements are properly discussed in the language appropriate to affirmative statements. Or take the case of existential statements. Here one needs to distinguish two kinds of demonstration or reference. There is, first, the kind whereby we enable our hearer to identify the thing or person or event or set of these which we then go on to characterize in some way. There is, second, the kind by which we simply indicate a locality. The first ('*Tabby* has the mange') answers the question 'Who which one, what are you talking about?' The second ('*There's* a cat') the question 'Where?' It is plain that no part of an existential statement performs the first function; though Austin's account of reference-cum-description is appropriate to reference of this kind rather than to that of the other. It is clear also that a good many existential statements do not answer the question 'Where?' though they may license the enquiry. The difference between various types of statement, and their mutual relations, is a matter for careful description. Nothing is gained by lumping them all together under a description appropriate only to one, even though it be the basic, type.

6. *Conclusion.*—My central objection to Mr Austin's thesis is this. He describes the conditions which must obtain if we are correctly to declare a statement true. His detailed description of these conditions is, with reservations, correct as far as it goes, though in several respects too narrow. The central mistake is to suppose that in using the word 'true' we are asserting such conditions to obtain. That this is a mistake is shown by the detailed examination of the behaviour of such words as 'statement', 'fact', etc., and of 'true' itself, and by the examination of various different types of statement. This also reveals some of the ways in which 'true' actually functions as an assertive device. What supremely confuses the issue is the failure to distinguish between the task of elucidating the nature of a certain type of communication (the empirically informative) from the problem of the actual functioning of the word 'true' within the framework of that type of communication.

POSTSCRIPT[15]

Although I still hold that the central contentions of my paper are correct, i.e. the contentions that 'statements', as here understood, and facts alike are not worldly items at all, and that the essential content of any predication of 'true' is identical with that of which it is predicated, yet I regret, and have long regretted, the mistake, made in the paper, of giving quite excessive weight to one particular (e.g. confirmatory) use we sometimes make of the expression 'true'. The mistake does not figure in 'A Problem about Truth: A Reply to Mr Warnock', in Pitcher (ed.), *Truth* (Englewood Cliffs, 1964), repr. in Strawson, *Logico-Linguistic Papers* (London, 1971), which gives a clearer account of my position; nor in subsequent writings.

[15] [*Editors' note*: this section was added by the author for this edn.]

XII

UNFAIR TO FACTS

J. L. AUSTIN

This chapter goes back to an old controversy between Strawson and me about truth. Of course comments on comments, criticisms of criticisms, are subject to the law of diminishing fleas, but I think there are here some misconceptions still to be cleared up, some of which seem to be still prevalent in generally sensible quarters.

In this old paper [Chapter IX in this volume] I gave (somewhat qualified) support to the common English expression that a true statement is one which 'corresponds with the facts'. I professed not to like this, in its own way doubtless unexceptionable, terminology, and preferred some jargon of my own, in which 'facts' and 'corresponds' do not occur at all, as a description of the conditions which must be satisfied if we are to say of a statement that it is true. Strawson in general, though with reservations, accepted, I believe, that description, but contended that, nevertheless, to say a certain statement is true is not to *assert that* those conditions are satisfied but to do something else such as *endorsing* the statement said to 'be true'. This was the principal issue, I think, between us, but we are not concerned with it here.

Now Strawson expended a good deal of ammunition on three words occurring in my paper—'statement', 'corresponds', and 'facts', giving at times, I think, the impression that I had given a pretty myth-eaten description even of the conditions which must obtain if we are to say of a statement that it is true. And this he claimed was due to my misunderstandings about the uses of these three words. I propose therefore to consider one of them, namely 'fact' (which I remember Ryle said at the time I should give more attention to). I choose 'fact' because, although the use of this word was not at all essential to my account of truth (indeed I only mentioned it to point out that it caused confusion), I do find that I think Strawson's own account of

From J. L. Austin, 'Unfair to Facts', *Philosophical Papers* (Oxford: Clarendon Press, 1961), 102–22. Reprinted by permission of Oxford University Press.

the word incorrect, and that I do not for a minute believe, with him, that 'facts' are pseudo-entities and the notion of 'fitting the facts' a useless notion.

By way of preliminary softening up, I shall take Strawson's two boldest and negative lines, and try to argue that they are unplausible and based on insufficient consideration of ordinary usage. Then I shall take his two more sophisticated and positive contentions.

I. What I am referring to as his two boldest and negative lines are these:

> (i) There is a (logically fundamental) type-difference between 'facts' and things-genuinely-in-the-world, such as things, persons and events.
>
> (ii) 'Corresponds with the facts' is a mere idiom, as it were a 'fused' idiom, not to be taken at all at its apparent face value.

(i) Taking the first of these: how is this alleged type-difference shown? Strawson points out, truly enough, that 'while we certainly say a statement corresponds to (fits, is borne out by, agrees with) the facts, as a variant on saying that it is true, we *never* say that it corresponds to the thing, person, &c., it is about'.[1] This is partly said, I think, to refute my analysis of 'corresponds with the facts' in terms of (among other things) the persons, &c., that the statement refers to: but it will not suffice for this, because, of course, that analysis was offered *as a whole* as an analysis of the *whole* expression 'corresponds with the facts': to substitute part of the analysis for part of the analysandum is a well-known short way with analyses. Still, here is a case, certainly, in which 'things', 'events', &c., are used differently from 'facts'. And certainly there are important differences between these words. But first, there are important similarities also.

For example, although we perhaps rarely, and perhaps only in strained senses, say that a 'thing' (e.g. the German Navy) is a fact, and perhaps never say that a person is a fact, still, things and persons are far from being all that the ordinary man, and even Strawson, would admit to be genuinely things-in-the-world whatever exactly that may mean. Phenomena, events, situations, states of affairs are commonly supposed to be genuinely-in-the-world, and even Strawson admits events are so. Yet surely of all of these we can say that they *are facts*. The collapse of the Germans is an event and is a fact—was an event and was a fact.

Strawson, however, seems to suppose that anything of which we say '. . . is a fact' is, automatically, *not* something in the world. Thus:

What 'makes the statement' that the cat has mange 'true' is not the cat, but the *condition* of the cat, i.e. the fact that the cat has mange. The only plausible candidate for the position of what (in the world) makes the statement true is the fact it states; but the fact it states is not something in the world.[2]

I cannot swallow this because it seems to me quite plain:

(1) that the condition of the cat is a fact;
(2) that the condition of the cat is something-in-the-world—if I understand that expression at all.

How can Strawson have come to say that the condition of the cat is *not* something in the world?

It seems to me that the trouble may arise through not observing certain rather easily overlooked boundaries between what may and may not be done with the word 'fact'.

There are two things we might very well, in of course a pedagogic way, say:

(*a*) what makes the statement that the cat has mange true is the condition of the cat (together, of course, with the meanings of the words);
(*b*) what makes the statement that the cat has mange true is the fact that the cat has mange.

(The second seems to me a *bit* unhelpful and off-colour, but let it pass.)

But now from these two we most certainly can*not* infer

The condition [or 'mangy condition'] of the cat is *the fact that* the cat has mange,

nor

The condition [or 'mangy condition'] of the cat is *the fact that* this statement [or 'the statement that the cat has mange'] states.

We cannot infer these things, because, for whatever reason, they don't make sense. We do not, I think (for whatever reason), *ever* say anything of the following form:

x is *the fact that* this statement [or 'the statement that S'] states

whatever be substituted for *x*.

Nor do we in general say anything of the form

x is the fact that S

whatever be substituted for *x* (to this there are some exceptions: e.g. It is the fact that S, Still more surprising is the fact that S, What I object to is the fact that S, The last straw is the fact that S).

---

[2] Ibid. [p. 166 in this vol.]

It appears to me, perhaps wrongly, that Strawson is led, by his 'i.e.', into supposing that the condition of the cat *is* the fact that the cat has mange, which according to me is not sense.

To this he is helped by his doctrine, to be discussed shortly, that ' "Fact" is wedded to "that"-clauses'. For it would of course be good sense to say that

> The condition of the cat *is a fact*:

and if we believe in adding 'that'-clauses we shall ask *what* fact, and reply 'The fact that the cat has mange'. But the question *what* fact, like its answer, does not make sense.

Having thus got so far as reducing 'the condition of the cat' to 'the fact that the statement states', Strawson is then ready to proclaim, on the strength of his other principal doctrine, that 'Facts are what statements state, not what they are about', that the condition of the cat is a pseudo-entity.

To sum this up. According to me

1. The condition of the cat is a fact, and is something in the world.
2. It is nonsense to say: the condition of the cat—or with only irrelevant exceptions anything else—*is the fact that* anything at all.
3. 'Fact' with 'that' and 'fact' without 'that' behave differently.
   a. *x is a fact* is all right   b. *x is the fact that* is wrong.

Here I should say (or admit?) that there is, I think, one important and perhaps obvious difference between 'fact' and say 'event' or 'phenomenon'—a difference which for all I know might qualify as a logically fundamental type-difference. But this is very far from making 'facts' to be *not* 'things-in-the-world'. It seems to me, on the contrary, that to say that something is a fact *is* at least in part precisely to say that it is something in the world: much more that than—though perhaps also to a minor extent—to classify it as being some special kind of something-in-the-world. To a considerable extent 'being a fact' seems to resemble 'existing' in the sorts of way that have led it to be held that 'existence is not a predicate'. One might compare:

Cows are animals	with	Fevers are diseases
Cows are things		Fevers are conditions
Cows exist		Fevers are facts
There are such things as cows		There are such conditions as fevers

Or one might say: it is as true and yet as queer to say that 'Facts are things-in-the-world' as that 'Entities are things-in-the-world'. Or one might say that 'fact' resembles 'person': 'persons' are not, of course, facts and facts are not persons but to say so-and-so is a person or a fact is in part at least to say so-and-so is real. (We do not on the whole like, there is oxymoron in, imaginary 'facts' or 'imaginary persons'—we prefer imaginary characters. In this way 'fact' does differ from say 'event'.)

I believe—but this is speculative—that it could be shown that some of the odd phenomena notorious about the word 'fact' could be shown to be connected with this 'existential' side of it (some of which, however, have been much exaggerated!), e.g. that we do not say that 'a fact was at a certain time' but that 'at a certain time it was a fact'.

(ii) Secondly, how is Strawson really to handle the good English expression 'corresponds with the facts' (and incidentally a good many others that go along with it)? For he claims that 'the demand for something in the world to which the statement corresponds when it is true' is a *wholly* mistaken demand and that 'fact' is a name for a pseudo-entity invented to satisfy this bogus demand. But this is to treat a wholesome English expression as though it were a philosopher's invented expression; to treat 'facts' as though they were in the same position as 'propositions' taking these to be pseudo-entities invented to answer the bogus demand 'what is it that sentences when meaningful mean?' How come that English has invented so unhappy an expression? It seems to me that Strawson has two rather different lines here, neither of which will do.

One thing we might try is to say that 'corresponds with the facts' is a 'fused' idiom precisely equivalent to 'is true'. It is in no way to be understood as meaning that anything 'corresponds' with anything in the way that that word ordinarily means, or as implying that there are such things as 'facts', or that anything is related in any way to anything—(for that matter, I suppose, no assertion is made about the statement *at all* when we say it 'corresponds with the facts', any more than when we say it 'is true'). This seems to me quite unplausible—why *should not* we be meaning by it that there is some sort of relation between something and something (no doubt not so simple as it sounds)? Strawson actually allows that when I say a map corresponds with the topography of the countryside I *am* talking about a relation between something and something, yet still contends that I am *not* when I say a statement corresponds with the facts. But how is this plausible—for we may remind ourselves that it is quite possible to say of a map that it does not correspond with the facts (e.g. a situation-map) and of a statement that it does not correspond with the topography. (Or should we go back, then, on the admission that 'corresponds' does mean a relation in the case of maps—say that topography is what maps map, not what maps are about, &c.!)

A second, and surely rather different, line, is the following. For the good English 'corresponds with the facts' or 'fits the facts' we substitute the quite unEnglish 'corresponds with *the fact that so-and-so*' or 'fits *the fact that so-and-so*' and proceed to claim that this is somehow tautological. This is a method which seems to be becoming fashionable. Strawson writes, 'What could fit more perfectly the fact that it is raining than the statement that it is raining? Of course statements and facts fit. They were made for each other.' But in answer to this: surely it is not sense either to ask whether the statement that S fits the fact that S or to state that it either does or does not. And I may add that it seems to me, *pace* Mrs Daitz, equally nonsense to ask whether the statement that S fits or corresponds to the fact that F, where 'F' is *different* from 'S' not identical with it (though of course it is *not* nonsense to ask something that sounds rather similar to this, viz. whether the statement that S *squares with* or '*does justice to*' the fact that F ('F'≠'S')). But even, further, if we allowed the expression: the statement that S fits the fact that S, surely we cannot allow the suggestion of 'statements and facts were made *for each other*'. To begin with, obviously, some statements *do not* fit the facts; we need not elaborate on this. But even if we take it as: '*True* statements fit the facts', '*True* statements and facts are made for each other' we cannot agree that there is any more sense in saying they are 'made for each other', or if there is sense, any more malice in saying it, than there would be in saying, on the ground that 'well-aimed shots hit their marks', that marks and shots (well-aimed) are made for each other.

It may be said—before we proceed further—why bother? Why raise this cry 'Unfair to facts'? There are two reasons I think.

1. It seems in the past to have been, at least often, inexpedient to say 'Facts are not things-in-the-world'. This misled, for example, Bradley, who had some by no means ill-deserved cold water to pour upon facts, at the crucial point. Still, on the other hand, no doubt it may for some purposes also be expedient to give ourselves a jolt by suggesting that 'there are no facts'.

2. More important altogether, to my mind, than this is the following. The expression 'fitting the facts' is *not* by any means an isolated idiom in our language. It seems to have a very intimate connexion with a whole series of adverbs and adjectives used in appraising statements—I mean, 'precise', 'exact', 'rough', 'accurate', and the like, and their cognate adverbs. All these are connected with the notion of fitting and measuring in ordinary contexts, and it can scarcely be fortuitous that they, along with fitting and corresponding, have been taken over as a group to the sphere of statements

and facts. Now to some extent the use of this galaxy of words in connexion with statements *may* be a transferred use; yet no one would surely deny
that these constitute serious and important notions which can be, and
should be elucidated. I should certainly go much farther and claim—as I
have done before—that these are the important terms to elucidate when
we address ourselves to the problem of 'truth', just as, not 'freedom' but
notions like duress and accident, are what require elucidation when we
worry about 'freedom'. Yet all these terms are commonly dismissed along
with the supposed useless 'fitting the facts'.

To give an illustration of this. Warnock, in his excellent book on
Berkeley, says that Berkeley's complaint is that ordinary language does
not *fit the facts* (or, as he says at other times, is inaccurate or inexact or
loose or imprecise). Warnock says this is a confusion: for 'fits the facts
(exactly?)' is simply equivalent to 'is true'—and he reduces the notion to
helplessness by the same device as Strawson did: he asks, e.g.

What statement could possibly fit the fact that there is a table in my
study more exactly than the statement 'There is a table in my
study'?[3]

and says

It is really tautologous to say that any true statement exactly fits the
facts; it exactly fits those facts, or that fact, which it states.

It would be most unreasonable to object to a statement because it fails
to state facts which it does not state.[4]

Having thus disposed of 'fitting the facts', Warnock considers all the rest—
inaccuracy,[5] looseness, &c. (but he does not distinguish between these!) as
apparently disposed of, and offers us as the only reasonable complaint
against statements which could very well, by confusion, be intended by, for
example, Berkeley, this: that the statement is 'logically complex' and can
be analysed into more verbose but logically simpler expressions. Such an
analysis does not he says 'fit the facts' any better but is merely more explicit
or more detailed—less concentrated. Well, maybe this does occur (if it is
a single phenomenon?); maybe it was what Berkeley meant, though this
would need proving; but all the same inaccuracy, looseness, and the rest do
also occur, are important, are distinct, and they cannot be dismissed

[3] G. J. Warnock, *Berkeley* (Harmondsworth, 1953), 240.
[4] Ibid.
[5] The relation between a rough, loose, inaccurate, inexact, imprecise, &c. statement and the
facts is a most important matter for elucidation.

from consideration by this perverted little rigmarole about 'fitting the facts'.

II. Now I shall set out what I take to be Strawson's main positive contentions about the word 'fact'. I think that others too hold the same beliefs.

i. 'Fact', says Strawson, 'is wedded to that-clauses'.[6] He does not explain this overmuch. But I think it is meant to be a statement about English usage: and one impression he conveys to his readers and I think himself is that, wherever we get the word 'fact' occurring in a sentence without a 'that-clause' we at least *could* insert a that-clause after it, even if we do not already actually 'supply' such a clause in some way mentally. We have seen already two instances of his acting on this principle.

ii. 'Facts', says Strawson, 'are what statements (when true) state; they are not what statements are about.' This seems to be a philosophical contention, based upon the linguistic contention I above. And it is this philosophical contention which leads him to say that facts are not anything genuinely-in-the-world, but pseudo-entities.

Now let us confront i: 'Fact is wedded to that-clauses' with the evidence of the Dictionary. If it is indeed so wedded, it leads, I fear, a double life. It was not born in wedlock, its marriage was a marriage of convenience and it continues to lead a flourishing bachelor existence.

The Dictionary (*Oxford English Dictionary*) does not take much account of 'fact that'. 'Fact that', along with 'fact of', is given as a comparatively recent linguistic device for avoiding gerundial constructions as the subjects of sentences or as the domains of prepositions: i.e. in order not to say 'I was unaware of the kitchen's being draughty' or 'the kitchen's being draughty annoyed him', we say 'I was unaware of the fact that the kitchen was draughty' or 'the fact that the kitchen was draughty annoyed him': it is compared with 'circumstance that'. No use of 'fact of' is given earlier than the eighteenth century: examples of 'fact that' are not given, but may even be later. I believe that if we consult even, say, the philosophers of the eighteenth century we can readily satisfy ourselves that 'fact that' is not in use; and the Dictionary's account is borne out by our experience of the general tendency nowadays to adopt similar novel 'that'-constructions with other words, like 'circumstance', 'event', 'situation'. (A later feature of such usages of course, is that the 'that' gets dropped out—'in case' for 'in the case that' and 'in the event' for 'in the event that'.)

To complete the history of the word according to the Dictionary. For the first 200 years of its use (sixteenth and seventeenth centuries) it meant

[6] *Proceedings of the Aristotelian Society*, suppl. vol. 24 (1950), 136 [p. 167 in this vol.].

(cf. 'feat') a deed or action, either the thing done or the doing of the thing, and more especially a criminal action; during the eighteenth century this use gradually died out in favour of a more extended meaning which began to appear already in the seventeenth century: a fact is now *something that has really occurred* (even classical Latin extended *factum* to mean 'event' or 'occurrence')[7] or something that is actually the case (a further extension to the meaning of '*factum*' found in scholastic Latin). *Hence* and thereafter it came to mean something *known* to have really occurred, and *hence* (according to the Dictionary) a particular *truth* known by observation or authentic testimony, by contrast with what is merely inferred or a conjecture or a fiction.

From this brief history, I take it as obvious that: (i) 'Fact' was in origin a name for 'something in the world', if we may take it that a past action or past actual event or occurrence is 'something in the world', and there is no reason whatever to doubt that it often still is so. (ii) Any connexion between 'fact' and 'knowledge', and still more between 'fact' and 'truth' (in particular the use of 'a fact' as equivalent to 'a truth'), is a derivative and comparatively late connexion. (iii) The expression 'fact that' is later still, and was introduced as a grammatical convenience, because of the already existing meaning of 'fact'. To explain the meaning of 'fact' in terms of the expression 'fact that' is to invert the real order of things—just as much as it would be to explain the meaning of 'circumstance' in terms of 'circumstance that' (or 'situation' in terms of 'situation that' and so on: indeed, one may suspect that we have here one pretty general method of misunderstanding or misrepresenting what language is up to).

I should further take it as fairly plain that (iv) when 'facts' or 'a fact' occur in general in modern English, the usage is just what it was in the eighteenth century. When we say 'The mangy condition of the cat is a fact' we mean it is an actual state of affairs; when we say 'What are the facts?' we mean 'what is the actual state of affairs?', 'what has actually occurred?' or the like. This is the meaning, too, in such common expressions as 'an *accomplished* fact' or 'He has had no personal experience of the facts he reports'. And finally, I take it that (v) the expression 'The fact that S' *means* 'a certain fact [or actual occurrence, &c.], namely that correctly described [or reported, &c.] by saying now "S" [or at other times "S" with a change of tense].' It was to this that I referred when I said that 'the fact that' is a way of speaking compendiously about words and world together. It is a usage grammatically *like* (not of course in all ways the same as) the

---

[7] Actual event or occurrence, of course.

apposition usage with proper names, as when we say 'The person Caesar' which we should interpret as 'a certain person [or actual man, &c.], namely the one designated by the name "Caesar"'.

And two further clear points about 'the fact that':

(vi) 'The fact that S' is a totally different occurrence of 'the fact that' from that in say '*The fact that* he stated'. In other words, even if 'fact' were wedded to that-clauses, there are different that-clauses.

(vii) I feel—but cannot I confess sufficiently 'explain', probably for want of terminology—that somehow this explanation of the special form of expression 'the fact that S' should be what accounts (*a*) for our inability to say things of the form 'the mangy condition of the cat *is* the fact that the cat has mange' (or 'the cat's having mange *is* the fact that the cat has mange') and likewise possibly (*b*) for the queerness of the problem that Ramsey and Moore discussed as to whether 'the fact that S' is a name or a description or what on earth?

Compare persons and facts again: is there a parallel between

'Cicero'	'The cat has mange'
Cicero	{ The cat's having mange
	{ The mangy condition of the cat

The person Cicero   The fact that the cat has mange?

Thus (*a*)

To say 'the mangy condition of the cat *is* the fact that the cat has mange' is like saying 'Cicero is the person Cicero'. These two forms of expression are not designed for combination in this manner. But why? Nor for that matter is 'Tully is the person Cicero', only rather ' "Cicero" is the name of the person Cicero'.

'Tully' is a name of the same person as 'Cicero': so 'Everest is so high' is a statement of the same fact as 'Gaurisankar is so high'. 'Everest is so high' is a statement of the fact that Everest is so high.

Also (*b*) asking whether 'The fact that S' is a name or a description is like asking whether 'the person Cicero' is a name. But we seem to lack a name for this type of expression and a description of its role and limitations.

Now let us ask, what was Strawson actually arguing in saying 'Fact is wedded to that-clauses'. He was thinking of its use in connexion with certain verbs.

'Facts', he says, 'are known, stated, learnt, forgotten, overlooked, commented on, communicated, or noticed. (Each of these verbs may be followed by a "that"-clause or a "the fact that"-clause.)[8] This is not, I think, very clear.

1. It is not clear whether it is meant that *wherever* we have a sentence in which one of these verbs occurs with 'fact' as its object we could put a that-clause or the-fact-that-clause in place of the object, or only that we *sometimes* can.

2. It is not clear whether it matters whether 'fact' occurring in the original sentence as object of one or another of these verbs is to be singular or plural, with the definite or indefinite article or neither.

3. It is not clear whether, if we do substitute a that-clause or a the-fact-that-clause for 'fact' the meaning of the original sentence is to be considered altered or unaltered.

But I *think* the impression Strawson conveys both to himself and to his readers is that, given any of these verbs, the following three forms of sentence are equally good English and somehow interchangeable.

(*a*) *Fact-form.* He verbed a/the fact/facts
(*b*) *That-form.* He verbed that S
(*c*) *The fact-that-form.* He verbed the fact that S.

But it will be found that the verbs in his list behave differently with respect to these three forms of sentence. (With some, such as 'comment on', it is not the case that all three forms make sense: we cannot 'comment on that'.)

The best example of what Strawson is after seems to be the verb 'forget':

He forgot a fact or the facts
He forgot that S
He forgot the fact that S.

These seem all good English, and reasonably interchangeable—of course the second two specify what it was he forgot whereas the first does not, but this is fair enough and nothing to boggle at.

And, of course, with the verb 'state' also, all three forms of sentence make sense (though not all are equally usual):

He stated a fact
He stated that S
He stated the fact that S.

But here there is a great difference between the second and the other two. With 'forget', the fact-form entails the that-form, and conversely; but with 'states' this is not so. 'He stated that S' does not entail 'he stated a fact'.

---

[8] *Proceedings of the Aristotelian Society*, suppl. vol. 24 (1950), 136 [p. 167 in this vol.].

Similarly, with 'state' certain forms of sentence are good sense which are not good sense in the same way with 'forget' or 'know':

What he stated was a fact

In stating that S he stated a fact.

But not

What he forgot or knew was a fact[9]

In forgetting that S he forgot a fact.

All that this shows is, of course, that 'state' is not, like 'know' and 'forget', a success or achievement word in Ryle's sense. To know that or to notice that is to know or notice a fact; but to state that is not necessarily to state a fact. 'State' may be wedded to that-clauses; but 'fact' is wedded to neither.

This is of course notorious enough. But surely it is also enough to cast doubt on 'Statements and facts are made for each other'. Even 'Knowledge and facts are made for each other' or 'Forgetfulness and facts were made for each other' would contain more truth—though even then one would be inclined to protest that there may very well be facts that nobody knows or ever will know, and that to say the facts are made for the knowledge is curious.

Strawson also produces a list of other verbs, presumably *un*connected with 'that'-clauses, which he suggests *are* connected with things-in-the-world (things, persons, events) but not with facts, namely 'witness', 'hear', 'see', 'break', 'overturn', 'interrupt', 'prolong', &c. But surely we can witness facts? And observe them and have personal acquaintance with them. I cannot see that there is a clear distinction here.

However, we have seen I think in general enough from the dictionary, and from the troubles that arise when we insert that-clauses indiscriminately, to abandon the doctrine that fact is wedded to that-clauses. Let us now turn to the second doctrine which was that:

'Facts are what statements (when true) state: they are not what statements are about.'

Take the second clause first, about which I shall not say much. The main thing I feel about it is that 'about' is too vague a word to bear the weight Strawson wants to put on it. If we take other verbs, for example, facts are both what we forget and what we forget about, both what we know and what we know about (as well as 'of'); verbally we can say that 'the number of the planets' is both what a statement is about and what that same state-

---

[9] Point of the joke about the Bourbons 'forgetting nothing'.

ment states. Moreover, Strawson would admit, I think, that a statement can be about a fact, or about the fact that . . . I do not, however, wish to insist that Strawson could not make out a case for this clause of his doctrine.

What I do wish to insist is that the first clause—'Facts are what statements, when true, state' is most misleading. Undoubtedly we should agree that 'True statements state facts'; but if we convert it in Strawson's manner we certainly give ourselves the impression that this is somehow or other a 'definition' of facts. It gives; and I think is meant to give, the impression of reducing 'facts' to an accusative so deeply and hopelessly internal that their status as 'entities' is hopelessly compromised.

Strawson represents us as asking: 'What do true statements state?' and giving ourselves the bogus and unhelpful answer 'Facts', much as philosophers are supposed to have asked themselves 'What do meaningful sentences mean?' and to have given themselves the bogus answer 'propositions'. Yet there is nothing in the form of such questions to make them necessarily, along with their answer, bogus. Strawson himself is prepared to ask, for example, 'What do statements refer to?' and to answer 'Things, persons or events'. Nor need we by any means take our answer (e.g. Things are what statements refer to) to be a definition of 'things' or in some manner unwholesomely analytic.

To shake off this hypnotism of the internal accusative, this vague menace of the analytic, consider a few parallel examples:

Births are what birth-certificates, when accurate, certify.
Persons are what surnames, when borne, are the surnames of.
Women are what men, when they marry, marry.
Wives are what men, when they marry, marry.
Animals are what portraits, when faithful, portray.
Sitters are what portraits, when faithful, portray.
Events are what narratives, when true, narrate.
History is what narratives, when true, narrate.

Which, if any of these, is Strawson's sentence to be taken to resemble? Does it in particular resemble the 'Events are what narratives, when true, narrate' case? And would it make sense to go on: 'they are not what narratives are about'? At any rate, one thing is plain, that, whatever the analyticity or internal accusatives or what not involved in any of these pronouncements, none of them have the slightest tendency to convince us that births, persons, or events, women (or even wives), animals (or even sitters) are *not* 'things or happenings on the surface of the globe'.

Why then worry about 'facts'?

There seems, on closer inspection, to be some trouble about the expression 'What statements state'. How is it to be taken?

Let us agree by all means that 'true statements state facts', and that somehow or in some sense this is, if you like, 'true by definition'—though keeping of course an open mind as to *which* definition—that, for example, of 'fact' or that of 'true statement'. But now if we put this in the shape.

  Facts are what true statements state

it has to be understood that this variety of 'what' ('what statements state' 'What he stated') is a highly 'ambiguous' one—or rather, that there are different uses for the expression 'what he stated'.

To take an illustration: compare:

 (*a*) what he stated was true, [or 'was a truth'].
 (*b*) what he stated was a fact.

In these two sentences 'what he stated' is not grammatically identical. For in (*a*) we can substitute for 'what he stated' the expression 'his statement'; whereas in (*b*) we cannot do this; 'his statement was a fact', if it had any meaning, would anyhow mean something quite different from 'what he stated was a fact'.[10]

Or again, contrast both (*a*) and (*b*) alike with yet another use of 'what he stated'. In reply to the question 'what did he state?' we might be told '(He stated) that S', i.e. we get

 (*c*) what he stated was that S.

That this differs from the use of 'what he stated' in (*a*) and (*b*) is plain; but the difference may be brought out by considering how odd it would be, to give to the question 'What did he state?' the answer 'A fact' or 'A truth'. These could only be given, on the contrary, as answers to the quite different yes-or-no-type questions 'Was what he stated a fact?' or 'Was what he stated true (a truth)'.

We can in fact distinguish at least five different ways in which 'What' is used in connexion with 'state', which are immediately relevant here. 'State', in this respect, is typical of a large group of words used in talking about communication, and I shall illustrate the five different uses concerned by means of the analogous verb to 'signal'.

Let us take a simple model situation in which all we are concerned to do is to signal targets as they bob up in an aperture. The targets are of

---

[10] This is of course in line with the fact that in 'It is true that S' we can insert 'to state' after 'is true'; whereas in 'It is a fact that S' we cannot insert 'to state'. Strawson says there is no nuance except of style between 'It is true that' and 'It is a fact that'; yet he himself admits that the former 'glances at' the making of a statement, whereas the latter does not.

various different recognizable types and there is an appointed signal (say a flag of a special colour) for each different type of target. Very well then—the targets keep on bobbing up, and we keep on wagging flags—the convention of reference being the simple one (non-'verbal' or rather non 'flag-al') that each signal refers to the contemporary occupant of the aperture. Now, in what ways can we use the expression 'what we signal'?

(I) There are two uses in which we can use the expression 'What we signal is always . . .'. Perhaps not very helpful or usual except for pedagogic purposes. Namely

  (1) 'What we signal is always a target'. Cf. 'What we state is always a fact'.
  (2) 'What we signal is always a signal'. Cf. 'What we state is always a statement'.

There is no conflict between these pronouncements; nor is it either necessary or legitimate, in order to 'reconcile' them, to conclude that 'targets are signals': they are *not*, nor are facts statements, by the same token! All that is needed is to realize that 'what we signal' has two uses—or that 'signal' can take two varieties of accusative, both, interestingly enough, completely 'internal'. (1) means that whenever we signal we signal something as a target, signals are as such signals of targets; so whenever we state we state something as a fact, statements are as such statements of fact.[11]

(2) of course is highly pedagogic, though harmless. It would be very pedagogic to say 'we signal signals' or 'we state statements'—though parallel to saying, for example, 'we plan plans'. Such remarks instruct us as follows: whenever we say 'we plan (signal, state) so-and-so' there will be something of which we can say that it was our plan (signal, statement). (1) and (2) alike are only of use in giving instructions about the meaning and use of the verb 'signal' and the substantive 'signal'.

But now further (II), when we do *not* use the 'always' and the 'we' of pedagogic generalization, we use 'what . . . signal (state)' in quite different ways, as follows:

  (3) 'What we signal is sometimes, but not always, a target'.
      'What we state is sometimes, but not always, a fact'.
  (4) 'What we signal is sometimes, but not always, (a) correct (signal).
      'What we state is sometimes, but not always, true' (a truth).

It is in use (3) that we speak when we say, for example, 'What he stated then was a fact but what she stated thereafter was not a fact'; and in use

---

[11] Of course we are excluding from treatment throughout the expression 'statement of opinion', interesting enough in itself but not relevant here.

(4) that we speak when we say, for example, 'What he stated then was true but what she stated thereafter was not'.

The uses of 'what we signal' in (3) and (4) are of course *connected*, but they are *not* identical. If they were *identical* we should get the absurd conclusion that

A target is (a) correct (signal)

and the conclusion, equally absurd I think, that

A fact is a true statement (a truth).

The actual connexion between (3) and (4) is not so simple, though simple enough:

If, and only if, and because what we signal (3) is a target, then what we signal (4) is correct; and, derivatively, if, and only if, but not because what we signal (4) is correct, then what we signal (3) is a target.

There is an obvious connexion between 'what we signal' in the sense (3) and 'what we signal' in the pedagogic sense (1); and likewise between sense (2) and sense (4). Perhaps, indeed, we might even say that the difference between (1) and (3) and again between (2) and (4), is not so much a difference between senses or uses of 'what we signal' as rather a difference between senses or uses of 'what we signal *is*'. But at any rate there is a radical distinction between 'what we signal' in (1) and (3) together and in (2) and (4) together—between what we signal as a *target* (actual or—pedagogically—putative) and on the other hand as a *signal* (correct or incorrect). And just as, in the signalling case, there is not the slightest temptation to say

'Targets are not things in the world'
'Targets are (correct) signals'

so there should be no temptation to say

'Facts are not things-in-the-world'
'Facts are true statements'.

But finally (III) there is yet another use of 'what we signal', or of 'what we signal is' where 'what we signal' is neither *always x*, as in (1) and (2), nor always either *x* or not *x*, as in (3) and (4).

In this use (5).

—what we signal is now red, now green, now purple
—what we state is now that S, now that T, now that U.

To sum up, then,

Facts are what true statements state

is like

Targets are what correct signals signal

and has no more tendency to prove that facts are pseudo-entities than that targets are. And if we choose to say that either is being defined in terms of the other, we should say the other way round.

Or again: from the two unexceptionable

(1) He stated a fact
(2) He stated that S

we can indeed get:

'what he stated was a fact'
'what he stated was that S'.

But we cannot possibly make an inference from these such as

a fact is that S or that T, &c.

(which makes it look like a 'bogus entity') because 'what he stated' does not mean the same in the two premisses.

PART IV

MODERN MINIMALISM AND DOUBTS ABOUT IT

XIII

TRUTH: A TRADITIONAL DEBATE
REVIEWED

CRISPIN WRIGHT

I

Every student of English-speaking analytical metaphysics is taught that
the early twentieth-century philosophical debate about truth confronted
the correspondence theory, supported by Russell, Moore, the early
Wittgenstein, and, later, J. L. Austin, with the coherence theory advocated
by the British idealists.[1] Sometimes the pragmatist conception of truth
deriving from Dewey, William James, and C. S. Peirce is regarded as a third
player. And as befits a debate at the dawn of analytical philosophy, the
matter in dispute is normally taken to have been the proper analysis of the
concept.

No doubt this conception nicely explains some of the characteristic turns
taken in the debate. Analysis, as traditionally conceived, has to consist in
the provision of illuminating conceptual equivalences; and illumination
will depend, according to the standard rules of play, on the *analysans'* uti-
lizing only concepts which, in the best case, are in some way prior to and

A version of this chapter was published in Matthias Vogel and Lutz Wingert (eds.), *Unsere
Welt-gegeben oder gemacht? Wissensproduktion zwischen sozialer Konstruktion und Entdeckung*
(Frankfurt am Main, 1999), and was originally written for delivery as a lecture in the series of
the same title held at the Johann Wolfgang Goethe-Universität in Frankfurt in spring 1996.
Thanks to the discussants on that occasion and also to participants at colloquia at University
College, Dublin, the University of Kent at Canterbury, Columbia University, and
the 1998 Austin J. Fagothey S. J. Philosophy Conference on Truth at Santa Clara University; and
to Bob Hale, Fraser MacBride, Stewart Shapiro, and Charles Travis. This material was first
published in the *Canadian Journal of Philosophy*, suppl. vol. 24 (1999) and is reprinted by kind
permission of the editor.

[1] Two *loci classici* of coherentism are H. H. Joachim, *The Nature of Truth* (Oxford, 1906) and
F. H Bradley, *Essays on Truth and Reality* (Oxford, 1914). Ralph Walker has argued that coher-
entism is implicit also in the forms of anti-realism canvassed by Michael Dummett and Hilary
Putnam (at least, the Hilary Putnam of *Reason, Truth and History*). See R. C. S. Walker, *The
Coherence Theory of Truth: Realism, Anti-Realism, Idealism* (London, 1989). Myself I doubt
this—for further discussion, see my 'Critical Study of Walker's *The Coherence Theory of Truth*',
Synthèse, 103 (1995), 279–302.

independent of the notion being analysed—or, if that's too much to ask, then concepts which at least permit of some form of explication which does not in turn take one straight back to that notion. Thus if it is proposed, in this spirit, that truth is correspondence to external fact, it will be possible for a critic both to grant the *correctness* of the proposal and to reject it nevertheless—because, it may be contended, it fails to comply with the conditions on an illuminating *analysis*. In particular, it will be an obligation on an analysis of truth in terms of correspondence that it be possible to supply appropriate independent explications of the notions of 'correspondence' and 'fact', and it is exactly here, of course, that many of the traditional difficulties for the correspondence proposal have been located. Likewise, if we propose to analyse truth in terms of coherence, or on broadly pragmatist lines, we must be prepared to allow that any and every occurrence of 'true' as applied to what the analysis recognizes to be its primary bearers—sentences, or propositions, or whatever—may be replaced, without change of meaning,[2] by an expression of the preferred analysans. And, again, many of the knots into which critics have tied proposals of these kinds depend upon exploitation of this constraint. As recently as 1982, for instance, Alvin Plantinga observed that if 'true' just means: *would be believed by cognitively ideal subjects operating under cognitively ideal conditions*, then there seems to be no prospect of recovering, without paradox, an account of the content of the thought: it is true that conditions are not cognitively ideal.[3]

When the debate is all about the analysis of the concept of truth, then at least two other kinds of position have to be possible—and, historically, they have indeed been occupied. One is the indefinabilist view adopted by Frege: that truth allows of *no* analysis, because it is too simple, or primitive, or because any notions involved in a formulation which is at least correct will rapidly bring one back to truth, so compromising illumination. Frege held this view for reasons whose cogency is a matter of dispute[4] but

---

[2] How this constraint may be made to consist with the requirement that analysis be illuminating is, of course, the heart of Moore's paradox of analysis. But the sort of objection about to be noted need read no more into sameness of content than sameness of truth conditions.

[3] 'How to be an Anti-Realist', *Proceedings and Addresses of the American Philosophical Association*, 56 (1982), 47–70. Plantinga's point also engages certain formulations of the coherence theory. e.g. to suppose that 'true' means: *would be believed by a subject who had arrived at a maximally coherent and comprehensive set of beliefs*, is again implicitly to surrender the means to construe the truth of the thought: no-one holds a maximally coherent and comprehensive set of beliefs. The problem is a special case of the so-called conditional fallacy: any analysis in terms of subjunctive conditionals is potentially in trouble if its intended range comprises statements which are incompatible with the protases of the relevant conditionals.

[4] For discussion, see P. Carruthers, 'Frege's Regress', *Proceedings of the Aristotelian Society*, 82 (1981), 17–32. See also the useful account in Ralph C. S. Walker's survey article, 'Theories of Truth' in B. Hale and C. Wright (eds.), *Companion to the Philosophy of Language* (Oxford, 1997), esp. §6.

the apparent paucity of successful analyses of *anything* in analytical philosophy, and the inchoate and uneasy state of the methodology of analysis itself, must encourage the thought that this negative stance will not
easily be dismissed. Quite different—and rather more interesting—is
the proposal that correspondence, coherentist, pragmatist, and even
indefinabilist conceptions of truth all err in their common conviction that
'true' presents a substantial concept at all. This is the deflationist tradition,
which is usually thought to have originated in Ramsey, was defended in
rather different ways by Ayer and Strawson, and which survives in contemporary writers such as Paul Horwich and Hartry Field.[5] According to
deflationism, there simply isn't anything which truth, in general, *is*. It's a
misconstrual of the role of the adjective 'true' to see it as expressing the
concept of a substantial characteristic of which one of the traditional
accounts might provide a correct analysis, or which might allow of no
correct analysis. Those who think otherwise are missing the point that
the role of a significant adjective doesn't have to be to ascribe a genuine
property.

My first principal point is that, notwithstanding the fact that it rational-
izes many of the moves made, and doubtless reflects therefore the intentions of many of the protagonists, the conception of the traditional debate
about truth as centred upon reductive analysis of the concept is not best
fitted to generate the most fruitful interpretation of it. To see this, suppose
for the sake of argument that the indefinabilists are right: that 'true', like—
say—'red', admits of no illuminating conceptual breakdown. It is striking
that philosophical discussion of colour has hardly been silenced by the corresponding point about the concept *red* or basic colour concepts generally.
The contention that there is, as Locke thought, an interesting distinction
between primary and secondary qualities of objects and that red is a secondary quality; the contention that whether an object is red is, in some way,
a 'response-dependent' matter, or more generally that there is some form
of implicit relativity in the idea of an object's being red; the contention
that red is, on the contrary, a non-relational property of objects or, more
specifically, that red things form a natural kind; even the 'error-theoretic'
view that a complete inventory of characteristics found in the real world
would contain no mention of the colours—all these views, and an acknowl-
edgement of the interest of the debates to which they contribute, are

---

[5] Horwich's *Truth* (Oxford, 1990) provides a detailed defence of the deflationary tradition
and a useful bibliography of its literature. While Field's 'The Deflationary Conception of Truth'
(in G. Macdonald and C. Wright (eds.), *Fact, Science and Morality: Essays on A. J. Ayer's
Language, Truth and Logic* (Oxford, 1986), 55–117) eventually suggests that there are purposes
for which a correspondence conception is needed; his more recent 'Deflationary Views of
Meaning and Content' (CH XIX in this vol.) takes a more committed deflationary line.

consistent with recognition of the indefinability of colour concepts. So, consistently with its indefinability—if it is indefinable—a similar range of issues can be expected to arise in connection with truth. 'True'—even when taken, in the broad sense which interests us, as a predicate of content-bearing things—is predicated of a variety of items: beliefs, thoughts, propositions, token utterances of type sentences. But whatever such items we have in mind, we can ask whether one of them being true is in any way an *implicitly relational* matter—and if so, what are the terms of the relation; whether it is a *response-dependent* matter, or in any other way dependent on subjectivity or a point of view; whether there is indeed nothing generally in which the truth of such an item consists—whether an inventory of all the properties to be found in the world would include mention of *no such thing as truth*.

Indeed, such issues arise for any putative characteristic, Φ. Should we (ontologists) take Φ seriously at all, or is some sort of error-theoretic or deflationary view appropriate? If we do take it seriously, should we think of the situation of an item's being Φ as purely a matter of how it is intrinsically with that item, or are we rather dealing with some form of relation? Is an item's being Φ an objective matter (and what does it mean to say so)? These are analytic-philosophical issues par excellence, but their resolution need not await—and might not be settled by—the provision of a correct conceptual analysis.

II

Suppose we discard the analysis-centred conception of the traditional debate and look at it instead in the way suggested by the foregoing reflections. Clearly the deflationary option remains in play, holding that truth is not a genuine characteristic of anything—that it would find no place in an inventory of what is real. The other views all allow the reality of truth but differ about its *structure*, or in respects relevant to the broad question of objectivity. Correspondence theory holds that truth is a relational characteristic whose terms are respectively propositions—to pick one among the possibilities[6]—and *non-propositional items*—facts, or states of affairs—in an independent world.[7] The proposal thus bears both on structure and, so proposers of correspondence intend, on objectivity too. Coherence theory agrees about the relationality of truth, but disagrees about the terms of the relation: on this type of view, the truth of a

[6] Sentences, token utterances, statements, beliefs, and thoughts are some among the other content-bearing items which we ordinarily think of as apt for truth.
[7] Excepting, of course, the case where a proposition is itself about propositions.

proposition consists not in a relation to something non-propositional but in its participation in a system, meeting certain conditions, whose other participants are likewise propositions—so ultimately in relations to those other propositions. This is again, in the first instance, a view about the structure of truth, but it was intended by its original proponents to provide a vehicle for their idealism. And pragmatism—the view that truth is, broadly, a matter of operational success of some kind—while making no clear suggestion about structure (though there may be commitments in this direction once the relevant dimensions of success are clarified), stands in opposition to the correspondence theorists' thoughts about objectivity without—intentionally anyway—implying anything like such idealism.

Let's focus for the time being on the question of structure, and return later to some of the issues connected with pragmatism. We may chart the possibilities in a tree as shown in Fig. XIII. 1. Essentially, then, just four structural proposals are possible: deflationism, intrinsicism, and the two forms of relationalism, coherentism, and correspondence. I think it's fair to say that this conception of correspondence, shorn of any further analytical or explanatory obligations, comes across as highly commonsensical. In general, we'd want to think both that there's a real distinction marked by the classification of some propositions as true and others as false, and that it is a distinction which cannot generally be understood without reference to things which are not themselves propositions, so cannot be understood in intrinsicist or coherentist terms.

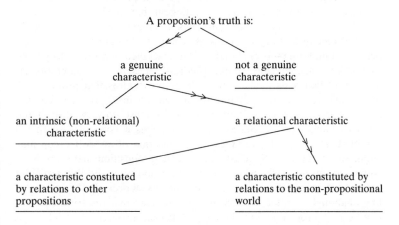

A proposition's truth is:

a genuine characteristic

not a genuine characteristic

an intrinsic (non-relational) characteristic

a relational characteristic

a characteristic constituted by relations to other propositions

a characteristic constituted by relations to the non-propositional world

Fig. XIII.1.

This piece of common sense is not to be confused with the idea that, understood one way, correspondence is nothing more than a platitude. The platitude is that predications of 'true' may always harmlessly be glossed in terms of correspondence to fact, telling it like it is, etc. These paraphrases incorporate no substantial commitment about the structure of truth—any more than the paraphrasability of 'she did it for John' by 'she did it on John's behalf' involves a commitment to the view that altruistic action is really a three-term relation. By contrast, the ordinary, commonsensical conception of the kind of thing a proposition's truth is involves exactly the structural commitments associated with the feathered path on the tree shown in Fig. XIII.1.

It will be a second main contention of this chapter that there is no stable alternative to allowing at least some scope to this commonsensical conception.

III

In order to make good that contention, we need to see that each of the three alternatives gives rise to intractable problems.

Intrinsicism is the easiest case to deal with. Fix attention on the case of contingent truths. If its truth-value were an intrinsic—but contingent—property of a particular proposition, then no contingent change in any other object should entail change in the proposition in that particular respect. That's an instance of a quite general principle. The mass, for instance, of a given body is a contingent but intrinsic property of that body only if no contingent change in any other object would entail change in that object's mass. By contrast, a property—for instance, being a grandfather—is essentially relational, even if expressed by what looks like a semantically simple predicate, if change in other objects may entail that a particular object sheds, or acquires that property. By this simple test, truth is, manifestly, not an intrinsic property. For the truth-value of any contingent proposition must co-vary with hypothetical changes in the characteristics of things it concerns—so that a hypothetical change, for instance, in the location of my coffee cup may entail an alteration in the truth-value of the proposition that there is no coffee cup on my desk, even though that proposition and the particular coffee cup in question are quite distinct existences. To be sure, this line of thought creates no difficulty for the idea that the truth-value of a *necessary* proposition might be an intrinsic property. So, indeed, it may be. But clearly intrinsicism cannot handle the general run of contingent cases.[8]

It might be rejoined that the canvassed account of the contrast between intrinsic and relational properties is incorrect or circular. For a property F may be an intrinsic characteristic of an object and yet its loss, say, may still be entailed by change in another object provided that latter change is permitted to be in *non-intrinsic respects*. For instance, if G is a ('Cambridge') property possessed by any object just in case *a* has intrinsic characteristic F, then any other object's losing G will entail that *a* has lost F. This observation is, however, beside the point. All the objection to intrinsicism needs is that the account be correct, not that it be explanatory. If it is at least granted that F is an intrinsic property of *a* just in case no *intrinsic* change in any other object can entail change in *a* in that respect, it will follow as before that truth cannot be an intrinsic property of any proposition whose content is that another object has some particular intrinsic but contingent property.

IV

It is a rather more complicated business to elicit what is fundamentally unsatisfactory about the deflationary conception of truth. The difficulties here are owing partly to the point that deflationism is more of a 'tendency' than a definite philosophical position, and different deflationists display differences of formulation and emphasis which make it hard to see what may be essential and what optional in their views. There are, however, a number of characteristic, interrelated claims: first

(i) that there is no property of truth which is an appropriate object of philosophical attention: something which we might try to analyse, or in whose structure we might be interested, or which might give rise to issues about objectivity. Contrary to the presupposition both of the traditional debate and of its revision canvassed above, there is *nothing* in which the truth of a proposition, e.g., consists. 'True' expresses no real property.[9]

---

[8] I do not know that anyone has ever seriously proposed an intrinsicist conception of truth quite generally.

[9] Horwich is more guarded on this than many writers in the deflationist tradition. But although he seems unwilling expressly to deny that truth is a property, it is not, he contends, a 'complex property'—not 'an ingredient of reality whose underlying essence will, it is hoped, one day be revealed by philosophical or scientific analysis' (*Truth*, 2). Thus there is, for Horwich, nothing to say about what truth really consists in; no real question for e.g. correspondence and coherence accounts to address themselves to.

That negative contention is then characteristically augmented by a variety
of considerations about the meaning or positive function of the word 'true';
for instance

  (ii) that, as applied to sentences, 'true' is just the device of *disquota-
       tion*—a device for affirming at the metalinguistic level (by locutions
       of the form: '*p*' is true) exactly what can be affirmed at the object-
       language level by an assertoric use of '*p*';
 (iii) that the disquotational scheme
            '*p*' is true ↔ *p*,
       (or if the primary grammar of 'true' is considered to be that of an
       operator on (or predicable of) propositions, the equivalence schema
            It is true that *p*/that *p* is true if and only if *p*)
       is (all but) a complete explanation of the meaning of 'true';
  (iv) that 'true' is just a device of endorsement—we only have any
       use for such a term because we sometimes choose to endorse
       propositions indirectly, without specifying their content ('The
       sixth sentence of *Remarks on the Foundations of Mathematics
       IV*, §3 is true' or 'Fermat's Last Theorem has turned out to
       be true') and sometimes want to endorse whole batches of pro-
       positions at once ('Almost everything Chancellor Kohl says is
       true'). In other kinds of case we can dispense with the word
       altogether.

Deflationism has been subjected to a variety of criticisms: for instance,
that its characteristic lionization of the disquotational scheme is in tension
with the manifest unacceptability of that principle when vagueness or
other phenomena leading to failures of bivalence are operative;[10] that it is
inconsistent with a truth-conditional conception of meaning or more generally with the semantic role of truth;[11] that it cannot accommodate the
idea of scientific progress; most generally, that it violates our intuitions
about correspondence, about truth as bestowed by fit with an external,
objective world.[12] Here I shall rehearse an argument I have given elsewhere to the effect that deflationism is internally unstable.[13] Specifically,
there is a contradiction between the kind of account of the function of
'true' which deflationists broadly want to give and the contention that

---

[10] This criticism is first lodged, I believe, in Michael Dummett's early paper, 'Truth',
Proceedings of the Aristotelian Society, 59 (1959), 141–62.
[11] This claim too is advanced in Dummett's 'Truth'.
[12] All these directions of criticism are usefully referenced and reviewed in Horwich's *Truth*.
[13] See Wright, *Truth And Objectivity* (Cambridge, Mass., 1992), ch. 1.

the concept of truth, properly understood, is not the concept of a genuine, substantial property.

Let us focus, for ease of exposition, on 'true' as predicable of propositions, and on the positive deflationist contention that, in its most basic use, the word is essentially a device of endorsement which, except in cases where the content of the proposition endorsed is not explicitly given, or where quantification over propositions is involved, may be dispensed with altogether in favour of a simple assertion of the proposition characterized as 'true'.

It is hardly deniable that 'true' does have this kind of function and that its uses may often be paraphrased away without materially affecting the content of what is said. The issue is rather whether the point can carry the intended deflationary implications. And the crucial question for that issue is, what is it to *endorse* a proposition? Endorsement generally involves an element of recommendation, or approval of an item as meeting a certain standard. That's what I'm doing when, for example, in helping my child choose an ice cream I point at the pistachio and say 'That's a nice one'. What kind of commendation is involved in the case of 'true'? Plausibly, that if I affirm a proposition's truth, I'm recommending its acceptance, commending it as meeting a certain doxastic standard, as it were. In this way, affirmations of truth—and likewise denials of truth—are normative claims. To endorse a proposition as true is to affirm that it is acceptable as a belief or statement; to deny that a proposition is true is to affirm that it's correspondingly unacceptable.

To be sure, nothing in that should impress as immediately uncomfortable for deflationism. No deflationist has wanted, or ought to have wanted, to deny that believing and statement-making are normatively constrained activities—activities governed by standards, non-compliance with which opens a thinker to criticism. However, once that is accepted, the question has to be confronted of what the relevant standards are. In particular, if 'true' is essentially just a device of endorsement, then in using it, I'm saying that a proposition is in good shape as far as certain relevant norms are concerned. What, for deflationism, are those norms?—what does 'good shape' here consist in?

Believing and stating are, naturally, subject to rather different norms. In very many contexts, justification for a belief is insufficient to confer justification for its public expression, partly because assertion is socially constrained—the public expression of a fully justified belief may give offence, or bore people, etc.—and partly because complex principles of conversational implication make it possible to encourage false beliefs in an audience by the judicious selection and assertion of fully justified ones.[14] However, if one wanted to criticize an assertion on this type of broadly social or pragmatic ground, one wouldn't do so by denying its truth. So, as a first approximation, it seems the deflationist should say that the use of 'true' in the basic kind of case is to endorse a proposition as *epistemically justified*, or to endorse an utterance as acceptable just insofar as the epistemic justification of the proposition it expresses is concerned.

In any case, what the deflationist clearly *cannot* allow is that 'true', when used to endorse, has the function of commending a proposition for its satisfaction of *some distinctive norm* which contrasts with epistemic justification and which only 'true' and equivalents serve to mark. For if there were a distinctive such norm, it could hardly fail to be reckoned a genuine property of a proposition that it did, or did not comply with it. And if the norm in question were uniquely associated with 'true' and its cognates, that would be as much as to allow that there was a special property of *truth*—at which point the deflationary game would have been given away. So for the deflationist, it appears, the basic use of 'true' has to be to signal a proposition's compliance with norms whose proper characterization will not proceed in terms of equivalents of 'true'. If it is propositions, rather than utterances, that we are concerned with, epistemic justification would then seem to be the only plausible candidate.[15]

It would follow that the basic use of 'not true' should be to signal a proposition's *non*-compliance with relevant norms of epistemic justification. But if that were so, there should in general be nothing to choose between the denial that a proposition is true and the denial that it is justified. And not only does that misrepresent the ordinary usage of the terms: it is inconsistent with principles to which deflationism itself is committed, and which are, indeed, at the heart of the deflationary account: the disquotational scheme and, its analogue for propositions, the equivalence schema.

I'll illustrate the relevant point as it flows from the latter. The schema provides that, for an arbitrary proposition p,

It is true that $p \leftrightarrow p$.

If we substitute 'not-p' for 'p' at both occurrences, we have

[14] The classic treatment of the phenomenon is, of course, H. P Grice's 'Logic and Conversation' repr. in *Studies in the Way of Words* (Cambridge, Mass., 1989).
[15] This would be less than a commitment to the idea that 'true' *means*: epistemically justified. There is a distinction between holding that a word expresses no property but is used to commend items for their possession of a certain property and holding that it expresses that very property.

It is true that not-p ↔ not-p,

while if we negate both sides, we derive

It is not true that p ↔ not-p.

And from the latter two principles, via transitivity of the biconditional, we have

It is not true that p if and only if it is true that not-p.

In brief: the equivalence schema entails, given only the most basic assumptions about its scope and about the logic of negation, that truth and negation commute as prefixes. Manifestly, this is not true in general of warrant and negation: there is, in general, no sound inference from

It is not the case that p is warranted,

to

It is the case that not-p is warranted.

This pattern of inference cannot be sustained in any case where the correctness of its premiss is owing to the *neutrality* of our state of information—to the fact that we have no evidence bearing either on p or its negation.

The equivalence schema itself, then, is a commitment to repudiating the idea that '. . . is not true' is a device for denying that a proposition complies with norms of warrant/justification—for if it were such a device, it ought not to commute with negation. But what other account can deflationism offer of what the denial of truth amounts to, given its express contention that '. . . is true' is merely a device of endorsement, so a device for affirming a proposition's compliance with some norm or other, and given that the only norms on the board—in a context in which the existence of any self-standing norm of truth has been rejected—are justificatory ones?[16]

---

[16] There is scope for some skirmishing. Ian Rumfitt has responded (in 'Truth Wronged', *Ratio*, NS 8 (1995), 100–7) that the divergence in the behaviour of 'true' and 'assertible' just noted may straightforwardly be accommodated in a fashion entirely consonant with the purposes of deflationism, without admission of a distinctive norm of truth, provided the deflationist is prepared to allow primitive norms of *warranted denial* to operate alongside those of warranted assertion. Rather, that is, than restrict his distinctive deflationary claims to the word 'true' the deflationist should contend '. . . that "is true" and "is not true" function purely as devices for endorsing *and rejecting* assertions, beliefs and so on . . . and which therefore register no norms distinct from justified assertibility *and justified deniability*' (ibid. 103; compare Wright, *Truth and Objectivity*, 30). How would this help to explain the commutativity of truth and negation? Rumfitt is not entirely explicit, but the point may seem clear enough. Since denying a statement is asserting its negation, a primitive warrant—an *anti-warrant* is Rumfitt's term—for the denial of p, registered by a claim of the form, it is not true that p, will be *eo ipso* a warrant for asserting the negation of p, so—via the disquotational scheme—for asserting that it is true that not-

In fact, it's intuitively perfectly evident that the use of 'true' *is* tied to a norm—to a way in which acceptance of a proposition may be in good, or bad standing—quite separate from the question of its justification in the light of the acceptor's state of information. An acceptance that grass is green, that is, may be open to censure if there is no warrant for accepting that grass is green; but it is in bad standing in quite another way if, warranted or not, it is actually not the case that grass is green. Correspondingly it is in good standing, in one way, just if accepted on the basis of sufficient justification, whether or not grass is green; but it is in good standing in another way if, irrespective of what justification may be possessed by the acceptor, grass is actually green. The concept of truth is a concept of a way a proposition may or may not be in good standing which precisely *contrasts* with its justificatory status at any particular time. That's the point which we've elicited from the equivalence schema. But it is independently evident, and any satisfactory philosophy of truth has to respect it.

There is no hope, then, for a deflationary account of truth which allows, or is anyway committed to the idea that 'true', in its most basic use, is a device for endorsing propositions as complying with other norms. A device of endorsement it may be, at least in the basic case. But the concept of the associated norm is of something *sui generis*.

Can the deflationist regroup? What the foregoing forces is an admission that, for each particular proposition, we have the concept of a norm which is distinct from warrant and is flagged by the word, 'true'. And once it's allowed that the role of 'true' is to mark a particular kind of achievement, or failing, on the part of a proposition, contrasting with its being warranted

---

p. So the problematical direction of commutativity is secured, while the invalidity of the corresponding principle for assertibility is vouchsafed, as before, by the possibility of states of information in which one has neither warrant nor anti-warrant for *p*.

However, the problem recurs. Consider again the problematical equivalence,

It is not true that *p* if and only if it is true that not-*p*.

and the result of negating both its sides:

It is not not true that *p* if and only if it is not true that not-*p*.

Supposing that the role of '(is) not true' were merely to register the presence of an anti-warrant, there seems no way of shirking the transition to

It is not anti-warranted that *p* if and only if it is anti-warranted that not-*p*.

But that, of course, is no less unacceptable when neutral states of information are possible than is

It is not warranted that *p* if and only if it is warranted that not-*p*.

In short, for any discourse in which neutral states of information are a possibility, the equivalence schema imposes a contrast both between 'is true' and 'is assertible'; *and* between 'is not true' and 'is anti-warranted'. Rumfitt's proposal that the deflationist should recognize anti-warrant as primitive—whatever its independent interest—is thus of no assistance with her present difficulty.

or not, there will have to be decent sense in the question, what does such an achievement, or failing, amount to? To be sure, that is a question which may turn out to admit of no very illuminating or non-trivial answer—but if so, that would tend to be a point in favour of Frege's indefinabilism, rather than deflationism. If a term registers a distinctive norm over a practice, the presumption ought to be that there will be something in which a move's compliance or non-compliance with that norm will consist. And whichever status it has, that will then be a real characteristic of the move. So what room does deflationism have for manoeuvre?

There are two possibilities. First, it might be contended that all, strictly, that has been noted—has been shown to follow from the equivalence schema—is that 'true' is so used as to *call for*—express—a norm over the acceptance of propositions which is distinct from warrant. It's quite another matter whether there *really is* such a norm—whether there really is such a way for a proposition to be in, or out of good standing. It's one thing for an expression to be used in the making of a certain distinctive kind of normative claim; quite another matter for there to be such a thing as a bearer's *really qualifying for* a judgement of that kind. An error-theorist about morals, for example, like John Mackie,[17] would presumably readily grant that moral language is *used* normatively—is used to applaud, or censure, particular actions, for instance. What he will deny, nevertheless, is that there are any real characteristics which respond to this use—any real characteristics by possessing which an action may qualify for a deserved such appraisal.

It is easily seen that deflationism cannot avail itself of any counterpart of this first line of defence. For the deflationist must surely be quite content to allow that all manner of statements *really are true*—when the right circumstances obtain: that grass is green, for instance, really is true just when grass is green; that snow is white really is true just when snow is white; that the earth's orbit is an ellipse is true just in case the earth's orbit really is an ellipse; and so on. For deflationism, there has to be, for each proposition—or at least for those of an objective subject matter—*an objective condition*, namely the very one specified by the appropriate instance of the equivalence schema, under which it qualifies as true. So there is no possibility of refuge in error theory in this context. The equivalence schema itself determines what the conditions of rightful application of 'true' to a particular proposition, p, are; if as a matter of fact they obtain, then this, coupled with the distinctive normativity of the predicate, enforces the recognition that there really is such a thing as p's complying, or failing to

---

[17] *Ethics: Inventing Right and Wrong* (Harmondsworth, 1977).

comply with the distinctive norm of truth. It is not merely that our concept of truth calls for such a norm; the call is answered.[18]

We should conclude that two characteristic claims of deflationism are lost. It is not true, first, that 'true' *only* functions as a device of (indirect, or compendious) endorsement—it also functions, for each proposition, to advert to the satisfaction of a distinctive norm, whose satisfaction is—at least for a proposition with an objective subject matter—a real matter of fact. Second, it is hard to hear a distinction between that last point and the admission that truth, for each such proposition, is a real property. But there is still a final line of defence—one last characteristic deflationary claim which a proponent might try to salvage. The question remains so far open whether the property in question should be regarded as *the same* in all cases. Perhaps the deflationist can dig a last ditch here. For if the property were not the same, we might yet have the resources to undercut the classical debates about the *general* constitution of truth; and that those debates were bad was one major point that deflationism wanted to make.

A line of thought with that tendency is nicely expressed by Simon Blackburn as follows:

... compare 'is true', ... with a genuine target of philosophical analysis: 'is conscious', or 'has rights', for example. We investigate these by looking for the principles which determine whether something is conscious, or has rights. These principles are intended to govern any such judgement, so that we get a unified class: the class of conscious things, or things that have rights. Each item in such a class is there because it satisfies the same condition, which the analysis has uncovered. Or, if this is slightly idealized, we find only a 'family' of related conditions or 'criteria' for the application of the term. Still, there is then a family relationship between the members of the class. But now contrast 'is true'. We know *individually* what makes this predicate applicable to the judgements or sentences of an understood language. 'Penguins waddle' is a sentence true, in English, if and only if penguins waddle. It is true that snow is white if and only if snow is white. The reason the first sentence deserves the predicate is that penguins waddle, and the reason why the judgement that snow is white deserves the predicate is that snow *is* white. But these reasons are entirely different. There is no single account, or even little family of accounts, in virtue of which each deserves the predicate, for deciding whether penguins waddle has nothing much in common with deciding whether snow is white. There are *as* many different things to do, to decide whether the predicate applies, as there are judgements to make. So how *can* there be a unified, common account of the 'property' which these quite different decision procedures supposedly determine? We might say: give us any sentence about whose truth you are interested, and simply

---

[18] This simple observation is a partial response to a recent tendency of Richard Rorty's, namely to dismiss those features of our practice with 'true' which are recalcitrant to 'pragmatist' interpretation as mere reflections of the concept's absorption of a misguided representationalist metaphysic. See e.g. his 'Is Truth a Goal of Enquiry? Davidson *vs.* Wright', *Philosophical Quarterly*, 45 (1995), 281–300. But it is to be expected, of course, that he would refuse to hear any but a metaphysically inflated reading of 'an objective subject matter'.

by 'disquoting' and removing the reference to truth, we can tell you what you have to judge in order to determine its truth. Since we can do this without any analysis or understanding of a common property of truth, the idea that there is such a thing is an illusion.[19]

Blackburn here captures with characteristic felicity a thought which has unquestionably influenced many deflationists—(though he does not himself explicitly endorse it). However, it surely provides no very good reason for the intended conclusion—that truth is no single property. For the pattern it calls attention to is a commonplace, exemplified by a host of properties which we should not scruple to regard as unitary, or as potentially open to philosophical account. *Many* properties, that is, are such that their satisfaction conditions vary as a function of the character of a potential bearer. Consider the property of having fulfilled one's educational potential. What it takes to instantiate this will depend naturally on other characteristics of the individual concerned; but that ought to be quite consistent with the substantiality and commonality of the property in question since there is a clear sense in which anyone who has fulfilled his educational potential has done the same thing as anyone else who has done so, and what they have both done may be expected straightforwardly to allow of a uniform account. In general, how x has to be in order to be F can depend in part on how things stand in other respects with x, and vary accordingly, without any motive thereby being provided for regarding it as an error to suppose, or to try to characterize, a general condition which being F involves satisfying. Otherwise you might just as well say that there is no single thing in which being twice as old as one's oldest child consists (being a *doubletenarian*) since for me it would involve being twice as old as Geoffrey, for Prince Charles being twice as old as William, and for Blackburn being twice as old as Gwen.

The general pattern, it should be evident, is that of properties whose satisfaction consists in an individual's meeting a condition implicitly involving existential quantification over the right field of a relation. To fulfil one's educational potential is for there to be certain levels of academic attainment such that under certain normal educational conditions it is possible for one to meet them, and such that one has met them. To be twice as old as one's oldest child is for there to be some individual of whom one is a father or mother and whose actual age is half one's own. In general, to be the bearer of such a property will be to stand in a relation of a certain kind to an appropriate instance or instances of this implicit quantifier, and the identity of that instance or instances may vary depending on the identity

[19] From *Spreading the Word* (Oxford, 1984), 230–1.

and character in other respects of the bearer in question. It is in the *nature* of properties of this general character to admit such variation, and it compromises their unity not at all.

There is accordingly no comfort for a deflationist in the platitude that how things have to be in order for particular propositions to be true varies. Propositions vary in *how they claim matters to stand*—as parents vary in how old their children are, or people vary in what their educational potential is—and propositions' truth-values will naturally be a function of the specific such claims they make. To impose the rubric explicitly: for any proposition p, it is true that p just in case *there is a way things could be* such that anyone who believed, doubted, etc. that p would believe, doubt, etc. that things were that way, and things are that way.[20] This paraphrase is doubtless wholly unilluminating—it offers little more than a long-hand version of the correspondence platitude. Its merit is to serve as a reminder how truth is naturally conceived to share a conceptual shape with e.g. doubletenarianship, or fulfilment of educational potential, and thus to bring out why no conclusions follow about its integrity from the line of thought outlined in Blackburn's remarks.

A sympathizer with deflationism may essay a final throw. It may be contended that the position at which we have arrived, although inconsistent with the traditional formulations of deflationism, is still nothing terribly at odds with its spirit. Maybe it has to be recognized that truth is a property after all, contrasting with justification, and normative over assertion and belief. But the conviction of the traditional debate is that it is a *metaphysically deep* property, whose essence is unobvious and controversial. By contrast, the characterization of it now offered by way of rebuttal of the tendency of Blackburn's remarks is nothing if not obvious and *trivial*; and this triviality surely just as effectively cuts the ground from under the traditional debate as would the findings that truth is no unified property, or no property at all. The victory over deflationism is therefore pyrrhic: the skirmishing has led us to say what truth in general is in such a way as to drain all metaphysical interest from the question in the process.[21]

Someone inclined to resist this would not be prudent to stake all on the possibility of a less trivial account of truth. Where the rejoinder goes astray is in its oversight, rather, of the contrast, drawn at the start, between the project of analysis of the concept of truth and the debate about the structure and objectivity of the property of truth. One meritorious claim in the

[20] For truth as a property of sentences, the rubric might naturally be applied to issue in something along the lines: for any sentence, s, an utterance of s in a particular context is true just in case there is a proposition, that p, which such an utterance would express, and which is true.

[21] Compare the remarks of Horwich quoted in n. 9, above.

deflationist portfolio—though not its exclusive possession—may well be that the success of any purported analysis of the concept must pay a price in terms of triviality. But the above account of truth for propositions, trivial as it may be, simply does not engage the structural alternatives charted earlier nor the debate they delimit. Anyone who has mastered the concept of truth and does not scruple to quantify over 'ways things could be' can accept it as necessary and sufficient for the truth of a proposition that there be a way things could be which anyone who believes that proposition will suppose realized, and which is indeed realized. To accept that much enjoins so far no commitment on the matter of what kind of characteristic—intrinsic, relational (if so, what are the terms of the relation?), etc.—the truth of a proposition is, nor on whether or to what extent its possession may be viewed as objective. Exactly those are the metaphysically substantial matters.

V

The third and last alternative to a correspondence account of the structure of truth is coherentism. Here is an expression of an old and sometime very influential objection to the coherence theory:

> . . . the objection to the coherence theory lies in this, that it presupposes a more usual meaning of truth and falsehood in constructing its coherent whole, and that this more usual meaning, though indispensable to the theory, cannot be explained by means of the theory. The proposition 'Bishop Stubbs was hanged for murder' is, we are told, not coherent with the whole of truth or with experience. But that means, when we examine it, that something is *known* which is inconsistent with this proposition. Thus what is inconsistent with the proposition must be something *true*: it may be perfectly possible to construct a coherent whole of *false* propositions in which 'Bishop Stubbs was hanged for murder' would find a place. In a word, the partial truths of which the whole of truth is composed must be such propositions as would commonly be called true, not such as would commonly be called false; there is no explanation, on the coherence theory, of the distinction commonly expressed by the words *true* and *false*, and no evidence that a system of false propositions might not, as in a good novel, be just as coherent as the system which is the whole of truth.[22]

The Right Reverend W. Stubbs died of natural causes. Russell's point is that we may nevertheless envisage a comprehensive *fiction* part of which is that he was hanged for murder, and that in point of coherence such a fiction may very well stand comparison with what we take to be the truth.

---

[22] From pp. 33–4 of Bertrand Russell, 'On the Nature of Truth', *Proceedings of the Aristotelian Society*, 7 (1906–7), 28–49.

In order, then, to recover the idea that such a fiction *is* fiction, we need recourse to a notion of truth which the coherence account is powerless to explicate. Whatever 'coherence' is taken to involve in detail, it seems likely that mutually incompatible, equally comprehensive, internally coherent systems of beliefs will be possible; more, *any* self-consistent proposition is likely to participate in *some* coherent system of belief with whatever degree of comprehensiveness you want. So the coherence theory cannot discriminate truth from falsehood—and it cannot justify principles like (non-contradiction):

> if *p* is true, not-*p* is not true.

Yet surely any correct account of truth has to sustain such principles.

Notice that this objection in no way depends upon the detail of any particular proposed conception of coherence, and thus does not presuppose that the coherence account is being offered as an *analysis* of truth. The objection is purely structural. The driving thought is that whatever coherence is taken to consist in, the suggestion that the truth of a proposition consists in its participation in a coherent system in effect falls foul of a dilemma: if *fiction* can constitute such a system, then participation in such a system is clearly insufficient for truth. If it cannot, then it appears that truth is not constituted purely in interpropositional relations—the propositions in question have to meet some other condition, so far unexplicated, and Russell's hostile suggestion is that the only available such condition is: truth as ordinarily understood.

There are two possible lines of response. First, the coherentist may go relativist, conceding that there is indeed no *absolute* truth, and embracing the contention that, to the contrary, truth is relative to the system. Thus the proposition that Bishop Stubbs was hanged for murder can indeed be true, relevant to a sufficiently coherent and comprehensive body of propositions which includes it. What we are pleased to regard as *the* truth merely reflects the actually entrenched such system. Principles, like non-contradiction, which seem to require that the truth cannot extend to every conceivable coherent system of propositions, are misconstrued when taken to have that implication. Sure, they are valid *within* systems: no proposition can participate in a coherent system for which its negation is already a member. But they have no valid application *across* systems.

Alternatively, a coherentist might try to avoid this extreme and rather unappealing form of relativism by earmarking certain propositions as in some way *privileged*, and construing truth not as participation in any old sufficiently comprehensive, coherent system of propositions, but as participation in such a system which is required in addition to include the privileged propositions. To be sure, thinking of truth as having such a structure does not by itself guarantee its uniqueness. But the resources may be available to do so if the theorist chooses the privileged base class cannily and interprets the relation of coherence in some correspondingly suitable way. For instance, the base class might consist of a large sample of our most basic beliefs. Then what might ultimately defeat the truth, conceived as by coherence, of the proposition that Bishop Stubbs was hanged for murder would be its inability to participate in a maximally coherent and comprehensive system of belief incorporating that particular membership.

This manoeuvre, however, appears open to an extremely powerful objection. The objection does, admittedly, make an assumption about the general character of the interpropositional relationships which coherence, conceived as a structural proposal, might regard as important—albeit an assumption suggested by the very term 'coherence', and validated by all the actual proposals which have been made under its head. That assumption is that the relations in question are *internal* relations: that the coherence, or otherwise, of a system of propositions is grounded *purely in their content*. The salient question is then: how can any proposal of this kind handle *contingency*? The general form of account proposed is that *p*'s truth consists in its participation in a coherent system based on a specified base class, i.e. its coherence with the other propositions in that system. But that situation, when it obtains, should be a matter of relations of a purely internal character holding between *p* and the other propositions in the system. If *p* coheres with those propositions, it will therefore do so in *all possible worlds*. So how could the truth of *p*, when it is true, ever be a contingent matter?

There is only one possible line of response. If *p*, although true, could be false, and if its truth consists in its sustaining internal—necessary—relations to a system of propositions, then what contingency needs is the possibility of a switch in the system—a change in which are the propositions coherence with which determines truth—and the possibility that *p* may fail to cohere with the new system. If we say that a system is *dominant* if it is coherence with *it* that constitutes truth, then what contingency demands is flexibility in the matter of dominance. (Dominance might be interpreted just as a matter of incorporating lots of what we actually believe, and its flexibility would then be secured by the flexibility in the identity of our beliefs.)

Now, though, interestingly, we find we have come full circle with the re-emergence of a version of the Bishop Stubbs objection. All contingency is now being construed as turning on contingencies of dominance. So the obvious next question is: what properly coherentist account is to be given of the truth of a proposition of the form,

(K) S is dominant?

Naturally, the coherentist has to view the truth of an instance of K, like that of any true proposition, as a matter of its coherence with a system—but which system? Presumably any coherent system S will be such that it will cohere with S to suppose it is dominant even if it is not in fact so—if, for example, dominance is construed as a matter of what is actually believed, it ought in general to cohere perfectly with a system of beliefs that we do not in fact hold to suppose that we do hold them. So in general, for each comprehensive, coherent system S, whether dominant or not, the relevant instance of K will cohere with S with the consequence, first, that the fact of dominance—the actual truth-value of that instance—goes unrecovered; and second, that we remain powerless to explicate the contingency of a system's dominance, since the coherence of the relevant instance of K with the system in question will be a matter of necessity.

There is thus no prospect of explicating what it is for a proposition of the form, S is dominant, to be true in terms purely of relations of coherence if the truth in question is conceived as contingent—as it has to be, if contingency in general is to be recovered in terms of a coherentist account. What has to be said, it seems, is that for that proposition, like any other, truth is a matter of relations with *what is in fact* the dominant system. But then exactly the move has been made that Russell triumphantly anticipated: for this appeal to the notion of *what is in fact so* has not been, and apparently cannot be explicated in terms of coherence.

The upshot is that coherentism, taken as a proposal about the general nature of truth-constituting relations, has no means—provided the relations in question are all internal—to recover the notion of contingent truth except at the cost of, one way or another, an appeal to a notion of what is in fact true of particular belief systems (that they are based on what we mostly believe, or otherwise dominant in some sense to be supplied) whose contingency is taken for granted and whose obtaining cannot be construed in terms of coherence. In brief, coherentism demands exceptions to its own account.[23] It thus has nothing to offer as a general account of the structure of truth.[24]

---

[23] This moral is repeatedly emphasized in Ralph Walker's excellent study *Coherence Theory of Truth* (see n. 1, above).

[24] The explicit argument has been against a response to the original Bishop Stubbs objection—the privileging manoeuvre—which was canvassed as an alternative to relativism about truth. Briskly, then, to review how a similar difficulty afflicts the relativistic move. The relativist proposal has it that truth is always coherence with a system, but that there are thus as many

VI

We have now reviewed each of the three possible structural alternatives to a correspondence conception of truth, and found that each is subject to seemingly decisive difficulties. It may seem to have been established, accordingly, that among the four paths on the original tree, only the feathered path to the correspondence conception is viable—that, contra deflationism, our ordinary concept of truth requires us to think of a proposition's being true as, so to speak, a distinctive accomplishment, and that, contra intrinsicism and coherentism, we may not satisfactorily conceive of this accomplishment as an intrinsic property of a proposition or a characteristic conferred upon it by dint of its relation to other propositions. It would follow that even if no satisfactory *analysis* of truth in terms of correspondence can be given, we are nevertheless squarely committed to a correspondence *conception* of truth—that there is no alternative but to think of the truth of a proposition as conferred upon it, in the general case, by its relations to non-propositional reality.

That is, in effect, the second main contention of the chapter, which was earlier advertised. But two very important qualifications are needed here. First, in the traditional debate, as we remarked, the correspondence theory was conceived as expressing a form of metaphysical *realism*, standing opposed to the idealism which kept company with the coherence theory. It merits emphasis that even if the effect of the foregoing arguments is indeed to impose a conception of truth as conferred on a proposition by aspects of non-propositional reality,[25] that conclusion certainly carries no

---

versions of the truth as there are coherent comprehensive systems. Thus the proposition that Bishop Stubbs was hanged for murder, while unfit to participate in any comprehensive coherent system which is controlled by what we actually believe, may—presumably will—participate in other comprehensive and coherent systems. Well, we should now immediately press the question: what account has this relativism to offer of the truth of contingencies about belief—of propositions of the form, S is believed? Again, it should cohere with any particular coherent comprehensive system to suppose that it is in fact believed—so such a proposition should be true relative to each particular system. So now the fact of actual belief seems fugitive. Suppose there is a single comprehensive and coherent system, S, incorporating (most of) what we actually believe, and that the proposition that Bishop Stubbs was hanged for murder is not a participant. Consider by contrast such a system, S′, in which that proposition is a participant. Add to each the proposition that it is believed by most human beings. Clearly a Martian, presented only with axiomatizations of each system, would have no way of telling, just on the basis of facts about coherence, which, if either, we *did* believe. So the truth of the proposition, that it is S we believe, if constituted just in facts about coherence, must reside in other such facts. The relativist-coherentist will offer, presumably, that it will be a matter of coherence with the Martian's own beliefs. But that is to appeal to a non-reconstructed notion of *what is in fact believed* by the Martian—and it was exactly the counterpart fact about us that the proposal seems to have no means to construe. So there is no progress.

[25] Except in cases, naturally, where the proposition is actually about other propositions.

direct implications for the realism debate in its modern conception. For example, nothing is yet implied about the *nature* of the relations in question, so there is consequently no immediate implication of the idea that the truth of a proposition consists in its successfully *representing* an aspect of reality, in any distinctively realist sense of 'represent'. There may in general be no alternative to thinking of propositions as made true when they are true, by, *inter alia*, non-propositional matters. But there is so far no commitment to any specific general conception of the kind of relations that may be involved in truth, or of the nature of the non-propositional items in their fields. Any broad view which assigns a role in the constitution of truth to a domain outside the bearers of truth would be consistent with our findings; and that much most modern anti-realisms, for example those canvassed by Dummett and Putnam, certainly do. In particular, nothing is implied about *cognitivism*—about whether the factors involved in appraising truth are invariably wholly cognitive—nor about *evidential constraint*: about whether it is possible for truth to outrun all evidence available in principle. Someone who thought, for example, of moral truth as broadly a matter of what *we* find acceptable in the light of a full appreciation of the non-moral facts and certain non-cognitive dispositions to moral sentiment would be making no demands on the notion to take him off the feathered path; on such a view, moral truth would be a complex matter, but one essentially implicating certain relations to aspects of the non-propositional world. Likewise, a proponent of a broadly Peircian conception of truth, that truth is what would be agreed upon by thinkers operating under epistemically ideal conditions, would be quite at liberty to think of the status of such propositions as owing in part to the impingements of a non-propositional world which such thinkers would feel. In sum: our findings at this point have almost no impact on the second of the great issues associated with the classical debate about truth: the issues of realism and objectivity.

However—this is the second necessary qualification—there ought in any case, I believe, to be no presumption in favour of a *monistic* view of truth.[26] If the difficulties which we have been exploring are to dispose of all the alternatives to correspondence once and for all, then it needs to be assumed that truth everywhere must possess a *uniform constitution*: that the truth of any true proposition always consists in the same sort of thing.

---

[26] i.e. in favour of the view that truth everywhere consists in the same thing. (This kind of 'monism' about truth contrasts of course with that of Bradley and Joachim, for whom the thesis of monism is rather that reality is an intrinsically unified whole which is distorted when conceived as a totality of individual states of affairs, each apt to confer truth on a single proposition considered in isolation.)

Yet why should that be so? For instance, both intrinsicist and coherentist conceptions of truth fell into difficulty over the construal of contingent truth, but a proponent of either view could conceivably retrench if it could be argued that truth is only *sometimes* to be conceived as an intrinsic property of a proposition, or a property bestowed upon it by its relations of coherence with certain other propositions, while in other cases the structure of truth is best conceived as by correspondence. The upshot of the argument is that if truth has a single uniform constitution, then that constitution must be conceived along broadly correspondence lines. But what enforces the assumption of uniformity?

I think the answer is: nothing. In fact, an opposed pluralistic outlook is intuitively quite attractive. It is quite appealing, for instance, to think of the true propositions of number theory as those which sustain certain internal relations—an appropriate kind of semantic consequence—to a certain base class of propositions—the Dedekind–Peano axioms, for instance. Such an account, it should be noted, would extend to the axioms themselves (assuming the reflexivity of the relevant internal relation). What it would not comfortably extend to would be truths of the form: p is a Dedekind–Peano axiom (more generally, p is a member of the relevant base class). But once coherentism forswears the ambition to a *comprehensive* account of the structure of truth, that limitation need not be a difficulty. An account along broadly similar lines might also be attractive for truth as it applies to general moral principles (as opposed to their applications).

A pluralistic conception of truth is also philosophically attractive insofar as an account which allows us to think of truth as constituted differently in different areas of thought might contribute to a sharp explanation of the differential appeal of realist and anti-realist intuitions about them. But I acknowledge, of course, that more detail and a sharper theoretical setting is required for the proposal before it can really be clear that it makes genuine sense, let alone possesses merit. In particular, an account is owing of what would make it *truth* that allowed of variable forms of instantiation in different areas—what would make for the relevant *unity*. (This is not work that one might excuse oneself by pleading that truth is a 'family resemblance' concept, or whatever. Even that suggestion would at least require that there be a network of marks of truth, any true proposition qualifying as such by its exemplification of some sufficiently substantial set of them; and the task of characterizing these marks would remain.)

In order to clarify the cast which a defensible alethic pluralism might assume, it will help to revisit the conception, dominating the traditional debate, that the winning position would be the provision of a satisfactory necessary-and-sufficient-conditions analysis of the concept. Earlier, I was concerned to point out that scepticism about that project remained consistent with the interest of many of the questions, about structure and objectivity in particular, which provided the driving force of the traditional debate, and that these questions could survive in a setting in which the idea of analysis of the notion of truth had been abandoned altogether. Now though it is time to reconsider and qualify that scepticism. For misgivings about the project are driven by the particular conception we had in play of what a successful analysis—of truth, or anything—would have to accomplish. And on that score there is clearly some scope for relaxation. Such a necessary-and-sufficient-conditions analysis, after all, even if it could be provided, would only culminate in one particular a priori—presumably, conceptually necessary—claim. Why should not other such claims—even if not biconditional-, or identity-claims—not provide illumination of essentially the same kind? To be sure, if one wants conceptual clarity about what truth—or beauty, or goodness, etc.— is, then the natural target is an identity (or a biconditional). But perhaps the point of the inquiry can be equally if less directly served by the assembly of a body of conceptual truths which, without providing any reductive account, nevertheless collectively constrain and locate the target concept and sufficiently characterize some of its relations with other concepts and its role and purposes to provide the sought-for reflective illumination.

Faced, then, with the manifest improbability of an illuminating necessary-and-sufficient-conditions analysis of truth, there is still a different, more relaxed programme of analysis which we might undertake before despairing of the whole business and falling back on the issues to do with structure. This more relaxed project will see us trying to build an overall picture of the concept of truth—of its contents and purposes—by the assembly and integration of as wide a variety as possible of basic a priori principles about it—'platitudes', as I've elsewhere termed them.[27] What would such principles be for the case of truth?

The method here should be initially to compile a list, including anything that chimes with ordinary thinking about truth, and later to scrutinize more rigorously for deductive articulation and for whether candidates do indeed have the right kind of conceptual plausibility. So we might begin by including, for instance,

---

[27] The limitation to a priori cases effects, of course, a restriction on the standard lay use of 'platitude', which applies to anything which no one would dispute (and also carries an unwanted connotation of tedium).

: the transparency of truth—that to assert is to present as true and, more generally, that any attitude to a proposition is an attitude to its truth—that to believe, doubt or fear, for example, that p is to believe, doubt or fear that p is true. (*transparency*)

: the opacity of truth—incorporating a variety of weaker and stronger principles: that a thinker may be so situated that a particular truth is beyond her ken, that some truths may never be known, that some truths may be unknowable in principle, etc. (*opacity*)

: the conservation of truth-aptitude under embedding: aptitude for truth is preserved under a variety of operations—in particular, truth-apt propositions have negations, conjunctions, disjunctions, etc. which are likewise truth-apt. (*embedding*)

: the correspondence platitude—for a proposition to be true is for it to correspond to reality, accurately reflect how matters stand, 'tell it like it is', etc. (*correspondence*)

: the contrast of truth with justification—a proposition may be true without being justified, and vice versa. (*contrast*)

: the timelessness of truth—if a proposition is ever true, then it always is, so that whatever may, at any particular time, be truly asserted may—perhaps by appropriate transformations of mood, or tense—be truly asserted at any time. (*timelessness*)

: that truth is absolute—there is, strictly, no such thing as a proposition's being more or less true; propositions are completely true if true at all. (*absoluteness*)

The list might be enlarged,[28] and some of these principles may anyway seem controversial. Moreover it can be argued that the equivalence schema underlies not merely the first of the platitudes listed—transparency—but the correspondence platitude[29] and, as we have seen in discussion of deflationism, the contrast platitude as well.

There's much to be said about this general approach, and many hard and interesting questions arise, not least, of course, about the epistemological provenance of the platitudes. But such questions arise on *any* conception of philosophical analysis, which must always take for granted our ability to recognize truths holding a priori of concepts in which we are interested.

Let us call an analysis based on the accumulation and theoretical organization of a set of platitudes concerning a particular concept an

---

[28] One possible addition is reviewed in Sect. VII, below.

[29] For elaboration of this claim, see Wright, *Truth and Objectivity*, 24–7.

analytical theory of the concept in question.[30] Then the provision of an analytical theory of truth in particular opens up possibilities for a principled pluralism in the following specific way: that in different regions of thought and discourse *the theory may hold good, a priori, of—may be satisfied by—different concepts*. If this is so, then always provided the network of platitudes integrated into the theory were sufficiently comprehensive, we should not scruple to say that truth may consist in different things in different such areas: in the instantiation of one concept in one area, and in that of a different concept in another. For there will be nothing in the idea of truth that is not accommodated by the analytical theory, and thus no more to a concept's being a concept of truth than its furnishing a model of the ingredient platitudes. In brief: the *unity* in the concept of truth will be supplied by the analytical theory; and the *pluralism* will be underwritten by the fact that the principles composing that theory admit of collective variable realization.

One important question is whether any unmistakably coherentist conception of truth is indeed such a truth-realizer for a particular region of thought.[31] Another candidate I have explored elsewhere[32] is the notion of *superassertibility*. A proposition is superassertible just in case someone investigating it could, in the world as it actually is, arrive at a state of information in which its acceptance was justified, which justification would then persist no matter how much more relevant information was acquired. Clearly a notion of this kind must make sense wherever the corresponding notion of justification makes sense—wherever we have a concept of what it would be to justify a particular proposition, it will be intelligible to hypothesize the attainment of such a justification and its stability through arbitrarily extensive further investigation. It turns out that in any region of discourse meeting certain constraints, superassertibility will satisfy each of the platitudes listed above, so a prima-facie case can be made that,

---

[30] Readers familiar with Michael Smith's work will note a point of contact here with the conception of a *network analysis* which he derives from Ramsey and Lewis; (see esp. ch. 2, sect. 10 of Smith's *The Moral Problem* (Oxford, 1994)). The principal contrast with the approach to truth here canvassed is that a network analysis has to be based on a comprehensive set of platitudes whose conjunction so constrains the target concept that the replacement within them of all expressions for that concept by a variable and its binding by the description operator results in a definite description which is at the service of an analytically true identity,

$$\Phi\text{—ness is the property, F, such that } \{\ldots F \ldots \& \ldots F \ldots \& \ldots\}$$

which thus effectively supplies a reductive analysis of the concept Φ. An analytical theory, by contrast, need not—though it may—subserve the construction of such an analytically true identity.

[31] For exploration of one local case—arithmetic—see the Appendix.

[32] In *Truth and Objectivity*, ch. 2; an earlier discussion is in ch. 14, 'Can a Davidsonian Meaning-Theory be Construed in terms of Assertibility' of Wright, *Realism, Meaning and Truth* (2nd edn., Oxford, 1993).

with respect to those regions, the concept of superassertibility is a truth concept.[33] In these areas, it is consequently open to us to regard truth as consisting in superassertibility. In other areas, by contrast, where the relevant background conditions arguably fail—in particular, if we can see that there is no essential connection between truth and the availability of evidence—then the concept of truth will not allow of interpretation in terms of superassertibility, and the constitution of truth must accordingly be viewed differently. It is perhaps superfluous to remark that a superassertibilist conception of truth chimes very nicely with the semantic anti-realism which Michael Dummett has presented as a generalization of mathematical intuitionism, whose cardinal thesis may indeed be taken to be that truth is *everywhere* best construed in terms of superassertibility.

To be sure, the method of analysis incorporated in the analytic-theoretical approach is, as far as it goes, consistent with a monistic view of the target concept—but the approach cautions against prejudice in that respect since such an account, may, in any particular case, prove to allow of multiple realization. That's a matter which will depend on the detail of the account, on whether it includes all relevant platitudes, and on whether the concept in question may justifiably be taken to have further components which are necessarily omitted by such an account (for instance, a component fixed by ostensive definition). Here, I have meant only to sketch how a principled pluralism about truth might conceivably emerge.

VII

I conclude by noting a different potential corollary of the analytic-theoretical approach to truth. If its satisfaction of the platitudes suffices for a concept to be a concept of truth, then wherever we can introduce a concept which is such a satisfier with respect to a particular class of contents, that fact on its own will justify us in regarding the contents in question as *apt for truth*. Or put another way: wherever the word 'true' operates in a fashion agreeable to each of the theorems of a satisfactory analytical theory, then we should think of it as expressing a genuine concept of truth, and of the contents being expressed as genuinely truth-apt accordingly. And this will always be so just when we are dealing with contents which meet certain constraints of syntax and discipline. Roughly: the contents in

---

[33] For relevant details see the Appendix.

question must allow for combination and recombination under the connectives—negation, the conditional, conjunction, disjunction—of ordinary sentential inference; they must allow of embedding within expressions of ordinary propositional attitudes; and their affirmation must be subject to recognized standards of warrant.[34] If that is right, then it falls out of the very analysis of the notion of truth that the aptitude for truth is a comparatively promiscuous property. Comic, moral, aesthetic, and legal discourses, for instance, all exhibit the requisite syntax and discipline and so presumably pass the test. The upshot is thus a tension with one traditional form of anti-realism about such discourses: the idea, typified by 'expressivism' in ethics, that a target discourse whose surface exhibition of these features is not questioned may nevertheless not really be dealing in truth-apt contents—in 'genuine' propositions—at all.

However some recent critics[35] have objected that this upshot depends on focusing only on a selection of the platitudes which constrain the notions of truth and assertion, and ignoring in particular equally platitudinous connections of those notions with *belief*. Their thought is that one may be forced to look below the propositional surface of e.g. ethical discourse if one takes it as a platitude that an assertion is a profession of belief[36] but also accepts, with Hume, that no belief can be, in and of itself, a *motivational* state and regards it as clear that whatever is professed by an ethical 'assertion', it *is* such a motivational state.

One who advances this line of thought need not, it merits emphasis, be offering any criticism of the analytic-theoretical approach to truth as such.

---

[34] How does it follow that a satisfier of the platitudes will be definable on such contents? Very straightforwardly. First, if we are dealing with a range of genuine contents—to the extent ensured by the hypothesis of discipline—for which we have the conditional construction, then nothing can stand in the way of the definitional introduction of a predicate, or operator which is subject to the equivalence schema:

That p is Φ if and only if p.

As noted, that will then suffice for versions of transparency, contrast, the minimal degree of opacity that attends contrast, and a correspondence platitude for Φ. It will further be open to us to insist that Φ be defined for all combinations of specified kinds of the contents in question and thereby secure embedding. Assuming that the contents in question allow of tensed expression, timelessness—effectively the principle that whatever may truly be thought or expressed at any particular time may, by appropriate variations of tense, be truly thought or expressed at every time—may be secured by stipulating that Φ is to be governed by analogues of the usual truth-value links between differently tensed counterparts. (If the contents in question are tenseless, then timelessness will hold by default.) Absoluteness, for its part, will hold by default in any case unless we explicitly fix the use of a comparative.

[35] e.g. F. Jackson, G. Oppy, and M. Smith, in their 'Minimalism and Truth Aptness', *Mind*, 103 (1994), 287–302.

[36] Of course, an assertion may be insincere. For an utterance to be a *profession* of a certain state means that one who accepts its sincerity must be prepared to ascribe that state to the utterer.

Moreover the general point being made is obviously perfectly fair: conclusions drawn from a proposed analytic theory of a concept are, of course, liable to be vitiated if that theory omits to recognize what are in fact valid conceptual ties between the target concept and others. But what of the specific objection?

It might seem that the only clean way to dispose of it would be to controvert one of its two auxiliary premises; that is, to argue directly that certain kinds of belief *are* intrinsically motivational after all[37] or to make a case that the attitudes expressed by sincere ethical claims are, appearances notwithstanding, not *intrinsically* motivational.[38] However it is not, on reflection, evident that it is necessary to take on either of those projects (even if either might very well succeed). Rather, the anti-expressivist may respond that, insofar as the questions, whether a belief can be, in and of itself, a motivational state, and whether the states professed by ethical utterances are indeed intrinsically motivational, are taken to be open, philosophically substantial questions, to that extent it is simply *not* a platitude that the assertion of any truth-apt content is a profession of belief. Or better: for one who accepts that those issues are open, *belief* is not the notion in terms of which to articulate the platitude which lurks in the vicinity. Instead, an alternative expression can be found by taking over for the purpose a term which Simon Blackburn conveniently introduces in his writings on these issues: *commitment*.[39] Blackburn's 'commitments' are typically expressed by indicative sentences; they may be argued for and against, reasoned to and from, accepted, doubted, and entertained. So the notion ought to provide everything here required: the relevant platitude is, in effect, that the assertion of any truth-apt content is the profession of a commitment. Since the two auxiliary premises are not simultaneously good for commitments, the objection accordingly lapses.

Someone who sympathizes with the view that only some commitments are pukka *beliefs* owes an account of what is distinctive of the narrower class. I know of no reason to reject out of hand the suggestion that a worthwhile such distinction may exist; and if it exists, the annexure of the term 'belief' to the narrower class might conceivably be a well-motivated linguistic *reform*. Until then, the fact remains that our ordinary practice does not scruple to use 'belief' across the range of cases where the expressivist would have us worry about it; and the anti-expressivist is free to respond

---

[37] This is a view often taken to be defended by John McDowell; see his 'Are Moral Requirements Hypothetical Imperatives?', *Proceedings of the Aristotelian Society*, suppl. vol. 52 (1978), 13–29.

[38] Michael Smith himself eventually takes such a view in *Moral Problem*.

[39] See *Spreading the Word, passim* but esp. chs. 5 and 6.

to the objection by charging that it is only with this more generous notion that there is a platitudinous connection with assertion, and that the two auxiliary premisses which the objection exploits cannot both be acceptable if it is the more generous notion of belief that is in play.

APPENDIX

Two Illustrative Satisfiers of the Platitudes for Truth

We shall reckon with just the seven platitudes proposed above: transparency, opacity, embedding, correspondence, contrast, timelessness, and absoluteness. First, we note the following dependencies:

(i) *Transparency* is tantamount to the validity of the equivalence schema,

It is true that p if and only if p,

for all propositional contents, p, which in turn ensures that of the disquotational scheme,

'p' is true if and only if p,

assuming only the validity of the corresponding instance of

'p' says that p,

and the stipulation that the truth of a sentence is to enjoin and be enjoined by that of the proposition it expresses.

(ii) *Correspondence* is a platitude, whether for propositions or for sentences, only if suitably neutrally interpreted—that is interpreted so as to be neutral on the status of the correspondence *theory*. As a platitude it thus carries no commitment to a real ontology of facts—'sentence-shaped' worldly truth-conferrers—nor to any seriously representational construal of 'correspondence', but merely claims that talk of truth may be paraphrased by any of a variety of kinds of correspondence idiom. We may thus take the correspondence platitude for propositions to be, for example, this:

(CPP) It is true that p if and only if matter stand in conformity with the proposition that p.

CPP is an immediate consequence of the equivalence schema, together with the analogous equivalence controlling the correspondence idiom itself:

Matters stand in conformity with the proposition that p if and only if p.

Likewise the correspondence platitude for sentences may suitably neutrally be taken to be:

(CPS) 'p' is true if and only if matters stand as 'p' says they do.

Now wherever we have that

'p' says that p,

it follows that

Matters stand as 'p' says they do if and only if p.

CPS is immediate from the last together with the disquotational scheme.[40]

(iii) *Contrast*—the contrast between truth and justification—is straightforwardly derived from the equivalence schema (or disquotational scheme) together with

---

[40] For parallel discussion, see Wright, *Truth and Objectivity*, 25–7.

embedding (specifically, its instance that every truth-apt content has a negation which is likewise truth-apt) and a very basic proof theory for negation. For propositions, the derivation runs as follows. Negation of both halves of the equivalence schema provides that

> It is not true that p if and only if not p,

while substitution of 'not p' for 'p' at each of its occurrences in the equivalence schema provides that

> It is true that not p if and only if not p.

Transitivity of the biconditional then yields what I termed the negation equivalence,

> It is not true that p if and only if it is true that not p

—the commutativity of truth and negation. It then suffices for contrast to reflect that, for any range of propositions for which neutral states of information are a possibility, negation does *not* commute with justification. For in such a neutral state, a lack of justification for p precisely does not convert into justification for its negation.

The upshot, then, is that our illustrations need address only the following: the equivalence schema, opacity, embedding, timelessness, and absoluteness.

Illustration I: pure arithmetical truth conceived as coherence

Assume a language, L, containing just the usual resources of first-order logic with identity plus the non-logical constants: Nx ('x is a natural number'), Sx ('the immediate successor of x'), and the decimal numerals, '0', '1', '2', '3', etc. Take as the coherence-base, **B**, the Peano axioms suitably formulated in this language, say as:

(i) N(0)
: Zero is a number
(ii) $(\forall x)\,(Nx \rightarrow NSx)$
: Every number is immediately succeeded by a number
(iii) $(\forall x)\,(\forall y)\,(\forall z)\,(\forall w)(Nx\&Ny \rightarrow (Sx = Sy \rightarrow x = y))$
: Numbers are the same if their successors are the same
(iv) $(\forall x)\,(Nx \rightarrow \neg 0 = Sx)$
: Zero is not a successor
(v) $(F0 \,\&\, (\forall x)\,((Nx \,\&\, Fx) \rightarrow FSx))) \rightarrow (\forall x)\,(Nx \rightarrow Fx)$
: Any characteristic possessed by zero and by the successor of any number which possesses it is possessed by all numbers

plus the standard recursive clauses for '+' and '×':

(vi) $(\forall x)\, x + 0 = x$
(vi) $(\forall x)\,(\forall y)\, x + Sy = S(x + y)$
(vii) $(\forall x)\, x \times 0 = 0$
(viii) $(\forall x)(\forall y)\, x \times Sy = (x \times y) + x$

and axioms to govern the definition of the regular decimal numerals from '1' onwards in terms of iterations of 'S' on '0'.

The proposal, then, is that a statement's being a *pure arithmetical truth of first-order* may be identified with its *cohering with* **B**. How is coherence here to be understood? Intuitively all the significant statements of first-order number theory fall into one of two classes: a *simple-arithmetical* base class whose members draw on no expressive resources save the numerals, the expressions for addition, multiplication and identity, and expressions for other operations which may be (recursively) defined in terms of those notions; and a remainder, each of which can be formed by (iterated) introductions of the logical constants into sentences of the base class in accordance with the standard first-order formation rules. From a classical point of view, it is quite intuitive that the truth-value of every first-order pure arithmetical sentence *supervenes upon* the truth-values of sentences in the base class: specifically, determine the truth-value of each of the latter and you have implicitly settled the truth-value of every pure arithmetical thought which may be expressed at first-order. (The crucial point, of course, is that simple arithmetic has the resources to name every element in the domain of quantification of full first-order arithmetic.) A natural version of truth as coherence, which should be attractive to those of broadly formalist disposition, simply follows through on this intuition, characterizing the coherence of simple-arithmetical sentences in terms of their syntactic derivability from ingredients in **B**, and that of the remainder in accordance with the sort of recursive clauses familiar from standard truth theories. It could run like this:

(i) If A is a simple-arithmetical sentence of L, then A coheres with **B** just if A may be derived from elements of **B** in standard (classical) first-order logic with identity.

(ii) If Ax is any open sentence of L in one free variable, x, and A is $(\forall x)Ax$, then A coheres with **B** just if each of $A0, A1, A2, \ldots$, coheres with **B**.

(iii) If Ax is any open sentence of L in one free variable, x, and A is $(\exists y)(Ay)$, then A coheres with **B** just if at least one of $A0, A1, A2, \ldots$, coheres with **B**.

(iv) If A is B&C, then A coheres with **B** just if both B and C cohere with **B**.

(v) If A is B $\vee$ C, then A coheres with **B** just if either B coheres with **B** or C coheres with **B**.

(vi) If A is B $\rightarrow$ C, then A coheres with **B** just if it is not the case that A coheres with **B** and C does not.

(vii) If A is ¬B, then A coheres with **B** just if B does not.

To the platitudes, then. First does this proposal validate the equivalence schema? Can it be affirmed, for all first-order expressible pure arithmetical statements, p, that

(E^C) p coheres with **B** if and only if p?

Dialectically, the status of a positive answer is somewhat akin to that of Church's thesis, that all effectively calculable arithmetical functions are general recursive. A formal proof of Church's thesis would demand some independent formal characterization of the effectively calculable functions—the very thing that Church's thesis purports to provide. Likewise a proof of (E^C) would demand some independent characterization of the first-order arithmetical truths. So, as with Church's thesis, it seems it cannot be definitely excluded that *intuitive* counterexamples to (E^C) might be forthcoming: sentences of the relevant kind which intuitively ought to rank as true yet which there is no reason to regard as cohering with **B** in the light of the stated clauses; or conversely, sentences which intuitively ought *not* to count as true, yet which do apparently so cohere. What can be said to make it plausible that there are no such cases?

Well, if (E^C) did have counterexamples, then—assuming the consistency of **B**—they could not come from within simple arithmetic, which comprises a complete and consistent system which is axiomatized within **B**. So their provenance would have to be of one of two kinds. *Either* truth in first-order arithmetic does not supervene upon simple-arithmetical truth—so that some arithmetical truths are determined by factors beyond the truth-value assignments in simple arithmetic and the semantics of the constants. That is surely excluded by the fact that '0', '1', and their suite collectively name everything in the domain. *Or* conversely, coherence as characterized outruns arithmetical truth (as it would if **B** were inconsistent or if, say, some quite different—perhaps intuitionistic—account of the truth conditions of universally quantified arithmetical sentences was thought appropriate than that which informs clause (ii)). Prescinding from the scenario of inconsistency, then, it does seem reasonable to doubt—or at least that one of realist inclination should doubt—that intuitive counterexamples of either kind will be forthcoming.

Of course, some kinds of arithmetical realist will doubtless regard truth, so characterized, as at best merely *extensionally equivalent* with the real thing. But even for such a realist, the coincidence in extension would be necessary. What, if anything, is wrong with the coherentist account would not be its extensional inaccuracy.

(ii) How much opacity should be required of a truth predicate is controversial but the arithmetical coherentist proposal is generous on this score. Matters of syntactic derivability, even though effectively decidable, can be mistaken or unknown by any single competent judge, or group of judges, in practice. And the presence of clause (ii) ensures that coherence in effect follows the omega rule, so that the proposal is hospitable to the idea that some arithmetical truths may be unknowable in principle.

(iii) Embedding: any statement couched purely in first-order arithmetical vocabulary can be regarded as in the relevant sense apt to cohere with the Peano axioms. Since the logical constants are part of that vocabulary, aptitude for coherence with the Peano axioms is thus conserved under the usual logical operations.

(iv) Timelessness: relations of coherence as defined are eternal.

(v) Absoluteness: relations of coherence as defined do not admit of degree.

Illustration II: truth conceived as superassertibility

Recall that a statement is superassertible just in case it is justified by some accessible state of information and will continue to be so justified no matter how that state of information is improved. (When I is such a state of information with respect to a statement, S, I shall say that I is S-stable.) Superassertibility models the truth platitudes under three assumptions concerning the region of discourse, D, with which we are concerned:

(I) that it is a priori that all truths of D are *knowable*;
(II) that the states of information which specifically bear on the characteristic claims of D are of a timelessly accessible kind;
(III) that it is a necessary condition of knowledge (at least of the subject matter of D, if not in general) that it exists only where a claimant does not thereby lay themselves open to a charge of irrationality.

(I) is a repudiation of evidence-transcendent truth for D. (II) has the effect that the opportunity for justification of a particular claim within D is never ephemeral but remains eternally open in principle for any suitable enquirer, no matter what her circumstances. (Note, however, the qualification: *suitable* enquirer. Suitability may demand, in particular, a certain innocence. It may be impossible for one who *knows too much* to justify a certain statement, even though evidence speaking defeasibly on its behalf is timelessly available.) (II) also implies that states of information may be conceived as *additive*—accessing one such state never costs you in principle the opportunity to access another (though again, since warrant is a function of one's *total* state of information, the import of a body of information under addition may naturally be different to what it would have been in isolation). (III) imposes a boundary on externalist conceptions of knowledge: let it be that, at least with respect to certain subject matters, knowledge should be viewed as grounded purely in the exercise of what are in fact reliable cognitive powers and stands in no need of further internal qualification—still, it should not be open to internal *dis*qualification. There is no knowledge, even of such subject matters, in any case where persistence in a knowledge claim would commit a subject to disregarding the balance of the available evidence and so convict her of irrationality.

Pure mathematics and issues of moral and aesthetic principle may arguably be thought to supply examples of discourses meeting these conditions under only relatively modest idealizations of the powers of their practitioners. Discourse concerning the spatially and/or temporally remote would do so, if at all, only under more elaborate idealizations—maybe of dubious coherence, like the possibility of time-travel.

The platitudes of opacity, embedding, timelessness, and absoluteness are all straightforward under these assumptions. To take them in that order:

First, it is clear that the superassertibility of a statement can *in practice* elude any single competent judge, or group of judges. On the other hand it cannot be undetectable *in principle*: if a statement is superassertible, then that fact will show in the S-stability of the relevant—superassertibility-conferring—state of information and hence will be detectable, albeit inconclusively, in just the same way that such S-stability is detectable. But that is no objection under the assumption (I) that we are operating in a region where it is a priori that all truths are knowable. For that is to suppose that the truths are detectable in any case.

Second, any statement is apt to be superassertible which is apt to be warranted in the first place, since its superassertibility is merely a matter of the S-stability of some warrant-conferring state of information. But aptitude for warrant itself is, of course, inherited under embedding within the standard logical operators. So such embeddings conserve aptitude for superassertibility.

Next, since one of our assumptions is exactly that states of information are accessible timelessly, it follows that superassertibility is, likewise, an eternal characteristic of any statement that has it.

Last, the definition of superassertibility—though the notion must inherit any vagueness in the notion of (all things considered) warrant—manifestly makes no provision for degrees: one statement may be more warranted than another, but if both are nevertheless all-things-considered warranted, and if their warrants are respectively stable, then they are equally and absolutely superassertible.

The key issue is accordingly the status of the equivalence schema with 'true' interpreted as: superassertible,

(E^S) It is superassertible that p if and only if p.

There are some subtleties here[41] but our discussion is simplified by the announced assumption (I), that we are working in a region where the schema,

---

[41] See Wright, *Truth and Objectivity*, ch. 2, sect. V.

$p \rightarrow$ It is knowable that p,

holds good a priori.

We consider each direction of (E^S) in turn. First, suppose that it is superassertible that p but that it is not the case that p. Then, by (I), it can be known that it is not the case that p. But that is absurd. For whatever state of information was possessed by one who had that knowledge, it would have—by the implication of additivity in (II)—to be able to coexist with the enduring all-things-considered warrant for p ensured by its superassertibility. And no one could be said to know that not-p whose total state of information warranted, to the contrary, a belief in p unless—contrary to (III)—the belief that not-p can be an example of knowledge even when irrationally held.

Now suppose that p but that it is not superassertible that p. Since p is not superassertible, we have it that there is no p-stable state of information—that any warrant for p can be defeated. So any subject who claims to know that p is nevertheless destined to lose a debate with a sufficiently resourceful agnostic; for—by additivity—the agnostic will always be able to come up with some consideration which will spoil whatever case the believer advances for p. It follows that it will not be possible rationally to sustain a belief in p. So, by (III), p cannot be known; whence by (I) it cannot be that p, contrary to hypothesis.

XIV

THE MINIMALIST CONCEPTION OF TRUTH

PAUL HORWICH

1. WHAT IS MINIMALISM?

The deflationary attitude toward truth—and the particular variant of it that I call minimalism—is a reaction against the natural and widespread idea that the property of truth has some sort of underlying nature and that our problem as philosophers is to say what that nature is, to analyse truth either conceptually or substantively, to specify, at least roughly, the conditions necessary and sufficient for something to be true.[1] Amongst the products of this traditional point of view there is the correspondence theory (*x* is true *iff x* corresponds to a fact), the coherence theory (*x* is true *iff x* is a member of a coherent set of beliefs), the verificationist theory (*x* is true *iff x* is provable, or verifiable in ideal conditions), and the pragmatist theory (*x* is true *iff x* is useful to believe). But nothing of this sort has ever survived serious scrutiny—which comes as no surprise to the deflationist, who denies that there is any prospect of an explicit definition or reductive analysis of truth, even a very approximate one.[2]

From Paul Horwich, *Truth* (2nd edn., Oxford: Oxford University Press, 1998). Reprinted (slightly revised) with permission.

[1] The minimalist form of deflationism about truth is presented in Horwich, *Truth* (Oxford, 1990). The present chapter is a slightly revised version of the postscript to the 2nd edn. of that work (Oxford: Oxford University Press, 1998). In the years since the 1st edn. was published several critical reactions to it have appeared. As far as I can tell, none of these discussions succeeds in undermining the minimalist perspective. Some of them show, however, that various points were poorly formulated and stand in need of clarification, and some raise new objections which should be addressed. In what follows I attempt to deal with the most serious of these issues. I will begin by articulating what I regard as the essence of the minimalist conception of truth, and then go on to discuss some of the recent objections to it. I shall focus particularly on questions raised by Anil Gupta, Hartry Field, Mark Richard, Donald Davidson, Crispin Wright, Scott Soames, Michael Dummett, Paul Boghossian, and Michael Devitt.

[2] For a discussion of what is right and wrong about these traditional analyses of truth, see Horwich, *Truth*, ch. 1 and R. L. Kirkham, *Theories of Truth* (Cambridge, Mass., 1992). It may be felt that since almost no concepts are susceptible to exact reductive analysis (not even 'table'

Deflationism begins by emphasizing the fact that no matter what theory of truth we might espouse professionally, we are all prepared to infer

The belief *that snow is white* is true

from

Snow is white

and vice versa. And, more generally, we all accept instances of the 'truth schemata'

The belief (conjecture, assertion, supposition, . . .) *that p* is true *iff* p.

But instead of taking the traditional view that an *analysis* of truth still needs to be given—a reductive account, deeper than the truth schemata, which will explain way we accept their instances—the deflationist maintains that, since our commitment to these schemata accounts for everything we do with the truth predicate, we can suppose that they implicitly define it. Our brute acceptance of their instances constitutes our grasp of the notion of truth. No conceptual analysis is called for—no definition of the form

'true' means 'F'

where 'F' is some expression composed of terms that are more basic than the truth predicate. Moreover there is going to be no non-definitional analysis of truth either, however rough and ready—no substantive discovery of the form

x's being true *consists in x*'s having property F.

Hence the term 'deflationism'.

This, of course, is highly reminiscent of the old 'redundancy theory' of Frege, Ramsey, Ayer, and Strawson:[3] the idea that

The proposition *that p* is true

means no more and no less than simply

p.

And the redundancy theory is indeed an early form of deflationism. However there are various respects in which we have been able to improve

---

or 'house'), it cannot be of much interest to deny that truth is. The alleged peculiarity of truth, however, is that there is nothing to be said—*not even very roughly speaking*—about what it consists in.

[3] G. Frege, 'On Sense and Reference', *Translations from the Philosophical Writings of Gottlob Frege*, ed. P. Geach and M. Black (London, 1960); F. Ramsey, 'The Nature of Truth', *Episteme*, 16 (1991), 6–16; id., *On Truth: Original Manuscript Materials (1927–1929) from the Ramsey Collection at the University of Pittsburgh*, ed. N. Rescher and U. Majer (1991) (based on part of his 'Facts and Propositions', *Proceedings of the Aristotelian Society*, suppl. vol. 7 (1927), 153–70; A. J. Ayer, 'The Criterion of Truth', *Analysis*, 3 (1935); P. Strawson, 'Truth', *Proceedings of the Aristotelian Society*, suppl. vol. 24 (1950), 129–56.

upon this original articulation of the view—leading to the formulation of deflationism defended here: namely, *minimalism*.

In the first place, as the name given to their doctrine suggests, the redundancy theorists had nothing much to say about the *function* of our concept of truth. But if it really is redundant, why on earth do we have such a notion? A virtue of minimalism is that it contains a satisfying response to this question—one that was first proposed by Quine[4]—namely, that the truth predicate plays a vital role in enabling us to capture certain generalizations. For we can generalize

> The moon is subject to gravity

by saying

> Every physical object is subject to gravity.

And similarly we can always obtain a generalization from a statement about a particular object by first selecting some kind or type G (e.g. 'physical object'), and then replacing the term referring to the object with the universal quantifier 'Every G'. However, there is an important class of generalization that cannot be constructed in this way: for example, the one whose instances include

> If Florence is smiling,
> then Florence is smiling

How can we extract the law of logic it instantiates? Or consider

> Physicists would like to *believe* that there are black holes only if there *are* black holes.

How are we to generalize this to obtain the epistemological policy it exemplifies? The solution provided by our concept of truth is to convert each such proposition into an obviously equivalent one—but one that *can* be generalized in the normal way. Thus, given the equivalence of

> *p*

and

> The statement *that p* is true

and

[4] *Philosophy of Logic* (Englewood Cliffs, 1970) [see this vol., Ch. IX]. See also his *Pursuit of Truth* (Cambridge, Mass., 1990). See also Stephen Leeds, 'Theories of Reference and Truth', *Erkenntnis* 13/1 (1978), 111–29. The redundancy theorists appreciated the need for some account of the function of the truth predicate. They tended to maintain that it serves various merely *pragmatic* purposes (e.g. to emphasize, as in 'It's true that I didn't see anything'; or to concede, as in 'It's true that they are a lousy team; but they will win anyway'.) But the Quinean account is clearly superior.

    The belief *that p* is true

we get, respectively

    The statement *that if Florence is smiling then Florence is smiling* is true

and

    Physicists would like to believe *that there are black holes* only if the belief *that there are black holes* is true

each of which generalizes in the standard fashion, yielding

    Every statement of the form 'If *p*, then *p*' is true[5]

and

    Physicists would like to believe only what is true.

From these we can derive (given the truth schemata) all the statements we initially wished to generalize—and nothing logically weaker would suffice. They may therefore be regarded as generalizations of the initial statements. Thus it is indeed useful to have a term that is governed by the truth schemata—despite their triviality. There is a clear *raison d'être* for a concept having precisely the characteristics that the minimalist attributes to truth.

    A second and related respect in which minimalism improves on the original redundancy theory is in not claiming that '*p*' and 'The statement (belief, . . .) *that p* is true' have exactly the same meaning. This claim is implausibly strong; for after all, the words 'true' and 'statement' do have meanings, and those meanings would appear to be, in some sense, 'components' of the meaning of 'The statement *that p* is true' but not of '*p*'. Moreover, there is no need to take such an extreme position. The generalizing function of truth is perfectly well fulfilled as long as instances of the truth schemata, understood as merely *material* biconditionals, are accepted. Relative to that body of assumptions, any generalization of the form 'All instances of schema S are true' will entail all the instances of S—which are precisely the statements we needed to generalize.

    Anil Gupta[6] rightly notes that the instances of the generalizations that we need the concept of truth to formulate (e.g. instances such as 'The statement *that if Florence is smiling then Florence is smiling* is true') will not say exactly the same thing as what we wished to generalize ('If Florence is smiling then Florence is smiling') unless corresponding instances of 'The statement *that p* is true' and '*p*' express the very same proposition—which,

---

[5] 'every statement of the form, " . . ."' can be read as 'every statement expressed by a sentence of the form, ". . .".'

[6] 'A Critique of Deflationism', this vol., Ch. XVI.

as we have just conceded, is not especially plausible. But this point does not undermine the minimalist story about the function of truth; for, as just mentioned, that function requires merely that the generalizations permit us to *derive* the statements to be generalized—which requires merely that the truth schemata provide material equivalences. This isn't to deny that the instances so understood are not only true but necessarily true (and a priori). The point is that their mere truth is enough to account for the generalizing function of truth.

It was perhaps an exaggeration to have suggested that the concept of truth is *needed* for this generalizing purpose. An alternative strategy would be to introduce some form of nonstandard (e.g. substitutional) quantification, by means of which we could say

(*p*) (If *p* then *p*)

and

Physicists would like it that (*p*) (they believe that *p*, only if *p*).

But in that case there would be required a battery of extra syntactic and semantic rules to govern the new type of quantifier. Therefore, we might consider the value of our concept of truth to be that it provides, not the only way, but a relatively 'cheap' way of obtaining the problematic generalizations—the way actually chosen in natural language.

It is emphasized by some philosophers that the truth predicate is a device for forming *prosentences*: just as one might use the pronoun 'he' instead of repeating a name (as in 'John said he was happy'), so one might say 'That's true' instead of repeating the sentence just asserted. Evidently this is a perfectly correct observation as far as it goes. However, there remains the issue of how best to explain it; and here is where minimalists such as myself part company with self-styled 'prosententialists' such as Dorothy Grover, Joseph Camp, Nuel Belnap, and Robert Brandom.[7] The latter tend to suppose that 'is true' should be analysed using substitutional quantification—roughly speaking, that '*x* is true' means '(*p*) (*x* = ⟨*p*⟩ → *p*)'. In contrast, the former contend that the overall use of the truth predicate (including its use as a prosentence forming device) is best explained by supposing that 'is true' is an unanalysable predicate governed by the equivalence schema; and that the virtue of such a predicate is that it allows us to avoid the complexities and obscurities of substitutional quantification.

A third defect of the original redundancy theory lies in its implication that truth is *not a property*—or, in other words, that attributions of truth (as in 'The proposition *that dogs bark* is true') do not have the logical form,

---

[7] Grover, Camp, and Belnap, Jr., 'A Prosentential Theory of Truth', *Philosophical Studies*, 27 (1975), 73–125; and Brandom, *Making It Explicit* (Cambridge, Mass., 1994).

244

244

'*x* is F', that is characteristic of attributions of properties to objects. A better form of deflationism will reject this thesis as inconsistent with the logical role of the truth predicate—in particular with the inferences we make from '*x* = *that p*' and '*x* is true' to '*that p* is true', and hence to '*p*'. No doubt truth is very different from most properties insofar as it has no underlying nature; but, in light of the inferential role of 'true' as a logical predicate, it is nonetheless a 'property', at least in some sense of the term. This is a point to which I return in Section 8.

My defence of the minimalist perspective will proceed as follows. In the next section I consider various criticisms of the idea that the truth schemata provide an implicit definition of the truth predicate. Then, in Sections 3 and 4, I take up the question of what sort of entity we apply it to, and argue in favour of propositions. Turning, in Section 5, from the question of how the word 'true' comes to mean what it does to the question of what explains the characteristics of truth, I substantiate the claim that truth has no underlying nature and that the basic theory of that property consists in instances of the equivalence schema, 'The proposition *that p* is true *iff p*'. In Sections 6 and 7 I address the objection that the *normative* status of truth implies that there must be something more to it than is appreciated by minimalists. And I conclude by looking back at the issue of whether or not truth is, in some sense, a *property*.

2. DOES MINIMALISM GIVE AN ADEQUATE ACCOUNT OF OUR CONCEPT OF TRUTH?

A central component of the minimalistic picture is its claim about the particular non-semantic fact that provides the word 'true' with its peculiar meaning. This is said to be the fact that a certain basic regularity governs the overall use of the truth predicate—i.e. that a certain pattern of behaviour provides the best explanation of our total linguistic practice with the term. Now, as we have just seen, the regularity which plays that explanatory role is the regularity in virtue of which the term is useful: namely, our disposition to accept instances of the truth schemata. Therefore, this is the fact about the truth predicate that constitutes our meaning by it what we do.[8] More specifically, the meaning-constituting fact is this: that the explanatorily basic fact about our use of the truth predicate is our ten-

---

[8] This claim about the meaning of 'true' is the product of two distinct ideas: first, the fundamental thesis of minimalism with respect to truth (namely, that the truth-schemata are the explanatory basis of our overall use of the truth predicate); and second, the use theory of meaning (namely, that a word means what it does in virtue of the basic regularity governing its

dency to infer instances of 'The proposition *that p* is true' from corresponding instances of '*p*', and vice versa, whenever (*a*) each '*p*' is replaced with tokens of an English sentence, (*b*) these tokens are given the same interpretation as one another, (*c*) under that interpretation they express the content of a statement (a proposition), and (*d*) the terms 'that' and 'proposition', are given their English meanings.

It might be objected that this condition is not strong enough to distinguish truth from various other concepts, since there are innumerable predicates, 'F', other than 'true', for which we would accept instantiations of (F*)

The proposition *that p* is F *iff p*.

Imagine, for example, that 'F' is the predicate 'is true and $1+1=2$'. However, this objection overlooks the fact that although there are indeed many predicative expressions that satisfy schema (F*), it is not generally true, for each such expression, that (F*) gives the *full*, basic regularity governing its use. For example, our knowledge that 'is true and $1+1=2$' satisfies schema (F*) does not explain our inclination to deduce, from the premiss that this predicate applies to an object, the conclusion that $1+1=2$. And, in general, if a complex predicate satisfies schema (F*), then it will exhibit various use-relations to its constituents; and these facts will not be explained by its satisfaction of the schema. Thus, in the case of the truth predicate, the schema provides the complete, basic regularity for its use. In contrast, the predicates other than 'true' that satisfy the schema are governed by additional regularities. And this is what distinguishes their meanings from that of 'true'.[9]

A separate objection, made by Hartry Field,[10] is that the minimalist account could capture the meaning of 'true' only in its application to statements that we are able to *formulate*; for only in those cases can we supply the relevant instance of the truth schemata. The idea is that if we take a statement, *s*, to say, for example, *that snow is white*, we might then suppose that the content of

    s is true

is more or less

---

deployment). Many of the radical consequences of minimalism depend only on its basic tenet (that the schemata are conceptually basic) and do not depend upon the further idea that they constitute our concept of truth.

  [9] This potential difficulty was brought to my attention by Anil Gupta in Oct. 1992.

  [10] 'Critical Notice: Paul Horwich's *Truth*', *Philosophy of Science*, 59 (1992), 321–30. Although Field is critical of my particular brand of minimalism, he has become one of the strongest advocates of the deflationary point of view. See e.g. his 'Deflationist Views of Meaning and Content', this vol., Ch. XIX.

snow is white

whereas, if we don't know what s means, then we don't know the content of 's is true'. Now this would indeed count against a theory that aimed, by means of the truth schemata, to provide a *reductive analysis* of each utterance containing the word 'true'. However, one need not, and should not, promise any such reductive analysis; indeed it is a central tenet of minimalism that there is no such thing. On the minimalist view, we aim to define the truth predicate, not by providing another expression with the same meaning (nor even by providing a rule transforming every sentence containing the word 'true' into a content-equivalent sentence without it), but rather by specifying which property of the truth predicate constitutes its having the meaning it has; and to that end we must identify the property that best explains our overall use of the term. In particular, the minimalist thesis is that the meaning of 'true' is constituted by our disposition to accept those instances of the truth schemata that we *can* formulate. In that way, the word is provided with a constant meaning wherever it appears—even when ascribed to untranslatable statements. And the justification for this thesis is that such a pattern of acceptance accounts for our entire use of the term—including its application to untranslatable utterances. Thus we might attribute truth to an untranslatable statement on the basis, for example, of a belief in the reliability of the person who made it; and we do, as Field suggests, need an account of truth that will explain this sort of attribution; but the minimalist proposal would do so perfectly well.

Mark Richard[11] has noted that some instances of the truth schemata will be found, by some people, to be less obvious than other instances. In particular, propositions involving empty names ('Atlantis is in the Atlantic'), vague attributions ('Smith is bald'), ethical pronouncements ('Killing is wrong'), and future contingents ('The sea-battle will occur tomorrow') may be affirmed, yet nonetheless regarded as 'non-factual' hence incapable of truth or falsity. In which case 'p' is not taken to imply the corresponding 'The statement (belief, conjecture, . . .) *that p* is true'. Consequently, argues Richard, minimalism is mistaken in maintaining that the concept of truth is fixed by our disposition to accept instances of the truth schemata.

However, the essence of minimalism is that certain uncontroversial schemata suffice to fix our concept of truth and that there is no deeper definition taking the traditional, explicit form. Therefore even if, in light of the above examples, we were to reformulate minimalism using the qualified schemata

[11] 'Deflating truth', in E. Villanueva (ed.), *Philosophical Issues*, viii (Atascadero, 1997), 57–78.

'*p*' has 'factual content' →
(The proposition *that p* is true *iff p*)

(where the notion of 'factual content' is explicated non-truth-theoretically, in terms of 'use' or 'conceptual role') we would leave intact the core of the minimalistic perspective.

Perhaps some such qualified schemata do give a better account of certain philosophers' concept of truth; but for the rest of us the unqualified schemata are accurate. Thus one might be inclined to suppose that there are *two* concepts of truth: that the original truth schemata provide a minimalist account of one of them, and the qualified schemata a minimalist account of the other. However, the truth predicate is needed as a device of generalization in *all* domains of discourse, including those in which certain philosophers are wary of attributing truth. Thus the original, unqualified schemata are what capture the concept we need. It seems reasonable, therefore, to blame any anxiety regarding those schemata on philosophical confusion rather than on deployment of a more restricted concept. Thus, despite the intuitions cited by Richard, I believe we can stand by the view that the meaning-constituting use of 'true'—the 'expert' use—is the disposition to accept instances of the unqualified truth schemata.

3. WHAT ARE THE BEARERS OF TRUTH?

In ordinary language what are said to be true are the *things* that we believe and that our utterances express—so-called *propositions*. Thus, on the face of it, propositions exist, some of them (presumably, half) are true, and the correlated truth-like attributes of utterances and of acts of believing, asserting, etc. are the complex, derivative properties, '*u* expresses a true proposition' and 'the object of act *x* is a true proposition'.

However, it remains to be seen (1) whether this first impression is correct—specifically, whether there really are such things as propositions; (2) whether, if correct, this naive picture is consistent with minimalism—specifically, with minimalism's requirement that propositions be conceptually prior to truth; and (3) which of the three truth-concepts is really fundamental—specifically, whether it is not explanatorily preferable to go against the current of ordinary language and to explicate propositional-truth and act-truth in terms of a previously developed account of utterance-truth.

On the basis of the inferential behaviour of that-clause (propositional attitude) constructions (which are sentences like 'John believes that God exists', 'Mary said that lying is wrong', and 'Charles imagines that he is Napoleon') a good case can be made for concluding that they articulate *relations* (such as believing, asserting, and hoping) between people and whatever are designated by the constituent that-clauses—i.e. propositions.[12] Assuming, as I shall, that this conclusion is right, there nonetheless might be no *nominalistic* answer to the question, 'But what are propositions?'—no theory specifying, for example, some species of physical or mental entity with which propositions are to be identified. An inability to give such an answer does not justify scepticism about the existence of propositions, for the nominalistic presupposition of any such sceptical argument can easily be resisted. It may be supposed, rather, that the conception we have of any given proposition lies in the circumstances in which we would take it to be expressed. In other words, it is by making explicit the grounds on which we maintain such things as 'John's utterance, *u*, expresses the proposition that dogs bark' that we will articulate our concept of proposition.

The minimalist view of truth has two important consequences regarding the grounds for such interpretive claims. One is that they not involve truth-theoretic notions (i.e. 'true', 'is true of', or 'refers'). For minimalism is primarily the view that the equivalence schema is conceptually basic vis-à-vis the truth predicate—and, analogously, that parallel schemata are conceptually basic vis-à-vis 'is true of' and 'refers'. This implies that the various truth-theoretic concepts be posterior to the concept of proposition, and therefore that it be possible to possess the concept of proposition without possessing the concepts of truth, being true of, and reference. And this implies that that-clause attributions not rest on grounds involving truth-theoretic notions. For example, minimalism implies that nothing along the lines of

> *u* expresses the proposition *that p*
> =*u* is true *iff p*

could be what articulates our conception of proposition.

The second important consequence of minimalism is that the grounds for that-clause attributions need not even involve anything that might *constitute* the truth-theoretic properties. In other words, it is not merely that

---

[12] I have in mind the need to accommodate such inferences as: 'Oscar believes that dogs bark and Barny denies that dogs bark; therefore there is something which Oscar believes and Barny denies'. This sort of argument in favour of propositions is developed in Horwich, *Truth*, ch. 6, and in Stephen Schiffer's 'A Paradox of Meaning', *Noûs*, 28 (1994), 279–324. For the sake of simplicity of exposition I am ignoring the various other ways of referring to propositions (e.g. 'John *wonders whether May loves him*') and am writing as though propositions were invariably designated by that-clauses.

the evidence for that-clause attributions does not explicitly advert to truth and reference; it need not even advert to anything non-semantic that might underlie truth and reference. For example, it need not be that 'dog' expresses the propositional constituent that it does in virtue of standing in some non-semantic relation R to dogs—where R would constitute the relation 'x is true of y'. For if truth is fully explained by the schema 'The proposition *that p* is true *iff p*', then the capacity of propositions and utterances to be true is guaranteed regardless of how it comes about that an utterance expresses the particular proposition it does.

Both of these consequences of the minimalist perspective are vindicated by the use theory of meaning. To see this, let us, for simplicity, restrict our attention to context-insensitive sentences (such as 'dogs bark' and 'snow is white')—sentences not involving indexical or demonstrative terms. In such cases it is plausible to identify the proposition expressed by an utterance with the meaning of the sentence-type to which the utterance belongs;[13] and it is plausible to suppose that the meaning of a sentence-type is determined by the meanings of its component words and by the procedure by which those words were combined. Thus the pair of minimalist implications about propositions amounts to the claim that word-meanings are constituted neither in terms of truth-theoretic properties nor by anything to which such properties might reduce. Now according to the use theory of meaning, each word-type means what it does in virtue of a certain non-semantic regularity regarding its tokens: more specifically, that the occurrences of its tokens derive from the acceptance of certain specified sentences (or inference rules) containing the word.[14] On this view there is no reason to expect that the property in virtue of which a predicate 'f' means what it does will consist in that predicate's standing in some non-semantic relation to fs. Consequently, there is no reason to think that 'f's meaning is constituted in terms of a non-semantic reduction of the 'true-of' relation.[15] Thus, if the use theory of meaning is correct, as I believe it is, then the two predictions of minimalism are verified.

We are now in a position briefly to address Donald Davidson's[16] dissatisfaction with the minimalist point of view. His critique is founded on two objections to the thesis that truth is implicitly defined by the equivalence schema. The first of them is that, contrary to minimalism, truth is

---

[13] For simplicity, I am not only ignoring context sensitivity but also the distinction between *de dicto, de re,* and *de se* propositional attitudes. For a discussion of these complexities, see Horwich, *Meaning* (Oxford, 1998), ch. 3.

[14] For elaboration and defence of this position see ibid.

[15] For a detailed discussion of this point see Horwich, 'Deflationary Truth and the Problem of Aboutness', in Villanueva (ed.), *Philosophical Issues*, viii. 95–106.

[16] 'The Folly of Trying to Define Truth', this vol., Ch. XVII.

conceptually prior to meaning and proposition. This claim is an immediate consequence of Davidson's own theory of meaning, according to which the meaning of a declarative sentence is constituted by its having a certain truth condition. However, Davidson's theory, although widely accepted, is far from unproblematic. Amongst the reasons for scepticism about it are:

(1) After thirty years there still remains the notorious unsolved problem of how to articulate a conception of truth condition ('u is true *iff* p') that is strong enough to constitute the corresponding attribution of meaning ('u means that p').

(2) Davidson's truth-conditional theory of meaning is largely motivated by the desire to explain how the meanings of sentences depend upon the meanings of their constituent words. The proposed explanations piggy-back on Tarski-style derivations of the truth conditions of sentences from the reference-conditions of words. But there are long-standing questions as to whether *all* the constructions of a natural language can be forced into the mould of a Tarski-style truth-theory.

(3) Moreover, Davidson's truth-theoretic approach to the explanation of the compositionality of meaning is not at all compulsory. One can 'deflate' the issue by supposing that understanding a complex expression is nothing over and above understanding its component words and appreciating how they are combined.[17]

(4) We have just seen how it is possible to give a use-theoretic account of proposition that does not presuppose the concept of truth.

It is therefore far from evident that meaning and proposition should be explicated in terms of truth.

Davidson's second objection to the brand of deflationism presented here is that expressions like 'The proposition that dogs bark', construed as singular terms, are unintelligible. However, this rather counterintuitive claim is entirely theory-driven: it is derived from his inability to find any account (of the sort required by his truth-theoretic paradigm) of how the referents of such expressions could be determined by the referents of their parts. Therefore, given the above-mentioned doubts already shrouding that paradigm, this particular inability to accommodate it would merely constitute one more reason to give it up.[18]

---

[17] For a full discussion of this thesis—namely, that the compositionality of meaning is easily explicable in non-truth-theoretic terms—see Horwich, 'The Composition of Meanings', *Philosophical Review*, 106 (Oct. 1997), 503–31, repr. as *Meaning*, ch. 7.

[18] For a more detailed response to Davidson's critique of minimalism, see Horwich, 'Davidson on Deflationism', in U. Zeglen (ed.), *Discussions with Donald Davidson: On Truth, Meaning and Knowledge* (London).

4. WHICH IS THE BASIC TRUTH-CONCEPT: PROPOSITIONAL-TRUTH, UTTERANCE-TRUTH, OR ACT-TRUTH?

Ordinary language suggests that propositional-truth is fundamental and that the notion of an utterance 'expressing a true proposition' and the notion of a belief 'being directed at a true proposition' are understood in terms of it. From this point of view the order of explanation will go as follows:

First: begin to characterize propositions by means of the principle

   p expresses the proposition *that p*

where the sentence-type, *p*, is individuated semantically as well as physically, and where the two tokens of '*p*' are understood in the same way.

Second: explicate propositional-truth via the equivalence schema

   The proposition *that p* is true *iff p*.

Third: complete the account of propositions (and propositional-truth) by adding

   u and *v* express the same proposition *iff u* and *v* have the same use-theoretic, construction property.

Fourth: introduce utterance-truth ('*truth*') and act-truth ('truth*') by means of the linking principles

   Utterance *u* expresses $x \rightarrow$ (*u* is *true iff x* is true);
   Act *a* is directed at $x \rightarrow$ (*a* is true* *iff x* is true).

Fifth: prove the adequacy of these notions by deducing the corresponding equivalence schemata

   u expresses the proposition *that* $p \rightarrow$ (*u* is *true iff p*)

(which in turn implies the disquotation schema: *p* is *true iff p*) and

   Act *a*, of believing (conjecturing, etc.) *that p*, is true* *iff p*.

However, despite its conformity with ordinary language, this order of explanation is not at all obligatory: we can equally well base everything on one of the other truth-concepts. For example, we might start by characterizing utterance-truth (for our own utterances) by means of the disquotation schema

   p is *true iff p*.

Then add a projection principle to cover *truth* for other utterances

   u and *p* have the same use-theoretic construction property $\rightarrow$ (*u* is *true iff* *p* is *true*).

Then bring in the above account of propositions

> *p* expresses the proposition *that p*
>
> *u* and *v* express the same proposition → *u* and *v* have the same use-theoretic, construction property

together with the above linking principle

> *u* expresses *x* → (*u* is *true iff x* is true)

from which we can easily derive the equivalence schema

> The proposition *that p* is true *iff p*.

The fact that the natural language truth predicate typically expresses propositional-truth makes the first approach more natural. And this is my rationale for taking truth, rather than *truth* or truth*, to be the conceptually basic truth-concept and for supposing that its bearers are propositions; and in the same vein I take it that our concept of truth is engendered by our disposition to accept instances of the equivalence schema and that this is what explains our confidence in the truth schemata and in the disquotation schema. However, we have seen that this conceptual ordering is not especially profound or important. Our language certainly could have had a word expressing a primitive concept of utterance-*truth* or act-truth*; and in that case it would have been a simple matter to construct the notion of propositional-truth.

5. WHAT DOES MINIMALISM HAVE TO SAY ABOUT THE NATURE OF TRUTH ITSELF, AS OPPOSED TO THE NATURE OF OUR CONCEPT OF TRUTH?

We do not hesitate to distinguish a theory about the concept of water (or the meaning of the word 'water') from a theory of the phenomenon of water itself. The first would be supplied by a semanticist and the second by a physicist; the first would be designed to account for our thoughts and statements about water and the second for the properties of water itself; and the first need not say anything about H_2O whereas the second would have to. Similarly, it is prima facie reasonable to distinguish between an account of our concept of truth and an account of truth itself. The former purports to specify the conditions in which someone uses the word 'true' with a certain meaning; the latter purports to specify the fundamental facts about what that word stands for—about the phenomenon, truth. Consequently, the former—the meaning of 'true'—is specified by a generalization about the *word* 'true', a generalization that will explain all our uses of it; whereas the latter—the theory of truth itself—consists in principles about the *property* of truth on the basis of which all the facts about truth are to be explained. And parallel distinctions should be drawn between our concepts of truth-expression and act-truth, and the phenomena themselves.

What then, from a minimalist point of view, is the basic theory of truth itself? Which body of *fundamental* facts about truth provides the best explanation of all the further facts about it? A natural conjecture is that, although there is always *in principle* a difference between the theory of the concept of X and the theory of X-ness itself, perhaps, in the case of truth, these theories more or less coincide. Perhaps the axioms of the theory of truth are instances of the equivalence schema

> The proposition *that p* is true *iff p*

comprising what we might call the minimal theory of truth.

An immediate problem for this proposal is created by the *Liar* paradoxes: the existence of contradiction-implying instances of the schema. Notice that this is not an overwhelming difficulty for the supposition that what we *mean* by 'true' is captured by the equivalence schema. For although certain instances yield contradictions, it might be argued that anyone who means what we do by 'true' has a certain inclination to accept even those instances—an inclination that is overridden by the discovery that they lead to contradiction. Indeed one might suppose that it is only because we have such an inclination that the 'Liar' sentences present us with a *paradox*! But no such manoeuvre is available to protect the schema if it is proposed as a theory of truth itself. All that can be said is that the theory may contain only a restricted set of the instances of the schema. But further theory will have to be deployed in order to specify that restriction.

A second deficiency of the proposed minimal theory, one might think, is that it has infinitely many axioms. Leaving aside the banned, contradiction-inducing instances of the equivalence schema, there is a separate axiom for each proposition. So would it not be better to pursue a Tarski-like strategy of explaining the truth of the infinitely-many propositions in terms of the referents of their finitely-many constitutents? The answer, it seems to me, is no. The Tarski-style approach offers false hope (1) because, as is well known, there are many kinds of proposition (e.g. statements of probability, counterfactual conditionals, etc.) whose truth we have no reason to believe can be explained on the basis of the referents of their parts; and, more importantly, (2) because such a strategy would

254   PAUL HORWICH

miss those propositions that are constructed from the primitive concepts that are not expressed in our langage. If *all* propositions are to be covered, then there would have to be axioms specifying the referents of all the infinitely-many possible primitives. So the Tarskian approach would turn out to need no fewer axioms than the minimal theory.

A third objection to the minimal theory (emphasized by Anil Gupta[19] and Scott Soames[20]) is that it is too weak to explain any *general* facts about truth. Consider, for example, the fact that

Every proposition of the form '$p \to p$' is true.

We might try to explain this by assembling particular explanatory inferences that invoke nothing more than axioms of the minimal theory. For example, given that

If snow is white, then snow is white

and given the axiom

The proposition *that if snow is white then snow is white* is true *iff* if snow is white then snow is white

we may explain why it is that

The proposition *that if snow is white then snow is white* is true.

But in order to arrive at the *general* fact to be explained we need to collect all these conclusions together; and there is no logically valid rule that would enable us to do so. Clearly, a set of premises attributing some property to each object of a certain kind does not entail that everything of that kind has the property. We would need a further premiss specifying that we have a premiss for every object of that kind—and this would be tantamount to our conclusion.

However, it seems to me that in the present case, where the topic is *propositions*, we can find a solution to this problem. For it is plausible to suppose that there is a truth-preserving rule of inference that will take us from a set of premises attributing to each proposition some property, F, to the conclusion that all propositions have F. No doubt this rule is not *logically* valid, for its reliability hinges, not merely on the meanings of the logical constants, but also on the nature of propositions. But it is a principle we do find plausible. We commit ourselves to it, implicitly, in moving from the disposition to accept any proposition of the form 'x is F' (where x is a proposition) to the conclusion 'All propositions are F'. So we can suppose that this rule is what sustains the explanations of the generaliza-

[19] 'Minimalism', in J. E. Tomberlin, *Philosophical Perspectives*, vii. *Language and Logic* (Atascadero, 1993), 359–69.
[20] 'The Truth About Deflationism', in Villanueva (ed.), *Philosophical Issues*, viii.

tions about truth with which we are concerned. Thus we can, after all, defend the thesis that the basic theory of truth consists in some subset of the instances of the equivalence schema.[21]

But there remains one further question. Even if all the familiar characteristics of truth do indeed stem from the equivalence facts, might not these facts in turn be explained by some more fundamental theory—perhaps a theory that attributes to truth some specific underlying nature? The answer, it seems clear, is no. For the equivalence axioms are *conceptually* basic and a priori. In these respects they are on a par with instances of fundamental logical laws, such as the law of excluded middle, and with the basic principles of arithmetic. And in no such case should we anticipate theoretical reduction, as we should in the empirical domain. For in the area of a posteriori facts, the behaviour of systems can be expected to be caused by the properties of their parts and the way those parts are combined with one another; therefore one might well anticipate some reductive explanation of this behaviour. In the a priori domain, however, there is no such reason to anticipate a reduction. And in the particular case of the equivalence axioms there are particular grounds for scepticism. For an explanation of them would have to provide a simple body of facts about truth and other matters, from which they could all be deduced. But that body of facts would itself need to be infinite—since the behaviour of infinitely many different propositional constituents must be accounted for. Consequently, the unification and gain of simplicity required of a decent explanation could be achieved only if the new theory were to explain not merely the equivalence axioms but various other phenomena as well. But we have absolutely no reason at all to think that there exist any other phenomena whose properties might be explained by the same theory that explains the equivalence axioms. It would be very surprising if there were. Thus it is indeed reasonable to regard the equivalence axioms as explanatorily basic; hence to suppose that truth has no underlying nature.

Thus minimalism is not merely the view that truth has no *conceptual* analysis. It involves the stronger thesis that no sort of reduction can be expected. And it bases that claim on a certain line of thought: namely, that the utility of the concept is non-descriptive and is explained by our acceptance of the truth schemata, that such acceptance constitutes our grasp of truth, and that the property so characterized will not be susceptible to

---

[21] In addition, Anil Gupta observes that the equivalence axioms will not suffice to explain such facts as that Julius Caesar is not true. We will (as he suggests) need the further axiom that all truths are propositions.

reductive analysis. This is why we should regard neither G. E. Moore[22] nor Davidson[23] as minimalists. For despite their insistence that truth is an indefinable primitive, they don't acknowledge the non-descriptive function of the concept, they don't take it to be implicitly defined by the truth schemata, and they do not oppose the prospect of a substantive reduction.

6. WHAT DOES MINIMALISM HAVE TO SAY ABOUT THE NORMATIVE SIGNIFICANCE OF TRUTH?

In Michael Dummett's famous paper of 1959 he argues against the redundancy theory that it fails to capture the *desirability* of truth.[24] The redundancy theory tells us *when* our beliefs are true: it says that our belief *that p* will be true if and only if *p*. But it leaves out the important fact that we *want* our beliefs to be true; we aim for the truth. And the same point could be made against minimalism.

In response, however, it can be said that in order for an account of truth to be adequate it suffices that it be able to *explain* the desirability of truth—it is not required that the desirability of truth be an integral *part* of the account. Moreover such an explanation (or, at least, a sketch of one) can indeed be given.

Roughly speaking, it is easily seen why I should want it to be the case, for example, that I *believe* that if I run I will escape, only if I *will* escape if I run. I want this because, given a desire to escape, that belief would lead to a certain action (running), and that action would satisfy my desire if indeed it implies escape. This is why I would like it to be that I believe that I will escape if I run, only if I will indeed escape if I run.

Clearly, one has parallel reasons for wishing that

If I believe that D, then D

whenever 'D' expresses what we might call 'a directly action guiding proposition'—namely, a conditional of the form 'If I do A, then I will get G', whose antecedent describes a possible action under one's control, and

---

[22] 'The Nature of Judgment', *Mind*, NS 8 (1899), 176–93. For discussion of this doctrine see Richard Cartwright, 'A Neglected Theory of Truth', in his *Philosophical Essays* (Cambridge, Mass., 1987).

[23] 'The Structure and Content of Truth', *Journal of Philosophy*, 87/6 (June 1990), 279–328; id., 'Folly of Trying to Define Truth'.

[24] Dummett's view ('Truth', *Proceedings of the Aristotelian Society*, NS 59 (1959), 141–62) is elaborated by Crispin Wright in his *Truth and Objectivity*. I respond to Wright's critique in Sect. 8.

whose consequent describes a state of affairs that one might wish to be realized.

Now recall the use of our concept of truth to capture such generalizations. We can reformulate the schema as

If I believe *that D*, then *that D* is true

which has the logical form.

If I believe X, then X is true

enabling it to be generalized in the normal way as

All my directly action-guiding beliefs are true.

This is what we have good practical reasons to want. But, in addition, bear in mind that directly action-guiding beliefs are derived from other beliefs by means of inferential rules that tend to preserve truth. And any one of our beliefs might be a premiss in some such inference. It thus becomes pretty clear why we might like *all* our beliefs to be true.[25]

Bernard Williams[26] has argued that insofar as truth *is intrinsically* valuable—that is, valuable for its own sake, regardless of practical benefits—then minimalism is in trouble, since it surely lacks the resources to explain that value. But this criticism is unjust. For the difficulty that attaches to explaining why true belief is intrinsically good is no more or less than the difficulty of explaining, for any other particular thing (e.g. kindness, happiness, etc.), why it is intrinsically good. The problem stems from our failure to understand the concept of intrinsic goodness, rather than our adoption of the minimalist conception of truth. More specifically, insofar as we don't know what it is for something to possess the quality of intrinsic goodness, then no explanation of why truth possesses it will suggest itself, regardless of which theory of truth is adopted. On the other hand, if some account of intrinsic goodness is assumed, then it is far from obvious that a minimalistically acceptable explanation of why truth has that quality could not be based upon the assumed account. Consider, for example, an analysis of 'being intrinsically good' roughly along the lines of 'being normally conducive to human welfare'. On the basis of this sort of theory the minimalistic account of truth's pragmatic value might well be developed into an account of its intrinsic value. Note that such an account would not undermine the *intrinsicality* of the value. For to recognize that truth is valuable 'for its own sake'—i.e. to suppose that truth is good even in those cases where it will have no practical benefits—is not to suppose

---

[25] See B. Loewer, 'The Value of Truth', in E. Villanueva (ed.), *Philosophical Issues*, iv (Atascadero, 1994) for refinements of this idea.

[26] 'Truth in Ethics', *Ratio* NS 8 (1995), 227–42.

that the explanation of this value is independent of the *normal* advantages of truth.

7. BUT DOESN'T THE EXISTENCE OF EMPIRICAL GENERALIZATIONS ABOUT TRUTH—INCLUDING THE FACT THAT TRUE BELIEFS FACILITATE SUCCESSFUL ACTION—SUGGEST THAT TRUTH IS, AFTER ALL, A PROPERTY WITH AN UNDERLYING NATURE?

The idea behind this objection is that an empirical generalization is typically explained by the underlying natures of the properties that it relates to one another. Therefore one might expect that if there are any general, empirical facts about truth, their existence would depend, contrary to minimalism, on truth's having some underlying nature. And, as we have seen, it does appear to be a general fact about truth that, as Hartry Field puts it, 'agents tend to be more successful when the truth conditions of their beliefs are realized'.[27]

It is a mistake, however, to suppose that generalizations involving truth may be explained by analysing that property. Given the function of our concept of truth, we can see that these generalizations are not focused on truth, not really about truth. Rather they belong to that class of special schematic generalizations that rely on the equivalence schema for their formulation. It was shown in Section 5 that such facts must be explained in terms of yet more basic schemata and in terms of the equivalence axioms; nothing can be gained by attempting to identify truth itself with some deeper property.

As we have just seen, it is more or less possible to explain the generalization in question in terms of the truth of the instances of the schemata

(I) If S believes that if p then q, and if S wants that q, then S wants that p;

(II) If S wants that he does A, then S does A;

(III) If S believes that q follows from $p^1, p^2, \ldots$, and pn, then (probably) q does follow from $p^1, p^2, \ldots$, and pn.

---

[27] Both Field ('Critical Notice: Paul Horwich's *Truth*', and Michael Devitt ('Minimalist Truth: A Critical Notice of Paul Horwich's *Truth*', *Mind and Language*, 6/3 (1991), 273–83) express the suspicion, just articulated, that minimalism may well be undermined by the role of truth in explaining successful action.

And, by the same token, each of these schematic facts 'about truth' will be explained by reference to yet more basic schemata and to instances of the equivalence schema. No analysis of truth is called for.

8. IS TRUTH A PROPERTY?

Minimalism does not involve, in itself, any particular answer to this question. For it may be combined with a variety of different conceptions of property, some of which will yield the conclusion that the truth predicate does stand for a property, and some that it doesn't.

Consider, for example, the liberal conception according to which every term that functions logically as a predicate stands for a property. Now it is a vital feature of truth that we can argue as follows

> x is true
> $x =$ the proposition *that p*
> $\therefore$ The proposition *that p* is true
> $\therefore$ p

Therefore the truth predicate must indeed be rendered in logic as a predicate. Thus there is a perfectly legitimate, weak conception of property according to which minimalism implies that truth certainly is one. However, this does not preclude the construction of various stricter, more robust conceptions of property, by adding further conditions. One might say, for example, that a predicate expresses a 'substantive' property (in one of many possible senses of 'substantive') if and only if there is no a-priori obstacle to its being reducible to non-semantic terms. Minimalism, insofar as it maintains, on the basis of a-priori considerations, that truth is not naturalistically reducible, will imply that it is not, in that sense, 'substantive'. Thus the only reasonable way to approach the question of whether, from a minimalistic point of view, truth is a property, is to distinguish various conceptions of property, and to answer on a case by case basis.

Paul Boghossian[28] has argued that minimalism is incoherent ('unstable') on the grounds that it implies both that truth *is*, and that it *is not*, a property. For according to Boghossian the essence of minimalism—that which distinguishes it from traditional accounts like the correspondence and coherence theories—is its claim that the truth predicate does not really stand for a property. However, he continues, it is also constitutive of the doctrine that any grammatically appropriate sentence be substitutable into the disquotation schema

[28] 'The Status of Content', *Philosophical Review*, 99 (Apr. 1990), 157–84.

'*p*' is true *iff p*.

And this is tantamount to accepting the generality of the schema

'*p*' expresses a fact *iff p*

which implies

'F*x*' expresses a fact *iff* F*x*

which, quite plausibly, implies

'F' stands for a property of *x iff* F*x*.

Therefore, since, for example, the proposition *that snow is white* is true, it follows (substituting 'true' for 'F' and 'the proposition *that snow is white*' for '*x*') that 'true' stands for a property.

There is, however, no reason for a minimalist to fall into this contradiction. The second leg of Boghossian's argument invokes the broad, logical notion of property; and we can accept that truth is a property of this sort. In that case we will say that what distinguishes the minimalist conception from traditional accounts is its characteristic view of the meaning and function of the truth predicate, together with what that implies about the non-existence of any reductive theory of truth. Alternatively, we can operate throughout with a more substantive conception of a property. And in that case we might agree with the characterization of minimalism as the view that truth is not a property. However, relative to this notion of property the minimalist should not accept the general schema

'F' stands for a property of *x iff* F*x*

and can well deny that this follows from the generality of the equivalence schema.

Crispin Wright[29] has also claimed that the minimalist view of truth is 'unstable'—but on quite different grounds from those of Boghossian. Wright argues that since truth is what he calls a 'distinctive norm'—i.e. since (*a*) it is desirable that our statements be true, and (*b*) truth is distinct from justification—then one must recognize that truth is a 'real' property.

But we must consider whether these claims really are in conflict with minimalism. And to that end we must review what might be meant by 'a *real* property'. There are various possibilities:

(1) Were it to mean 'the sort of property that any logically normal predicate stands for', then, as we have seen, the minimalist has no disagreement that truth is indeed this sort of 'real' property.

(2) Perhaps, then, Wright has in mind what I have called a 'substantive'

---

[29] *Truth and Objectivity*, and id., 'Responses to Commentators', *Philosophy and Phenomenological Research* 56 (1997), 863–8, 911–41.

property: namely, the sort of property for which there might well be a constitution theory of the form

x is true = x is F

But it surely does not follow, from the normative character of truth, that truth is 'real', in that sense. On the contrary, we saw in Section 5 that no reductive theory of truth is likely to be correct because no such account will explain the equivalence axioms.

(3) Another possibility is that we count the following infinitely disjunctive property as 'real':

> x = the proposition *that snow is white*
> and snow is white

or x = the proposition *that God exists*
> and God exists

or ...

But again this is unlikely to be what Wright is supposing since, apart from terminology, it is more or less exactly the minimalist account of truth.

(4) Of course one might introduce a special sense of 'real property' for which it is *stipulated* that any 'distinctively normative' property (as defined above) is to count as a 'real' property. But again the minimalist could have no quarrel—except concerning the *point* of such a stipulation.

(5) The only other possibility I can think of is that Wright's notion of 'real' property resembles my notion of 'substantive' property—except for not requiring that there be any prospect of reduction. It may be, in other words, that his conception of 'property with a real nature' appeals to an intuitive picture whereby it is possible for a property to have a 'real nature' even though we can see a priori that no such nature is likely to be specifiable. If this is indeed the right interpretation of Wright's thesis then there are two replies. First, in the absence of some explicit articulation of the criterion for being such a property, and in the absence of any argument for Wright's contention that any distinctively normative property would have to satisfy the criterion, we have absolutely no reason to accept that contention. Second, there is intuitive evidence for the opposite conclusion. For suppose that a concept of 'truth' (perhaps not identical to our own) is introduced by means of the stipulation that it will apply to the proposition *that snow is white* if and only if snow is white, to the proposition *that* $E = mc^2$ if and only if $E = mc^2$, and so on. Then it would seem to be consistent with our intuitive conception of 'real nature' and of 'property constitution' that the 'truth' of the proposition that snow is white simply consists in snow being white, that the 'truth' of the proposition that

$E = mc^2$ simply consists in E being equal to mc^2, etc.,—which will imply that 'truth' *as such* has no real nature. And this despite the fact that it would nonetheless follow from the equivalence schema that 'truth' is a 'distinctive norm' (in Wright's sense). Consequently, it does not follow from the fact that our actual concept of truth is 'distinctively normative' that it stands for a property with a real nature.

9. CONCLUSION

The minimalist picture of truth has three principal components: first an account of the utility of truth (namely, to enable the explicit formulation of schematic generalizations); second, an account of the concept of truth (namely, that 'true' is implicitly defined by the equivalence schema); and third, an account of the nature of truth (namely, that truth has no underlying nature, and that the explanatorily basic facts about it are instances of the equivalence schema).

These ideas are supported as follows. The thesis about utility is justified by a couple of considerations. First there appear to be no other convenient ways of expressing the generalizations that can be captured with the concept of truth; the alternative would be to supplement our language with the relatively cumbersome apparatus of substitutional quantification. And second there appear to be no other advantages of having the concept.

The thesis about the meaning of 'true' is based on two assumptions, both of which are themselves justifiable. First the facts in virtue of which we mean what we do by 'true' are those that best account for our use of the term. And second our use of the term is best explained by our acceptance of the equivalence schema. The first of these assumptions comes out of a general use theory of meaning.[30] The second is justified by the difficulty of finding any uses of the truth predicate that cannot be explained in terms of the equivalence schema. Or to put it another way: it is justified by showing that the generalizing function of the truth predicate is explained by our acceptance of that schema.

The thesis that truth has no underlying nature derives from the foregoing. Given the function of truth, we may infer that the general facts which we need the concept of truth to articulate are not really *about truth*; therefore their explanation would not be facilitated by an account of truth's underlying nature. Rather, the facts about truth that will enter into the

---

[30] A version of the use theory of meaning is defended in Horwich, *Meaning*.

explanation of those generalizations will be instances of the equivalence schema. These instances are conceptually basic and a priori; hence very likely to be insusceptible to reductive explanation. It is reasonable to conclude therefore that truth is not constituted by some more fundamental property.

This is not the place to elaborate the philosophical ramifications of minimalism—but they are evidently considerable. For the concept of truth is deployed throughout philosophy, often in ways that are in tension with the minimalist picture. One example is the formulation of emotivism as the theory that ethical pronouncements have no truth-value. Another is the view that the realism/anti-realism debate concerns the nature of truth. Another is the doctrine that meaning should be explained in terms of truth. Another is the idea that truth is precluded by vagueness and other forms of indeterminacy. In each of these cases, progress towards clearer formulations, and a better sense of where the problems really lie, is achieved by appreciating that truth is metaphysically trivial—nothing more than a device of generalization.

XV

OF WHAT KIND OF THING IS TRUTH A PROPERTY?

MICHAEL DUMMETT

When we say that something is true, of what kind of thing are we saying that it is true? Are we saying of some *sentence*, some form of words, that it is true? Or are we saying that it is what some form of words *expresses* that is true?

In order to maintain that it is sentences that are said to be true, we need to distinguish between type sentences and token sentences. If you were attending a class in the German language, and the teacher asked you to put into German the sentence, 'That man has just broken all the wine glasses', the sentence in question would be a *type* sentence. It would be senseless to ask the teacher which man or which wine glasses were meant: no reference to any particular man, or wine glasses, or occasion, is intended or conveyed, and it would therefore be equally senseless to ask whether the sentence is true or false. If truth is a property of sentences, it can be a property only of *token* sentences, that is, sentences considered as uttered by a particular speaker at a particular time. It would, however, be inconvenient to restrict truth to utterances that are actually made. What often makes it senseless to ask of a mere type sentence whether it is true or false is that no reference has been assigned to component demonstrative expressions like 'that man' or 'the wine glasses', or indexical expressions such as 'here', 'I', 'yesterday'. We must therefore think of truth and falsity as attaching to type sentences taken together with an assignment of references to any expressions of these kinds that occur in them. We might, for this purpose, press into service the term 'statement', taking a 'statement', in this technical usage, to consist precisely of a type sentence together with such an assignment of references to demonstrative and indexical terms.

The alternative is to treat truth as attaching to what a 'statement' expresses. In philosophical writing in English this is usually called a 'proposition'. The term is highly ambiguous, but philosophers writing in other languages usually have an even more confusing terminology. Some philosophers use the word 'proposition' simply to mean 'declarative sentence'; but we have here to consider its use for what such a (token) sentence expresses, as contrasted with the form of words by which that is expressed. Even when the word 'proposition' is used in this way, however, there is great disagreement, in the philosophical tradition, over what propositions are. The external reality of which we speak contains *objects*— human beings and wine glasses, among many others. Are propositions, or at least true ones, also constituents of external reality, though of a different type? Or do propositions stand to token sentences as meanings stand to words—not that *about* which we (normally) speak, but that which we express and convey in speaking?

Fortunately, we do not really need to decide this issue. Philosophers who have regarded true propositions as constituents of external reality have seldom denied that propositions are also what are expressed by utterances of declarative sentences: rather, they have denied that there is any distinction between the two sorts of thing. In a similar way, such philosophers have usually refused to distinguish between the meanings of the names we use as parts of sentences and the objects we use them to denote; for them, the meaning of the name simply is the object named. Bertrand Russell held this view: according to him, the object named is actually part of the proposition we express by means of a sentence in which the name occurs. Other philosophers, such as Gottlob Frege, have drawn a sharp distinction between the senses of our words and that which, in external reality, we use them to talk about. For our purposes, however, we can sidestep this whole issue. A proposition, as opposed to a sentence, is to be what we express by uttering a sentence: that is agreed by both groups of philosophers, that to which Russell belonged as well as that to which Frege belonged. Whether, as Russell thought, a proposition can also be a constituent of external reality, being that which, if true, makes the utterance true, or whether, as Frege thought, it is something quite distinct from what makes the utterance true, is an important question indeed, but one which, for our purposes, we can leave unanswered.

If a proposition, so understood, is to be that to which truth attaches, it cannot, in general, be what is expressed by a type sentence, for the same reason that, if truth attaches to sentences, it cannot, in general, be to type sentences that it attaches. We accordingly need to consider a proposition as involving not only the sense of a type sentence, but also a determination of the references of indexical and demonstrative expressions occurring in it.

Objections to treating truth as a property of propositions rather than of sentences are likely to be heard from philosophers who doubt whether there are any such entities as propositions, or whether there are any such items as senses of type sentences. Such philosophers are impelled by a dread of the error known as 'reification'. Reification consists of understanding a word as applying to or denoting a *thing* of some kind, when in fact it has some quite different function or role in a sentence. For example, I might say to someone 'Make the cheque out in my favour', or remark that the president of an organization resigned in favour of another person. It would be a crude example of reification to think that such remarks imply that people possess things called 'favours', and to try to discover what kind of an object a favour was. It may well seem that, in seeking to decide whether truth is a property of sentences or of propositions, we cannot avoid trying to resolve *this* issue, namely whether there are any such things as propositions at all. But perhaps, if we reformulate the question we are seeking to answer, there will be a way to avoid the issue after all.

Let us first observe that language notoriously uses clauses governed (in English) by the conjunction 'that' in opaque contexts; examples are 'George knows that Napoleon was twice married', 'evidence that the universe is expanding', and 'the hypothesis that the Danes reached America'. An opaque context is usually explained as one in which replacement of an expression by an extensionally equivalent one will not, in general, preserve the truth-value of the whole sentence. Thus, while the name 'Napoleon' is extensionally equivalent to the phrase 'the victor at the battle of Austerlitz' (both denote the same man), the sentence 'George knows that Napoleon was twice married' may be true while 'George knows that the victor at Austerlitz was twice married' is false, because George does not know that Napoleon won the battle of Austerlitz. The replacement of an expression by a *synonymous* one, on the other hand, *will* normally leave the truth-value of the whole unchanged. For instance, if the sentence 'George hopes that his wife will visit her paternal grandfather' is true, then the sentence 'George hopes that his wife will visit her father's father' must be true likewise, because the phrases 'paternal grandfather' and 'father's father' have not only the same application but the same sense. Opaque contexts are perplexing, and no generally acceptable account of them has been put forward. They can, however, neither be eliminated nor dispensed with, and must therefore be explained somehow. For this reason, there can be no objection to using them to give the correct form for ascribing truth. We can accordingly reformulate our question whether truth attaches to sentences or to propositions as the question whether 'is true' is primarily to be used in such a context as

'Some fungi are poisonous' is true,

or in one such as

It is true that some fungi are poisonous,

where the clause governed by 'that' is understood as constituting an opaque context. We may call the first of these two forms the 'S form' and the second the 'P form'. I have taken as an example a sentence, 'Some fungi are poisonous', that contains no demonstrative or indexical expression. For a sentence that does contain such expressions, the choice must lie between forms allowing their references to be specified in an ancillary manner. The S form will be, for example:

'I will go to Sofia tomorrow', considered as said by John on Monday, was true

and the P form:

It was true of John on Monday that he was going to Sofia the next day.

We may, for convenience, continue to speak of the P form as consisting in the ascription of truth to propositions. But if we do in this way continue to use the terminology of 'propositions', we must do so only in ways that admit of reformulation in terms of the use of clauses governed by the conjunction 'that'. If we violate this proviso, we shall lose the right to ignore the arguments of those who think that to speak of propositions is to be guilty of reification.

There is no question of declaring either the S form or the P form illegitimate: we use both, and so both have to be explained. It is a question only of which form we take to be *primary*. When we seek to explain or analyse the notion of truth, we must decide which of these two ways of ascribing truth is the primary one, which we must explain in the first instance. We shall then have, as a subordinate task, to devise a means of explaining the other form in terms of that which we have taken as primary, regarded as already understood: but, unless we can show that the choice between them is in some way unreal, we must take one of them to be that in which the notion of truth is most faithfully expressed, and in terms of which it is to be explained.

The choice, as I stated it, is not just between two verbal forms. The grammar or logical structure of the S form is unproblematic: the property of truth is being predicated of a sentence, considered, if necessary, as uttered by a particular speaker at a particular time. The possibility exists of understanding the P form in such a way as to make its grammar or logical structure equally unproblematic, namely by taking the clause governed by 'that' to constitute a transparent context. On that understanding of the P form, the grammatical conjunction 'that' will not be taken as belonging to the clause it governs, but as part of a sentential operator 'it is true that . . .'. It will thus be an expression of the same logical type as the negation operator, as logicians understand it. The negation operator functions to form a new sentence, when prefixed to any sentence; the new sentence will be false if the original sentence was true, and true if the original sentence was false. The operator 'It is true that . . .', understood in this way, is even more simple. It, too, serves to form a new sentence, when prefixed to any sentence; but this time the new sentence will be true if the original sentence was true, and false if the original sentence was false. Just because, on this interpretation of the P form, we are taking the subordinate clause as forming a transparent context, there will be no problem about the logical grammar of the words in that clause: they will be functioning in just the way that they normally function.

The choice I proposed was not, however, simply one between the S form and the P form: it was the choice between the S form and the P form *so interpreted as to make the subordinate clause an opaque context*. The grammar or logical structure of the P form, when so understood, is *not* unproblematic. Admittedly, if we regard the clause beginning with and including the conjunction 'that' as standing for a proposition, the main structure of the sentence is straightforward: the property of truth is being predicated of a proposition. But the logical grammar of the subordinate clause *is* problematic: how do the words in it—for example, 'fungi', 'poisonous', and so on—serve, when prefixed by the word 'that', to form an expression denoting a proposition? Plainly, they cannot be playing their normal roles. Moreover, we cannot assume that the subordinate clause does denote a proposition. It was precisely to evade the objections of those who deny that there are any such entities as propositions that we reformulated our question as a choice between two linguistic forms for ascribing truth; and, if we refrain from taking the clause governed by 'that' to denote a proposition, the whole logical structure of the P form becomes difficult to perceive.

Should we not, then, make the choice one between three, rather than only two, possibilities, taking as the third possibility the P form, with the subordinate clause understood as being a *transparent* context? Admittedly, this third possibility could scarcely be, even loosely, described as treating truth as a property of propositions: but ought we not at least to recognize the possibility as an interpretation that might be adopted in preference to both the other two? No: for we are after the *primary* way of ascribing truth, that on the basis of which the notion of truth is eventually to be explained. The interpretation of 'It is true that . . .' as a sentential operator is undoubtedly a possible one. But it cannot be the primary use of 'is true', at least if, as I did, we use the notions of truth and falsity in explaining how the operator functions. For our purposes, therefore, we may set it aside as incapable of yielding what we want.

But have we any right to regard the subordinate clause in a sentence of the P form as forming an opaque context? Does it not go against our characterization of opaque contexts to treat such a clause as constituting one? Surely such clauses are clear instances of transparent contexts. If in the sentence 'It is true that Napoleon married twice' we substitute the phrase 'the victor at Austerlitz' for the name 'Napoleon', we are certain to obtain a sentence with the same truth-value as the one we started with, given that 'Napoleon' and 'the victor at Austerlitz' refer to the same man: so with what right can we construe the clause following 'that' in this sentence as being an opaque context?

This challenge assumes that the property we used to characterise opaque contexts amounts to a *definition* of the term 'opaque context'. By a 'context' is meant in this connection a segment of a sentence: and the property in question was that the replacement of any expression occurring in that segment by an extensionally equivalent one does not guarantee that the truth-value of the whole sentence will be preserved. Possession of this property does not *define* what it is for a context to be opaque: it is merely a symptom. If a given context has this property, we must indeed recognize it as opaque. But the fact that, in a particular context, the replacement of a constituent expression by an extensionally equivalent one will always leave the truth-value of the whole sentence unchanged does not debar us from construing that context as opaque. What we are concerned with is the logical structure of a segment of a sentence and of the sentence as a whole. To anlayse the logical structure of a sentence is to explain how the words that compose it combine to give it the meaning that it has. If we say of a certain segment of a sentence that it constitutes a transparent context, we shall have made a small positive contribution to analysing the logical structure of that sentence; for it amounts to saying that the words in that segment play their normal roles. If, on the other hand, we say that the segment forms an opaque context, we shall merely have made a negative contribution. An opaque context is simply one in which, for one reason or another, the words occurring in it are *not* to be considered as playing their normal roles. This does not tell us what roles they do play: it merely tells us that some special explanation of their roles in the given sentence will be needed. If the context has the property that extensionally equivalent expressions cannot be substituted within it without the danger that the truth-value of the whole will be changed, this is enough to show that the words in that context cannot be playing their normal roles; the context must therefore be opaque. But if the context lacks this property, we have a choice between regarding it as transparent and regarding it as opaque; we may regard it as opaque if there is some other good reason for thinking that the words in it do not play their normal roles. In a sentence of the P form, such as 'It is true that some fungi are poisonous', we therefore have just such a choice.

We can express the choice as lying between taking the conjunction 'that', in an analysis of the logical structure of the sentence, as going with the clause that follows it or with the words that precede it. If, in the sentence 'It is true that some fungi are poisonous', the words 'some fungi are poisonous' are playing their normal roles, and so constituting a subsentence that contributes to determining the truth or falsity of the whole sentence solely by whether that subsentence is true or false, then our task is simply to explain the meaning of the words preceding it, among which the word 'that' is included: we must ask what 'it is true that' means. But if the words 'some fungi are poisonous' are not playing their normal roles, this must be because of some peculiarity of the clause in which they are embedded, and then we must take the conjunction 'that' which introduces that clause as going with *them*.

What reason can we have for thinking that, to change the example, in such a sentence as 'It is true that Tokyo is crowded', the words in the clause 'that Tokyo is crowded' are not functioning in the normal way? In sentences like 'Jones believes that Tokyo is crowded' that ascribe to some subject what Russell called a 'propositional attitude' such as belief, hope, or expectation, the clause governed by 'that' unquestionably forms an opaque context. Russell indeed chose the term 'propositional attitude' because he thought that the subordinate clause denoted a proposition and that the whole sentence expressed that subject's attitude to that proposition: on this view, the sentence 'Jones believes that Tokyo is crowded' states that Jones has a certain relation or attitude, in this case that of belief, to the object of his belief, namely the proposition that Tokyo is crowded, denoted by the clause 'that Tokyo is crowded'. But we do not merely use such a clause in both types of context, to ascribe truth and to ascribe a propositional attitude to someone: we combine them in a single sentence. We can say, for example, 'Jones believes that Tokyo is crowded and it is quite true' or, again, 'That Tokyo is crowded is well known, and that implies that it is true'. In both sentences, the pronoun 'it' refers back to the clause 'that Tokyo is crowded', and could be replaced by a repetition of it. It seems implausible to suppose that, if it were so replaced, the two occurrences of the clause would be functioning quite differently and would require different logical analyses.

This consideration is far from conclusive. More telling is the role of such clauses in inferences. The inference

(A)   Jones believes that Tokyo is crowded
        It is true that Tokyo is crowded
        Therefore, Jones has a true belief

is unquestionably valid. It is unproblematic if, in both premisses, the clause governed by 'that' forms an opaque context, but problematic if it forms a transparent context in the second premiss, since it indisputably forms an opaque context in the first. It may be objected that

(B)   Jones believes that Tokyo is crowded
        Tokyo is crowded
        Therefore, Jones has a true belief

is equally valid, though problematic. Its problematic character can be localized, though not, of course, dispelled, by expanding it so as to make (A) a subargument; set out in tree form, the expanded argument will run:

(C)   Tokyo is crowded
        Hence it is true that   Jones believes that
        Tokyo is crowded   Tokyo is crowded
          Therefore, Jones believes something true

where, again, the clause following 'it is true that' is taken to form an opaque context. The only problematic step is that from 'Tokyo is crowded' to 'It is true that Tokyo is crowded'; and, in all inferences that are problematic for a reason of this kind, the problem can be localized to an inference of this form, or to one of the converse form. This supplies a strong reason for construing the phrase 'it is true that' as inducing an opaque context.

This argument is not intended to establish the necessity, but only the possibility, of understanding 'it is true that' in this way, and thereby of speaking of truth and falsity as ascribed to propositions, without admitting the need to reify them. If 'it is true that' is treated as a sentential operator, then of course argument (A) becomes a mere variant on argument (B), and the expansion (C) pointless. The problematic character of the arguments will remain: we do, legitimately, switch from a sentence in a transparent context to one containing the same sentence in an opaque context, and conversely, however this is to be explained. It is just that we shall no longer have a way of localizing this transition.

Now everyday usage affords us no help in choosing between the two alternatives, ascribing truth or falsity to a sentence and ascribing it to a proposition, because we habitually use both idioms. This is natural, since, given the conception of a sentence's expressing a proposition, either idiom can readily be explained in terms of the other. A true sentence is one that expresses a true proposition; a true proposition is one such that any sentence expressing it is true. As I previously remarked, our question is whether it is to sentences or to propositions that truth *primarily* attaches.

But, still, does it matter? More exactly, need there be any preferred answer to the question? There is a parallel question concerning the ascription of propositional attitudes: is belief, for example, an attitude to sentences or to propositions? It is difficult to take this question seriously. If belief is an attitude to sentences, we may call the relevant attitude that of 'believing-true'. We must not here explain believing-true a sentence as believing *that* the sentence is true, since this would be to explain the attitude to sentences, which is supposed to be being treated as fundamental, in terms of what looks like an attitude to a proposition. Rather, the attitude of believing-true must be so understood that someone is capable of having such an attitude to a sentence without ever having heard or thought of it, without being able to understand it, and without knowing the language to which it belongs. The advantage claimed for treating belief as an attitude to sentences is that it eliminates reference to such entities as propositions. The cost is that we must now explain the required sense of 'believes-true'. The explanation will necessarily involve an account of the relation between any sentence and its equivalent within the same language, and that between it and its translation into another language. Very little will have been gained.

The parallel between the question whether belief is an attitude to sentences or to propositions and the question whether truth is a property of sentences or of propositions is very inexact. In the first place, natural language uses both forms, the S form and the P form, for ascribing truth, whereas it has only one form for ascribing a belief to a subject, namely the form using a clause governed by 'that'. The exponents of the view that belief is an attitude to sentences intend that 'He believes-true the sentence "Some fungi are poisonous"' shall have the sense expressed in natural language by 'He believes that some fungi are poisonous'. This intention provides a further decisive reason for distinguishing between 'He believes-true the sentence "Some fungi are poisonous"' and 'He believes that the sentence "Some fungi are poisonous" is true'; for there is plainly a difference between believing that a sentence is true and believing the proposition expressed by that sentence. Here I am employing the locution 'He believes the proposition expressed by "Some fungi are poisonous"' simply as meaning 'He believes that some fungi are poisonous', without any commitment to the existence of such entities as propositions. The difference between believing that a sentence is true and believing the proposition it expresses arises from the fact that one who does not understand a sentence may still have grounds for believing it to be true, though this in no way implies that he believes the proposition it expresses. Conversely, he may well believe that proposition, without having any reason to think that particular sentence to be true.

The situation as regards truth is quite different. One who holds that truth is a property of sentences is not wishing to claim that the S form 'The sentence "Some fungi are poisonous" is true' has the very same meaning as the P form 'It is true that some fungi are poisonous'; indeed, in view of the fact that either might express a belief that someone held without his believing what was expressed by the other, he could not claim that. Rather, he simply claims that the S form is primary, and that the P form must be explained in terms of it (not necessarily as equivalent to it).

In view of this difference, we cannot argue that it does not matter whether we take truth as a property of sentences or of propositions along the same lines as those on which we can argue that it does not matter whether we take belief as an attitude to sentences or to propositions. Naturally, someone who understands the sentence 'Some fungi are poisonous' will immediately conclude, from being told that the sentence is true, that some fungi are poisonous. It does not follow that it is all one whether we take the locution

'Some fungi are poisonous' is true

(the S form) or the locution

It is true that some fungi are poisonous

(the P form) as primary, still less that we can always switch from one to the other with complete indifference.

A philosopher strongly of the opinion that there is no significant difference between the two locutions—the S form and the P form—is Professor Elizabeth Anscombe. This opinion is expressed in her currently unpublished essay 'Making True'. She remarks first that she need not concern herself with the direct speech form; she at least 'would translate it into a foreign language altogether', she says, 'unless there was some particular purpose for which I needed to leave the quoted bits in English'. By 'the direct speech form', she means the S form, when truth is being ascribed, but also, I think, any occurrence of a sentence in quotation marks within a larger sentence, as when we report what someone said by quoting his actual words.

Let us pause, first to consider this remark. It is indeed an important fact that the conventional manner of translating a sentence reporting speech by direct quotation is to translate the quoted speech as well, not to leave it in the original. When, in the English translation of a French history book, you read, 'Napoleon said, "Ney has blundered"', you do not suppose that Napoleon spoke in English. What this shows is that, in such a case, the conventional canons of translation do *not* require that the sense of the original be strictly preserved. If they did, then the sentence quoted from Napoleon would have had to be in French, since it is to a French sentence that the original refers.

This fact is relevant to a celebrated argument of the famous American logician Alonzo Church to show that belief is not an attitude to sentences but to propositions. Church argued that if the sentence 'Galileo believed that the Earth moves' stated Galileo's attitude of believing-true the *English* sentence 'The Earth moves', then, when translated into Italian, that English sentence ought to be mentioned, not the Italian sentence 'La terra si muove' which expresses the same proposition.[1] Admittedly, the attitude of believing-true needs to be so explained that, if Galileo believed-true the English sentence, he believed-true the Italian one, and conversely. Nevertheless, the accepted mode of translating a sentence reporting a belief in indirect speech—a clause governed by the conjunction 'that'— would not strictly preserve the sense of the original. This argument fails because the accepted canons of translation cannot be presumed to involve strict preservation of sense, as Church's argument assumes that they do; and this is shown by the fact that they normally require the translation of the quoted sentence when direct speech is used.

Professor Anscombe's remark tells us only what she would normally do in translating a sentence reporting speech by direct quotation, which is what anyone else would do. There is, however, a strong suggestion that, in so translating it, she *would* be strictly preserving sense, and hence that the sentences 'Galileo said "The Earth moves"' and 'Galileo said that the Earth moves' have exactly the same meaning, or at least that this holds good of the S form ' "The Earth moves" is true' and the P form 'It is true that the Earth moves'.

---

[1] A. Church, 'On Carnap's Analysis of Statements of Assertion and Belief', *Analysis*, 10 (1950), 97–9.

The S form and the P form cannot *always* be equivalent on her view, however, since she hastens to make the point that I made earlier in this chapter, that there are exceptional cases in which someone has reason for thinking that a sentence he did not understand was true, although he could not be said to think the proposition it expressed was true. One would think that, if two forms of sentence failed to have the same meaning in *some* contexts, they could not have precisely the same meaning in *other* contexts, unless the meaning of one of them changed from one type of context to the other; but Professor Anscombe does not make it plain whether she thinks that such a change of meaning occurs.

However this may be, Professor Anscombe goes on, immediately after remarking that she need not concern herself with the direct speech form, to state that she considers the three forms of sentence:

(i) Some fungi are poisonous
(ii) 'Some fungi are poisonous' is true
(iii) It is true that some fungi are poisonous

to be equivalent (perhaps we ought to say 'usually to be equivalent'). (I have here substituted a particular sentence, 'Some fungi are poisonous' for the schematic letter 'Q' she uses to indicate the generality of her thesis.) The view that (ii) and (iii) are equivalent is simply an assertion that the S form and the P form have the same meaning. It is therefore indifferent, in Professor Anscombe's opinion, whether we ascribe truth to sentences or to propositions: But she says more than this. She also claims that (i), the simple sentence, is equivalent to both (ii) and (iii), the S form and the P form.

This claim appears to put Professor Anscombe in the camp of those philosophers who advocate what is generally known as a 'minimalist' theory of truth. Minimalists, too, are divided between those who treat the S form (ii) as primary and those who treat the P form (iii) as primary. Those of the former school not only regard (i) and (ii) as equivalent, but claim that the equivalence between them (and between all similar pairs) contains essentially the *whole* explanation of the concept of truth. Those of the latter school regard (i) and (iii) as equivalent, and claim that the equivalence between *them* (and between all similar pairs) contains essentially the *whole* explanation of the concept of truth. Professor Anscombe, by equating the forms (ii) and (iii) appears to have adopted a super-minimalist position.

We need to take care over thus describing her view, however. Frege asserted that the forms (i) and (iii) had exactly the same sense. Nevertheless, he was not a minimalist: he did not say that the equivalence

between them and similar pairs constituted an explanation of the concept
of truth. On the contrary, he insisted that the notion of truth is indefinable,
and called logic the theory of truth. But what Professor Anscombe goes
on to say makes it clear that she *is* a minimalist. Once it has been laid down
that (i), (ii), and (iii) are all equivalent, everything has been said about
truth that needs to be said.

Professor Anscombe is also an adherent of a truth-conditional theory
of meaning, that is, of the principle that the meaning of a sentence is to
be given by stating the conditions under which a particular utterance of it
is true. Note that what is in question here is how the meaning of a *sentence*, not that of a *proposition*, is to be explained. There is no such thing
as the meaning of a proposition, as we have agreed to use the term 'proposition'. On this use, a proposition is what a sentence expresses, or, more
exactly, what is expressed by an utterance of the sentence on a particular
occasion: when you know what proposition will be expressed by uttering
the sentence on each particular occasion, then you know what the sentence
means.

There are many versions of the truth-conditional theory of meaning;
and I have argued that no version of it can be combined with a minimalist account of truth. Suppose that an inquirer genuinely does not understand a certain sentence, say 'Some fungi are poisonous', and wants to
know what it means: he is not merely using the sentence as a philosophical example. And suppose that he addresses his inquiry what the sentence
means to an adherent of a truth-conditional theory of meaning, who replies
by giving an account of the conditions under which an utterance of the
sentence will be true. In order for such an account to constitute a successful
explanation of what the sentence means, it is necessary that the enquirer
should know what the word 'true' means. He need not, of course, be
capable of giving a philosophical analysis of its meaning; but if it is a word
he does not know at all, one of which he does not have even an implicit
understanding, then obviously he will not derive any grasp of the meaning
of the sentence from the explanation he has been given of it. Suppose now
that he asks a minimalist to explain the word 'true' to him. The minimalist replies that what saying that a particular sentence is true amounts to
depends on the sentence said to be true. 'Well, then', the enquirer asks,
'what does it amount to to say that the sentence' "Some fungi are poisonous" is true?' 'It amounts to saying that some fungi are poisonous', the
minimalist replies. Now have the truth-conditional theorist and the minimalist between them given the enquirer the explanation that he was
seeking? Obviously not. He cannot understand the final reply of the minimalist because he does not know what 'Some fungi are poisonous' means;

what it means was indeed the very question he was in the first place seeking to have answered.

What the inquirer needed was a *general* explanation, or at least a general understanding, of what is meant by saying that a sentence (or a particular utterance of one) is true, not a separate explanation for each individual sentence. He needed this in order to understand what he was being told when he was told the condition that must hold for the sentence 'Some fungi are poisonous' to be true. In order for him to recognize this explanation as providing him with the meaning of the sentence, he needed something more. He needed, if not to know explicitly, then at least to grasp, the connection between the condition for a sentence to be true and the significance of uttering it in any context: the connection between the truth conditions of a sentence and its *use*. Truth-conditional theorists of meaning usually presume a grasp of this connection: they seldom, if ever, spell it out.

Professor Anscombe criticizes, as being based on a misunderstanding, the foregoing argument to show that an explanation of what the word 'true' means solely by appeal to equivalences such as that between (i) and (ii) is incompatible with a truth-conditional account of meaning. She devises a dialogue to reproduce that argument, which I shall again adapt by substituting the sentence 'Some fungi are poisonous' for the schematic letter 'p' which she uses for the sake of generality.

So adapted, the dialogue begins with someone's asking, 'What is the meaning of such a sentence as "Some fungi are poisonous"?' The answer is 'Its meaning is given by giving a comprehensive account of the conditions under which it is true.' We may take it that Professor Anscombe would endorse this answer. We may thus see her as envisaging an explanation as taking the general form of a biconditional:

(1) 'Some fungi are poisonous' is true if and only if . . .

the dots being filled by a sentence constituting a 'comprehensive account' of the appropriate condition.

The questioner now asks, 'But what does " 'Some fungi are poisonous' is true" mean?', and receives the answer, 'It means the same as "Some fungi are poisonous" '. We may take Professor Anscombe as also endorsing *this* answer, which explains (ii) as being equivalent to (i).

The questioner objects that what 'Some fungi are poisonous' means was just what he wanted to know in the first place. 'In short', Professor Anscombe says, summarizing the argument and, in the process, switching from the S form to the P form, 'If "Some fungi are poisonous" and "It is true that some fungi are poisonous" are equivalent, and you tell me conditions on which it is true that some fungi are poisonous, I do not know what you have given me conditions of, if I do not *already* know what it means to say, "Some fungi are poisonous"'. This argument, she says, is based on a misunderstanding. We may safely take it that she thinks that, in her imaginary dialogue, the questioner goes astray only with his final objection. Explaining how he went astray, she says, 'You do not know, until you are told them, either the conditions on which it is true that some fungi are poisonous, or the conditions given which, some fungi are poisonous— but they are the same'. 'To say that you do not know what "It is true that some fungi are poisonous" means is the same as to say that you do not know what asserting "Some fungi are poisonous" comes to', she says further. She concludes that the term 'truth conditions' 'is just a convenient locution'.

Professor Anscombe's essay propounds an idea which I think is wrong but which others have also propounded. I have chosen to comment on her essay because she specifically applies this mistaken idea in criticism of an argument which I think is both sound and important. This underlying idea is that, in virtue of the alleged equivalence between the three forms of statement (i), (ii), and (iii), it will always be possible to avoid the use of the word 'true', and of expressions such as 'the condition for the truth of . . .', when we are concerned with any one particular sentence; it is only in enunciating the general principle of truth-conditional explanations of meaning that the notion of truth is needed.

The reasoning behind this idea is as follows. Suppose that someone is reading a book, and comes across the sentence (quite false, of course) 'Every fungus is poisonous'. He asks me what it means. I could quite adequately answer him by saying, 'Every fungus is poisonous just in case all plants without chlorophyll cause anyone who eats them to become ill or die'. Admittedly, I should be somewhat unlikely to do so; I should be more likely to say, 'The statement "Every fungus is poisonous" is true just in case all plants without chlorophyll cause anyone who eats them to become ill or die' or 'It is true that every fungus is poisonous just in case all plants without chlorophyll cause anyone who eats them to become ill or die'. But if I answered in either of these two ways, all that the person who asked me to explain would have to know about the meaning of the word 'true' is that 'The statement "Every fungus is poisonous" is true' or 'It is true that every fungus is poisonous' holds good if and only if every fungus is poisonous. We are more inclined to explain particular words without using 'semantic' terms such as 'denote' and 'apply to' than we are to explain a whole sentence without using the word 'true'; asked what the word 'lacrosse' meant, for example, I should be more likely to say something beginning 'Lacrosse is a team game played . . .' than something beginning 'The word "lacrosse" is the name of (or: denotes) a team game played . . .'. All the same, we *can* adopt the analogous way of explaining the meaning of a sentence; and this is because the forms of statement (ii) and (iii) express no more than the simple form (i). A minimalist theory of truth is compatible with a so-called truth-conditional account of meaning just because truth is not an essential component of the account, when it is applied to any one particular sentence. The condition for the truth of 'Every fungus is poisonous' is just the condition for every fungus to be poisonous.

That is the reasoning underlying Professor Anscombe's criticism of my argument for the incompatibility of a minimalist account of truth with a truth-conditional account of meaning. In accordance with it, her conception of the most straightforward way to explain the meaning of the sentence 'Every fungus is poisonous' is:

> (2) Every fungus is poisonous if and only if all plants without chlorophyll cause those who eat them to become ill or die

But how can (2) be a way of giving the meaning of the sentence 'Every fungus is poisonous', when (2) does not even *mention* that sentence? The objection may appear trifling and pedantic; for, while (2) does not *mention* the sentence 'Every fungus is poisonous', it *uses* it, just as an explanation of the word 'lacrosse' that begins 'Lacrosse is a team game . . .' uses, though it does not mention, the word.

Nevertheless, this apparently pedantic objection contains the crucial point. It would be a strange account of meaning that applied only to English sentences—more exactly, to sentences of the language in which the account was given—and could not be extended to sentences of other languages. How, then, could we frame in English a truth-conditional account of the meaning of the French sentence 'Chaque champignon est vénéneux'? We must aim at giving such an account in accordance with the way Professor Anscombe conceives it. We might try, as a first attempt:

> (3) 'Chaque champignon est vénéneux' is true if and only if all plants without chlorophyll cause those who eat them to become ill or die.

But, to obtain an explanation of the kind desired by Professor Anscombe, we must remove the word 'true'; and how can we do that? We cannot simply substitute in (3) the sentence 'Chaque champignon est vénéneux' in place of the clause ' "Chaque champignon est vénéneux" is true', for we should obtain a sentence half in French and half in English. The best we can do is to substitute 'Every fungus is poisonous' for ' "Chaque

champignon est vénéneux" is true'. By this means, we shall transform (3)
into (2).

But how could (2) be regarded as giving the meaning of the *French* sentence 'Chaque champignon est vénéneux'? It does not mention that sentence; nor does it use it. Because it does use the English sentence 'Every
fungus is poisonous', (2) can certainly serve to convey the meaning of that
sentence to someone who is ignorant of it, but understands English in
general. Such a person would grasp that the clause following 'if and only
if' was intended as an equivalent of the clause preceding it. But that is
merely a means of conveying the meaning of an English sentence to an
English speaker. It certainly does not exemplify a philosophical account of
what it is for a sentence to have the meaning that it has; and that is shown
by the utter inability of this form of explanation to state the meaning of a
sentence of a language other than that in which it itself is framed.

What someone has to know in order to know the meaning of a declarative sentence may be dissected into two components. He has, on the one
hand, to grasp the proposition that the sentence expresses. And he has, on
the other, to know that the sentence expresses that proposition. He may
grasp the proposition without understanding the sentence, perhaps by
being able to express that proposition in another language. But a philosophical account of what it is for a sentence to have the meaning that it
has cannot avoid referring to, that is, *mentioning*, that sentence; for otherwise it cannot explain, or even acknowledge, the second component of a
knowledge of its meaning. It therefore cannot renounce the use of the term
'true', considered as applying to the *sentence*; for it is by means of the term
'true' that we say what proposition it is that the sentence expresses.

More exactly stated, according to a truth-conditional theory of meaning,
the term 'true' is what we use in order to say what proposition it is
that the sentence expresses. I do not wish myself to advocate a truth-
conditional theory. I am deeply suspicious of the notion expressed by the
phrase 'knowing what it is for . . .', completed by such a phrase as 'one
event to be the cause of another'; but this notion is indispensable in a truth-
conditional account of understanding. On a theory of meaning of some
other kind, we may possibly need, not the notion of truth, but some other
notion, in order to say what proposition it is that a given sentence
expresses. Without deciding between competing theories of meaning, all
we can say is that we shall need a term that applies to *sentences*.

In speaking of a dissection of an understanding of a sentence into two
components, I am not wishing to argue that a theory of meaning for a
language ought to break into two distinct parts, one of them explaining
what propositions the sentences of the language express, while the other

explains in what grasping those propositions consists. The second component of understanding is dependent on the first. One can grasp a proposition without knowing that a certain sentence expresses it; but one cannot know what proposition a sentence expresses without grasping that proposition. A theory of meaning for a language that merely specifies which proposition each sentence of the language expresses must therefore rely on a grasp of those propositions by those to whom the theory is addressed. That is what I have labelled a 'modest' theory of meaning; it is evident that such a theory fails to make explicit all that is involved in a knowledge of the language. A full-blooded theory of meaning, which does seek to make that explicit, must explain in what grasping the propositions expressible in the language consists; but it does not follow that it must explain this independently of an ability to speak the language. One who has that ability thereby grasps the propositions expressible in it. His employment of the language itself manifests his grasp of them; so there is no need of an independent account of what such a grasp involves.

The upshot of this discussion is, then, as follows. If anything resembling a truth-conditional theory of meaning is correct, the notion of truth is indissolubly linked to that of meaning. It is vain to try to explain either notion by taking the other as already understood: they have to be explained *together*. The joint explanation will be highly complex: it will be nothing less than an account of how language functions as a whole. In this explanation, truth must be taken as a property of sentences, or rather of particular utterances of them, not as a property of propositions: for to speak of propositions is to assume the meanings of sentences to be already known (and therefore as explained without appeal to the notion of truth). A minimalist account of truth is incompatible with a truth-conditional account of meaning, for it cannot supply that link between the condition for a sentence to be true and the use of that sentence in discourse which needs to be grasped if a statement of that condition is to determine the meaning of the sentence. Only if the right theory of meaning should turn out to be one in which the notion of truth plays no essential role is it possible that a minimalist account of that notion would be adequate; and that seems highly unlikely.

XVI

A CRITIQUE OF DEFLATIONISM

ANIL GUPTA

I

Throughout much of this century there have been two types of philosophical debates over the concept of truth. In the first, *substantive*, type of
debate we find rival theories of truth put forward that seem to have, and
whose proponents have taken them to have, significant metaphysical and
epistemological implications. An early example of this type is the debate
in the early 1900s between the British idealists (F. H. Bradley and his followers) and the logical atomists (Bertrand Russell and his followers). The
idealists defended a coherence theory of truth, whereas the logical atomists argued for a correspondence theory. This dispute over the theory of
truth was not, and was not taken by the participants to be, a local disagreement. It was integral to the larger metaphysical debate between the
two sides over monism and pluralism and over idealism and realism. A
recent example of the substantive type is the debate between the realist
and the anti-realist found in Michael Dummett's writings. The crux of the
debate here is what notion of truth is admissible. Dummett's anti-realist
argues for a notion of truth that is constrained by evidence, while the realist
defends the admissibility of a radically non-epistemic notion.

In the first type of debate, then, we find theses put forward and defended
that have (or at least seem to have) substantial philosophical implications.
Debates of this type presuppose that truth has a substantial role to play in
philosophical inquiry. In the debates of the second, *metaphilosophical*, type
the presupposition is called into question. An early example of this type is
the debate over the claim, made by some logical positivists, that truth is a
metaphysical concept and hence ought to be banished from all rigorous
and scientific thought. A decisive contribution to this debate was made by
Alfred Tarski, who gave a definition of truth (for certain languages) that

From Anil Gupta, 'A Critique of Deflationism', *Philosophical Topics*, 21/2 (1993), 57–81.
Reprinted by permission of The University of Arkansas Press and the author.

was adequate by the positivists' own strictures. Tarski's definition used only terms that the positivists found legitimate, and it defined a notion that was provably coextensive with truth. Tarski's work was widely viewed as establishing the legitimacy and the usefulness of truth in philosophical inquiry. One result of its influence was a shift away from a syntactical conception of language and towards a semantical one.[1]

Ironically, Tarski's work, while refuting one sort of scepticism about the usefulness of truth, provided a basis for a different, more compelling, kind of scepticism. This new kind of scepticism, *deflationism*, maintains that truth is a simple and clear concept and has no substantial role to play in philosophy. Substantive debates over truth, according to deflationism, are in error not because they work with a notion that is metaphysically loaded (and hence corrupt), but because they work with a notion that is metaphysically lightweight. Deflationism has provoked a large debate among philosophers—a debate that provides a contemporary instance of the second, metaphilosophical, type of debate distinguished above.

A deflationary view typically consists of two parts: (i) a description of the meaning and function of 'true' and (ii) a derivation from that description of deflationary consequences concerning truth. As an example of (i), consider the following passage from Michael Williams: It contains a popular account of the meaning and function of 'true'. (In the next section I shall explain and discuss the account in detail.)

[W]hen we have pointed to certain formal features of the truth-predicate (notably its 'disquotational' feature) and explained why it is useful to have a predicate like this (e.g. as a device for asserting infinite conjunctions), we have said just about everything there is to be said about truth.[2]

Examples of (ii) can be found in Sections III and IV below. The following extracts illustrate the sorts of deflationary consequences that are often drawn. The first extract is from Richard Rorty and the remaining two are from Scott Soames and Paul Horwich.[3]

[T]ruth is not the sort of thing one should expect to have a philosophically interesting theory about.[4]

---

[1] See e.g. R. Carnap, *Introduction to Semantics* (Cambridge, Mass., 1942).
[2] 'Epistemological Realism and the Basis of Scepticism', *Mind*, 97 (1988), 415–39; the extract appears on p. 424.
[3] I shall base my account of deflationism on the writings of a number of philosophers. I want to emphasize that while there are important similarities in the ideas of the philosophers I rely on, there are also important differences. No views, unless explicitly attributed to the individual authors, should be ascribed to them.
[4] Rorty, *Consequences of Pragmatism* (Minneapolis, 1982), p. xiii.

What does seem right about Tarski's approach is its deflationist character. . . . Truth is a useful notion, but it is not the key to what there is, or to how we represent the world to ourselves through language.[5]

[Truth is not] a deep and vital element of philosophical theory. . . . [T]he realism/ anti-realism issue (together with various related issues in the philosophy of science) have nothing at all to do with truth.[6]

In short, deflationism holds that once we understand the meaning and function of 'true'—and this understanding, according to deflationism, is not hard to achieve—we shall see that truth has no substantial role to play in philosophy. Many contemporary philosophers find the deflationary account of 'true' attractive and plausible, and they have accepted (some-times enthusiastically, sometimes regretfully) its negative verdict on the role of the concept of truth in philosophy.

I want to oppose deflationary attitudes in philosophy. The main problem with deflationism, in my view, lies in the descriptive account it gives of 'true'. The deflationary account makes (and, to sustain its conclusions, needs to make) some very strong claims about the meaning of 'true'—claims that on examination prove to be highly problematic. The account appears plausi-ble, I think, only because we read its claims in a weaker way. But the weaker readings do not, I believe, yield any deflationary conclusions.

The argument I shall develop against deflationism, then, is this. The deflationary description of 'true', when it is taken in the strong and intended way, motivates the deflationary conclusions, but is highly problematic. On the other hand, when it is taken in the weaker way, the description is correct enough, but does not yield the deflationary conclusions. I shall substantiate this by considering deflationary arguments on two issues: the possibility of a physicalistic theory of truth (Section III), and truth and meaning (Section IV). Deflationists take the concept of truth to be transparent, one capable of a complete and simple philosophical analysis. Towards the end of the chapter (Section V) I shall point out some reasons to think that truth is a highly puzzling notion, one that defies all our attempts at its analysis.

II

Let us consider the *disquotational* account of the meaning of 'true', which we encountered briefly in the extract from Williams.[7] Its original

[5] Soames, 'What is a Theory of Truth?', *Journal of Philosophy*, 81/8 (1984), 411–29; the extract appears on p. 429.

[6] Horwich, *Truth* (Oxford, 1990), 54.

[7] Deflationists have offered several closely related descriptions of 'true.' In this chapter I choose to focus on just one description—that contained in the disquotational account.

source is the following well-known passage from W. V. Quine's *Philosophy of Logic*.[8]

By calling the sentence ['snow is white'] true, we call snow white. The truth predicate is a device of disquotation. We may affirm the single sentence by just uttering it, unaided by quotation or by the truth predicate; but if we want to affirm some infinite lot of sentences that we can demarcate only by talking about the sentences, then the truth predicate has its use. We need it to restore the effect of objective reference when for the sake of some generalization we have resorted to semantic ascent.[9]

Stephen Leeds provides, in the following extract, a useful elaboration of the disquotational account.

It is not surprising that we should have use for a predicate P with the property that ' "——" is P' and '——' are always interdeducible. For we frequently find ourselves in a position to assert each sentence in a certain infinite set z (e.g., when all the members of z share a common form); lacking the means to formulate infinite conjunctions, we find it convenient to have a single sentence which is warranted precisely when each member of z is warranted. A predicate P with the property described allows us to construct such a sentence: $(x)(x \in z \rightarrow P(x))$. Truth is thus a notion that we might reasonably want to have on hand, for expressing semantic ascent and descent, infinite conjunction and disjunction. And given that we want such a notion, it is not difficult to explain how it is that we have been able to invent one.[10]

The core thought here is that the function of the truth predicate is to serve certain expressive purposes, namely, that of expressing certain infinite conjunctions and disjunctions. The truth predicate serves these functions in virtue of its disquotational character; i.e., in virtue of the fact that it undoes the effect of quotation marks.[11] For example, the role of 'true' in

---

Nevertheless, the arguments developed below apply in a straightforward way to many other deflationary descriptions. One notable exception is the strand of deflationism that relies on the prosentential theory of truth of Dorothy Grover, Joseph Camp, and Nuel Belnap. A development of this strand can be found in Dorothy Grover's essays in *A Prosentential Theory of Truth* (Princeton, 1992) and in Robert Brandom's 'Pragmatism, Phenomenalism, and Truth Talk', in P. A. French, T. E. Uehling, Jr., and H. K. Wettstein (eds.), *Midwest Studies in Philosophy*, xii, *Realism and Antirealism* (Minneapolis, 1988). My view is that the prosentential theory has important insights into the logical grammar of truth. But these insights need to be supplemented with subsidiary theses before we can derive deflationary conclusions from them. I would want to argue that the subsidiary theses are problematic.

[8] Although Quine's writings have provided much inspiration to the deflationists, a reasonable case can be made that Quine himself is no deflationist. First, the concept of truth seems to play a substantial role in Quine's philosophy of logic. Second, Quine takes a sceptical attitude towards many of the notions used in the defence of deflationism.

[9] W. V. Quine, *Philosophy of Logic* (Englewood Cliffs, 1970), 12.

[10] 'Theories of Reference and Truth', *Erkenntnis*, 13/1 (1978), 111–29; the extract appears on p. 121.

[11] The presence of ambiguity, context-sensitivity, self-reference, etc., in our language poses a challenge to the disquotational account. It forces us to recognize, for instance, that truth is not

   (1) 'snow is white' is true

is to cancel the quotation marks: (1) says no more nor less than the
sentence

   snow is white.

   We shall get clearer on the disquotational theory if we consider a situation in which, as Quine puts it, 'we want to affirm some infinite lot of sentences'. Suppose we wish to affirm all sentences of the form

   —— & snow is white [= A, say].

That is, we want to affirm the conjunction of all sentences obtained by
filling the blank in A with sentences of English:

   (2) [Sky is blue & snow is white] & [Chicago is blue & snow is white]
       & . . .

We lack explicit and direct means of formulating the infinite conjunction,
but the truth predicate, according to Quine and Leeds, provides us with an
indirect means. Observe that we cannot generalize on the '——' position
in A using ordinary first-order variables. We cannot say, for example,

   For all x: x & snow is white.

For the variable 'x' is pronominal and occupies name positions; it cannot
meaningfully be put in sentence positions. The way the truth predicate
helps here, according to the disquotational account, is this. The disquotational feature of truth makes (2) equivalent to

   (3) ['Sky is blue' is true & snow is white] & ['Chicago is blue' is true
       & snow is white] & . . .

But the position '——' in

   —— is true & snow is white

is nominal and can be quantified using the pronominal variable 'x'. We can
say,

   (4) For all sentences x: [x is true & snow is white].

But (4) is equivalent to (3) and, consequently, in virtue of disquotation, to
(2). The truth predicate thus provides us with a means of expressing the
infinite conjunction (2). Truth is, on the disquotational account, essentially
a logical device. It enables us to generalize over sentence positions *while
using pronominal variables such as 'x'* and, thus, endows us with additional
expressive power.

a simple predicate of sentences. I shall assume, for the sake of the argument, that the deflationists can meet the challenge. I shall often write as if the problematic elements are not present in
our language. Also, when context allows it, I shall suppress relativity to language. I shall write
'true' in place of the longer 'true in English'.

It will be useful to separate out four component ideas of the disquotational theory.

> *The disquotation thesis:* The truth predicate is a device of disquotation.
>
> *The infinite conjunction thesis:* The truth predicate enables us to express certain infinite conjunctions and disjunctions; (4), for instance, expresses (2) and (3).[12]
>
> *The generalization thesis:* The truth predicate provides a means for generalizing over sentence positions even when the variables are pronominal.
>
> *The connection thesis:* The truth predicate serves its expressive functions in virtue of its disquotation feature.[13]

The first two of these theses contain important ambiguities. Let us demarcate a little the sense in which the deflationists understand these theses (and need to understand them).

Let us call instances of the form

(T) '——' is true if and only if ——

T-biconditionals.[14] Then, the disquotation thesis is understood by the deflationists as saying not just that the T-biconditionals are true, nor just that they are necessarily true.[15] The claim is rather that the T-biconditionals issue from our very understanding of 'true', that they explain (at least partially) the meaning of 'true'.[16] This way of reading the disquotation thesis is not always explicit in the writings of the deflationists. But, as we shall see, it is required by key deflationary arguments.

---

[12] I suppose I should call this thesis 'the infinite conjunction and disjunction thesis', but I want to save a few syllables.

[13] See Horwich, *Truth*, 52 and 127. Recall also Quine's statement, 'We *need* [a disquotational truth predicate] to restore the effect of objective reference when for the sake of some generalization we have resorted to semantic ascent' (emphasis added).

[14] Sometimes the notion 'T-biconditional' is understood in a wider sense. This allows a non-quotational name of a sentence to appear in the left hand side of the biconditional and a translation of the sentence to appear in the right hand side. Tarski constructed a definition (for certain languages) that implies the T-biconditionals in this wider sense. Since the definition implies the biconditionals, there could be no doubt that it was coextensive with truth. This refuted the scepticism of the positivists. At the same time it made it seem that truth was a clear and simple notion. This paved the way for modern-day deflationism. John Etchemendy's paper 'Tarski on Truth and Logical Consequence', *Journal of Symbolic Logic*, 53 (1988), 51–79, contains a good account of how Tarski's definition can be read in a deflationary way.

[15] Observe that the mere truth (or even the necessary truth) of the T-biconditionals will not yield that disquotation is a 'formal feature' of the truth predicate (Williams); nor will it yield the interdeducibility of the two sides of the T-biconditionals (Leeds); nor Quine's claim that '[b]y calling the sentence ["snow is white"] true, we call snow white'.

[16] I put in the qualification 'at least partially' because a full explanation of 'true' may require not only the T-biconditionals but also some such claim as 'only sentences are true'. I shall sometimes take the qualification as read and will not state it explicitly.

Furthermore, some authors *are* explicit on the point. Horwich has stated that our understanding of 'true' *consists* in our 'disposition to accept, without evidence, any instantiation of the schema [(T)]'. And he speaks of the T-biconditionals as constituting a *definition* of 'true'.[17] Even philosophers opposed to deflationism have often been attracted to this reading of the disquotation thesis.[18] Hartry Field's influential paper 'Tarski's Theory of Truth' argues for a view as far removed from deflationism as any. Yet it contains a description of 'true' that would fit comfortably in any deflationary text:[19]

[L]et's note one obvious fact about how the word 'true' is standardly learned: we learn to apply it to utterances of our own language first, and when we later learn to apply it to other languages it is by conceiving the utterances of another language more or less on the model of utterances of our own language. The obvious model of the first stage of this process is that we learn to accept instances of the schema

(T) X is true if and only if p.

where 'X' is replaced by a quotation-mark name of an English sentence S and 'p' is replaced by S.[20]

In summary, we shall understand the disquotation thesis as stating that disquotation provides an analysis of 'true', that it explains (at least partially) what the word means and what our understanding of it consists in. The thesis should be sharply distinguished from weaker claims such as that the T-biconditionals are necessarily true.

The infinite conjunction thesis separates out for consideration the claim, often made by the deflationists (and sometimes by the nondeflationists

[17] Horwich actually states this for a propositional notion of truth, but he wants to give a parallel account of the sentential notion. See *Truth*, 36–8, 52, 116, and 125.

[18] Perhaps this explains why opponents of deflationism have been on the defensive in recent years.

[19] Hilary Putnam accepted at one time an account of 'true' similar to the one sketched by Field. See his *Meaning and the Moral Sciences* (London, 1978), 15–17. Putnam's arguments against deflationism can be found in, among other places, his 'On Truth', in L. S. Cauman, I. Levi, and R. Schwartz (eds.), *How Many Questions: Essays in Honor of Sidney Morgenbesser* (Indianapolis, 1983), 35–56; and in 'Does the Disquotational Theory Really Solve All Philosophical Problems', *Metaphilosophy*, 22 (1991), 1–13.

Christopher Hill is another non-deflationist who accepts parts of the disquotational account. See his 'Rudiments of a Theory of Reference', *Notre Dame Journal of Formal Logic*, 28 (1987), 200–19. I should note that Hill thinks that 'refers' and 'true' are ambiguous. He accepts the disquotational account only for one sense of 'true', and he extends this account beyond the home language in a manner different from that of Field and Putnam.

[20] H. Field, 'Tarski's Theory of Truth', in M. Platts (ed.), *Reference, Truth, and Reality: Essays on the Philosophy of Language* (London, 1980), 104. The paper originally appeared in *Journal of Philosophy*, 69 (1972), 347–75. This paper no longer represents Field's present position. See his 'The Deflationary Conception of Truth', in G. MacDonald and C. Wright (eds.), *Fact, Science, and Morality: Essays on A. J. Ayer's Language, Truth and Logic* (Oxford, 1986), 55–117. Field is now much more sympathetic to deflationism.

also), that the truth predicate is a device for expressing certain infinite conjunctions and disjunctions. The thesis is ambiguous because of an ambiguity in 'express'. Is the thesis to be read so that it yields only that (4) and (2) are *materially* equivalent? Or that they are necessarily equivalent? Or that they have the same sense? Or something yet different? The deflationists have not been explicit on the point. We shall see, however, that the use they make of the infinite conjunction thesis requires that 'express' be read in a strong way.

One argument of the deflationists—that for the connection thesis—requires much too strong a reading of the infinite conjunction thesis. According to the connection thesis the truth predicate *needs* to be disquotational if it is to serve its expressive functions—in particular, its function of expressing certain generalizations. The argument for the thesis was implicit in our exposition above: The function of (4) is to express (2). But this is possible only if (2) and (3) are equivalent. Here is where disquotation comes in. It is needed to ensure that the equivalence of (2) and (3) holds. Hence, disquotation is needed to ensure that truth plays its desired role in generalizations such as (4). The role of the infinite conjunction thesis in the argument is to show that (2) and (3) need to be equivalent, if the truth predicate is to play its expressive role. But this motivates the need for a disquotational truth predicate only if the equivalence of (2) and (3) is required to be something like sameness of sense. Anything weaker will yield the need, not for disquotational truth, but for something weaker. If, for example, the role of truth in (4) requires only that (2) and (3) be necessarily equivalent, then the argument will yield only that the T-biconditionals must be necessarily true if 'true' is to serve its role. It will not yield the disquotation thesis.

In the strong sense needed for the connection thesis, the infinite conjunction thesis is plainly false. A universal statement (e.g., (4)) does not have the same sense as the conjunction of its instances (e.g., (3)). The two typically do not even imply the same things; they are equivalent only in a much weaker sense.[21] I think that the proponents of the disquotational theory have gone astray because they have ignored the difference between wanting to affirm a generalization and wanting to affirm each of its instances. Quine writes in the passage quoted above, 'if we want to affirm some infinite lot of sentences that we can demarcate only by talking about

---

[21] This causes a problem for any attempt to derive the strong reading of the infinite conjunction thesis—and, more specifically, the synonymy of (2) and (4)—from the disquotation thesis. The disquotation thesis yields, we can grant, that (2) and (3) are synonymous. But to derive that (2) and (4) are synonymous we need the synonymy of (3) and (4), which unfortunately does not hold.

the sentences, then the truth predicate has its use'. In the situation envisaged by Quine, where we can demarcate some infinite lot of sentences only by talking about them, what we typically want to do is affirm a generalization—and the truth predicate enables us to do this. We can, for example, generalize on the '——' position in

—— & snow is white

with the aid of the truth predicate, as we saw above. But this is not the same as affirming 'some infinite lot of sentences', which requires an infinitary conjunction. It is because two distinct things (which, to repeat, are affirming the universal and affirming all the instances) are confused that the infinitary conjunction seems to be strongly equivalent to the generalization, and leads in turn to the disquotation thesis. [I think the same confusion is going on in Leeds's claim in the passage quoted above that 'we frequently find ourselves in a position to assert each sentence in a certain infinite set z (e.g., when all the members of z share a common form)'.]

The connection thesis, then, rests on a confusion. This, I think, is a blemish on deflationism: It means that the deflationary accounts of the meaning and the function of 'true' are not connected in the neat way that the deflationists supposed. But this does not damage deflationism in a material way. For the arguments for the deflationary attitude towards the role of truth in philosophy rest not on the connection thesis but on the disquotation and the infinite conjunction theses. Let us now examine some of these arguments.

III

One question that philosophers have debated in recent years is whether truth is amenable to a physicalistic reduction—in other words, whether truth is a complex physical property. Two compelling philosophical pictures, when combined, suggest a positive answer: (i) the correspondence theory of truth and (ii) a physicalistic ontology. The former suggests that underlying truth there is a systematic relation between words and the world; the latter suggests that this relation can be understood in physical terms. The combination of the two pictures, in fact, makes each a little more attractive. Traditional correspondence theories are confronted with the embarrassment that they have had little to say (beyond such vacuous claims as 'snow' refers to snow) about the relation between words and the world. Physicalistic ontology is useful here: It provides a framework in which a substantial account of the relation might be spelled out. Physicalistic ontology has faced, on the other hand, the problem of giving an account of psychological and semantic properties. A correspondence theory helps here: It provides a scheme for making sense of at least one semantic property. In short, the idea that truth is a complex physical property makes the two philosophical pictures a little more coherent and attractive.

The deflationist position on the question is, as one would expect, that truth is not amenable to a physicalistic reduction, that to suppose otherwise is to misunderstand the meaning and function of 'true'. We shall examine the deflationary arguments for this claim after we have briefly reviewed the debate within which the arguments arose.

Hartry Field initiated the debate by arguing (in his paper 'Tarski's Theory of Truth') that truth is amenable to a physicalistic reduction. Field argued that just as the usefulness of the concept of valence in chemistry is a reason to expect a physicalistic reduction for it, so with truth: The usefulness of the notion of truth is a reason to think that it has a physicalistic reduction. Stephen Leeds pointed out a problem with this argument.[22] What provides us with a reason to expect a reduction of 'valence' is that it is a *causal-explanatory* notion, as is shown by its role in the *law* of valences. Mere usefulness does not establish the requisite analogy of truth with valence. What must be shown is that there are laws of truth analogous to the law of valences. (Leeds went on to suggest that the utility of truth can be explained by seeing it as a device for expressing infinite conjunctions and disjunctions.) Hilary Putnam took up Leeds's challenge.[23] He argued that, like valence, truth does play a causal-explanatory role. He offered several generalizations as examples of causal-explanatory laws involving truth—generalizations such as the following:

(5) The laws of a mature science are typically approximately true.

(6) True beliefs about how to attain our goals tend to facilitate success in achieving them.

(7) Beliefs formed as a result of our methods of inquiry tend to be true.

The first law, Putnam suggested, helps explain the success of the mature sciences; the last two *our* success in attaining our goals.[24] The deflationists responded that Putnam's examples do not pose a difficulty for them; the

---

[22] See his 'Theories of Reference and Truth'.

[23] See *Meaning and the Moral Sciences*.

[24] Putnam rejects the idea that causal-explanatory laws are a reason to expect a physicalistic reduction. So, while Putnam thinks, *pace* Leeds, that truth is causal-explanatory, he rejects Field's quest for a physicalistic reduction of truth. See *Meaning and the Moral Sciences*, lectures 3–5.

examples, they argued, can be explained within their framework. Their arguments seem to have been widely accepted and have contributed to the prevalent scepticism of the possibility of a physicalistic reduction of semantic concepts.

Let us consider how the deflationary arguments go for one of Putnam's examples. (The others are treated in a parallel way.) Here is how Williams responds to (6).

> I see no reason to think of [(6)] as a law. . . . If I want a cold drink and believe that the refrigerator, rather than the oven, is the place to look, I will increase the likelihood of getting what I want. This is because cold drinks are more likely to be found in the refrigerator than in the oven. To say that my having true beliefs makes it more likely that I will attain my goals is just a compact way of pointing to the indefinite number of mundane facts of this sort. It involves nothing so arcane as a physical correspondence theory of truth.[25]

Williams argues here that (6) is not a law, since it is 'just a compact way of pointing to the indefinite number of mundane facts' of the sort he cites. Let $A_1, A_2, A_3, \ldots$ be these mundane facts. Williams's argument rests on the idea that (6) expresses—in some sense of 'expresses'—the infinite conjunction

(8) $A_1 \& A_2 \& A_3 \ldots$.

It is plain that Williams's argument does not work if 'express' is understood in an extensional way; i.e., if we suppose only that (6) is materially equivalent to (8). Nor does the argument work if we take 'express' in an intensional way; i.e., if we suppose only that (6) is necessarily equivalent to (8). For, of two sentences that are necessarily equivalent, one can be a law and the other not. Here is an example:

(9) Cicero is Tully.

(10) No chemical reaction will produce caustic soda from saltpetre and sulphuric acid.

Both these statements are necessary truths and, hence, are necessarily equivalent.[26] The second states a law, but not the first. Only when the equivalence between two sentences is very strong can we infer the nomological character of one from the nomological character of the other. Williams's argument presupposes therefore a strong reading of the infinite conjunction thesis.

---

[25] 'Do We (Epistemologists) Need a theory of Truth?', *Philosophical Topics*, 14 (1986), 223–42; the extract appears on p. 232. The formulation of (6) that Williams is commenting on is this: 'If we have true beliefs about how to attain our goals, we will generally attain them.' Williams gives one other argument for not regarding (6) as a law. Since this argument does not rely on the disquotational account of 'true', I shall not consider it here.

[26] I am assuming here the Kripke–Putnam theory of reference.

Horwich responds to Putnam in a different way. He does not deny that (6) is a law. He argues instead that (6) is sufficiently explained by the T-biconditionals and, hence, that we do not need a substantial correspondence theory of truth to explain it. Horwich writes:

[I]t is clear, in general, how true beliefs contribute to practical success. Nothing beyond the minimal theory [which consists essentially of the T-biconditionals] is called for to explain this phenomenon.[27]

The way the T-biconditionals explain (6), according to Horwich, is this. Suppose that

(11) Bill believes that he will get a beer if he nods

and that

(12) Bill wants a beer.

Sentences (11) and (12) explain Bill's nod. The truth of Bill's belief yields, in virtue of the T-biconditionals, that

If Bill nods, he will get a beer.

Hence, we obtain the conclusion that Bill will get a beer and, consequently, that his want will be fulfilled. Other examples of beliefs and desires may require a more complex explanation, but, as the above example illustrates, none will need a substantial theory of truth.[28]

This argument needs the support of the disquotation and the infinite conjunction theses to work. The argument invites two challenges. First, it may be argued that even if the T-biconditionals explain (6), the need for a substantial theory of truth remains. It may be that a substantial theory of truth will provide a deeper explanation of the T-biconditionals and, consequently, of (6). Second, it may be argued that what Horwich proposes is an explanation only of the instances of (6), not of (6) itself.

The disquotation thesis provides a response to the first challenge: Since the T-biconditionals are definitional of truth, the response goes, they are not open to a deeper explanation;[29] the substantial theory of truth has no work to do. Observe that this response will not work on the weaker readings of the disquotation thesis. It will not work, for example, if all we have available is the thesis that the T-biconditionals are necessary truths. For, necessary truths *can* sometimes be given a deeper explanation. Sentence (10) expresses a necessary truth, yet chemistry provides a deep explanation of why it holds.

The infinite conjunction thesis provides a response to the second

---

[27] *Truth*, 45.   [28] See ibid. 23–4 and 44–7 for a fuller account.   [29] Ibid. 52.

challenge: Since the T-biconditionals explain all the instances of (6), they explain their infinite conjunction. But by the infinite conjunction thesis, (6) expresses this infinite conjunction. Hence, the T-biconditionals explain (6) also. Again, observe that this response requires a strong reading of 'express'. The necessary equivalence of (6) with an infinite conjunction is insufficient ground for it. For, to explain one of two sentences that are necessarily equivalent is not thereby to explain the other (see examples (9) and (10)).

We may conclude, then, that the deflationary arguments against a substantial theory of truth need the support of the disquotation thesis and the infinite conjunction thesis read in a strong way; weaker versions of the theses are insufficient. This is a major weakness in the arguments, for on the strong reading the infinite conjunction thesis is false. Williams's argument requires the generalization (6) to be equivalent to the infinite conjunction (8) in a sense strong enough to guarantee sameness of nomological character. But the two plainly are not equivalent in such a strong sense. The conjuncts of (8) are particular in character. So, (8) itself is particular in character. But this is not true of (6), which is general. Further, (6) gives us information about counterfactual situations that lie beyond the infinite conjunction (8).

Horwich's argument presupposes that a generalization is equivalent to the conjunction of its instances in a sense strong enough to guarantee that an explanation of one is an explanation of the other. But, as the following example shows, this is not true. We can explain each instance of the generalization 'everyone on the boat died' by providing a separate explanation for the death of each person on the boat: Jack died of a heart attack; Mohini drowned; etc. But these separate explanations do not necessarily explain the generalization. The generalization may in fact have no explanation at all—it may be true accidentally. Or it may have an altogether different explanation, such as that the boat capsized. In any case, an explanation of the instances is not necessarily an explanation of the generalization.[30]

We can accept the infinite conjunction thesis when 'express' is under-

---

[30] An analogy may make it clear that Horwich's argument is unsuccessful. Consider the generalization:

In aircrafts with autoland systems, accurate instrumentation promotes safe landings.

If Horwich's argument were successful then one could give a parallel deflationary explanation of this generalization and could argue that no further substantial explanation should be expected. But the deflationary explanation here is plainly unsatisfactory. An adequate explanation of why accurate instrumentation promotes safe landings would show how the actions of the autoland system are linked with the readings of the instruments and how these actions affect the flight behaviour of the aircraft.

stood as implying only material equivalence. We can even suppress several doubts and grant the thesis when 'express' is understood as implying necessary equivalence. But the thesis is false when 'express' is understood in the strong way needed in Williams's and Horwich's arguments.[31] I think the cause of error here is the same oversight that we found in Quine's passage in Section II: a neglect of the distinction between 'affirming the universal' and 'affirming all the instances'. Once the distinction is neglected it becomes easy to read the infinite conjunction thesis in a strong way. Once the distinction is marked, the strong readings are seen to be plainly false.

In conclusion: The deflationary arguments against a substantial theory of truth presuppose an unacceptably strong reading of the infinite conjunction thesis. I myself see nothing in the meaning and function of 'true' to rule out the possibility or the usefulness of a substantial theory of truth.[32]

IV

The theory of meaning is another area in which the deflationists deny truth a substantial role. Two paradigms dominate philosophical studies of meaning. One paradigm seeks to understand meaning in terms of language-*world* relations. On this paradigm the concept of truth plays a central role in an account of meaning. Indeed, on many theories within this paradigm, meaning (of a sentence) is identified with truth conditions. The other paradigm seeks to understand meaning in terms of language-*user* relations. On this paradigm language-world relations are not so central in an account of meaning. What is central is the *use* to which sentences are put. The debate between the two paradigms is large and of large significance. The deflationist contribution to the debate is the argument that the meaning and function of 'true' rule out a truth-conditional account of the meanings of sentences.

An early formulation of the argument occurs in Michael Dummett's paper 'Truth':

[31] It seems to me that the infinite conjunction thesis is false also if 'express' is taken to mean 'interdeducible' or 'warranted on the same occasions' (see the extract from Leeds's paper 'Theories of Reference and Truth' given in Sect. II). Let z be a set that contains sentences of a certain form. Then, the generalization 'all members of z are true' is not interdeducible with (nor is it warranted on the same occasions as) the infinite conjunction of the members of z. Neither the infinite conjunction nor the generalization carries information about what all the members of z are. But this is needed if we are to deduce one from the other.

[32] To avoid misunderstanding let me say explicitly that I am not here defending a correspondence, or a physicalistic, or any other particular theory of truth. What I am defending is the claim that the meaning of 'true' does not make the search for a substantial theory of truth futile.

[I]n order that someone should gain from the explanation that *P* is true in such-and-such circumstances an understanding of the sense of *P*, he must already know what it means to say of *P* that it is true. If when he enquires into this he is told that the only explanation is that to say that *P* is true is the same as to assert *P*, it will follow that in order to understand what is meant by saying that *P* is true, he must already know the sense of asserting *P*, which was precisely what was supposed to be being explained to him.[33]

Dummett goes on to write, in the concluding paragraph of his paper, that

[F]or most ordinary contexts the account of these words ['true' and 'false'] embodied in the laws 'It is true that *p* if and only if *p*' and 'It is false that *p* if and only if not *p*' is quite sufficient: but it means facing the consequences of admitting that this is the *whole* explanation of the sense of these words, and this involves dethroning truth and falsity from their central place in philosophy and in particular in the theory of meaning.[34]

Dummett's argument brings out a tension between two ideas: the idea that the T-biconditionals explain the meaning of 'true' and the idea that meaning is to be explained in terms of truth conditions. If T-biconditionals are definitional of truth, if they explain what our understanding of 'true' consists in, then our understanding of 'true' presupposes a prior grasp of the meanings of the sentences of our language. Hence, truth cannot play a fundamental role in the theory of meaning; it cannot provide an explanation of our grasp of the meanings of sentences.

The tension is particularly vivid if one follows Donald Davidson and conceives of the theory of meaning for a language as a theory of truth for it.[35] The tension is now over two ways of reading the T-biconditionals: as elucidating the meanings of sentences and as elucidating 'true'. The two ways preclude each other. The former presupposes the concept of truth and uses the T-biconditionals to explain meaning; the latter presupposes meaning and uses the T-biconditionals to explain truth. By holding one element (truth or meaning) fixed, it appears, one can obtain the other. But one cannot use the T-biconditionals to extract both. As Horwich says, this is like having one equation and two unknowns.[36] Fixing one unknown we can solve for the other, but we cannot solve for both simultaneously.

Notice that these considerations provide an argument against truth-conditional semantics only when they are supplemented with the full force of the disquotation thesis. A weaker thesis such as that the T-bicondition-

---

[33] In his *Truth and Other Enigmas* (London, 1978), 7 (the essay originally appeared in *Proceedings of the Aristotelian Society*, 59 (1959), 141–62.)

[34] Ibid. 19. Dummett later rejected this conclusion. See ibid., preface, esp. pp. xx–xxii.

[35] For Davidson's views on the theory of meaning see his essays in *Inquiries into Truth and Interpretation* (New York, 1984). Davidson criticizes deflationism in 'The Structure and Content of Truth', *Journal of Philosophy*, 87/16 (1990), 279–328.

[36] *Truth*, 71.

als are necessarily true is insufficient. Not only is there no tension between this weaker thesis and truth-conditional semantics, the very formulation of truth-conditional semantics requires a sense of 'true' for which the weaker thesis holds. Consider an arbitrary sentence 'p' and an arbitrary possible situation w.[37] Truth-conditional semantics identifies the meaning of 'p' with its truth conditions, say, X. Now suppose w is in X. The very formulation of truth-conditional semantics requires that there be a sense of 'true' on which 'p' is true in w. Since w is in the truth conditions of 'p,' the T-biconditional

'p' is true if and only if p

holds in w. By a parallel argument the biconditional holds also if w is not in X. Since w is arbitrary, the biconditional must be necessarily true. It follows that truth-conditional semantics requires a sense of 'true' on which the T-biconditionals are necessarily true.

The deflationary argument, if it is to work, requires the strong idea that the T-biconditionals explain the *meaning* or *sense* of 'true'. This suggests the following picture of our acquisition of 'true': We first learn some first-order words ('snow', 'white', etc.) and then we arrive at 'true' definitionally through the T-biconditionals.[38] Given this picture, it follows immediately that we cannot explain our understanding of 'snow is white' in terms of our understanding of 'true', for our understanding of 'true', according to the picture, rests on our prior understanding of 'snow is white'.

But now a basic difficulty with the argument comes into view. If anything like the above picture of the meaning of 'true' is correct, then an understanding of 'true' requires the possession of massive conceptual resources. For consider again the picture with which we are presented. We are told that we gain our understanding of 'true' through the T-biconditionals, that we acquire 'true' by laying down the totality of T-biconditionals as definitional of 'true'. But each biconditional plays an important role in the resulting definition: It defines what it means to apply truth to one particular sentence. If some of the biconditionals are omitted, the result is at best a partial definition of 'true'. An individual who does not lay down some of the T-biconditionals as definitional of 'true' would have at best a partial notion of truth. To have a full notion of truth—to have a full understanding of the meaning of 'true'—requires, on this picture, a grasp of all the T-biconditionals. But this is possible only if the individual possesses all the concepts expressed by the terms in the

---

[37] Let us understand the variable p substitutionally in this argument.
[38] Recall the extract from Field's paper 'Tarski's Theory of Truth' given in Sect. II.

right-hand sides of the biconditionals. Hence, on the above picture of the meaning of 'true', a full understanding of 'true' is possible only for someone with massive conceptual resources.

An immediate response to this argument is to say that what defines 'true' is not the T-biconditionals, but something in their neighbourhood—perhaps the form (T), or perhaps the general fact lying behind the T-biconditionals, or perhaps the rule of inference embodied in them. These suggestions are interesting but, as I shall argue in the next section, they do not provide a viable explanation of the meaning of 'true'. Furthermore, they cannot play the role that the disquotation thesis plays in Dummett's deflationary argument. Let us therefore for the moment set aside these suggestions and return to our original concerns: Should we think of the T-biconditionals as definitional of 'true'? Do the T-biconditionals explain what our understanding of 'true' consists in? In short, is the disquotation thesis true? Let us approach these questions indirectly. Let us ask: What are we denying in denying the disquotation thesis?

(i) It is plain that we are not denying the T-biconditionals. Nor are we denying that the T-biconditionals are necessarily true. If the slogan 'truth is a device of disquotation' is meant to say nothing more than this, then we are not denying the slogan. But the slogan so read does not provide a foundation strong enough to support deflationism.

(ii) In denying the disquotation thesis, we need not even deny that there is a sense of 'definition' on which the T-biconditionals define 'true': We can accept the idea that the T-biconditionals fix the *extension*, and even the *intension*, of 'true'.[39] What we deny is that the T-biconditionals fix the *sense* of 'true'. When we evaluate a definition that aims to fix the extension or the intension of a predicate, we consider only how it carves the domain of its application into those objects that fall under the predicate and those that do not. The *ideology of* the definition, that is, the totality of the concepts employed in the definiens of the definition, is entirely irrelevant.[40] So, the fact that the ideology of the T-biconditionals is vast does not cast any doubt on the idea that the biconditionals fix the extension and the intension of 'true'. But when we evaluate a definition that aims to capture the sense of a term, the ideology is of critical importance. For, the definition is now meant to capture what our understanding of the term consists in. If the definition is correct, a full understanding of the definiendum requires

---

[39] I follow Carnap and think of 'intension' as 'extension-across-possible-situations'. For a theory of how the T-biconditionals fix the extension (more precisely, the signification) of 'true', even in the presence of vicious self-reference, see Gupta and N. Belnap, *The Revision Theory of Truth* (Cambridge, Mass., 1993).

[40] Quine uses 'ideology' in an analogous, though not identical, way.

possession of the concepts in the definition's ideology. Let the *ideology of* a term consist of those concepts that are necessary and sufficient for an understanding of the term (assuming that there is such a totality).[41] Then, it is an adequacy condition on a definition that aims to capture the sense of a term that the ideology of the definition coincide with the ideology of the term. It follows that a definition that aims to capture sense may be inadequate simply because of the ideology that it employs.[42] This explains why the T-biconditionals are not an adequate definition of the sense of 'true'. If the T-biconditionals were adequate, then, given that their ideology is vast, it would follow that a full understanding of 'true' would require a massive repertoire of concepts. But, plainly, one can have a perfect understanding of 'true' even though one lacks, e.g., the concept of set or that of relativistic mass. The T-biconditionals fail to define the sense of 'true' because they attribute much too large an ideology to 'true'.

(iii) In denying the disquotation thesis, we are not denying the observation that lies at the foundation of deflationism: that in asserting ' "snow is white" is true' one typically asserts nothing more nor less than 'snow is white'. Deflationism goes on to explain this pragmatic fact in a certain way. And it is this explanation that we deny. According to deflationism, the pragmatic fact obtains because the sentences ' "snow is white" is true' and 'snow is white' are synonymous, and the synonymy obtains because of the meaning of 'true'. Deflationism thus explains the pragmatic fact solely on the basis of the meaning of 'true'. But the deflationary explanation is not the only possible, or the most plausible, one. The pragmatic fact is sufficiently explained by the observation that in a typical situation the T-biconditional

(13) 'snow is white' is true if and only if snow is white,

is common knowledge, and indeed trivial common knowledge. Deflationism goes wrong because it reads the pragmatic fact into the very analysis of 'true'.

(iv) This point is connected to the previous one. In denying the disquotation thesis we are not forced to deny that the T-biconditionals are trivial. Nor are we forced to deny that there is a sense of 'analytic' on

---

[41] I shall understand 'ideology of a concept' in a parallel way.

[42] Here is a simple illustration. Consider the definition,

x is a human iff x is an animal with such and such a DNA structure.

Supposing that the 'such and such' is properly filled out, the definition fixes correctly the intension of 'human'—the ideology of the definition is irrelevant to this assessment. But when we consider whether the definition captures the sense of 'human', the ideology is highly relevant. The fact that the ideology of the definition includes the concept 'DNA structure' makes the definition implausible as an explanation of the sense of 'human'.

which the T-biconditionals are analytic. We can grant, for example, that a person who knows the meanings of all the parts of (13) will thereby know that

'snow is white' is true if and only if snow is white.

We can grant therefore that there is a sense in which the T-biconditionals are 'true solely in virtue of meaning'.[43] But this is not to say that the T-biconditionals are 'true solely in virtue of the meaning of "true"'; that someone who knew only the meaning of 'true' would thereby know the biconditionals. I think the point is important because the intuitive pull of the disquotation thesis comes from the seeming triviality and analyticity of the T-biconditionals. This makes us think that the T-biconditionals explain the meaning of 'true' and that an adequate definition of 'true' must imply the biconditionals (Tarski's Convention T). But in thinking thus we make an unwarranted leap, a leap from common sense to deflationism.

In denying the disquotation thesis, then, we are not denying any of our commonsensical ideas about truth. We are denying a very specific claim about the meaning of 'true', a claim that plays a key role in the deflationary argument from Dummett considered above. And we are denying a picture of how we arrive at our understanding of 'true', a picture that makes the deflationary attitude compelling. Once we shed the claim and the picture nothing remains, I believe, to make plausible the deflationary attitude in the theory of meaning.

V

The T-biconditionals make it tempting to believe that the concept of truth is simple, that a complete analysis of the meaning of 'true' is easily given. We readily grant that analysis of meaning is, in general, a difficult task. Even the meaning of such a simple word as 'table', we believe, is difficult to specify. But when it comes to 'true' the T-biconditionals make it tempting to suppose that a reductive analysis of its meaning is possible. Even if we accept the point that an explanation of the meaning of 'true' should not employ the massive ideology of the T-biconditionals—and that therefore the T-biconditionals themselves do not explain the meaning of 'true'—the thought persists that something in the neighbourhood of the

---

[43] In this sense of 'analytic', some analytic truths are open to substantial explanations. Contrast the analytic truths, 'all bachelors are males' and ' "snow" means snow'. It is unreasonable to expect a substantial answer to the question 'Why are all bachelors males?' but not to the question 'Why does "snow" mean snow?'

T-biconditionals does explain it. What matters to the meaning of 'true', we feel, is not the details of the particular T-biconditionals, but the general idea captured by them. We want to say that the meaning of 'true' is explained by the *form* (T),

(T) '——' is true if and only if ——,

not by the particular biconditionals. And evidently the form does not carry with it a heavy ideology.

But how does a form explain the meaning of a predicate? This type of explanation of meaning is quite different from the usual sort. Form (T) does not explicitly state the application conditions of 'true' (or it would not have overcome the ideology problem), but this is what we expect from an explanation of the meaning of a predicate.[44] So how does (T) constitute an explanation of the meaning of 'true'? Several approaches suggest themselves as ways of answering this question. Let us examine a few. Our examination will cast doubt on the idea that a reductive analysis of 'true' is possible.

(A) The Generalization Approach

This approach tries to make sense of the idea that (T) explains the meaning of 'true' by appealing to the general truth corresponding to (T). What explains the meaning of 'true', on this approach, is not the totality of the T-biconditionals but the general fact that

(GT) All instances of the form (T) [i.e., all T-biconditionals] are true.

The suggestion has some attractive features. It explains the meaning of 'true' using a formula whose ideology is highly limited. Moreover, the formula is plainly analytic of the terms it involves. Anyone who understands the meaning of 'form (T)', 'true', etc., must grant the truth of (GT).

Unfortunately, however, the suggestion faces an obvious but overwhelming problem: It explains the meaning of 'true' using a formula that itself involves 'true'. The circularity is not intrinsically objectionable.[45] But the particular form it takes here violates material aspects of the meaning of 'true': The proposal fails to yield the T-biconditionals. Imagine we give (GT) as an explanation of 'true' to someone who does not yet understand the word. This person will be able to deduce from (GT) that

---

[44] I am setting aside circular predicates here.
[45] As Gupta and Belnap have argued in *Revision Theory of Truth*.

(14) ' "Snow is white" is true if and only if snow is white' is true.

But how can he eliminate the last occurrence of 'true' and arrive at the T-biconditional

(15) 'Snow is white' is true if and only if snow is white?

To eliminate it he needs to derive the T-biconditional

(16) ' "Snow is white" is true if and only if snow is white' is true if and only if ['snow is white' is true if and only if snow is white].

But, again, (GT) does not yield (16) but only that (16) is true. A parallel difficulty blocks attempts to eliminate this new unwanted occurrence of 'true'. Our imaginary learner can derive of any T-biconditional that it is true, but he cannot derive the T-biconditional itself.

Note that if we *presuppose* the notion of truth, then the present strategy is a good way of spelling out the idea that a form explains the meaning of a predicate. The trouble is that the strategy works only if the meaning of 'true' is taken as given, not otherwise. The strategy cannot therefore be used to explain the meaning of 'true'. Rather, the meaning of 'true' is needed to make sense of the strategy.

(B) The Syntactic Approach[46]

This approach reads (T) as expressing a syntactic rule, a rule to the effect that a declarative sentence can be transformed by the addition (and deletion) of the marks,

(17) '—' is true,

without altering the sense of the original sentence. The approach thus views addition of the marks (17) as analogous to the passive transformation. Both transformations have a limited utility, but are insubstantial modifications of the original.

The syntactic approach gets around the ideology problem. And, it, unlike the previous approach, avoids circularity in its explanation. However, it cannot be regarded as explaining the meaning of 'true'. At best, the approach explains the meaning of (17) *when* (17) *is viewed as one syntactic unit*; it does not explain the meanings of the parts of (17). The approach does not even entitle us to treat 'is true' as a predicate. It therefore does not explain the role 'is true' plays when it occurs in combination with pronouns and general terms. If we follow the syntactic approach, we face problems explaining such simple inferences as the following:

---

[46] Mark Wilson and Eric Dalton, independently, suggested this approach to me. They do not endorse it.

The sentence Bill uttered is 'snow is white'. 'Snow is white' is true. Hence, the sentence Bill uttered is true.

The approach does not entitle us to treat the occurrence of 'snow is white' in the second premiss as a singular term. Consequently, we cannot explain the inference as an instance of Leibniz's principle of indiscernibility of identicals.

(C) The Inferential Approach

This approach uses the idea that the meaning of certain items in our language is specified by their inferential roles. The meaning of the truth predicate, it is suggested, is given by the rules of inference embodied in (T): to infer ' "——" is true' from '——'; and, conversely, to infer '——' from ' "——" is true'.

This approach to the explanation of meaning, while attractive for some parts of our language, is distinctly less attractive when applied to the truth predicate. For, if truth is explained in terms of inference, how do we explain our understanding of inference? How do we explain inference without appeal to the notion of truth? The natural response to the query is as follows. Inference is to be explained in terms of its role in our conceptual practices—practices of assertion, denial, supposition, verification, etc. These practices, the suggestion goes, are governed by various norms, and an explanation of inference will specify the role that it plays in these norms. Thus, our understanding of inference consists in understanding such things as that if q can be inferred from p then the assertion of p commits one to q, that one cannot assert p and also deny q, that a verification of p counts as a verification of q, etc.

Obviously, the suggestion is viable only if one can explain 'assertion', 'denial', 'commitment', etc., without appeal to truth. But can this be done? How is one to make sense of our conceptual practices without any appeal to the notion of truth? And supposing sense can be made, do our practices make *more* sense when one allows the use of the notion of truth? The inferential approach remains a large promissory note until it provides a satisfactory answer to these questions. I will not attempt to speculate on how the approach might be developed, but I would like to make two remarks about it.

First, the inferential approach to meaning does not need to forgo the notion of truth in order to stay true to its philosophical motive. *Use of the notion of truth in an explanation of our conceptual practices (and of meaning) doesn't immediately commit one to a referential picture of language.* It seems to me that the burden of explaining truth for a body of discourse in non-referential terms is lighter than that of giving a reductive explanation of the concept of truth. The inferential approach to meaning, it seems to me, takes a wrong turn when it denies itself the use of truth and takes on the burden of explaining the meaning of truth in inferential terms.

Second, even if truth does not play a substantive role in the explanation of our conceptual practices, it most likely does play an expressive role in their description. That is, truth is probably needed to describe basic facts about our conceptual practices—facts which are constitutive of them. For example, a description of our understanding of inference will, in all probability, need to mention our knowledge of the general fact of which the following is an instance.

> If 'snow is white' can be inferred from 'everything is white,' then snow is white if everything is white.

But how else can one express the general fact than by using the truth predicate: If a sentence A can be inferred from a sentence B, then A is true if B is? If this thought is correct, then the prospects for an inferential approach to the meaning of 'true' are bleak indeed.

None of the above approaches, then, is likely to yield a viable account of the meaning of 'true'. Let us observe also this: Even if these approaches were to lead to a viable account, it is an open question whether the resulting account would support any deflationary claims, and, if it did support some, it is an open question which ones it would support. For example, suppose that the inferential approach overcomes the obstacles in its way and offers an acceptable account of the meaning of 'true'. This account will not, as far as I can tell, support a blanket deflationism in the theory of meaning. The account, plainly, could not play the role that the disquotation thesis played in the deflationary argument from Dummett considered in Section IV. That argument rested on the idea that our understanding of ' "——" is true' presupposes an understanding of '——'. The inferential approach, far from supporting this idea, is designed to overcome the problem that the idea creates. Further, the account the inferential approach proposes will, presumably, explain our understanding of 'true' in terms of our understanding of a limited range of terms, conceptual practices, etc. It is intuitively plausible that 'true' could not be used to provide an explanation of our understanding of the terms, practices, etc., within this range. But this allows truth to play an important role in an explanation of those terms and conceptual practices that lie outside the range. The account therefore will not make plausible a blanket deflationism in the theory of meaning.

Let us return to the original, disquotational, account of truth and take stock. The account, to review briefly, goes as follows: 'The usefulness of truth lies in the expressive power that it provides. The truth predicate, by providing us with an indirect means of quantifying over sentence positions, enables us to express certain infinite conjunctions and disjunctions. To perform this function truth must be a device of disquotation: Applied to a quoted sentence it must undo the effect of the quotation marks. This function therefore requires the T-biconditionals to be definitional of "true".' There are readings of this account on which it contains no errors, only insights. The key is how we understand 'express', 'device of disquotation', and 'definition'. Suppose we understand them extensionally. Then the account reads (in part): 'The generalizations involving truth are materially equivalent to the corresponding infinite conjunctions/disjunctions. To ensure this equivalence, truth needs to be a device of disquotation in the sense that the T-biconditionals need to be true. The T-biconditionals define "true" in the sense that they fix the extension of "true".' There is also an 'intensional' reading of the disquotational account. This reading is parallel to the one just given, but it takes 'express' to require necessary equivalence, 'device of disquotation' to require necessary truth of the T-biconditionals, and 'definition' to require the fixing of intension. The disquotational account, when it is read in either of these ways, is good, true, and insightful. The only point that I have insisted on is that on these readings the account is not strong enough to carry the burden of deflationism.

Deflationists read (and, to sustain their conclusions, need to read) the disquotational account in very strong ways. Here is one such reading:[47] 'The generalizations involving truth are abbreviations for (and, hence, mean the same as) the corresponding infinite conjunctions/disjunctions. To ensure this equivalence, truth needs to be a device of disquotation in the sense that guarantees the synonymy of "'——' is true" and "——". Thus, if "true" is to perform its function, the T-biconditionals must be definitional in the sense that they explain the meaning of "true".' The reading goes on to add: 'This makes truth a simple concept. What it means, what our understanding of it consists in, and how we acquire it—these all have a simple explanation. The meaning of "true" is given by the T-biconditionals, our understanding of it consists in our acceptance of the T-biconditionals, and we acquire it by laying down the biconditionals as its definition.'

The objection from ideology, given in Section IV, puts in doubt each element of this reading. The T-biconditionals do not provide an adequate account of the meaning of 'true' because they impute to 'true' a massive

---

[47] This is not the only possible strong reading, but it will highlight the points made earlier.

ideology. The sentences ' "——" is true' and '——' are not always synony-mous, for the concepts needed to understand the latter are not necessar-ily needed to understand the former. The generalizations involving 'true' do not mean the same as the corresponding infinite conjunctions/disjunc-tions, for again the two do not involve the same conceptual resources.

It is remarkable that not only do the deflationary claims fail, but that an explanation of the usefulness of 'true' lies in their failure. An example: One important reason why generalizations involving 'true' are useful is pre-cisely that they do *not* mean the same as the corresponding infinite con-junctions/disjunctions. Consider the generalization 'all men are mortal' for comparison. One reason why this generalization is useful is that it enables us to express a fact about all men without requiring of us the ability to say of each man that he is mortal. The generalization expresses, in a weak sense, the conjunction of its instances *without* being synonymous with the conjunction. It thus enables us to express (weakly) a conjunction that we lack the resources to formulate explicitly—here lies its usefulness. The same holds for generalizations involving 'true'. One reason for their use-fulness is that they are not synonymous with the corresponding infinite conjunctions/disjunctions. They allow us to express (weakly) these infinite conjunctions/disjunctions, even though our conceptual resources are meagre.

More generally, one important source of the usefulness of 'true' is its remarkable double character: (i) that an understanding of 'true' requires only a limited range of conceptual resources, and yet (ii) 'true' enables us to talk and think about things that lie far beyond this range. (So, one reason 'true' is useful is precisely that the T-biconditionals do not define its sense.) This double character also constitutes, it seems to me, the most funda-mental mystery of truth. The meaning of 'true,' like that of many other words, is difficult to explain; it becomes mysterious when we consider what 'true' enables us to do. 'True' appears simple to the deflationists, I think, because they overlook its most puzzling feature.

I have focused in this chapter on homophonic truth ('true in English') because it is here that the deflationist account appears most plausible. And I have tried to show that even here it fails. When we turn to heterophonic truth ('true in Inuit', 'true in such and such an infinitary language') the problems facing deflationism become more vivid, but in essence remain the same. Suppose we have somehow gained 'true in English', and suppose L is a language that can express things that are inexpressible in English (perhaps L is spoken by some alien creatures; perhaps L is an infinitary language that we find theoretically useful to talk about). How then can we gain 'true in L' when all we have to work with is 'true in English'? We cannot say that a sentence of L is true iff it has a true translation in English, for this will make all untranslatable sentences of L untrue. How then will the explanation go?[48] Deflationism needs to explain 'true in L' without using the conceptual resources of L. The problem that must be solved is in essence the same as the fundamental problem we pointed to above. How to reconcile two features of 'true in L': (i) that it enables us to talk about the inexpressible contents of L, but (ii) the explanation of its meaning does not appeal to those contents.

In conclusion: Deflationists think that truth is a simple concept, one that has a simple analysis. The analysis the deflationists offer *is* simple, but, unfortunately, it makes truth far too complicated—it attributes to truth a vast ideology. We examined several attempts to get around this problem, but none resulted in a plausible account of the meaning of 'true'. Now we are left with questions: *What does our understanding of 'true' consist in? How can one explain the meaning of 'true' using a limited ideology?* It is a fact that we understand truth attributions even when truth is attributed to a sentence (or thought or representation) that lies beyond our conceptual resources. *What do we understand by such attributions?* We seem to grasp something general about what it is for a sentence (or thought or representation) to be true. *But what is it that we understand?* Once we overcome the spell of deflationism we are no longer inclined to brush these questions aside with simple answers. We regain our original sense that there is something very mysterious about truth and that an exploration of this mystery may illuminate the nature of our thought and our language.[49]

[48] This kind of problem rules out the most obvious deflationist response to the ideology objection. According to the response, each of us learns 'true' first, not as it applies to English, but as it applies to one's own personal idiolect. That is, one first acquires the concept 'true-in-my-present-idiolect' and then using it acquires the full-fledged 'true'. The problem of explaining how one goes from 'true-in-my-present-idiolect' to 'true' seems to me to be much harder than that of explaining 'true' using a limited ideology. The response reduces a very hard problem to a virtually impossible one.

[49] I presented some of the ideas of this chapter in talks at the University of Minnesota, Boston Colloquium for the Philosophy of Science, University of Delhi, and Indiana University. I wish to thank my auditors (esp. André Chapuis, John Etchemendy, Geoffrey Hellman, Paul Horwich, Ranjit Nair, and Scott Soames) for their helpful comments, suggestions, and queries. Members of my Spring 1993 Metaphysics Seminar at Indiana University also helped me—not only through their ideas and suggestions, but also through their friendly scepticism towards my favourite arguments. I do not want to reproduce the whole roster for the seminar, but I should mention David Chalmers, Eric Dalton, Craig DeLancey, Jim Hardy, Ingo Farin, Adam Kovach, Malcolm MacIver, Gregg Rosenberg, and Jerry Seligman. I owe a special debt to Nuel Belnap, Dorothy Grover, Jerry Kapus, and Mark Wilson. Over the years I have had, and have benefited from, numerous discussions with these philosophers. None of them, of course, should be held responsible for the flaws of this chapter. I know Dorothy will disagree with much of what I say. My views are, I think, closest to those of Jerry Kapus. See his 'Truth and Explanation' (Ph.D. diss., University of Illinois at Chicago, 1992). Finally, I wish to thank Marian David, Allen Hazen, and Chris Hill for their comments on this chapter.

XVII

THE FOLLY OF TRYING TO DEFINE TRUTH

DONALD DAVIDSON

In the *Euthyphro*, Socrates asks what holiness is, what 'makes' holy things holy. It is clear that he seeks a definition, a definition with special properties. He spurns the mere provision of examples or lists, asking in each case what makes the examples examples, or puts an item on the list. He rejects merely coextensive concepts ('something is holy if and only if it is dear to the gods'): what makes something dear to the gods is that it is holy, but not vice versa. The dialogue ends when Socrates begs Euthyphro to enlighten him by coming up with a satisfactory answer; Euthyphro decides he has another appointment.

The pattern of attempted definition, counterexample, amended definition, further counterexample, ending with a whimper of failure, is repeated with variations throughout the Socratic and middle Platonic dialogues. Beauty, courage, virtue, friendship, love, temperance are put under the microscope, but no convincing definitions emerge. The only definitions Plato seems happy with are tendentious characterizations of what it is to be a sophist. He also gives a few trivial samples of correct definitions: of a triangle; of mud (earth and water).

In the *Theaetetus*, Plato attempts to define empirical knowledge. Like many philosophers since, he takes knowledge to be true belief plus something more—an account that justifies or warrants the belief. It is the last feature which stumps him (again foreshadowing the subsequent history of the subject). It seems no more to occur to Plato than it has to most others that the combination of causal and rational elements that must enter into an analysis of justified belief (as it must into accounts of memory, perception, and intentional action) may in the nature of the case not be amenable to sharp formulation in a clearer, more basic, vocabulary.

What is important in the present context, however, is the fact that in

From Donald Davidson, 'The Folly of Trying to Define Truth', *Journal of Philosophy*, 93/6 (1996). © 1996 Donald Davidson. Reprinted with permission.

attempting to define knowledge, it is only with the concept of warrant that Plato concedes defeat. He does not worry much about the equal involvement of knowledge with truth and belief.

Again, though, Plato was simply blazing a trail that other philosophers over the ages have followed: you follow his lead if you worry about the concept of truth when it is the focus of your attention, but you pretend you understand it when trying to cope with knowledge (or belief, memory, perception, and the like). We come across the same puzzling strategy in David Hume and others, who forget their scepticism about the external world when they formulate their doubts concerning knowledge of other minds. When a philosopher is troubled by the idea of an intentional action, he would be happy if he could analyse it correctly in terms of the concepts of belief, desire, and causality, and he does not for the moment worry too much about those (at least equally difficult) concepts. If memory is up for analysis, the connections with belief, truth, causality, and perhaps perception, constitute the problem, but these further concepts are pro tem taken to be clear enough to be used to clarify memory, if only the connections could be got right. It is all right to assume you have an adequate handle on intention and convention if your target is meaning. I could easily go on.

There is a lesson to be learned from these familiar, though odd, shifts in the focus of philosophical puzzlement. The lesson I take to heart is this: however feeble or faulty our attempts to relate these various basic concepts to each other, these attempts fare better, and teach us more, than our efforts to produce correct and revealing definitions of basic concepts in terms of clearer or even more fundamental concepts.

This is, after all, what we should expect. For the most part, the concepts philosophers single out for attention, like truth, knowledge, belief, action, cause, the good and the right, are the most elementary concepts we have, concepts without which (I am inclined to say) we would have no concepts at all. Why then should we expect to be able to reduce these concepts definitionally to other concepts that are simpler, clearer, and more basic? We should accept the fact that what makes these concepts so important must also foreclose on the possibility of finding a foundation for them which reaches deeper into bedrock.

We should apply this obvious observation to the concept of truth: we cannot hope to underpin it with something more transparent or easier to grasp. Truth is, as G. E. Moore, Bertrand Russell, and Gottlob Frege maintained, and Alfred Tarski proved, an indefinable concept. This does not mean we can say nothing revealing about it: we can, by relating it to other concepts like belief, desire, cause, and action. Nor does the indefinability of truth imply that the concept is mysterious, ambiguous, or untrustworthy.

Even if we are persuaded that the concept of truth cannot be defined, the intuition or hope remains that we can characterize truth using some fairly simple formula. What distinguishes much of the contemporary philosophical discussion of truth is that though there are many such formulas on the market, none of them seems to keep clear of fairly obvious counterexamples. One result has been the increasing popularity of minimalist or deflationary theories of truth—theories that hold that truth is a relatively trivial concept with no 'important connections with other concepts such as meaning and reality'.[1]

I sympathize with the deflationists; the attempts to pump more content into the concept of truth are not, for the most part, appealing. But I think the deflationists are wrong in their conclusion, even if mostly right in what they reject. I shall not pause here to give my reasons for refusing to accept correspondence theories, coherence theories, pragmatic theories, theories that limit truth to what could be ascertained under ideal conditions or justifiably asserted, and so on.[2] But since I am with the deflationists in being dissatisfied with all such characterizations of truth, I shall say why deflationism seems to me equally unacceptable.

Aristotle, as we all know, contended that

(1) To say of what is that it is not, or of what is not that it is, is false, while to say of what is that it is, or of what is not that it is not, is true.

When Tarski[3] mentions this formulation in 1944, he complains that it is 'not sufficiently precise and clear', though he prefers it to two others:

(2) The truth of a sentence consists in its agreement with (or correspondence to) reality.

(3) A sentence is true if it designates an existing state of affairs.

In 1969, Tarski[4] again quotes (1), and adds,

[T]he formulation leaves much to be desired from the point of view of precision and formal correctness. For one thing, it is not general enough; it refers only to sentences that 'say' about something 'that it is' or 'that it is not'; in most cases it would hardly be possible to cast a sentence in this mold without slanting the sense of the sentence and forcing the spirit of the language.

---

[1] These words are quoted from Michael Dummett's jacket blurb for Paul Horwich's *Truth* (Oxford, 1990). This is not, of course, Dummett's view.

[2] I spell out my reasons for rejecting such views in 'The Structure and Content of Truth', *Journal of Philosophy*, 87/6 (June 1990), 279–328.

[3] 'The Semantic Conception of Truth and the Foundations of Semantics', this vol., Ch. VIII, 118.

[4] 'Truth and Proof'. *Scientific American*, 220 (1969) 63–77; quote from p. 63.

He adds that this may be the reason for such 'modern substitutes' for Aristotle's formulations as (2) and (3).

In the *Wahrheitsbegriff*, however, Tarski[5] prefers the following informal statement:

> (4) A true sentence is one which says that the state of affairs is so and so, and the state of affairs indeed is so and so.

It seems to me that Aristotle's formulation is clearly superior to (2), (3), and (4); it is more in accord with Tarski's own work on truth; and Tarski's comment that (1) is 'not general enough' is strangely out of keeping with the spirit of his own truth definitions.

(1) is superior to (2)–(4) for three reasons. First, (3) and (4) mention states of affairs, thus suggesting that postulating entities to correspond to sentences might be a useful way of characterizing truth. ('A true sentence is one that corresponds to the facts', or 'If a sentence is true, there is a state of affairs to which it corresponds'.) But facts or states of affairs have never been shown to play a useful role in semantics, and one of the strongest arguments for Tarski's definitions is that in them nothing plays the role of facts or states of affairs. This is not surprising, since there is a persuasive argument, usually traced to Frege (in one form) or Kurt Gödel (in another), to the effect that there can be at most one fact or state of affairs. (This is why Frege said all true sentences name the True.) Tarski's truth definitions make no use of the idea that a sentence 'corresponds' to anything at all. We should not take seriously the mention of 'states of affairs' in such remarks of Tarski's[6] as this: '[S]emantical concepts express certain relations between objects (and states of affairs) referred to in the language discussed and expressions of the language referring to those objects'. ·

A second reason for preferring Aristotle's characterization of truth is that it avoids the awkward blanks marked by the words 'so and so' in Tarski's version (4); one is hard pressed to see how the blanks are to be filled in. Aristotle's formula, on the other hand, sounds much like a generalization of Tarski's convention-T.

The third reason for preferring Aristotle's characterization is that it makes clear, what the other formulations do not, that the truth of a sentence depends on the inner structure of the sentence, that is, on the

---

[5] 'The Concept of Truth in a Formalized Languages', in *Logic, Semantics, Metamathematics* (2nd edn.), trans. J. H. Woodger and ed. John Conoran (Indianapolis: Hackett, 1983), 153–278 (1st. pub. in German in 1936); quote from p. 155.

[6] 'The Establishment of Scientific Semantics', in *Logic, Semantics, Metamathematics*, 401–8; quote from p. 403.

312   DONALD DAVIDSON

semantic features of the parts. In this it is once again closer to Tarski's approach to the concept of truth.

Tarski's convention-T, which he understandably substitutes for the rough formulas I have been discussing, stipulates that a satisfactory definition of a truth predicate 'is true' for a language L must be such as to entail as theorems all sentences of the form

s is true-in-L if and only if p

where 's' is replaced by the description of a sentence, and 'p' is replaced by that sentence, or a translation of the sentence into the metalanguage. Since it is assumed that there is an infinity of sentences in L, it is obvious that, if the definition of the truth predicate is to be finite (Tarski insisted on this), the definition must take advantage of the fact that sentences, though potentially infinite in number, are constructed from a finite vocabulary. For the languages Tarski considered, and for which he showed how to define truth, all sentences can be put into the form of an existential quantification, or the negation of an existential quantification, or a truth-functional compound of such sentences. So how 'incomplete', from Tarski's point of view, is Aristotle's formulation (1)? It deals with four cases. There are the sentences that 'say of what is that it is not': in modern terms it is a false sentence that begins 'It is not the case that there exists an x such that . . .'. An example might be: 'There does not exist an x such that $x=4$'. Then there are sentences that 'say of what is not that it is'; for example: 'There exists an x such that $x=4$ & $x=5$'. There are sentences that 'say of what is that it is'; for example: 'There exists an x such that $x=4$'. And, finally, there are sentences that 'say of what is not that it is not'; for example, 'It is not the case that there exists an x such that $x \neq x$'. According to the classical formulation, sentences of the first two kinds are false and of the second two kinds are true. Tarski is so far in agreement. What would Tarski add? Just the truth-functional compounds (beyond those involving negation) of the types of sentences already mentioned; these are true or false on the basis of the truth or falsity of the kinds of sentences already provided for. Of course, Tarski also showed in detail how the truth or falsity of the first four types of sentences depended in turn on their structure.

Thus, the classical formulation regarded as an informal characterization is 'incomplete' in only a minimal way compared to Tarski's own work, and is better than Tarski's informal attempts to state the intuitive idea. Needless to say, someone might question the extent to which natural languages can be adequately characterized using such limited resources; but this is a comment equally applicable to Tarski.

Despite his nod in the direction of a correspondence theory, in which sentences are said to correspond to facts, Tarski ought not to be considered as giving comfort to serious partisans of correspondence theories, nor should Aristotle. For neither Aristotle's formula nor Tarski's truth definitions introduce entities like facts or states of affairs for sentences to correspond to. Tarski does define truth on the basis of the concept of satisfaction, which relates expressions to objects, but the sequences that satisfy sentences are nothing like the 'facts' or 'states of affairs' of correspondence theorists, since if one of Tarski's sequences satisfies a closed sentence, thus making it true, then that same sequence also satisfies every other true sentence, and thus also makes it true, and if any sequence satisfies a closed sentence, every sequence does.[7]

If Tarski is not a correspondence theorist (and he certainly does not hold a coherence theory or a pragmatic theory or a theory that bases truth on warranted assertability), is he a deflationist? Here opinions differ widely: W. V. Quine thinks he is, and so does Scott Soames. John Etchemendy thinks Tarski simply says nothing about truth as a semantic concept, and Hilary Putnam, though for somewhat different reasons, agrees.[8]

If Tarski has said 'all there is to say' about truth, as Stephen Leeds, Paul Horwich, and Soames all contend, and Quine has strongly hinted, then a sort of deflationary attitude is justified; this is not quite the same as the 'redundancy' view, but close to it. The redundancy view, taken literally, is the same as the disquotational view taken literally: we can always substitute without loss a sentence for that same sentence quoted, and followed by the words 'is true'. What Tarski added, as Michael Williams and others have pointed out, is a way of predicating truth of whole classes of sentences, or of sentences to which we do not know how to refer; you may think of this as an elaboration of the redundancy theory in that it allows the elimination of the truth predicate when applied to sentences of a language for which that predicate has been defined.

At the same time that we credit Tarski with having shown how to make sense of remarks like 'The English sentence Joan uttered about Abbot was true' or 'Everything Aristotle said (in Greek) was false' or 'The usual truth table for the conditional makes any conditional true that has a false antecedent', we have to recognize that this accomplishment was accompanied by a proof that truth cannot (given various plausible assumptions) be defined in general; there can be no definition of 'For all languages L,

---

[7] At one time I suggested calling Tarski's concept of truth a correspondence theory on the strength of the role of sequences in satisfying closed sentences, but I subsequently withdrew the suggestion as misleading. For the suggestion, see 'True to the Facts', in *Inquiries into Truth and Interpretation* (New York, 1984). For the retraction, see 'Afterthoughts, 1987', in A. Malichowski (ed.), *Reading Rorty* (Cambridge, 1990), 120–38.

[8] For references, and further discussion, see Davidson, 'Structure and Content of Truth'.

and all sentences *s* in *L*, *s* is true in *L* if and only if ... *s* ... *L* ...'. In other words, Tarski justified the application of a truth predicate to the sentences of a particular language only by restricting its application to the sentences of that language. (It is ironic that in much recent writing on deflationary theories, Tarski has been taken to have lent support to the idea that there is a single, simple, even trivial, concept of truth.)

A deflationary attitude to the concept of truth is not, then, encouraged by reflection on Tarski's work. One can adopt the line advanced by Putnam and Etchemendy that Tarski was not even doing semantics, despite his insistence that he was; but this construal of Tarski does not support a deflationary theory: it simply denies the relevance of Tarski's results to the ordinary concept of truth. If, on the other hand, one takes Tarski's truth definitions to say something about the relations of specific languages to the world, one cannot at the same time claim that he has told us all there is to know about the concept of truth, since he has not told us what the concept is that his truth definitions for particular languages have in common.

I think that Tarski was not trying to define *the* concept of truth—so much is obvious—but that he was *employing* that concept to characterize the semantic structures of specific languages. But Tarski did not indicate how we can in general reduce the concept of truth to other more basic concepts, nor how to eliminate the English predicate 'is true' from all contexts in which it is intelligibly applied to sentences. Convention-T is not a rough substitute for a general definition: it is part of a successful attempt to persuade us that his formal definitions apply our single pretheoretical concept of truth to certain languages. Deflationists cannot, then, appeal to Tarski simply because he demonstrated how to handle the semantics of quantification for individual languages. Leeds, Horwich, Williams, and others who have contended that all Tarski did was reveal the usefulness of an otherwise dispensable concept are wrong. They are right that we need a truth predicate for the purposes they, along with Tarski, mention; but they fail to note the obvious fact that at the same time Tarski solved one problem he emphasized another: that he had not, and could not, given the constraints he accepted, define or fully characterize truth.

Over the years, Quine has said a number of things about truth, but there has been, from early days until the most recent, what seems a consistent embrace of a deflationary attitude. Thus, Quine has made much of the 'dis-quotational' aspect of the truth predicate, the fact that we can get rid of the predicate 'is true' after the quotation of an English sentence simply by removing the quotation marks as we erase the truth predicate. As Quine put it in *From a Logical Point of View*,[9] we have a general paradigm, namely,

(T) '—' is true-in-*L* if and only if —

which, though not a definition of truth, serves to endow 'true-in-*L*' with

every bit as much clarity, in any particular application, as is enjoyed by the particular expressions of *L* to which we apply [it]. Attribution of truth in particular to 'Snow is white'. . . is every bit as clear to us as attribution of whiteness to snow.

In *Word and Object*, Quine[10] remarks that 'To say that the statement "Brutus killed Caesar" is true, or that "The atomic weight of sodium is 23" is true, is in effect simply to say that Brutus killed Caesar, or that the atomic weight of sodium is 23'. The theme is repeated thirty years later in *Pursuit of Truth*:[11]

. . . there is surely no impugning the disquotation account; no disputing that 'Snow is white' is true if and only if snow is white. Moreover, it is a full account; it explicates clearly the truth or falsity of every clear sentence.

'Truth', he summarizes, 'is disquotation'. On this matter, Quine has not changed his mind.

It is the disquotational feature of truth, in Quine's opinion, which makes truth so much clearer a concept than meaning. Comparing theory of meaning and theory of reference, Quine says that they constitute 'two provinces so fundamentally distinct as not to deserve a joint appellation at all'.[12] The former deals with such tainted topics as synonymy, meaning, and analyticity. The concepts treated by the latter, which include truth, are by contrast 'very much less foggy and mysterious . . .'. For although 'true-in-*L*' for variable '*L*' is not definable, 'what we do have suffices to endow "true-in-*L*", even for variable "*L*", with a high enough degree of intelligibility so that we are not likely to be averse to using the idiom'. 'What we do have' is, of course, the paradigm (T) and the 'expedient general routine' due to Tarski for defining 'true-in-*L*' for particular languages.

The disquotational feature of truth, wedded to the thought that this may exhaust the content of the concept of truth, encourages the idea that truth and meaning can be kept quite separate. But can they in general? Scattered remarks in Quine's work suggest otherwise. In 1936, Quine published the brilliant and prescient 'Truth by Convention'.[13] In it he remarks that 'in point of meaning . . . a word may be said to be determined to whatever

[9] (Cambridge, Mass., 1953); quote from p. 138.
[10] (Cambridge, Mass., 1960); quote from p. 24.
[11] (Cambridge, Mass., 1990); quotes from pp. 93 and 80.
[12] *From a Logical Point of View*; quotes from pp. 130 and 137–8.
[13] Repr. in *The Ways of Paradox* (Cambridge, Mass., 1976); quote from p. 89.

extent the truth or falsehood of its contexts is determined'. It is hard to see how truth could have this power of determining meaning if the dis-quotational account were all there were to say about truth. Other passages in Quine suggest the same idea: 'First and last, in learning language, we are learning how to distribute truth values. I am with Davidson here; we are learning truth conditions.'[14] Or again, 'Tarski's theory of truth [is] the very structure of a theory of meaning.'[15]

Up to a point it may seem easy to keep questions of truth and questions of meaning segregated. Truth we may think of as disquotational (in the extended Tarski sense) and therefore trivial; meaning is then another matter, to be taken care of in terms of warranted assertability, function, or the criteria for translation. This is the line followed, for example, by Horwich in his 1990 book *Truth*, by Soames,[16] and by Lewis.[17] It may, at least at one time, have been Quine's view. In *Word and Object*, in a passage that immediately precedes the remark that to say that the sentence 'Brutus killed Caesar' is true is in effect simply to say that Brutus killed Caesar, Quine despairs of a substantive concept of truth, and concludes that we make sense of a truth predicate only when we apply it to a sentence 'in the terms of a given theory, and seen from within the theory'.[18] This is, I think, what Quine means when he says that truth is 'immanent'. The point is not merely that the truth of a sentence is relative to a language; it is that there is no transcendent, single concept to be relativized.[19]

Most recently, however, Quine muses that truth 'is felt to harbor something of the sublime. Its pursuit is a noble pursuit, and unending'; he seems to agree: 'Science is seen as pursuing and discovering truth rather than as decreeing it. Such is the idiom of realism, and it is integral to the semantics of the predicate "true".'[20]

I turn now to Horwich's version of deflationism, for he seems to me to have accepted the challenge other deflationists have evaded, that of saying something more about an unrelativized concept of truth than we can learn from Tarski's definitions. Horwich's brave and striking move is to make the

[14] *The Roots of Reference* (La Salle, Ill., 1974), 65.
[15] 'On the Very Idea of a Third Dogma' in *Theories and Things* (Cambridge, Mass., 1981), 38.
[16] 'What is a Theory of Truth?', *Journal of Philosophy*, 81/8 (Aug. 1984), 411–29.
[17] 'Languages and Language', *Minnesota Studies in the Philosophy of Science*, vii (Minneapolis, 1975).
[18] *Word and Object*, 24.
[19] The preceding paragraphs on Quine are partly quoted and partly adapted from a longer and more detailed study of Quine on truth: 'Pursuit of the Concept of Truth', in P. Leondardi and M. Santambrogio (eds.), *On Quine: New Essays* (New York, 1995). The relevant pages are 7–10.
[20] *From Stimulus to Science* (Cambridge, Mass., 1995), 67.

primary bearers of truth propositions—not exactly a new idea in itself, but new in the context of a serious attempt to defend deflationism. He is clear that he cannot provide an explicit definition of a truth predicate applying to propositions, but he urges that we really have said all there is to know about such a predicate (and hence the property it expresses) when we grasp the fact that the 'uncontroversial instances' of the schema:

The proposition that p is true if and only if p

exhaust its content. (The limitation to 'uncontroversial instances' is to exclude whatever leads to paradox.) The schema is taken as an axiom schema: the totality of its instances constitute the axioms of his theory.

This theory is, of course, incomplete until the controversial instances are specified in a non-question-begging way; and since the set of axioms is infinite, it does not meet one of Tarski's requirements for a satisfactory theory of truth. But perhaps the first difficulty can be overcome, and the second may be viewed as the price of having an unrelativized concept of truth. There are, further, the doubts many of us have about the existence of propositions, or at least of the principles for individuating them.

All these considerations give me pause, but I plan to ignore them here. I want to give deflationism its best chance, since it seems to me to be the only alternative to a more substantive view of truth, and most substantive views are in my opinion, as in Horwich's, clear failures. But although I enthusiastically endorse his arguments against correspondence, coherence, pragmatic, and epistemic theories, I cannot bring myself to accept Horwich's 'minimal' theory.

I have two fundamental problems with Horwich's theory, either of which alone is reason to reject it if it cannot be resolved; and I do not myself see how to resolve them.

The first problem is easy to state: I do not understand the basic axiom schema or its instances. It will help me formulate my difficulty to compare Horwich's axiom schema with Tarski's informal (and ultimately supplanted) schema:

'——' is true if and only if ——

Tarski's objection (among others) is that you cannot turn this into a definition except by quantifying into a position inside quotation marks. The complaint ends up with a question about the clarity of quotations: How does what they refer to depend on the semantic properties of their constituents? It has sometimes been proposed to appeal to substitutional quantification, and one may wonder why Horwich cannot generalize his schema:

(p) (the proposition that p is true if and only if p)

by employing substitutional quantification. But here Horwich quite rightly explains that he cannot appeal to substitutional quantification to explain truth, since substitutional quantification must be explained by appeal to truth.

Why, though, does Horwich not try generalizing his schema by quantifying over propositions? The answer should be: because then we would have to view ordinary sentences as singular terms *referring* to propositions, not as *expressing* propositions. This brings me to the crux: How are we to understand phrases like 'the proposition that Socrates is wise'? In giving a standard account of the semantics of the sentence 'Socrates is wise', we make use of what the name 'Socrates' names, and of the entities of which the predicate 'is wise' is true. But how can we use these semantic features of the sentence 'Socrates is wise' to yield the reference of 'the proposition that Socrates is wise'? Horwich does not give us any guidance here. Could we say that expressions like 'the proposition that Socrates is wise' are semantically unstructured, or at least that after the words 'the proposition that' (taken as a functional expression) a sentence becomes a semantically unstructured name of the proposition it expresses? Taking this course would leave us with an infinite primitive vocabulary, and the appearance of the words 'Socrates is wise' in two places in the schema would be of no help in understanding the schema or its instances. A further proposal might be to modify our instance of the schema to read:

> The proposition expressed by the sentence 'Socrates is wise' is true if and only if Socrates is wise.

But following this idea would require relativizing the quoted sentence to a language, a need that Horwich must circumvent.

So let me put my objection briefly as follows: the same sentence appears twice in instances of Horwich's schema, once after the words 'the proposition that', in a context that requires the result to be a singular term, the subject of a predicate, and once as an ordinary sentence. We cannot eliminate this iteration of the same sentence without destroying all appearance of a theory. But we cannot *understand* the result of the iteration unless we can see how to make use of the same semantic features of the repeated sentence in both of its appearances—make use of them in giving the semantics of the schema instances. I do not see how this can be done.

My second difficulty with Horwich's theory is more dependent on my own further convictions and commitments. Horwich recognizes that to maintain that truth has, as he says, 'a certain purity', he must show that we can understand it fully in isolation from other ideas, and we can understand other ideas in isolation from it. He does not say there are no relations between the concept of truth and other concepts; only that we can understand these concepts independently. There are several crucial cases so far as I am concerned, since I do not think we can understand meaning or any of the propositional attitudes without the concept of truth. Let me pick one of these: meaning.

Since Horwich thinks of truth as primarily attributable to propositions, he must explain how we can also predicate it of sentences and utterances, and he sees that to explain this without compromising the independence of truth, we must understand meaning without direct appeal to the concept of truth. On this critical matter, Horwich is brief, even laconic. Understanding a sentence, he says, does not *consist* in knowing its truth conditions, though if we understand a sentence we usually *know* its truth conditions. Understanding a sentence, he maintains, consists in knowing its 'assertability conditions' (or 'proper use'). He grants that these conditions may include that the sentence (or utterance) be true. I confess I do not see how, if truth is an assertability condition, and knowing the assertability conditions *is* understanding, we can understand a sentence without having the concept of truth.

I realize, however, that this is disputed territory, and that heavy thinkers like Michael Dummett, Putnam, and Soames, following various leads suggested by Ludwig Wittgenstein and H. P. Grice, believe that an account of meaning can be made to depend on a notion of assertability or use which does not in turn appeal to the concept of truth.

My hopes lie in the opposite direction: I think the sort of assertion that is linked to understanding already incorporates the concept of truth: we are *justified* in asserting a sentence in the required sense only if we believe the sentence we use to make the assertion is true; and what ultimately ties language to the world is that the conditions that typically cause us to hold sentences true *constitute* the truth conditions, and hence the meanings, of our sentences. This is not the place to argue this. For now I must simply remark that it would be a shame if we had to develop a theory of meaning for a speaker or a language independently of a theory of truth for that speaker or language, since we have at least *some* idea how to formulate a theory of truth, but no serious idea how to formulate a theory of meaning based on a concept of assertability or use.

I conclude that the prospects for a deflationary theory of truth are dim. Its attractions seem to me entirely negative: it avoids, or at least tries to avoid, well-marked dead ends and recognizable pitfalls.

Let me suggest a diagnosis of our aporia about truth. We are still under the spell of the Socratic idea that we must keep asking for the *essence* of an idea, a significant *analysis* in other terms, an answer to the question what *makes* this an act of piety, what *makes* this, or any, utterance, sentence, belief, or proposition true. We still fall for the freshman fallacy that demands that we *define* our terms as a prelude to saying anything further with or about them.

It may seem pointless to make so much of the drive to define truth when it is unclear who is trying to do it: not Tarski, who proves it cannot be done; not Horwich, who disclaims the attempt. Who, then, *admits* to wanting to define the concept of truth? Well, that is right. But. But the same ugly urge to define shows up in the guise of trying to provide a brief criterion, schema, partial but leading hint, in place of a strict definition. Since Tarski, we are leery of the word 'definition' when we are thinking of a concept of truth not relativized to a language, but we have not given up the definitional urge. Thus, I see Horwich's schema on a par *in this regard* with Dummett's notion of justified assertability, Putnam's ideally justified assertability, and the various formulations of correspondence and coherence theories. I see all of them as, if not attempts at definitions in the strict sense, attempts at *substitutes* for definitions. In the case of truth, there is no short substitute.

Now I want to describe what I take to be a fairly radical alternative to the theories I have been discussing and (with unseemly haste) dismissing. What I stress here is the *methodology* I think is required rather than the more detailed account I have given elsewhere. The methodology can be characterized on the negative side by saying it offers no definition of the concept of truth, nor any quasi-definitional clause, axiom schema, or other brief substitute for a definition. The positive proposal is to attempt to trace the connections between the concept of truth and the human attitudes and acts that give it body.

My methodological inspiration comes from finitely axiomatized theories of measurement, or of various sciences, theories that put clear constraints on one or more undefined concepts, and then prove that any model of such a theory has intuitively desired properties—that it is adequate to its designed purpose. Since among the models will be all sorts of configurations of abstract entities, and endless unwanted patterns of empirical events and objects, the theory can be applied to, or tested against, such specific phenomena as mass or temperature only by indicating how the theory is to be applied to the appropriate objects or events. We cannot demand a precise indication of how to do this; finding a useful method for applying the theory is an enterprise that goes along with tampering with the formal theory, and testing its correctness as interpreted.

We are interested in the concept of truth only because there are actual objects and states of the world to which to apply it: utterances, states of belief, inscriptions. If we did not understand what it was for such entities to be true, we would not be able to characterize the contents of these states, objects, and events. So in addition to the formal theory of truth, we must indicate how truth is to be predicated of these empirical phenomena.

Tarski's definitions make no mention of empirical matters, but we are free to ask of such a definition whether it fits the actual practice of some speaker or group of speakers—we may ask whether they speak the language for which truth has been defined. There is nothing about Tarski's definitions that prevents us from treating them in this way except the prejudice that, if something is called a definition, the question of its 'correctness' is moot. To put this prejudice to rest, I suggest that we omit the final step in Tarski's definitions, the step that turns his axiomatizations into explicit definitions. We can then in good conscience call the emasculated definition a theory, and accept the truth predicate as undefined. This undefined predicate expresses the *general*, intuitive, concept, applicable to any language, the concept against which we have always surreptitiously tested Tarski's definitions (as he invited us to do, of course).

We know a great deal about how this concept applies to the speech and beliefs and actions of human agents. We use it to interpret their utterances and beliefs by assigning truth conditions to them, and we judge those actions and attitudes by evaluating the likelihood of their truth. The empirical question is how to determine, by observation and induction, what the truth conditions of empirical truth vehicles are. It bears emphasizing: absent this empirical connection, the concept of truth has no application to, or interest for, our mundane concerns, nor, so far as I can see, does it have any content at all.

Consider this analogy: I think of truth as Frank Ramsey thought of probability. He convinced himself, not irrationally, that the concept of probability applies in the first instance to propositional attitudes; it is a measure of degree of belief. He went on to ask himself: How can we make sense of the concept of degree of belief (subjective probability)? Subjective probability is not observable, either by the agent who entertains some proposition with less than total conviction and more than total disbelief, or by others who see and question him. So Ramsey axiomatized the pattern of preferences of an idealized agent who, more or less like the rest of us, adjusts his preferences for the truth of propositions (or states of affairs or events) to accord with his values and beliefs. He stated the conditions on which a pattern of such preferences would be 'rational', and in effect proved that, if these conditions were satisfied, one could reconstruct from the agent's preferences the relative strengths of that agent's desires and subjective probabilities. Ramsey did not suppose everyone is perfectly rational in the postulated sense, but he did assume that people are nearly enough so, in the long run, for his theory to give a content to the concept of subjective probability—or probability, as he thought of it.

A brilliant *strategy*! (Whether or not it gives a correct analysis of probability.) The concept of probability—or at least degree of belief—unobservable by the agent who has it and by his watchers, linked to an equally theoretical concept of cardinal utility, or subjective evaluation, and both tied to simple preference by the axiomatic structure. Simple preference in turn provides the crucial empirical basis through its manifestations in actual choice behaviour.

We should think of a theory of truth for a speaker in the same way we think of a theory of rational decision: both describe structures we can find, with an allowable degree of fitting and fudging, in the behavior of more or less rational creatures gifted with speech. It is in the fitting and fudging that we give content to the undefined concepts of subjective probability and subjective values—belief and desire, as we briefly call them; and, by way of theories like Tarski's, to the undefined concept of truth.

A final remark. I have deliberately made the problem of giving empirical content to the concept of truth seem simpler than it is. It would be *relatively* simple if we could directly observe—take as basic evidence—what people *mean* by what they say. But meaning not only is a more obscure concept than that of truth; it clearly involves it: if you know what an utterance means, you know its truth conditions. The problem is to give *any* propositional attitude a propositional content: belief, desire, intention, meaning.

I therefore see the problem of connecting truth with observable human behavior as inseparable from the problem of assigning contents to all the attitudes, and this seems to me to require a theory that embeds a theory of truth in a larger theory that includes decision theory itself. The result will incorporate the major norms of rationality whose partial realization in the thought and behavior of agents makes those agents intelligible, more or less, to others. If this normative structure is formidably complex, we should take comfort in the fact that the more complex it is, the better our chance of interpreting its manifestations as thought and meaningful speech and intentional action, given only scattered bits of weakly interpreted evidence.

XVIII

PRAGMATISM, DAVIDSON, AND TRUTH

RICHARD RORTY

I LESS IS MORE

Davidson has said that his theory of truth 'provides no entities with which to compare sentences', and thus is a 'correspondence' theory only in 'an unassuming sense.'[1] His paper 'A Coherence Theory of Truth and Knowledge' takes as its slogan 'correspondence without confrontation'.[2] This slogan chimes with his repudiation of what he calls the 'dualism of scheme and content'—the idea that something like 'mind' or 'language' can bear some relation such as 'fitting' or 'organizing' to the world. Such doctrines are reminiscent of pragmatism, a movement which has specialized in debunking dualisms and in dissolving traditional problems created by those dualisms. The close affiliations of Davidson's work to Quine's and of Quine's to Dewey's make it tempting to see Davidson as belonging to the American pragmatist tradition.

Davison, however, has explicitly denied that his break with the empiricist tradition makes him a pragmatist.[3] He thinks of pragmatism as an identification of truth with assertibility, or with assertibility under ideal conditions. If such an identification is essential to pragmatism, then indeed Davidson is as anti-pragmatist as he is anti-empiricist. For such an identification would merely be an emphasis on the 'scheme' side of an unacceptable dualism, replacing the emphasis on the 'content' side represented by traditional empiricism. Davidson does not want to see truth identified with anything. He also does not want to view sentences as 'made true' by anything—neither knowers or speakers on the one hand nor 'the

From Richard Rorty, 'Pragmatism, Davidson and Truth', in *Truth and Interpretation*, ed. E. Lepore (Blackwell, 1986), 333–55. Reprinted by permission of Blackwell Publishers and the author.

[1] *Inquiries into Truth and Interpretation* (New York, 1984), p. xviii.

[2] This article appears in *Kant oder Hegel?*, ed. Dieter Henrich (Stuttgart, 1983); the quoted slogan is on p. 423.

[3] *Inquiries*, p. xviii.

world' on the other. For him, any 'theory of truth' which analyses a relation between bits of language and bits of non-language is already on the wrong track.

On this last, negative, point, Davidson agrees with William James. James thought that no traditional theory of truth had come close to explaining 'the particular go'[4] of such a special relation, and that it was a hopeless quest. On his view, there was no point in trying to give sense to a notion of 'correspondence' which was neutral between, e.g., perceptual, theoretical, moral, and mathematical truths. He suggested that we settle for 'the true' as being 'only the expedient in our way of thinking'.[5] When his critics chorused that 'truths aren't true because they work; they work because they are true', James thought they had missed his point, namely that 'true' was a term of praise used for endorsing, rather than one referring to a state of affairs the existence of which explained e.g., the success of those who held true beliefs. He thought that the moral of philosophers' failures to discover, as it were, the microstructure of the correspondence relation was that there was nothing there to find, that one could not use truth as an *explanatory* notion.

James, unfortunately, did not confine himself to making this negative point. He also had moments in which he inferred from the false premiss that

If we have the notion of 'justified', we don't need that of 'truth'

to

'True' must mean something like 'justifiable'.

This was a form of the idealist error of inferring from

We can make no sense of the notion of truth as correspondence

to

Truth must consist in ideal coherence.

The error is to assume that 'true' needs a definition, and then to infer from the fact that it cannot be defined in terms of a relation between beliefs and non-beliefs to the view that it must be defined in terms of a relation among beliefs. But, as Hilary Putnam has pointed out in his 'naturalistic fallacy' argument, 'it might be true but not *X*' is always sensible, no matter what one substitutes for *X* (the same point G. E. Moore made about 'good').[6]

Suppose that we prescind from the moments in which James fell into

---

[4] *Pragmatism* (Indianapolis, 1981), 92, this vol., 53.   [5] Ibid. 100, this vol., 62.

[6] Putnam, *Meaning and the Moral Sciences* (London, 1978), 108.

this error, as well as from Peirce's unfortunate attempt (of which more later) to define truth in terms of 'the end of inquiry'. Suppose that we follow up James's negative point—his polemic against the notion of 'correspondence'—and forget his occasional attempts to say something constructive about truth. We can then, I think, isolate a sense for the term 'pragmatism' which will consist *simply* in the dissolution of the traditional problematic about truth, as opposed to a constructive 'pragmatist theory of truth'. This dissolution would start from the claim that 'true' has no explanatory use, but merely the following uses:

(a) an endorsing use
(b) a cautionary use, in such remarks as 'Your belief that S is perfectly justified, but perhaps not true'—reminding ourselves that justification is relative to, and no better than, the beliefs cited as grounds for S, and that such justification is no guarantee that things will go well if we take S as a 'rule for action' (Peirce's definition of belief)
(c) A disquotational use: to say metalinguistic things of the form 'S is true iff ——'.[7]

The cautionary use of the term was neglected by James, as was the disquotational use. The neglect of the former led to the association of pragmatism with relativism. The misleading association of the latter (by Tarski) with the notion of 'correspondence' has led people to think that there must have been more to this notion than James realized. Davidson, on my view, has given us an account of truth which has a place for each of these uses while eschewing the idea that the expediency of a belief can be explained by its truth.

In the sense of 'pragmatism' in which Davidson and James are both pragmatists, the term signifies adherence to the following theses:

(1) 'True' has no explanatory uses.
(2) We understand all there is to know about the relation of beliefs to the world when we understand their causal relations with the world;

---

[7] There is much to be said about the relations between these three uses, but I shall not try to say it here. The best attempt to do so which I have seen is found in an unpublished paper by Robert Brandom called 'Truth Talk'. Brandom shows how the 'primitive pragmatism' which tries to define truth as assertibility is defeated by the use of 'true' in such contexts as the antecedents of conditionals. But he then suggests a way of developing a sophisticated pragmatism which, invoking Frege and the Grover–Camp–Belnap prosentential theory of truth, saves Dewey's intentions. Brandom not only shows how 'anaphoric or prosentential theories' can, as he says 'retain the fundamental anti-descriptive thrust of the pragmatist position, while broadening it to account also for the embedded uses on which primitive pragmatism founders', but suggests ways of reconciling these theories with Davidsonian disquotationalism.

our knowledge of how to apply terms such as 'about' and 'true of'
is fallout from a 'naturalistic' account of linguistic behaviour.[8]
(3) There are no relations of 'being made true' which hold between
    beliefs and the world.
(4) There is no point to debates between realism and anti-realism, for
    such debates presuppose the empty and misleading idea of beliefs
    'being made true'.[9]

Notice that, so defined, pragmatism offers no 'theory of truth'. All it gives
us is an explanation of why, in this area, less is more—of why therapy is
better than system-building.

Both James and Davidson would urge that the only reason philosophers
thought they needed an 'explanation of what truth consists in' was that
they were held captive by a certain picture—the picture which Davidson
calls 'the dualism of scheme and content' and which Dewey thought of as
'the dualism of Subject and Object'. Both pictures are of disparate ontological realms, one containing beliefs and the other non-beliefs. The picture
of two such realms permits us to imagine truth as a relation between particular beliefs and particular non-beliefs which (a) is non-causal in nature,
and (b) must be 'correctly analysed' before one can rebut (or concede
victory to) the epistemological sceptic. To adopt (1)–(4) above is to erase
this picture, and thereby to erase most of the traditional philosophical
dualisms which Dewey thought ought to be erased. It is also to drop the
picture which the epistemological sceptic needs to make his skepticism
interesting and arguable—to make it more than the philosopher's pursuit
of *Unheimlichkeit* of a sense of the strangeness of the world.

II PEIRCE'S HALFWAY MEASURE

Before turning to the question of whether Davidson in fact adheres to
(1)–(4), it may be helpful to say something about Peirce's 'end of inquiry'

---

[8] This thesis does not, of course, entail that you can define intentional terms in non-
intentional terms, nor that a semantical metalanguage can somehow be 'reduced' to
Behaviorese. It is one thing to say 'You learn which sentences using the term "X" are true by
finding out which sentences using the term "Y" are true' and another to say 'You can explain
the meaning of "X" in terms of "Y" ' or 'You can reduce Xs to Ys'. Our intentional concepts
are not fall-out from our observation of causal relationships, but our knowledge of how to apply
them is. See Sect. IV below for a discussion of Davidson's non-reductive brand of physicalism.
[9] Jamesian pragmatists heartily agree with Dummett's claim that lots and lots of the traditional 'problems of philosophy' (including the problems which Peirce thought to solve with his
'Scotistic realism') are best seen as issues between realists and anti-realists over whether there
are 'matters of fact' in e.g. physics, ethics, or logic. But whereas Dummett sees himself as having
rehabilitated these fine old problems by semanticizing them, the pragmatist sees him as having
conveniently bagged them for disposal.

pragmatism. This is the version of the so-called 'pragmatist theory of truth' (a misleading textbook label for a farrago of inconsistent doctrines) which has received most attention in recent years. It represents, on my view, a halfway house between idealist and physicalist theories of truth on the one hand, and (1)–(4) on the other.

Idealism and physicalism have in common the hope that

(A) 'There are rocks' is true

is true if and only if

(B) At the ideal end of inquiry, we shall be justified in asserting that there are rocks

This suggestion requires them, however, to say that

(C) There are rocks

is implied by (B) as well as by (A). This seems paradoxical, since they also wish to assert

(D) 'There are rocks' is linked by a relation of correspondence—accurate representation—to the way the world is

and there seems no obvious reason why the progress of the language-game we are playing should have anything in particular to do with the way the rest of the world is.

Idealism and physicaism are attempts to supply such a reason. The idealists suggest that

(E) The world consists of representations arranged in an ideally coherent system

thus permitting them to analyse (C) as

(F) 'There are rocks' is a member of the ideally coherent system of representations.

Idealists support this move by saying that the correspondence relation of (D) cannot be a relation whose existence could be established by confronting an assertion with an object to see if a relation called 'corresponding' holds. Nobody knows what such a confrontation would look like. (The relation of 'customary response to' which holds between tables and assertions of the presence of tables is clearly not what is wanted.) Since the only criterion of truth is coherence among representations, they say, the only way of saving (D) while avoiding scepticism is (E).

The physicalists, on the other hand, analyse (A) as (D) and then argue that playing the language-games we play will eventually lead us to correspond with reality. It will do so because, so to speak, the world takes a hand in the game. This is the view of philosophers like Friedrich Engels, Jerry Fodor, Michael Devitt, Jay Rosenberg, and Hartry Field. They reject the possibility of a priori discovery of the nature of reality, illustrated by the idealists (E), but they think that one or another empirical science (or the 'unified' ensemble of them all) will provide an answer to the sceptic. These philosophers think that, although there are no entailments, there are deeply buried connections between the conditions of the truth of (B) and of (C). These connections will not be discovered by an analysis of meanings but by empirical scientific work which will pry out the causal connections between, e.g., rocks and representations of rocks.

Peirce, in his earlier period, wanted to avoid both the revisionary metaphysics of idealism and the promissory notes of physicalism. He tried for a quick fix by analysing (D) as (B). He shared with the idealist and the physicalist the motive of refuting the sceptic, but he thought it enough to say that 'reality' means something like 'whatever we shall still be asserting the existence of at the end of inquiry'. This definition of reality bridges the gap the sceptic sees between coherence and correspondence. It reduces coherence to correspondence without the necessity either for metaphysical system-building or for further empirical inquiry. A simple reanalysis of the term 'reality' does the trick.

I do not think (though I once did)[10] that Peircian pragmatism is defensible, but before transcending it I want to remark that Peirce was moving in the right direction. The Peircian pragmatist is right in thinking that the idealist and the physicalist share a common fallacy—namely that 'correspondence' is the name of a relation between pieces of thought (or language) and pieces of the world, a relation such that the relata must be ontologically homogeneous. The idealist generalizes Berkeley's point by saying: nothing can correspond to a representation except a representation. So he saves us from scepticism by redescribing reality as consisting of representations. The physicalist thinks that nothing can correspond to a bit of spatio-temporal reality except by being another bit linked to the first by appropriate causal relationships. So he saves us from scepticism by offering a physicalistic account of the nature of our representations—one which shows that, as Fodor once said, the correspondence theory of truth corresponds to reality. The Peircian rises above this debate by saying

[10] As e.g. when I said, falsely, that 'we can make no sense of the notion that the view which can survive all objections might be false' (*Consequences of Pragmatism* (Minneapolis, 1982), 165—passage written in 1979). I started retracting this Peircianism in the introd. to that book (e.g., p. xlv, written in 1981) and am still at it. I was persuaded of the untenability of Peircian view by Michael Williams's 'Coherence, Justification and Truth' (*Review of Metaphysics*, 34 (1980), 243–72) esp. by his claim (p. 269) that 'we have no idea what it would be for a theory to be ideally complete and comprehensive . . . or of what it would be good for inquiry to have an end'. Cf. his suggestion that we drop the attempt to think of truth as 'in some sense an epistemic notion' (p. 269). Davidson spells out what happens when the attempt is dropped.

that the 'about' and 'true of' relations can link utterly disparate relata, and that problems of ontological homogeneity need not arise.[11] All that is necessary is to redefine 'reality' as what the winners of the game talk about, thus insuring that the conditions laid down by (B) and (D) coincide.

The Peircian redefinition, however, uses a term—'ideal'—which is just as fishy as 'corresponds'. To make it less fishy Peirce would have to answer the question 'How would we know that we were at the end of inquiry, as opposed to merely having gotten tired or unimaginative?' This is as awkward as 'How do we know we are corresponding to reality, rather than merely making conventionally correct responses to stimuli?' Peirce's idea of 'the end of inquiry' might make sense if we could detect an asymptotic convergence in inquiry, but such convergence seems a local and short-term phenomenon.[12] Without such a clarification of 'ideal' or 'end', the Peircian is merely telling that the conditions laid down by (B) and (D) coincide without giving us any reason for thinking they do. Nor is it clear what such a reason could consist in.

Peirce went halfway towards destroying the epistemological problematic which motivated the metaphysical quarrels between idealists and physicalists. He did so by leaving out 'mind' and sticking to 'signs'. But he went *only* halfway because he still thought that (D) was an intuition which any philosophy had to assimilate. James went the rest of the way by saying that not only was 'true of' not a relation between ontologically homogenous relata, but was not an analysable relation at all, not a relation which could be clarified by a scientific or metaphysical description of the relation between beliefs and non-beliefs. Deciding that no reason could be given for saying that the constraints laid down by (B) and (D) would coincide, he simply dropped (D), and with it the problematic of epistemological scepticism. He thereby set the stage for Dewey's argument

[11] Peircian pragmatism is often criticized on the ground that, like idealism, it raises problems about ontological homogeneity and heterogeneity through a counter-intuitive Kantian claim that 'objects in the world owe their fundamental structure—and, if they couldn't exist without displaying that structure, their existence—to our creative activity' (A. Plantinga, 'How to be an Anti-Realist', *Proceedings and Addresses of the American Philosophical Association*, 56 (1982), 52). But this confuses a criterial claim with a causal one: the Peircian claim that 'If there are rocks, they will display their structure at the end of inquiry' and the idealist claim that 'If there were no inquiry, there would be no rocks.'

[12] See Mary Hesse's distinction between 'instrumental progress'—increase in predictive ability—and 'convergence of concepts' (*Revolutions and Reconstructions in the Philosophy of Science* (Bloomington, Ind., 1980), pp. x–xi). The possibility of scientific revolutions endangers conceptual convergence, which is the only sort of convergence which will do the Peircian any good. To insure against the indefinite proliferation of such revolutions in the future one would need something like Peirce's 'metaphysics of evolutionary love', or Putnam's attempt to certify contemporary physics as 'mature'.

that it is only the attempt to supplement a naturalist account of our interaction with our environment with a non-naturalist account (involving some third thing, intermediate between the organism and its environment—such as 'mind' or 'language') which makes that problematic seem interesting.

III DAVIDSON AND THE FIELD LINGUIST

What justification is there for attributing (1)–(4) to Davidson? He has asserted (3) on various occasions. But it may seem odd to attribute (4) to him, since he has often been treated as a prototypical 'realist'. (2) may also sound unDavidsonian, since he has had no truck with recent 'causal theories' in semantics. Further, his association with Tarski, and Tarski's with the notion of 'correspondence', may seem to make him an unlikely recruit for the pragmatist ranks—for pragmatism, as I have defined it, consists very largely in the claim that only if we drop the whole idea of 'correspondence with reality' can we avoid pseudo-problems.

Nevertheless, I propose to argue that all four pragmatist theses should be ascribed to Davidson. To defend this claim, I shall begin by offering an account of what I shall call 'the philosophy of language of the field linguist'. I shall claim that this is all the philosophy of language (and, in particular, all the doctrine about truth) which Davidson has, and all that he thinks anybody needs.

Davidson, like the traditional philosopher who wants an answer to the epistemological sceptic, wants us to step out of our language-game and look at it from a distance. But his outside standpoint is not the metaphysical standpoint of the idealist, looking for an unsuspected ontological homogeneity between beliefs and non-beliefs invisible to science, nor the hopeful standpoint of the physicalist, looking to future science to discover such an homogeneity. Rather, it is the mundane standpoint of the field linguist trying to make sense of our linguistic behaviour. Whereas traditional theories of truth asked 'what feature of the world is referred to by "true"?', Davidson asks 'how is "true" used by the outside observer of the language-game?'

Davidson is surely right that Quine 'saved philosophy of language as a serious subject' by getting rid of the analytic-synthetic distinction.[13] Quine's best argument for doing so was that the distinction is of no use to the field linguist. Davidson follows up on this argument by pointing out

---

[13] 'Coherence Theory', 431.

that, *pace* Dummett and Quine himself,[14] the distinction between the physical objects the natives react to and their neural stimulations is of no
use either. The linguist cannot start with knowledge of native meanings
acquired prior to knowledge of native beliefs, nor with translations
of native observation sentences which have been certified by matching
them with stimulations. He must be purely coherentist in his approach,
going round and round the hermeneutic circle until he begins to feel at
home.

All the linguist has to go on is his observation of the way in which
linguistic is aligned with non-linguistic behaviour in the course of the
native's interaction with his environment, an interaction which he takes
to be guided by rules for action (Peirce's definition of 'beliefs').
He approaches this data armed with the regulative principle that most
of the native's rules are the same as ours, which is to say that most of
them are true. The latter formulation of the principle is an extension
of Quine's remark that any anthropologist who claims to have
translated a native utterance as '*p* and not-*p*' just shows that she has
not yet put together a good translation manual. Davidson generalizes
this: any translations which portrays the natives as denying most
of the evident facts about their environment is automatically a bad
one.

The most vivid example of this point is Davidson's claim that the best
way to translate the discourse of a brain which has always lived in a vat
will be as referring to the vat-cum-computer environment the brain is actually in.[15] This will be the analogue of construing most native remarks as
about, e.g., rocks and diseases rather than about trolls and demons. In
Davidson's words:

> What stands in the way of global skepticism of the senses is, in my view, the fact
> that we must, in the plainest and methodologically most basic cases, take the objects
> of a belief to be the causes of that belief. And what we, as interpreters, must take
> them to be is what they in fact are. Communication begins where causes converge:
> your utterance means what mine does if belief in its truth is systematically caused
> by the same events and objects.[16]

---

[14] See ibid. 430: 'Quine and Dummett agree on a basic principle, which is that whatever there
is to meaning must be traced back somehow to experience, the given, or patterns of sensory
stimulation, something intermediate between belief and the usual objects our beliefs are about.
Once we take this step, we open the door to skepticism ... When meaning goes epistemological in this way, truth and meaning are necessarily divorced.'

[15] As far as I know, Davidson has not used this example in print. I am drawing upon unpublished remarks at a colloquium with Quine and Putnam, Heidelberg, 1981.

[16] 'Coherence Theory', 436. This line of argument—together with Davidson's account of reference as fallout from translation (as at *Inquiries*, 219 ff., 236 ff.)—is my chief textual evidence
for imputing (2) to Davidson.

In this passage, Davidson weds the Kripkean claim that causation must have *something* to do with reference to the Strawsonian claim that you figure out what somebody is talking about by figuring out what object most of his beliefs are true of. The wedding is accomplished by saying that Strawson is right if construed holistically—if one prefaces his claim with Aristotle's phrase 'on the whole and for the most part'. You cannot, however, use Strawson's criterion for individual cases and be sure of being right. But if *most* of the results of your translation-scheme, and consequent assignment of reference, do not conform to Strawson's criterion, then that scheme must have something terribly wrong with it. The mediating element between Strawson and Kripke is the Quinean insight that knowledge *both* of causation *and* of reference is (equally) a matter of coherence with the field linguist's own beliefs.

Thesis (2) above can be construed in either a Kripkean or a Davidsonian way. One the former, building-block, approach to reference, we want to trace causal pathways from objects to individual speech-acts. This approach leaves open the possibility that speakers may get these pathways all wrong (e.g., by being largely wrong about what there is) and thus that they may never know to what they are referring. This allows the possibility of a wholesale divorce between referents and intentional objects—just the kind of scheme-content gap which Davidson warns us against. By contrast, Davidson is suggesting that we maximize coherence and truth first, and then let reference fall out as it may.

This guarantees that the intentional objects of lots of beliefs—what Davidson calls 'the plainest cases'—will be their causes. Kripkean slippage (e.g., the Goedel-Schmidt case) must be the exception. For if we try to imagine that a split between entities referred to and intentional objects is the rule we shall have drained the notion of 'reference' of any content. That is: we shall have made it, like 'analytic', a notion which the field linguist has no use for. The linguist can communicate with the natives if he knows most of their intentional objects (i.e., which objects most of their rules for action are good for dealing with, which objects most of their beliefs are true of). But he can make as little sense of the sceptical claim that this is not 'really' communication (but just accidentally felicitous cross-talk) as of the suggestion that the 'intended interpretation' of some platitudinous native utterance is 'There are no rocks'.

Davidson's application of this view of the job of the field linguist to epistemological scepticism is as follows. Unless one is willing to postulate some intermediary between the organism and its environment (e.g., 'determinate meanings', 'intended interpretations', 'what is before the speaker's mind', etc.) then radical interpretation begins at home. So, like all other natives, we turn out to have mostly true beliefs. The argument is neat, but does it *answer* the sceptic, as the idealist and the physicalist want to do? Or does it simply tell the sceptic that his question, 'Do we ever represent reality as it is in itself?' was a bad one, as the Jamesian pragmatist does?

A sceptic is likely to reply to Davidson that it would take a lot more than an account of the needs of the field linguist to show that belief is, as Davidson says, 'in its nature veridical'.[17] He will think that Davidson has shown no more than that the field linguist must assume that the natives believe mostly what we do, and that the question of whether most of *our* beliefs are true is still wide open. Davidson can only reply, once again, that radical interpretation begins at home—that if we want an outside view of our own language-game, the only one available is that of the field linguist. But that is just what the sceptic will not grant. He thinks that Davidson has missed the philosophical point. He thinks that Davidson's outside standpoint is not, so to speak, far enough outside to count as philosophical.

As far as I can see, the only rejoinder readily available to Davidson at this point is to remark on the intuitive appeal of (2): the naturalistic thesis, which he shares with Kripke, that there is nothing more to be known about the relation between beliefs and the rest of reality than what we learn from an empirical study of causal transactions between organisms and their environment. The relevant result of this study is the field linguist's translation-manual-cum-ethnographic-report.[18] Since we already have (in dictionaries) a translation manual for ourselves, as well as (in encyclopedias) an auto-ethnography, there is nothing more for us to know *about our relation to reality* than we already know. There is no further job for philosophy to do. This is just what the pragmatist has been telling the sceptic all the time. Both the pragmatist and Davidson are saying that if 'correspondence' denotes a relation between beliefs and the world which can vary though nothing else varies—even if all the causal relations remain the same—then 'corresponds' cannot be an explanatory term. So if truth is to be thought of as 'correspondence', then 'true' cannot be an explanatory term. Pressing (2) to the limit, and freeing it from the atomistic presuppositions which Kripkean 'building-block' theories of reference add to it, results in (1).

Thus Davidson's strategy with the sceptic would seem to give him reason to subscribe to (1) as well as to (2). Whereas the physicalist invokes (2)

---

[17] 'Coherence Theory', 432.
[18] That such a manual cannot be separated from such a report is entailed by the Quine–Davidson argument that you cannot figure out beliefs and meanings independently of one another.

with an eye to finding something for 'correspondence' to refer to, Davidson takes the absence of such a thing in the field linguist's results as a reason for thinking that there is nothing to look for. Like Dewey's (and unlike Skinner's) his is a *non-reductive* naturalism, one which does not assume that every important semantical term must describe a physical relationship.[19] He thinks that there will be lots of terms used by theorists who study causal relations (e.g., field linguists, particle physicists) which do not themselves denote causal relations.

On my interpretation, then, Davidson joins the pragmatist in saying that 'true' has no explanatory use.[20] His contribution to pragmatism consists in pointing out that it has a disquotational use in addition to the normative uses seized upon by James. The traditional philosophical attempt to conflate these two kinds of use, and to view them both as explained by the use of 'true' to denote a non-causal relation called 'correspondence', is, on this account, a confused attempt to be inside and outside the language-game at the same time.

My interpretation, however, must deal with the fact that Davidson, unlike the pragmatist, does not present himself as repudiating the sceptic's question, but as answering it. He says that 'even a mild coherence theory like mine must provide a skeptic with a reason for supposing coherent beliefs are true'.[21] Again, he says 'the theory I defend is not in competition with a correspondence theory, but depends for its defense on an argument that purports to show that coherence yields correspondence'.[22] This sounds as if Davidson were not only adopting something like (D) above, but claiming to deduce (D) from (B), in the manner of idealism and Peircean pragmatism. In wanting 'correspondence without confrontation', he shows that he shares with these latter 'isms' the view that we cannot compare a belief with a non-belief to see if they match. But what does Davidson suppose is left of correspondence after confrontation is taken away? What is it that he thinks the sceptic wants? What is it that he proposes to give the sceptic by making coherence yield it?

Davidson says that the sceptical question he wishes to answer is: 'how,

---

[19] Davidson's 'Mental Events' illustrates his strategy of combining identity-with-the-physical with irreducibility-to-the-physical.

[20] One might object, as Alan Donagan has suggested to me, that the fact that both the linguist's and the native's beliefs are mostly true is an explanation of the fact that they are able to communicate with one another. But this sort of explanation does not invoke a causally efficacious property. It is like explaining the fact of communication by saying that the two inhabit the same space-time continuum. We do not know what it would be like for them not to, any more than we know what it would be like for one or the other to have mostly false beliefs. The only candidates for causally efficacious properties are properties which we can imagine away.

[21] 'Coherence Theory', 426.   [22] Ibid. 423.

given that we "cannot get outside our beliefs and our language so as to find some test other than coherence" we nevertheless can have knowledge and talk about an objective public world which is not of our making?'[23] But this does not help us much. Only if one held some view which made it mysterious that there could be such knowledge and such talk (e.g., one which required ontological homogeneity between beliefs and non-beliefs, or one which thought that there was an intermediary 'scheme' which 'shaped' the non-beliefs before they became talkable-about), would this be a challenging question. If there is to be a problem here, it must be because the sceptic has been allowed to construe 'objective' in such a way that the connection between coherence and objectivity has become unperspicuous.[24] What sense of 'correspondence' will both preserve this lack of perspicuity and yet be such that Davidson can argue that coherence will yield it?

To make a start, we can note that Davidson thinks 'correspondence' is not, as correspondence-to-*fact* theorists believe, a relation between a sentence and a chunk of reality which is somehow isomorphic to that sentence. In 'True to the Facts', he agrees with Strawson that facts— sentence-shaped chunks of the world—are ad hoc contrivances which do not answer to the sceptic's needs. What does, he thinks, is the more complex notion of correspondence made intelligible by Tarski's notion of satisfaction. Rather than thinking of the correspondence of language to reality as symbolized by the relation between two sides of a T-sentence, Davidson says, we should attend to word–world rather than sentence–world mappings, and in particular to the constraints on such mappings required for 'the elaboration of a nontrivial theory capable of meeting the test of entailing all those neutral snowbound trivialities' (namely the T-sentences).[25]

These constraints are what guide the field linguist who tries to guess the causes of the native's behaviour, and then goes around the hermeneutic circle long enough to come up with T-sentences which maximize the truth of the native's beliefs. The eventual theory will link native words with bits of the world by the satisfaction-relation, but these links will not be the

[23] Ibid. 426–7. Davidson correctly says, in this passage, that I do not think this is a good question. I am here trying to explain what is wrong with it, and why I think Davidson too should regard it as a bad question.
[24] I think that Davidson may be worrying, in this passage, about the sort of identification of criterial and causal relations for which I criticized Plantinga in n. 11, above. This is the sort of identification which is characteristic of idealism, and which generates fear that coherence theories will result in human beings having 'constituted the world'. On my interpretation, he has already disposed of that identification, and thus of the need for worry.
[25] *Inquiries*, 51.

basis for the translations. Rather, they will be fallout from the translations. Going around this circle means not attempting (in the manner of building-block theories of reference) to start with some 'secure' links, but rather going back and forth between guesses at translations of occasion-sentences and of standing sentences until something like Rawlsian 'reflective equilibrium' emerges.

The correspondence between words and objects provided by the satis-faction-relations incorporated in a T-theory are thus irrelevant to the sort of correspondence which was supposed to be described by 'true of', and which is supposed to be revealed by 'philosophical analysis', culminating in a 'theory of truth'. So whatever the sceptic's desired correspondence may be, it is not something which is captured in Tarski's account of satis-faction. For 'true' does not offer material for analysis. As Davidson says

Truth is beautifully transparent compared to belief and coherence and I take it as primitive. Truth, as applied to utterances of sentences, shows the disquotational feature enshrined in Tarski's Convention T, and that is enough to fix its domain of application.[26]

So we cannot define 'true' in terms of satisfaction, nor of anything else. We can only explain our sense that, as Davidson says, 'the truth of an utter-ance depends on just two things, what the words mean and how the world is arranged' by explaining how we go about finding out these two things, and by pointing out that these two inquiries cannot be conducted independently.

I think Davidson should be interpreted as saying that the plausibility of the thesis just cited—that there is no third thing relevant to truth besides meanings of words and the way the world is—is the best explanation we are going to get of the intuitive force of (D): the idea that 'truth is corre-spondence with reality'. This thesis is all there is to the 'realistic' intuition which idealists, physicalists, and Peirceans have been so concerned to pre-serve. But, so construed, (D) makes the merely *negative* point that we need not worry about such *tertia* as, in Davidson's words, 'a conceptual scheme, a way of viewing things, a perspective' (or a transcendental constitution of consciousness, or a language, or a cultural tradition). So I think that Davidson is telling us, once again, that less is more: we should not ask for more detail about the correspondence relation, but rather realize that the *tertia* which have made us have sceptical doubts about whether most of our beliefs are true are just not there.

To say that they are not there is to say, once again, that the field linguist does not need them—and that therefore philosophy does not need them

---

[26] 'Coherence Theory', 425.

either. Once we understand how radical interpretation works, and that the interpreter can make no good use of notions like 'determinate meaning', 'intended interpretation', 'constitutive act of the transcendental imagination', 'conceptual scheme', and the like, then we can take the notion of 'correspondence to reality' as trivial, and not in need of analysis. For this term has now been reduced to a stylistic variant of 'true'.

If this is indeed what Davidson is saying, then his answer to the sceptic comes down to: you are only a sceptic because you have these intentionalistic notions floating around in your head, inserting imaginary barriers between you and the world. Once you purify yourself of the 'idea idea' in all its various forms, scepticism will never cross your enlightened mind. If this *is* his response to the sceptic, then I think he is making exactly the right move, the same move which James and Dewey were trying, somewhat more awkwardly, to make. But I also think Davidson was a bit misleading in suggesting that he was going to show us how coherence yields correspondence. It would have been better to have said that he was going to offer the sceptic a way of speaking which would prevent him from asking his question, than to say that he was going to answer that question. It would have been better to tell him that when confrontation goes, so does representation, and thus the picture which made possible both the fears of the sceptic and the hopes of the physicalist, the idealist and the Peircean.

Davidson's favourite characterization of the picture which the sceptic should abjure is 'the dualism of scheme and content'. A common feature of all the forms of this dualism which Davidson lists is that the relations between the two sides of the dualism are non-causal. Such *tertia* as a 'conceptual framework' or an 'intended interpretation' are non-causally related to the things which they organize or intend. They vary independently of the rest of the universe, just as do the sceptic's relations of 'correspondence' or 'representation'. The moral is that if we have no such *tertia*, then we have no suitable items to serve as representations, and thus no need to ask whether our beliefs represent the world accurately. We still have beliefs, but they will be seen from the outside as the field linguist sees them (as causal interactions with the environment) or from the inside as the pre-epistemological native sees them (as rules for action). To abjure *tertia* is to abjure the possibility of a third way of seeing them—one which somehow combines the outside view and the inside view, the descriptive and the normative attitudes. To see language in the same way as we see beliefs—not as a 'conceptual framework' but as the causal interaction with the environment described by the field linguist, makes it impossible to think of language as something which may or may not (how could we ever tell?) 'fit the world'. So once we give up *tertia*, we give up (or trivialize) the notions of representation and correspondence, and thereby give up the possibility of formulating epistemological scepticism.

If my understanding of Davidson is right, then—apart from his appeal to physicalistic unified science, the appeal formulated in the pragmatist's (2)—his only arguments for the claim that the philosophy of language of the field linguist is all we need will be the arguments offered in 'On the Very Idea of a Conceptual Scheme' to the effect that various 'confrontationalist' metaphors are more trouble than they are worth. All that we might add would be further arguments to the same point drawn from the history of philosophy—illustrations of the impasses into which the attempts to develop those metaphors drew various great dead philosophers. It will not be an empirical or a metaphysical discovery that there is no *tertium quid* relevant to the truth of assertions, nor a result of 'analysis of the meaning' of 'true' or 'belief' or any other term. So, like James (though unlike Peirce) Davidson is not giving us a new 'theory of truth'. Rather, he is giving us reasons for thinking that we can safely get along with less philosophizing about truth than we had thought we needed. On my interpretation, his argument that 'coherence yields correspondence' comes down to

From the field linguist's point of view, none of the notions which might suggest that there was more to truth than the meaning of words and the way the world is are needed. So if you are willing to assume this point of view you will have no more sceptical doubts about the intrinsic veridicality of belief.

IV DAVIDSON AS NON-REDUCTIVE PHYSICALIST

Before turning to a well-known set of objections to the claim that the philosophy of the field linguist is all the philosophy of language we need— those of Michael Dummett—it will be useful to compare Davidson with a philosopher to whom he is, beneath a few superficial differences in rhetoric, very close: Hilary Putnam. Putnam is a proponent of many familiar pragmatist doctrines. He makes fun, as James and Dewey did, of the attempt to get an outside view—a 'God's-eye-view' of the sort which the traditional epistemologist, and the sceptic, have tried for. But when he confronts disquotationalist theories of truth he is troubled. They smell reductionist to him, and he sees them as symptoms of a lingering positivism, a 'transcendental Skinnerianism'. Putnam says:

If a philosopher says that *truth* is different from *electricity* in precisely this way: that there is room for a theory of electricity but *no room* for a theory of truth, that knowing the assertibility conditions is *all there is to know* about truth, then, in so far as I understand him at all, he is denying that there is a *property* of truth (or a property of rightness or correctness), not just in the realist sense, but in *any* sense. But this is to deny that our thoughts and assertions are *thoughts* and *assertions*.[27]

Putnam is here assuming that the only reason why one might disclaim the need for a theory of the nature of X is that one has discovered that Xs are 'nothing but' Ys, in good reductivist fashion. So he thinks that Davidson's abjuration of 'an account of what it is for an assertion to be correct and what it is for it to be incorrect' must be made on the basis of a reduction of true assertions to conventionally accepted noises.[28] On this view, to assume the point of view of the field linguist is to reduce actions to movements. But Davidson is not saying that assertions are nothing but noises. Rather he is saying that truth, unlike electricity, is not an explanation of anything.

The idea that the property of truth can serve as an explanation is a product of the misleading picture which engenders the idea that its presence requires an explanation. To see this, notice that it would be a mistake to think of 'true' as having an explanatory use on the basis of such examples as 'He found the correct house because his belief about its location was true' and 'Priestley failed to understand the nature of oxygen because his beliefs about the nature of combustion were false'. The quoted sentences are not explanations but promissory notes for explanations. To get them cashed, to get real explanations, we need to say things like 'He found the correct house because he believed that it was located at . . .' or 'Priestley failed because he thought that phlogiston . . .'. The explanation of success and failure is given by the details about what was true or what was false, not by the truth or falsity itself—just as the explanation of the praiseworthiness of an action is not 'it was the right thing to do' but the details of the circumstances in which it was done.[29]

If truth *itself* is to be an explanation of something, that explanandum must be of something which can be caused by truth, but not caused by the content of true beliefs. The function of the *tertia* which Davidson wishes to banish was precisely to provide a mechanism outside the causal order of the physical world, a mechanism which could have or lack a quasi-causal property with which one might identify truth. Thus to say that our conceptual scheme is 'adequate to the world', is to suggest that some

[27] *Philosophical Papers*, iii, *Realism and Reason* (Cambridge, 1983), p. xv.

[28] Ibid., p. xiv.

[29] The line of argument I have been employing in this paragraph may also be found in Michael Levin, 'What Kind of Explanation is Truth?', in J. Leplin (ed.), *Essays in Scientific Realism* (Berkeley and Los Angeles, 1984), 124–39 and in Michael Williams, 'Do We (Epistemologists) need a Theory of Truth?', *Philosophical Topics*, 14 (1986), 223–42.

cogs and gears are meshing nicely—cogs and gears which are either non-physical or which, though physical, are not mentioned in the rest of our causal story. To suggest, with the sceptic, that our language-game may have nothing to do with the way the world is, is to call up a picture of a gear-wheel so out of touch with the rest of the mechanism as to be spinning idly.[30]

Given his distaste for intentionalist notions, Putnam should have no relish for such pictures, and thus no inclination to regard truth as an explanatory notion. But because he still retains the idea that one should give an 'account of what it is for an assertion to be correct', he demands more than Davidson is in a position to give. He retains this idea, I think, because he is afraid that the inside point of view on our language-game, the point of view where we use 'true' as a term of praise, will somehow be weakened if it receives no support from 'a philosophical account'. Consider the following passage:

If the cause-effect-description [of our linguistic behavior qua production of noises] is complete from a philosophical as well as from a behavioral-scientific point of view; if all there is to say about language is that it consists in the production of noises (and subvocalizations) according to a certain causal pattern; *if the causal story is not to be and need not be supplemented by a normative story* . . . then there is no way in which the noises we utter . . . are more than mere 'expressions of our subjectivity' . . .[31]

The line I have italicized suggests that disquotationalist theorists of truth think that there is only one story to be told about people: a behaviouris-tic one. But why on earth should such theorists not allow for, and indeed insist upon, supplementing such stories with 'a normative story'? Why should we take the existence of the outside point of view of the field linguist as a recommendation never to assume the inside point of view of the earnest seeker after truth? Putnam, I think, still takes a 'philosophical account of *X*' to be a synoptic vision which will somehow synthesize every other possible view, will somehow bring the outside and the inside points of view together.

It seems to me precisely the virtue of James and of Dewey to insist that we cannot have such a synoptic vision—that we cannot back up our norms by 'grounding' them in a metaphysical or scientific account of the world. Pragmatism, especially in the form developed by Dewey, urges that we not

---

[30] Davidson's position as Alan Donagan has pointed out to me, is the same as Wittgenstein's: no gears are necessary, for the sentences in which our beliefs are expressed touch the world directly. See *Tractatus Logico-Philosophicus*. 2.1511–2.1515.

[31] Putnam, 'On Truth', in L. S. Cauman, I. Levi, and R. Swartz (eds.), *How Many Questions* (Indianapolis, 1983), 44.

repeat Plato's mistake of taking terms of praise as the names of esoteric things—of assuming, e.g., we would do a better job of being good if we could get more theoretical knowledge of The Good. Dewey was constantly criticized, from the Platonist right, for being reductionistic and scientistic, inattentive to our needs for 'objective values'. This is the kind of criticism Davidson is currently getting from Putnam. He was also constantly criticized, from the positivist left, for a light-minded relativistic instrumentalism which paid too little attention to 'hard facts', and for trivializing the notion of 'truth' by this neglect.[32] This is the kind of criticism Davidson gets from physicalists such as Field.

Attack from both sides is the usual reward of philosophers who, like Dewey and Davidson, try to stop the pendulum of philosophical fashion from swinging endlessly back and forth between a tough-minded reductionism and a high-minded anti-reductionism. Such philosophers do so by patiently explaining that norms are one thing and descriptions another. In Davidson's case, this comes down to saying that the understanding you get of how the word 'true' works by contemplating the possibility of a Tarskian truth-theory for your language is utterly irrelevant to the satisfaction you get by saying that you know more truths today than you did yesterday, or that truth is great, and will prevail. Putnam's insistence that there is more to truth than disquotationalism can offer is not based on having looked at 'true', or at the language-games we play, and having seen more than Davidson saw. Rather, it is based on a hope that there is more to the notion of a 'philosophical account' than Dewey or Davidson think there can be.

This parallel between Dewey and Davidson seems to me reinforced by Stephen Leeds's formulation of what he calls 'Naturalistic Instrumentalism': the Quine-like combination of the view that 'the only goal relative to which our methods of theory construction and revision fall into place as a rational procedure is the goal of predicting observations'[33] with the claim that the world is, really and truly *is*, made up of the entities of current science. As Leeds says, this new 'ism' may sound like an oxymoron (as a similar 'ism' did to Dewey's critics). But it only sounds that way if, as Leeds says, one thinks that 'a theory of truth is needed to explain why our theories work'[34]—if one thinks, that 'truth' can be an explanatory notion. Leeds and Arthur Fine[35] have pointed out the circularity of attempts to

---

[32] So, simultaneously, was Neurath—who is beginning to get a better press these days.

[33] Leeds, 'Theories of Reference and Truth', *Erkenntnis*, 13 (1978), 117.

[34] Dewey would not have restricted theory construction and revision to the sciences which aim at prediction and control, but this difference between Dewey and Leeds is not relevant to the point at hand.

[35] In his 'The Natural Ontological Attitude', in Leplin (ed.), *Essays in Scientific Realism*.

use semantics to explain our predictive successes. Such circularity is the natural consequence of trying to be both outside our inquiries and inside them at the same time—to describe them both as motions and as actions. As Davidson has reiterated in his writings on the theory of action, there is no need to choose between these two descriptions: there is only a need to keep them distinct, so that one does not try to use both at once.

V DAVIDSON AND DUMMETT

The question of whether 'truth' is an explanatory property encapsulates the question of whether the philosophy of the field linguist is philosophy of language enough or whether (as Michael Dummett thinks) we need a philosophy of language which links up with epistemology, and with traditional metaphysical issues. Dummett says that a theory of meaning should tell us how:

an implicit grasp of the theory of meaning, which is attributed to a speaker, issues in his employment of the language and hence ... in the content of the theory. Holism in respect of how one might, starting from scratch, arrive at a theory of meaning for a language, on the other hand, has no such implications, and is, as far as I can see, unobjectionable and almost banal. It is certain that Davidson intends his holism as a doctrine with more bite than this.[36]

Dummett thinks that what you get out of Davidsonian radical interpretation does not include 'the content' of a theory of meaning—'the specific senses speakers attach to the words of the language'. But on the interpretation of Davidson I have been offering, what Dummett calls a 'sense' is just the sort of *tertium quid* which Davidson wants us to forget about. So the bite of Davidson's theory is not the sort Dummett wants. Dummett wants a theory that bites down on the problems which he thinks can only be formulated when one has a theory of 'sense'—e.g., epistemological and metaphysical issues. Davidson wants a theory of meaning which will serve the field linguists' purposes and to which such problems are irrelevant.

Dummett's argument that more is needed than Davidson gives us is that somebody could know the ensemble of truth-conditions produced by a Davidsonian interpreter without knowing the content of the right-hand, metalinguistic, portions of the T-sentences. He thinks that 'a T-sentence for

[36] 'What is a Theory of Meaning (I)?' in Samuel Guttenplan, *Mind and Language* (Oxford, 1975), 127.

which the metalanguage contains the object-language is obviously unexplanatory' and that if this is so then 'a T-sentence for an object-language
disjoint from the metalanguage is equally unexplanatory'.[37] Davidson will
reply that no single T-sentence—no single 'neutral snowbound triviality'—
will tell you what it is to understand any of the words occurring on the left-
hand sides, but that the whole body of such sentences tells you *all* there is
to know about this. Dummett regards that reply as an admission of defeat.
He says:

On such an account, there can be no answer to the question what constitutes a
speaker's understanding of any one word or sentence: one can say only that the
knowledge of the entire theory of truth issues in an ability to speak the language,
and, in particular, in a propensity to recognize sentences of it as true under conditions corresponding, by and large, to the T-sentences.[38]

And again:

now way is provided, even in principle, of segmenting his ability to use the language
as a whole into distinct component abilities.[39]

Now it is of the essence of Davidson's position, as of the positions of
Wittgenstein and Sellars, that there are no such distinct component abilities.[40] For when you get rid of such *tertia* as 'determinate meanings',
'intended interpretations', 'responses to stimuli', and the like, you are left
with nothing to split up the overall know-how into component bits—
nothing to reply to 'How do you know that that's called "red"?' save
Wittgenstein's: 'I know English'. Davidson has to insist that the individual
T-sentences do not replicate any inner structures, and that any attempt to
provide such structures will pay the price of reintroducing *tertia*, entities
which will get between our words and the world.

   Dummett notes that Davidson tries 'to make a virtue of necessity', but
insists that doing so 'is an abnegation of what we are entitled to expect
from a theory of meaning'.[41] For Dummett thinks that we are entitled to

---

[37] Ibid. 108. Dummett actually says 'M-sentence' (i.e., a sentence of the form ' "——" means
——') rather than 'T-sentence'. I have changed the quotation for the sake of perspicacity. As
Dummett rightly says, for Davidson's purposes the two sorts of sentence are interchangeable.
[38] Ibid. 115.   [39] Ibid. 116.
[40] A similar position is adopted by Ernst Tugendhat in his *Traditional and Analytical
Philosophy* (Cambridge, 1983). Tugendhat thinks of this position as the only alternative to the
'objectualist' account of the understanding of language which has dominated the philosophical
tradition up through Husserl and Russell.
[41] Dummett, 'What is a Theory of Meaning? (I)', 117. Some of the complaints about Davidson
I have been citing from Dummett are modified in the appendix (ibid. 123 ff.). But the insistence
on the point that Davidson 'can make no sense of knowing part of the language' (p. 138) and
the unargued-for presumption that philosophy of language must preserve an unQuinean lan-
guage-fact distinction (p. 137) remain.

a theory of meaning which will preserve the traditional notions of empiricist epistemology. He thinks that any such theory must grant that 'an ability to use a given sentence in order to give a report of observation may reasonably be taken, as a knowledge of what has to be the case for that sentence to be true'.[42]

Dummett's paradigm case of grasping the content of an expression is what you do when you observe that something is red. He thinks that the contrast between 'That's red!' and cases like 'Caesar crossed the Rubicon', 'Love is better than hate', and 'There are transfinite cardinals' is something which any adequate philosophy of language must preserve. But for Davidson's and Wittgenstein's holism there simply is no contrast. On their view, to grasp the content is, in *all* these cases, to grasp the inferential relationships between these sentences and the other sentences of the language.[43]

The same point can be made in reference to Dummett's presentation of the issue about realism and anti-realism in terms of bivalence. Dummett seems to think that the question of bivalence, of whether statements are 'determinately true or false, independently of our knowledge or our means of knowing'[44] arises only for statements made by means of sentences 'belonging to the less primitive strata of our language'.[45] He has no doubt that for the 'lower storeys'—e.g., for statements like 'That's red!'—bivalence obtains. Our inarticulable knowledge of what it is for such a statement to be true, presumably, is enough to make us realists about redness. For these types of statements we can have a strong sense of 'correspondence to reality'—'strong' in that we are confident that what makes the statement true is 'reality' rather than merely ourselves. Here we have the empiricist picture, shared by Quine and Dummett, according to which language stands as a veil between us and reality, with reality punching its way through (or being known to punch its way through) only at the tips of a few sensory receptors. The farther into the upper storeys

---

[42] Dummett, 'What is a Theory of Meaning? (II)' in Gareth Evans and John McDowell (eds.), *Truth and Meaning* (Oxford, 1976), 95.

[43] Dummett thinks that Wittgenstein's view that 'acceptance of any principle of inference contributes to determining the meaning of words'—a view which Davidson shares—is unacceptably holistic. (See ibid. 105.) Elsewhere Dummett has said that this sort of holism leads to the view that 'a systematic theory of meaning for a language is an impossibility' and thus to the view that philosophy 'seeks to remove, not ignorance or false beliefs, but conceptual confusion, and therefore has nothing positive to set in place of what it removes' (*Truth and Other Enigmas* (London, 1978), 453). By 'a systematic theory of meaning for a language' Dummett means one which gives him 'what we are entitled to expect', namely a handle on traditional philosophical problems. But he begs the question against Davidson when he rebuts the holism shared by Davidson and Wittgenstein on the ground that it leads to the therapeutic approach to traditional problems shared by Dewey and Wittgenstein.

[44] 'What is a Theory of Meaning? (II)', 101.   [45] Ibid. 100.

we get, on the other hand, the more doubt there is that we are in touch with the world, and the more temptation to be an 'anti-realist' in regard to certain entities—that is, to adopt a theory of meaning which explains the truth of such statements 'in terms of our capacity to recognize statements as true, and not in terms of a condition which transcends human capacities'.[46]

By contrast, if one follows Davidson, one will not know what to make of the issue between realist and anti-realist. For one will feel in touch with reality *all the time*. Our language—conceived as the web of inferential relationships between our uses of vocables—is not, on this view, something 'merely human' which may hide something which 'transcends human capacities'. Nor can it deceive us into thinking ourselves in correspondence with something like that when we really are not. On the contrary, using those vocables is as direct as contact with reality can get (as direct as kicking rocks, e.g.). The fallacy comes in thinking that the relationship between vocable and reality has to be piecemeal (like the relation between individual kicks and individual rocks), a matter of discrete component capacities to get in touch with discrete hunks of reality.

If one thinks that, one will, for example, agree with Plato and Dummett that there is an important philosophical question about whether there really are moral values 'out there'. For Davidson, on the other hand, there is goodness out there in exactly the same trivial sense in which there is redness out there. The relevant sense is explicated by saying that the field linguist will come up with a T-sentence whose right-hand side is 'that's morally right' in just the same manner as he comes up with one whose right-hand side is 'that's red'. He will assume that insofar as the natives fail to find the same things red, or morally right, as we do, our disagreements with them will be explicable by various differences in our respective environments (or the environments of our respective ancestors).

I conclude that for Dummett no philosophy of language is adequate which does not permit the perspicuous reformulation of the epistemological and metaphysical issues discussed by the philosophical tradition. For Davidson this ability is not a desideratum. For James and Dewey, the *in*ability to formulate such issues was a desideratum. I should like to attribute this latter, stronger, view to Davidson, but I have no good evidence for doing so. I commend it to him, because I think that his only recourse in arguing with those who think they have a right to expect more philosophy of language than he offers is to adopt this therapeutic stance.

---

[46] Ibid. 116.

More specifically, all he can do is point out that Dummett's expectations stem from the habit of construing correspondence as confrontation, and then exhibit the unhappy history of this construal, a history which stretches from Plato through Locke to Quine. In the end, the issue is going to be decided on a high metaphilosophical plane—one from which we look down upon the philosophical tradition and judge its worth.

VI DAVIDSON, REALISM, AND ANTI-REALISM

If the argument of the preceding section is right, then Davidson has been put in a false position by Dummett's attempts to place him on the 'realist' side of a distinction between realism and anti-realism. That distinction, stated in terms of a distinction between truth-conditions and assertibility-conditions, will seem a plausible way of classifying philosophical doctrines only if one accepts what Michael Devitt has called Dummett's 'propositional assumption': the assumption that 'an L–speaker's understanding of a sentence of L consists in his knowing that the sentence is true-in-L in such and such circumstances'.[47] Davidson, however, thinks it hopeless to isolate such circumstances. His holism makes him reject the idea of such knowledge. Yet Dummett gives an account of Davidsonian 'truth-conditions' which is radically non-holistic. As Devitt rightly says, Dummett tries to infer from 'X knows the meaning of S' and 'The meaning of S=the truth-conditions of X' to 'S knows that the truth-conditions of X are TC', an inference which only goes through if we construe 'S knows the meaning of S' as 'there exists an entity which is the meaning of S and X is acquainted with it'.[48] The latter construal will be made only by someone who accepts the propositional assumption.

Davison would not accept it,[49] and therefore cannot be seen as a theorist of 'truth-conditions' in Dummett's sense. Davidson thinks that one

[47] 'Dummett's Anti-Realism', *Journal of Philosophy*, 80 (1983), 84.   [48] Ibid. 86.
[49] Devitt disagrees. He says 'Davidson is open to [Dummett's] argument because he accepts the propositional assumption' (ibid. 90). This willingness to accept Dummett's description of Davidson seems to me a blemish in Devitt's incisive criticism of Dummett's attempt to semanticize metaphysics. (Though, as I say below, I also disagree with Devitt's claim that desemanticizing metaphysics restores the purity of that discipline. I think that doing so merely exposes its barrenness.) I suspect the reason why Devitt thinks of Davidson as accepting the propositional assumption is that Davidson, in his earlier articles, identified a theory of meaning for L with what a speaker of L understands, an identification which suggests that the speaker *does* have 'distinct component abilities' corresponding to the various T-sentences. But this identification is, as far as I can see, either incompatible with the holism I have described in the previous section or as misleading a metaphor as that billiard balls have 'internalized' the laws of mechanics.

great advantage of his view is that it gives you a theory of meaning without countenancing such things as 'meanings'. Since he agrees with Quine that a theory of meaning for a language is what comes out of empirical research into linguistic behaviour, Davidson would be the first to agree with Devitt, against Dummett, that 'any propositional knowledge of a language that a person has is something over and above his competence, something gained from theorizing about the language'.[50] If we bear Davidson's holism and behaviourism in mind, he will seem the last philosopher to believe that users of S are typically able to envisage acquaintance with sets of circumstances which would conclusively verify S.

Dummett misconstrues Davidson because he himself believes that (in Devitt's words), 'The only sort of behavior that could manifest the speaker's understanding of S is that behavior which brings him into the position in which, if the condition obtains that conclusively justifies the assertion of S, he recognizes it as so doing.'[51] As Devitt says, this expresses Dummett's commitment to 'anti-holist epistemology'.[52] Dummett thinks that there are some familiar cases (e.g., so-called 'observation sentences') where there are indeed such conditions, and such acts of recognition. But for Davidson there are never any of either. So the contrast which Dummett draws between, e.g., realism about tables and anti-realism about values makes no sense for Davidson. For holists, so to speak, truth is *always* evidence-transcendent. But that is to say that X's understanding of S is *never* manifested in the kind of recognitional abilities which Dummett envisages.[53]

Dummett takes the upshot of Frege's linguistification of philosophy to be that the only way to make sense of a metaphysical disagreement is by semantic ascent—jacking up the old metaphysical issue into a new semantical issue. Davidson, on my interpretation, thinks that the benefit of going linguistic is that getting rid of the Cartesian mind is a first step toward eliminating the *tertia* which, by seeming to intrude between us and the world, created the old metaphysical issues in the first place. We

---

[50] Ibid. 89–90.   [51] Ibid. 91.   [52] Ibid. 92.

[53] See P. Horwich, 'Three Forms of Realism', *Synthese*, 51 (1982), 199: '[Dummett's] inference from not being able to establish when *p* is true to not being able to manifest knowledge of its truth-conditions is not at all compelling. All it takes to know *p*'s truth-conditions is to understand it; and all it takes to understand *p* is the ability to use it in accordance with community norms, implicit in linguistic practice, for judging in various circumstances, the degree of confidence it should be given.' Horwich's own suggestion that we combine what he calls 'semantic realism' (the claim that truth may extend beyond our capacity to recognize it) with a 'use theory of meaning and a redundancy account of truth' (p. 186) seems to me a succinct description of Davidson's strategy. (For an earlier statement of Horwich's anti-Dummett point, see P. F. Strawson's criticism of Crispin Wright: 'Scruton and Wright on Anti-Realism', *Proceedings of the Aristotelian Society*, 77 (1977), 16.)

can take the final step, and dissolve those issues for good, by not letting philosophy of language re-create the factitious contrasts in terms of which those issues were formulated, e.g., the contrast between 'objective realities' and 'useful fictions', or that between the 'ontological status' of the objects of, respectively, physics, ethics, and logic. For Davidson, Quine's idea of 'ontological commitment' and Dummett's idea of 'matter of fact' are both unfortunate relics of metaphysical thought; they are among the ideas which metaphysics wove together to form the scheme-content dualism.

These ideas form such a large, mutually reinforcing, network that it is hard to pick one out as crucial. But the best candidate for being at the centre of this network may be the idea repudiated in the pragmatists' thesis (3): the idea that sentences can be 'made true'. Davidson says that 'all the evidence there is is just what it takes to make our sentences or theories true. Nothing, however, no thing, makes sentences or theories true: not experience, not surface irritations, not the world, can make a sentence true.'[54] I interpret this passage as saying that the inferential relations between our belief that S and our other beliefs have nothing in particular to do with the aboutness relation which ties S to its objects. The lines of evidential force, so to speak, do not parallel the lines of referential direction. This lack of parallelism is the burden of epistemological holism. To know about the former lines is to know the language in which the beliefs are expressed. To know about the latter is to have an empirical theory about what the people who use that language mean by what they say— which is also the story about the causal roles played by their linguistic behaviour in their interaction with their environment.

The urge to coalesce the justificatory story and the causal story is the old metaphysical urge which Wittgenstein helped us overcome when he told us to beware of entities called 'meanings'—or, more generally, of items relevant to the fixation of belief which are, in Davidson's words, 'intermediate between belief and the usual objects which beliefs are about'.[55] For such entities are supposed to be *both* causes *and* justifications: entities (like sense-data or surface irritations or clear and distinct ideas) which belong both to the story which justifies me in believing that S and to the story which the observer of my linguistic behaviour tells us about the causes of my belief that S. Devitt succumbs to this pre-Wittgensteinian urge when he follows Field in suggesting that we can explicate the 'intuitive idea of correspondence to a "world out there"' by making truth dependent on

[54] *Inquiries*, 194.   [55] 'Coherence Theory', 430.

'genuine reference relations between words and objective reality'.[56] Dummett succumbs to it when he thinks of a given state of the world as capable of 'conclusively verifying' a belief. The latter notion embodies just the idea of bits of the world making a belief true which Davidson rejects.

Devitt is, I think, right in saying that, once we drop Dummett's anti-holism, the issue about 'realism' is de-semanticized. But it is also trivial-ized. For there is now nothing for 'realism' to name save the banal anti-idealist thesis which Devitt formulates as 'Common-sense physical entities objectively exist independently of the mental.'[57] Devitt thinks this an interesting and controversial thesis. It is an embarrassment for my inter-pretation of Davidson as a pragmatist that he apparently does too: witness his pledge of allegiance, cited above, to the idea of 'an objective public world which is not of our making'.[58] This formula strikes me as no more than outdated rhetoric. For on my view the futile metaphysical struggle between idealism and physicalism was superseded, in the early years of this century, by a metaphilosophical struggle between the pragmatists (who wanted to dissolve the old metaphysical questions) and the anti-pragmatists (who still thought there was something first-order to fight about).[59] The latter struggle is *beyond* realism and anti-realism.[60]

---

[56] Devitt, Dummett's Anti-Realism', 77.   [57] Ibid. 76.

[58] See also *Inquiries into Truth and Interpretation*, 198: 'In giving up the dualism of scheme and world, we do not give up the world, but re-establish unmediated touch with the familiar objects whose antics make our sentences and opinions true or false.' Yet surely these familiar objects are simply not the world which anti-idealist philosophers have tried to underwrite. The idealists had these objects too. The world which their opponents were concerned about was one which could vary independently of the antics of the familiar objects; it was something rather like the thing-in-itself. (I developed this distinction between two senses of 'world', the familiar objects on the one hand and the contrived philosophical counterpart of 'scheme' on the other, in an earlier (1972), and rather awkward, attempt to latch on to Davidson's arguments; see 'The World Well Lost', repr. in *Consequences of Pragmatism*.)

[59] I should try to account for this change by reference to (*a*) Hegel's demonstration that idealism eventually eats its itself up (like the Worm Ourouboros) by deconstructing the mind-matter distinction which it started out with and (*b*) the disenchantment with that distinction brought about by the theory of evolution. Dewey's importance, I think, lies in having brought Hegel and Darwin together. But this is a long and controversial story.

[60] Current debates about Heidegger's 'destruction of the Western metaphysical tradition' and Derrida's 'deconstruction of the metaphysics of presence' form another wing of the same strug-gle. For some connections between Davidson and Derrida, see Samuel Wheeler, 'Indeterminacy of French Interpretation: Derrida and Davidson', in Ernest LePore (ed.), *Truth and Interpretation: Perspectives on the Philosophy of Donald Davidson* (Oxford, 1986), 477–94, and also his 'The Extension of Deconstruction', *Monist*, 69/1 (1986), 3–21. For parallels between Heidegger's attempt to get beyond both Plato and Nietzsche and Fine's and Davidson's attempts to get beyond realism and anti-realism see Rorty, 'Beyond Realism and Anti-Realism', in Ludwig Nagl and Richard Heinrich, *Wo steht die Analytische Philosophie heute?* (Vienna, 1986), 103–15.

So, despite his occasional pledges of realist faith, is Davidson.[61] On my version of the history of twentieth-century philosophy, logical empiricism was a reactionary development, one which took one step forward and two steps back. Davidson, by subverting the scheme-content dualism which logical empiricism took for granted, has, so to speak, kept the logic and dropped the empiricism (or better, kept the attention to language and dropped the epistemology). He has thus enabled us to use Frege's insights to confirm the holistic and pragmatist doctrines of Dewey. His work makes possible the kind of synthesis of pragmatism and positivism which Morton White foresaw as a possible 'reunion in philosophy'.[62] From the point of view of such a synthesis, the Peirce-Frege turn from consciousness to language (and from transcendental to formal logic) was a stage in the dissolution of such traditional problems as 'realism v. anti-realism', rather than a step towards a clearer formulation of those problems.[63]

[61] Arthur Fine has offered the best recent account of why we ought to get beyond this struggle. See the anti-realist polemic of his 'Natural Ontological Attitude' (cited in n. 35, above) and the anti-anti-realist polemic of 'And not Anti-Realism either', *Nous*, 18 (1984), 51–65. The latter (p. 54) makes the point that 'The anti-realism expressed in the idea of truth-as-acceptance is just as metaphysical and idle as the realism expressed by a correspondence theory.' On my interpretation of Davidson, his position pretty well coincides with Fine's 'Natural Ontological Attitude'.

Frederick Stoutland ('Realism and Anti-Realism in Davidson's Philosophy of Language (I) and (II)', *Critica Revista Hispano-Americana de Filosofia*, 14/41 (Aug. 1982), 13–55, and 14/42 (Dec. 1982), 19–49 respectively has given excellent reasons for resisting attempts (by e.g. John McDowell and Mark Platts) to construe Davidson as a realist. However, I think that he is wrong in construing him as an anti-realist who holds that 'sentences are not true in virtue of their extra-linguistic objects: they are true in virtue of their role in human practise' (Ibid. (I), 21). To repeat, Davidson thinks that we should drop the question 'In virtue of what are sentences true?' Therefore, as I said earlier, he does not wish to be associated with pragmatism, for too many people calling themselves 'pragmatists' (including myself) have said things like 'a sentence is true in virtue of its helping people achieve goals and realize intentions' (Stoutland, 'Realism and Anti-Realism (III)', 36). Despite my disagreement with Stoutland, however, I am much indebted to his discussion. In particular, his remark (Ibid. (II), 22) that Davidson opposes the idea that it is the 'intentionality of *thoughts*—their being directed to objects, independently of whether they are true or false—which accounts for the relation of language to reality' seems to me an admirably clear and succinct expression of the difference between Davidson's holism and the 'building-block' approach common to Russell, Husserl, Kripke, and Searle.

[62] See M. White, *Toward Reunion in Philosophy* (Cambridge, Mass., 1956).

[63] I am very grateful to Robert Brandom, Alan Donagan, and Arthur Fine for comments on the penultimate version of this chapter. I made substantial changes as a result of their comments, but have not tried to acknowledge my indebtedness in every case.

XIX

DEFLATIONIST VIEWS OF MEANING AND CONTENT

HARTRY FIELD

1. TWO VIEWS OF MEANING AND CONTENT

I see the philosophy of language, and the part of philosophy of mind concerned with intentional states like believing and desiring and intending and the like, as pretty much bifurcated into two traditions. The traditions differ over the role that the notion of truth conditions plays in the theory of meaning and in the theory of the content of intentional states.

One of the traditions, whose early advocates include Frege, Russell, the early Wittgenstein, and Ramsey, has it that truth conditions play an extremely central role in semantics and the theory of mind; a theory of meaning or content is at least in large part a theory of truth conditions. A strong prima facie reason for the attractiveness of this position is that the way we standardly ascribe meanings and contents is via 'that' clauses, and the ascription of 'that' clauses is in effect the ascription of truth conditions: to describe an utterance as meaning that snow is white, or a belief state as a state of believing that snow is white, is in effect to say that the utterance or belief state has the truth conditions that snow is white. Since 'that' clauses and hence truth conditions play such a central role in our *ascriptions* of meaning and content, it would seem as if they ought to play a central role in the *theory* of meaning and content. However, it isn't easy to say precisely what this central role is that truth conditions allegedly play; that I think is a main motivation for the alternative tradition.

As a crude paradigm of the other tradition, consider the verifiability theory of meaning. Here the main concept is not truth conditions but verification conditions. The verification conditions of a type of utterance might be given by the class of sensory stimulations that would or should lead to the acceptance of an utterance in that class. Notice that if the

From Hartry Field, 'Deflationist Views of Meaning and Content', *Mind*, 103 (July 1994), 249–84.

verification conditions of a type of utterance are given in this way, then they are given without a 'that' clause; and indeed, there is no immediately clear way in which to obtain a 'that' clause from them. It is because of this that an advocate of the Frege–Russell–Ramsey–*Tractatus* tradition is likely to react to a verification theory of meaning as leaving out what is central to semantics: a theory of meaning according to which you can fully describe the 'meaning' of an utterance without saying that it means *that snow is white* (or that something else) has left out the central element of meaning. That central element is truth conditions.

Some advocates of the Frege–Russell tradition might prefer to describe what has been left out as not truth conditions but as *propositional content*. There is a way of understanding this that makes it unobjectionable, but it could be misleading. For a verificationist is likely simply to deny the charge that he has left out propositional content (or even, the charge that he has demoted it from a central place in his theory). A proposition, he can say, is simply a class of verification conditions; for an utterance or belief state to express the proposition is for it to have verification conditions in that class. So propositions in the verificationist's sense needn't be described by 'that' clauses: the most direct way to specify a proposition in the verificationist's sense is directly in terms of verification conditions. No one can deny that propositions *so understood* play a central role in the verificationist's theory. An advocate of the Frege–Russell tradition is likely to say that these 'propositions' aren't what *she* means by propositions, and that is doubtless so; that is because propositions as she conceives them must *encapsulate truth conditions*. (They may encapsulate more than truth conditions, but they encapsulate at least this much.) So it seems to me that to describe the difference between the two traditions in terms of truth conditions rather than in terms of propositional content brings to the forefront what is really central.

I do not mean to suggest that a verificationist is precluded from speaking of truth or truth conditions; he can do so in either of two ways. One way, which seems to me a very bad idea, is to introduce some epistemic notion of truth conditions: that is, to define truth in terms of verification (e.g. 'would be verified in the long run'), so that truth conditions are derivatively defined in terms of verification conditions. I won't discuss this line here. The other way is to make use of what has been called a *deflationary* conception of truth. I take this to have several variants, but the variant I will primarily focus on is called *pure disquotational* truth. As a rough heuristic, we could say that for a person to call an utterance true in this pure disquotational sense is to say that it is true-as-he-understands-it. (This is *not* intended to provide a *definition* of pure disquotational truth in terms of some other notion of truth plus a notion of understanding; it is intended only as a heuristic, to motivate the features of pure disquotational truth I now proceed to enumerate.) As the heuristic suggests, a person can meaningfully apply 'true' in the pure disquotational sense only to utterances that he has some understanding of; and for such an utterance u, the claim that u is true (true-as-he-understands-it) is cognitively equivalent (for the person) to u itself (as he understands it).[1] A qualification is needed, since the claim that u is true involves an existential commitment to the utterance u, whereas u itself doesn't; this keeps the two from being fully cognitively equivalent. The qualified version is that the claim that u is true is cognitively equivalent to u *relative to the existence of the utterance u*; just as 'Thatcher is such that she is self-identical and snow is white' is cognitively equivalent to 'Snow is white' *relative to the existence of Thatcher*. (To say that A is cognitively equivalent to B relative to C means that the conjunction of A and C is cognitively equivalent to the conjunction of B and C; so that as long as C is presupposed we can treat A and B as equivalent.) Having made this qualification, I will generally leave it tacit, and simply say that in the purely disquotational sense of 'true', the claim that u is true (where u is an utterance I understand) is cognitively equivalent for me to u itself (as I understand it).[2]

There are both oddities and attractive features to this as a reading of 'true'; I will discuss these later on, starting in §5. But odd or not, the cognitive equivalence of the claim that u is disquotationally true to u itself provides a way to understand disquotational truth independent of any nondisquotational concept of truth or truth conditions (and independent of any concept of proposition). That is: if I understand 'Snow is white', and if I also understand a notion of disquotational truth as explained above, then I will understand ' "Snow is white" is true', since it will be equivalent

---

[1] Because of the paradoxes, exceptions must be made for certain utterances u that contain 'true'; I won't be concerned here with just how the exceptions are to be carved out.

[2] There is more than one acceptable way to understand 'cognitively equivalent' here. My own preferred reading, for what it's worth, is that to call two sentences that a person understands 'cognitively equivalent' for that person is to say that the person's inferential procedures license a fairly direct inference from any sentence containing an occurrence of one to the corresponding sentence with an occurrence of the other substituted for it; with the stipulation, of course, that the occurrence to be substituted for is not within the context of quotation marks or an intentional attitude construction. (Cognitive equivalence *relative to some other assumption* is the same, except that that assumption is allowed to be used in the inferences.) I would also take the claim of cognitive equivalence to imply that the inferences are more or less indefeasible. (More specifically, that they are empirically indefeasible, and close to indefeasible on conceptual grounds as well, and that the person is not in possession of defeaters for them. These stipulations are motivated by the assumption that we should describe someone who doesn't know the semantic paradoxes as a person for whom ' "p" is true' is cognitively equivalent to 'p' across the board; as the person comes to terms with the paradoxes he revises his standards of cognitive equivalence on conceptual grounds.)

to 'Snow is white'. This will hold on any view of understanding, even a crude verificationist view according to which understanding it is simply a matter of having verification conditions for it: for the verification conditions of ' "Snow is white" is true' will be precisely those of 'Snow is white'. Certainly there is no need to presuppose that understanding an utterance involves correlating a proposition or truth condition with it, as propositions and truth conditions are understood in the Frege–Russell tradition. Because of this, there can be little doubt that the notion of pure disquotational truth is a notion which a verificationist is entitled to—and which other opponents of the Frege–Russell tradition who have a more sophisticated alternative than verificationism are entitled to as well. (Adherents of the Frege–Russell tradition are entitled to it too, though not all want it.)

Using this notion of truth, even a crude verificationist can grant the legitimacy of talk of truth *conditions* of his own utterances. For the cognitive equivalence of ' "Snow is white" is true' and 'Snow is white' will lead to the (more or less indefeasible) acceptance of the biconditional ' "Snow is white' is true iff snow is white'; and a natural way to put this (more or less indefeasible) acceptance is to say ' "Snow is white' has the truth conditions that snow is white'. A pure disquotational notion of truth gives rise to a purely disquotational way of talking about truth conditions.

An opponent of the Frege–Russell tradition can try to use this purely disquotational way of talking about truth conditions, or some variant or extension of it, to allow the legitimacy of talk of the truth conditions of utterances and mental states without giving truth conditions the central role that they play in the Frege–Russell tradition. For instance, if one of our mental states can be described as an attitude of believing or accepting the sentence 'Snow is white', then it can be described both as a state of believing that snow is white and as a state with the truth conditions that snow is white. The connection of 'that' clauses to truth conditions noted in the second paragraph thus remains, but the initial impression that it leads inevitably to the Frege–Russell view is at least lessened. It may not be obvious that all legitimate talk of the truth conditions of mental states can be handled in this way or by an extension of it, but that is what the opponent of the Frege–Russell tradition contends. (This may involve disallowing as illegitimate certain uses of truth conditional talk that an advocate of the Frege–Russell view would allow.)[3] Such a view might naturally be called a *deflationist view of meaning and content*; or more accurately, a deflationist view of *meaning that* and *having the content that*, or a deflationist view about

---

[3] Certain uses of truth conditional talk in explanations seems to me the most likely target for excision.

the role of truth conditions in meaning or content. The first of the three labels
(which I have used in the title for brevity) could be misleading, since some
versions of the view are in a sense quite undeflationist about meanings: for
instance, the crude verificationism I described is not in the least deflationist about verification conditions; and it identifies them with meanings. What
it is deflationist about is truth conditions; or, the locutions 'means *that*' and
'has the content *that*'. From now on I'll simply use the label 'deflationist'. So
that my labels not be thought to prejudge the merits of the views, I'll call
the Frege–Russell tradition 'inflationist'.

The division between the inflationist and deflationist positions is in some
ways most fundamental division within the theory of content and
meaning (though as with many fundamental divisions in philosophy, the
line between the two views is not absolutely sharp). I myself strongly feel
the attractions of each position, though I have come to favour deflationism. In this chapter I will formulate a fairly radical version of deflationism,[4] say a few things to try to motivate it, and try to defend it against some
obvious objections. I will also mention some deeper lines of objection that
I cannot deal with here; these seem to me the places where the battle
between deflationism and inflationism must ultimately be fought.

2. MORE ON THE DEFLATIONIST/INFLATIONIST
DISTINCTION

The version of deflationism I outlined in my opening remarks was built
around a crude verificationism. It hardly needs arguing that such a version
of deflationism isn't satisfactory. But the main idea behind deflationism
doesn't require verificationism; it requires only that what plays a central
role in meaning and content not include truth conditions (or relations
to propositions, where propositions are conceived as encapsulating truth
conditions).

I must admit at the start that the question of whether truth conditions
(or propositions encapsulating truth conditions) play a central role in
meaning and content is not a very clear one, for three reasons. First, the
notions of meaning and content aren't clear as they stand. Some ways of
clarifying them involve legislating truth conditions into or out of meaning
and content, which would make the issue of deflationism totally uninteresting. My way of resolving this unclarity will be to interpret 'meaning' and

[4] More radical, I think, than the one advanced in P. Horwich, *Truth* (Oxford, 1990). While I
like much that Horwich says I have substantial disagreements: see Field, 'Critical Notice: Paul
Horwich's *Truth*', *Philosophy of Science*, 59/2 (1992), 321–30.

'content' as broadly as possible short of explicitly legislating truth conditions into meaning or content. Second, the idea of a *central* role isn't initially clear either. My goal is to clarify this as I go along, by making explicit
the limited role that I think the deflationist can give to truth conditions,
and identifying kinds of role that deflationism cannot allow truth conditions to have. Unfortunately I cannot complete the job in this paper: to
keep the paper to a manageable size I have had to leave to another occasion discussion of the crucial subject of the role of truth conditions in psychological explanation.

There is also a third source of unclarity in the question, one which I think
makes a complete sharpening impossible. If deflationism is to be at all
interesting, it must claim not merely that what plays a central role in
meaning and content not include truth conditions *under that description*,
but that it not include *anything that could plausibly constitute a reduction
of* truth conditions to other more physicalistic terms. It is well known that
there is no sharp line between reduction and elimination, so that this
crucial tenet of deflationism is not an altogether precise one. In other
words, a theory of content and meaning might end up not employing the
notion of truth conditions directly (in a central role), but employing (in
that role) certain physicalistic relations that *could* be regarded as reducing the relation 'S has the truth conditions *p*', but could *only* be so regarded
on a rather loose conception of reduction. Such a theory of content and
meaning would occupy the borderline between a deflationist and inflationist theory: it would be rather a matter of taste which way we describe it.
I'll have a bit more to say about this possibility later.

I remarked earlier that a deflationist need not be a verificationist. What
elements instead of or in addition to verification conditions does he have
available for inclusion in meaning or content? One element that can certainly be included in content is conceptual or computational role: role in
a (perhaps idealized) computational psychology that describes how the
agent's beliefs, desires, etc. evolve over time (partly in response to sensory
stimulations).[5] The conceptual role of a belief state includes its verification
conditions, but includes much more besides. (It includes a wider variety of
evidential relations;[6] it includes the conceptual consequences of having the
belief; etc.) But conceptual role isn't enough: it is both 'internalist' and

---

[5] Of course, conceptual or computational role can be described at different levels of abstraction, and until we settle on a level of abstraction the notion of conceptual role is highly pro-
grammatic. But my purposes here don't demand the detail that would be required were I to try
to set out a reasonable deflationism in detail.

[6] If the probability of S given E is higher than the probability of S, then (especially if this fact
is rather 'robust', that is, if except for very special sentences F, P(S|E&F) remains higher than
P(S|F)) it is natural to include this fact in the conceptual role of S, even if E is in no sense 'obser-

'individualist', and a plausible deflationism is going to have to give to content both 'externalist' and 'social' aspects.

In describing these further aspects of content, it will help if I make what I hope is a harmless assumption. The assumption is that we can speak of a language-user as believing and desiring sentences of his or her own language—or at least, as believing and desiring internal analogs of them in which some or all of the ambiguities may have been removed—and that this relation can be made sense of without a prior notion of content for the belief or desire states or of meaning for the sentences. In other words, this relation is one that a deflationist can perfectly well appeal to. There is a good bit that needs to be said about just what this assumption comes to, but let me simply say that I think that when it is unpacked it is pretty unobjectionable.[7]

Now let's get back to the aspects of content that go beyond conceptual role. The most obvious 'externalist' element that a deflationist can put into content is indication relations. It is a fact about me that I am a pretty good barometer of whether there is rain falling on my head at that moment: when there is rain falling on my head, I tend to believe 'There is rain falling on my head'; conversely, when I do believe this sentence, usually there is rain falling on my head. This is simply a correlation, there to be observed; and a deflationist is as free to take note of it as is anyone else, and as free as anyone else to deem it an ingredient of what he calls content. The correlation of people's belief states to the world outside presumably extends past the directly observed; the beliefs of astronomers in sentences of the form 'The location of Halley's comet at time t will be x' generally correlate pretty well with the location of Halley's comet at time t, and in certain circumstances the beliefs of physicists in sentences of the form 'a particle has recently tunnelled through the potential barrier' will correlate with whether a particle has indeed done so.

These observations might make one think that a deflationist is bound to recognize (a non-disquotational version of) the relation 'S has truth

vational' and could never be established with enough certainty or whatever to count as evidence for anything. It was central to verificationism to exclude such facts from verification conditions when E was not observational.

[7] Part of the idea behind this assumption is that when you read or hear a given unambiguous sentence, there is a type of thought state that you typically undergo in processing it, where this type is identifiable in purely computational terms; and that this type of thought state also typically occurs when you utter such a sentence. This assumption and some other plausible assumptions about the computational processes of the language-user make it possible to define in computational terms a correspondence between many of the person's states of believing and desiring and his unambiguous sentences. A natural computational story about the processing of ambiguous sentences allows us to extend this to such sentences too. I will not attempt to give the details of any of this here.

conditions p', in fact if not in name, since these indication relations constitute the truth conditions relation. But this overlooks the fact that the
project of giving anything close to a believable reduction of talk of truth
conditions to talk of indication relations is at best a gleam in the eye of
some theorists. A way to see the point is to notice that there are plenty of
examples where the indication relations don't reflect what we would intuitively regard as truth conditions. Maybe I systematically exaggerate, so
that my believing a sentence of the form 'It is n feet high' is strongly correlated with the object before me being $f(n)$ feet high, where $f(x)$ starts
dropping off rapidly from x after about 6 feet or so. Or worse, maybe my
beliefs of the form 'In Bosnia, p' don't stand in any interesting correlations
with the actual facts about what's happening in Bosnia, but just reflect what
appears in the newspapers I read. The deflationist can recognize the facts
about indication, and attribute explanatory importance to them; he can
even use the disquotation schema to formulate the distinction between one
of his belief states indicating its own truth conditions and its indicating
something else (as in the exaggeration example and the Bosnia example).[8]
What he *can't* do, it seems to me, is say that *this distinction* is of much
explanatory importance: for that would give truth conditions (rather than
just indication relations in general) a central role in the theory of mind;
and the claim that truth condition have a central role in the theory of mind
is the defining characteristic of inflationism.[9] That the distinction between
a belief state reliably indicating its own truth conditions and its reliably
indicating something else is of little explanatory importance is a consequence of deflationism that seems at first quite implausible. But it can grow
on one, after one has spent some time trying to say just what its explanatory importance is!

Anyway, the deflationist can include indication relations in content; this
is enough to make content externalist, but not enough to make it social.
However, since we are regarding many of our most important beliefs as in

---

[8] Whether the deflationist can formulate the distinction for *other people's* belief states is less
clear, and turns on some issues we will discuss.

[9] I have heard the objection that a deflationist is free to give truth conditions an explanatory
role as long as it is only 'deflationary truth conditions' and not 'heavy duty truth conditions'
that are given that role. This seems to me a confusion. I think it is quite misleading to speak of
two kinds of truth conditions, the heavy duty ones and the disquotational ones: this suggests
that the advocate of 'heavy duty' truth conditions thinks that we should ascribe to 'Snow is
white' some truth conditions other than that snow is white, and that of course is absurd. It would
be better to say that there are two kinds of relation between truth conditions on the one hand
and utterances and mental states on the other, the disquotational relation and the heavy duty
relation. But the only ways I can see to make sense of the distinction between these relations
directly or indirectly preclude giving the disquotational relation certain kinds of explanatory
role. (In my view, the preclusion is indirect, and stems from the deflationist's account of how
truth conditions attach to sentences and mental states.)

effect attitudes toward sentences in our language, the means to make content social is at hand. That is, it seems reasonable to decree that the content of these belief states is to be influenced by the meaning these sentences have for us; that meaning is of course partly influenced by the content of our intentional states, but since language is social it will be influenced by the contents of the states of other members of our community as well. In particular—and removing the appearance of circularity— we can understand 'content' in such a way that *the conceptual roles and indication relations of other people's states of believing a certain sentence are counted as relevant to the content of my state of believing that sentence;*[10] such a way of understanding 'content' is not only possible, it is natural when one thinks of how which sentences I believe influence and are influenced by which sentences others believe. Again, construing content as social in this way is quite compatible with deflationism, that is with keeping truth conditions (and hence 'that' clauses) out of the fundamental characterization of content.

3. THE SEMANTICS OF LOGICAL OPERATORS

'Deflationism' and 'inflationism' are broad labels, each encompassing many different views. I think it would help to make the contrast between the deflationist and inflationist traditions clearer if I focused on several problems in the theory of content, and showed how they looked from each of the two broad perspectives.

The first problem I will discuss is the problem of saying what determines the 'referent' of a logical operator like 'or' or 'not' or 'all'; or to put it less Fregeanly, the problem of saying what determines the contributions that such a logical operator makes to the truth conditions of sentences that contain it.

I think it is clear in broad outline what an inflationist's best strategy is for answering this question. The answer will have two stages. The first stage involves spelling out the 'conceptual role' that 'or' has (for a given person, or for the linguistic community generally): in this case, it would largely be a matter of role in deductive inference and perhaps inductive and practical inference as well. For instance, among the relevant facts about my use of the word 'or' is that I tend to accept inferences to a disjunction 'A or B' from either disjunct, and to the negation of the disjunction from the

---

[10] This last way of putting things gives a way to make content social without relying on an independent notion of meaning. It thus leaves room for explaining meaning in terms of content if so desired.

negations of both disjuncts, but not to the disjuncts from the disjunction; and when I do occasionally slip and infer according to the latter rule, I can be brought to correct myself. Also relevant perhaps is that I tend to assign to a disjunction a degree of belief at least as high as the degrees of belief of each disjunct but no higher than the sum of the degrees of belief of the disjuncts. (Indeed my degree of belief in a disjunction 'A or B' tends to be about equal to the sum of my degrees of belief in the disjuncts minus my degree of belief in A times my conditional degree of belief in B given A.) And so on.

But what does the word's having this conceptual role have to do with its standing for the usual truth function (that is, with its contributing to truth conditions by means of the usual truth table)? Perhaps the conceptual role of 'or' determines that it stands for that truth function *in this sense*: any word in any linguistic community that had that conceptual role would stand for that truth function. But that doesn't seem very helpful, for it doesn't tell you why that conceptual role should be associated with that truth function.

There is though a rather natural story to try to tell. The idea is that if we assign truth conditions to our sentences (and hence our belief states) according to this rule of truth for 'or' (and the standard rules of truth for 'not'), it will make our deductive inferences involving 'or' truth-preserving, and presumably will make our inductive inferences involving 'or' highly reliable;[11] whereas if we used any other truth table, the deductive and inductive inferences would come out totally unreliable. Reliability considerations seem to give just the sort of link between conceptual role and reference that we want in this case.

There are of course some holes here. One hole is that though it is true that no alternative *truth function* makes our inferences involving 'or' at all reliable, this just shows that reliability considerations make the usual truth table for 'or' more satisfactory *than alternative truth functions*; but maybe there is an alternative to a truth functional account that would make us equally reliable? A second hole is that in explaining the contribution of 'or' to truth conditions, we can't legitimately assume the contribution that 'not' makes to truth conditions unless that can be independently established; so unless it can be independently established (which is doubtful), or unless we can avoid mentioning it in our account of what determines the truth table for 'or', then we really need an account of how reliability

---

[11] I mention 'not' because the deductive inference rules I listed include the rule that we can infer 'not (A or B)' from 'not A' and 'not B' together. It is possible to replace this by a rule involving 'if . . . then' instead of 'not'; or (as in natural deduction systems and sequent calculi) by a rule involving a notion of implication.

considerations give us the rules of truth for 'or' and 'not' together. (Using another operator like 'if . . . then' or 'implies' instead of 'not' would give rise to similar problems.) This deepens the first hole: for now we need to compare the package containing the usual truth functional accounts of 'or' and 'not' to alternative packages in which both truth rules are varied, and where there is no constraint that either truth rule be truth functional.

Even if the second hole can be avoided, the problem with the first hole is greater for more complicated operators, like quantifiers: for instance, in the case of 'some' our usual deductive inferences turn out truth preserving if we suppose that its contribution to truth conditions is that of the unrestricted objectual existential quantifier, but making it a restricted quantifier or substitutional quantifier of a certain sort would also make the inferences truth preserving, and (depending on the details of the restriction) might make us at least equally reliable—even with the truth rules for the truth functional connectives and 'implies' unchanged.

So what determines that our word 'or' or 'not' or 'some' makes the contribution to truth conditions that we assume it makes? An inflationist has three choices. Either she can find some sort of naturalistic facts that could be cited in answer to this question (facts involving reliability considerations might work in the end, despite the questions above); or she can say that there is simply no fact of the matter, that we have a surprising example of referential indeterminacy here; or she can say that it is a non-naturalistic fact about us that our word 'some' contributes to truth conditions according to the rules of the unrestricted objectual quantifier and that 'not' and 'or' contribute according to the usual truth-tables. But this third option strikes me as rather repellent; the first may be hard to carry out; and the second may not be altogether free of philosophical difficulties.

The same sort of problem arises in the case of the predicate 'is identical to' (and the numerical quantifiers such as 'there are exactly two' that are definable from it). The axioms that we accept as governing this predicate determine (given a reliability assumption) that it stands for a congruence relation, that is, an equivalence relation for which substitutivity holds; but this is not enough to determine that it stands for genuine identity, that is, for the relation that everything bears to itself and to nothing else. It is especially not enough if the extensions of the other predicates in the language are up for grabs: as Quine has famously pointed out, it isn't so easy to say what facts about us make 'identical to' stand for identity and 'rabbit' for rabbits, rather than 'rabbit' for rabbit stages and 'is identical to' for the relation of being stages of the same object. And even if we can find facts about usage that would rule out this example as violating a plausible reliability requirement, it is a tall order to find facts about usage which would rule out *all* choices of nonstandard congruence relations. Again, an inflationist is apparently faced with the three options of finding such facts, or accepting it as simply a brute fact that our word stands for genuine identity, or accepting a surprising level of referential indeterminacy in our basic logical vocabulary. This is a choice that not everyone would be happy to have to make.

A main motivation for deflationism is that it apparently avoids having to make this sort of choice.[12] According to the simplest version of deflationism—that relying on the pure disquotational truth predicate mentioned earlier—it is an entirely trivial matter to explain why one's own word 'or' obeys the truth table it does: this follows from truth functional logic together with the logic of the disquotational truth predicate, with no mention of any facts at all about our usage of 'or'. Recall that if 'true' is used purely disquotationally, then ' "p" is true' is cognitively equivalent to 'p', for any sentence 'p' that we understand. As a result, we get that each instance of the 'disquotation schema'

(T) 'p' is true if and only if p

holds of conceptual necessity, that is, by virtue of the cognitive equivalence of the left and right hand sides. But for any sentences q and r, instances of the following schemas are also instances of (T), and hence conceptually necessary:

'q or r' is true if and only if q or r
'q' is true if and only if q
'r' is true if and only if r.

You can use the latter two to substitute into the right-hand side of the first, so as to get the conceptual necessity of each instance of the following:

(TF) 'q or r' is true if and only if 'q' is true or 'r' is true.

The conceptual necessity of the instances really isn't enough to justify the claim that 'or' obeys the usual truth-table: we need the conceptual necessity of the generalization

(TFG) For all sentences S_1 and S_2 of our language, $\ulcorner S_1$ or $S_2 \urcorner$ is true iff S_1 is true or S_2 is true.

But it is easy to get that if we start not from (T) but from some generalized form of (T). One such generalized form of (T) employs a universal substitutional quantifier:

[12] It may not avoid the threat of indeterminacy in the end: I discuss this in Field, 'Disquotational Truth and Factually Defective Discourse', *Philosophical Review*, 103/3 (1994), 405–52. Even so, the account to follow offers an attractive alternative to the inflationist's approach to the determination of the way that our logical symbols contribute to truth conditions; and I will generalize it in §6.

(TG) Πp ('p' is true if and only if p).[13]

(I assume a theory of substitutional quantification that avoids the semantic paradoxes.) There are also ways to get the generalization without substitutional quantifiers. One alternative is to incorporate schematic letters for sentences into the language, reasoning with them as with variables; and then to employ two rules of inference governing them: (i) a rule that allows replacement of all instances of a schematic letter by a sentence; (ii) a rule that allows inference of $\forall x(\text{Sentence}(x) \supset A(x))$ from the schema $A('p')$, where $A('p')$ is a schema in which all occurrences of the schematic letter p are surrounded by quotes. Such a formalism corresponds to a very weak fragment of a substitutional quantifier language, and is probably preferable to using the full substitutional quantifier. In such a formalism, (T) and (TF) themselves are part of the language, rather than merely having instances that are part of the language; and from (T) we can derive (TF) and thence (by rule (ii) and a bit of syntax) (TFG).

Note that on any of these versions of the pure deflationary account, facts about the meaning of our word 'or'—e.g., its conceptual role—need not be explicitly referred to in explaining why our word 'or' obeys the usual truth-table. Of course, we do need to use logical reasoning, and in particular, the deductive inferential rules that are in fact associated with the word 'or'. But we needn't mention in the explanation *that these rules are associated with 'or'*; in that sense, the meaning of 'or' plays no role in the explanation.

Does this mean that a deflationist can't make sense of the idea that 'or' obeys the truth-table it does *because of* its conceptual role? Not really: the fact that *the deductive inferential rules for 'or'* are used in the explanation of 'or' having the truth-table it has is enough to give one quite natural sense to the claim that it obeys that truth-table *because* it obeys those deductive inferential rules. However, the sense of 'because' here does not support counterfactuals. That is, because *the fact that these rules are associated with 'or'* plays no role in the explanation of 'or' having this truth-table, we don't get the conclusion that if different rules had been associated with 'or', its contributions to truth conditions would have been different. (At least, we don't get this conclusion on the most straightforward reading of the counterfactual.) Indeed, it is clear that this counterfactual (on its

---

[13] The argument from (T) to (TF) generalizes as an argument from (TG) to

$\Pi p \Pi q$('p or q' is true if and only if 'p' is true or 'q' is true).

By use of the additional axiom

$\forall x(x$ is a sentence of our language $\supset \Sigma p(x = 'p'))$,

we get (TFG).

straightforward construal anyway) is unacceptable if 'truth conditions' is understood in a purely disquotational sense. (This may seem an objection to the purely disquotational notion of truth, but later on I will argue that it is not. I will also consider whether a deflationist can make sense of a modified notion of truth conditions according to which such a counterfactual would be straightforwardly true; if so, the conceptual role of 'or' might have to be explicitly referred to in explaining why the truth conditions of 'or' in this modified sense of truth conditions are those of the usual truth-table.)

What I've said here about the explanation of the truth-theoretic properties of the logical connectives goes for other words as well. Consider 'rabbit': an inflationist presumably thinks that the set or property that my term 'rabbit' stands for is determined from the facts about this word's conceptual role for me, together with its conceptual role for other members of my community, together with the facts about what my believing various 'rabbit' sentences tends to be correlated with, together with the same sort of facts for other members of my community, and so on. This raises the question of precisely how it is determined; and it seems to me that if inflationism is to be believable then the inflationist needs to have some story to tell here. Of course, Quine's well-known difficulty about rabbits v. rabbit-stages would be solved if we solved the problem for identity: reliability with respect to sentences like 'For all x and y, if x and y are nearby rabbits then $x = y$' ties the extension of 'rabbit' to that of 'identical' in such a way as to handle such individuation problems. But there are further problems: what makes 'rabbit' stand for the rabbits rather than the rabbits-or-realistic-imitations, for instance. I don't say that the inflationist can't tell a reasonable story about this, only that there is a story to be told, and perhaps there is room for skepticism about the possibility of telling it adequately. If so, that provides a motivation for deflationism. For the deflationist view is that there is nothing here to explain: it is simply part of the logic of 'refers' (or 'is true of') that 'rabbit' refers to (is true of) rabbits and to nothing else.

The deflationary view of truth and reference as I've presented it here applies only to words and sentences that we understand. This may well seem worrisome, and it is important to ask both whether it should seem worrisome and whether it could be avoided. I'll return to these matters in later sections, but first I want to further explore the contrast between the deflationist and inflationist viewpoints.

4. INVERTING THE THEORY OF REFERENCE

One qualm that one might reasonably have about the deflationist perspective is that a lot of work that has gone into the theory of reference in recent years seems to be onto something, and it seems at first hard to explain just what it could be onto if truth conditions play no central role in the theory of meaning. After all, if truth conditions play no central role, reference can hardly play a central role: whatever importance reference has surely derives from its contribution to truth conditions.

Let's consider first Kripke's observation that description theories of the reference of our proper names[14] are incorrect. If truth conditions play no central role in meaning, and truth is fully explained by the disquotation schema (and of value only as a logical device, in a manner soon to be explained), then the same is true of reference: for the reference of singular terms, the relevant schema is

> (R) If b exists then 'b' refers to b and nothing else; if b doesn't exist then 'b' doesn't refer to anything.

If this tells us everything we need to know about the reference for our own words, what could Kripke's critique of description theories be telling us?

We need a concrete example before us. Consider Kripke's case against a version of the description theory according to which the referent of our term 'Gödel' is determined by the associated description 'prover of the incompleteness theorem': the referent of the name (if it has one) is to be whatever uniquely fits the description. Kripke's case against this view is a thought experiment, in which we discover the following fact:

> (F) The incompleteness theorem was proved by a man baptized 'Schmidt' and who never called himself anything other than 'Schmidt'; a certain person who called himself 'Gödel' and got a job under that name at the Institute for Advanced Study stole the proof from him.

In this situation, Kripke asks, who is it natural to say we have been referring to when we used the name 'Gödel', the guy who called himself 'Schmidt' and proved the incompleteness theorem, or the guy who called himself 'Gödel'? Nearly everyone says the latter, so the description theory (or this version of it) is wrong. Surely there is something important in this critique, and if the deflationist can't make sense of it then something is wrong with deflationism.

---

[14] Or at the very least, description theories that use only non-metalinguistic descriptions. S. Kripke, *Naming and Necessity* (Cambridge, Mass., 1980).

I think that the deflationist can make sense of Kripke's observations. On the deflationist viewpoint, though, *the observations aren't at the most basic level about reference but about our inferential practice.* That is, what Kripke's example really shows is that we would regard the claim (F) as *grounds for inferring* 'Gödel didn't prove the incompleteness theorem' rather than as grounds for inferring 'Gödel was baptized as "Schmidt" and never called himself "Gödel" '. Reference is just disquotational. It does come in indirectly: from (F) I can indirectly infer

'Gödel' doesn't refer to the guy that proved the incompleteness theorem.

But that isn't because of a causal theory of reference over a description theory, but only because I can infer

Gödel isn't the guy that proved the incompleteness theorem

and then 'semantically ascend'.

This does seem to me a fairly plausible account of what the Kripke point shows. We see that at least in this case, the deflationist picture leads to a reasonably plausible inversion of standard views, and tends to demote the importance of theories of reference and truth conditions from accounts of language use and cognitive functioning.

How about the positive view of reference that emerges from the writings of Kripke, Putnam etc.? The positive view is that a typical name of mine refers to what it does because of a causal network of beliefs and utterances involving that name: in the simplest cases, some people acquired beliefs involving a name as a result of direct causal interaction with the thing named; these beliefs led to their using the name in utterances, which led other people to have beliefs involving the name; these in turn passed beliefs on to others, and so forth. It is because my uses of (say) 'Hume' stand in a causal network of roughly this sort, a network whose dominant causal source is Hume, that my uses of the name refer to Hume. The previous discussion shows how a deflationist can partially capture the force of this: he can say that it is just part of our inferential procedure to regard claims of roughly the form 'The dominant causal source of our beliefs involving "*b*" is *b*' as pretty much indefeasible. But this doesn't seem to fully capture the importance of the causal theory of reference. It has seemed to many that the causal network emanating from Hume to my uses of the name 'Hume' explains what is otherwise mysterious, namely, how my name could be *about* Hume. Obviously a deflationist can't say this: the whole point of deflationism is that the only explanation we need of why my word is about Hume is given by the disquotation schema.

Nonetheless, the deflationist can agree that this causal network story is explanatory of something: what it explains is the otherwise mysterious correlation between a knowledgeable person's beliefs involving the name 'Hume' and the facts about Hume. You probably believe quite a few sentences that involve the name 'Hume', and a large proportion of them are probably disquotationally true: that is, the conditional probability that Hume was φ given that you believe 'Hume was φ' is quite high. Surely this correlation between your 'Hume' beliefs and the Hume-facts cries out for explanation.[15] The general lines of the explanation are clearly suggested in the Kripke–Putnam account: you acquired your 'Hume' beliefs largely through interactions with others, who in turn acquired theirs from others, and so on until we reach believers with a fairly immediate causal access to Hume or his writings or whatever. Moreover, the causal network has multiple independent chains, and contains historical experts who have investigated these independent chains systematically, so the chance of large errors surviving isn't that high. The role of 'experts' that figures heavily in Putnam's account of reference thus also has its analog when focus is put instead on explaining our reliability—indeed, when the focus is put on reliability it is obvious *why* the reliance on 'experts' should have such a central place.

Earlier I pointed out that the reliability of my beliefs under the disquotation schema is simply an objective fact about me, stateable without semantic terms, which a deflationist can hardly be debarred from taking note of in his account of meaning. Here I am expanding the point, to observe that he can hardly be debarred from wanting an explanation of it; and the explanation is bound to involve some of the ingredients that inflationists tend to put into their theories of reference.

This of course raises again the possibility mentioned earlier, that by the time the deflationist is finished explaining this and similar facts, he will have reconstructed the inflationist's relation 'S has the truth conditions *p*', in fact if not in name. My guess is that this will turn out not to be the case, but to assert that conclusion with confidence requires a more thorough investigation than I will be able to undertake in this chapter. All I really hope to motivate here is that we should be 'methodological deflationists': that is, we should start out assuming deflationism as a working hypothesis; we should adhere to it unless and until we find ourselves reconstructing what amounts to the inflationist's relation 'S has the truth conditions *p*'. So methodological deflationism is simply a methodological policy, which if

---

[15] This incidentally is why the Benacerraf problem about mathematical knowledge (P. Benacerraf, 'Mathematical Truth', *Journal of Philosophy*, 70/19 (1973), 661–79) isn't dissolved by a disquotational theory of truth.

pursued could lead to the discovery that deflationism in the original sense ('metaphysical deflationism') is workable or could lead to the discovery that inflationism is inevitable. It could also turn out that we end up constructing something that *might or might not* be regarded as the inflationist's relation 'S has the truth conditions *p*'; in that case, the line between inflationism and metaphysical deflationism will turn out to have blurred.[16]

5. MORE ON DISQUOTATIONAL TRUTH

It is time now to be a bit more precise about what exactly deflationism involves. In order to do this, it will help to ask what a deflationist should say about why we need a truth predicate. If truth conditions aren't central to meaning, why not drop talk of truth altogether? As is well known, the deflationist's answer is that the word 'true' has an important logical role: it allows us to formulate certain infinite conjunctions and disjunctions that can't be formulated otherwise.[17]

There are some very mundane examples of this, for instance, where we remember that someone said something false yesterday but can't remember what it was. What we are remembering is equivalent to the infinite disjunction of all sentences of form 'She said "*p*", but not-*p*'.

A more important example of this which has been widely noted arises in discussions of realism. 'Realism' has been used to mean many things, but one version of it is the view that there might be (and almost certainly are) sentences of our language that are true that we will never have reason to believe, in contrast to 'anti-realist' doctrines that identify truth with long-run justifiability or whatever. To assert realism in this sense one needs

[16] Methodological deflationism doesn't even preclude that we might in the end come to accept an *unreduced* inflationist relation *S has the truth conditions that p*: we might conceivably see the need for introducing non-physical relations as explanatory. I think it does put the burden of proof against such a position, but I think that doing so is appropriate.

[17] This needs two small qualifications. The first is that the generalizations can be formulated otherwise if the language contains certain devices of infinite conjunction such as substitutional quantifiers. However, this qualification is not a terribly severe one, since the presence of such substitutional quantifiers would allow you to define 'true': S is true iff $\Pi p(S={}^\prime p^\prime \supset p)$. (Again, I assume a theory of substitutional quantification that avoids the paradoxes.)

Note that the use of schematic letters as an alternative to substitutional quantification, mentioned in §3, does not allow us to formulate infinite disjunctions without 'true', and therefore does not allow us to explicitly define 'true'.

The second qualification is that what I've given (in either the substitutional quantifier version or the free schematic variable version) allows statements that are really a bit stronger than infinite conjunctions, in the same way that first order quantifications are stronger than the totality of their instances even when every object has a name: see the discussion in §3 of the generalization (TFG).

a notion of truth. But the reason for this is purely logical: that is, if only finitely many sentences could be formulated in our language, we could put the realist doctrine without use of a predicate of truth: we could say:

> It might be the case that either the number of brontosauruses that ever lived is precisely 75,278 but we will never have reason to believe that; or the amount that Michael Jackson spent on underwear in his lifetime is exactly $1,078,852.72 but we will never have reason to believe that; or . . . ,

where in place of the '. . .' go similar clauses for every sentence of the language. It is because we can't complete the disjunction that we need a notion of truth. Or perhaps I should say, because we can't *otherwise* complete the disjunction: for the claim that it might be the case that some sentence of our language is true but that we will never have reason to believe it can be viewed as simply a way of formulating the disjunction.[18]

Another example of 'true' as a device of infinite conjunction and disjunction is the desire to utter only true sentences or to have only true beliefs: what we desire is the infinite conjunction of all claims of the form 'I utter "p" only if p' or 'I believe "p" only if p'. It is sometimes claimed that a deflationist cannot grant that there is any 'substantial norm' of assertion beyond warranted assertibility.[19] This seems to me a serious mistake: any sane deflationist will hold that truth and warranted assertibility (even long run warranted assertibility) can and do diverge: as the previous paragraph should make clear, their divergence is a consequence of the truth schema together with quite uncontroversial facts. Consequently, a norm of asserting the truth is a norm that goes beyond warranted assertibility. But there is no difficulty in desiring that all one's beliefs be disquotationally true; and not only can each of us desire such things, there can be a general practice of badgering others into having such desires. Isn't this enough for there being a 'norm' of asserting and believing the truth? Admittedly, this account of norms in terms of badgering is a bit crude, but I see no reason to think that on a more sophisticated account of what a norm is, norms of

---

[18] For present purposes I am regarding sentence types as 'necessary existents', so that the fact that the disjuncts don't all entail the existence of sentence types doesn't debar a sentence that does entail this from counting as their 'infinite disjunction'.

[19] Both Hilary Putnam, *Philosophical Papers*, iii., *Realism and Reason* (Cambridge, 1983), pp. xiv–xv and 279–80) and Crispin Wright, *Truth and Objectivity* (Cambridge, Mass., 1992) 12–24 object to deflationism on this ground. However, their discussions are directed at a version of deflationism which says that truth is not a property (Putnam) or not a 'substantial property' (Wright), and I'm not clear enough as to what that is supposed to mean to know whether the authors would have intended to be arguing against deflationism as I have defined it. (In a long footnote, Wright does say that he thinks his objection applies to the version of deflationism in Horwich, *Truth*, despite the fact that Horwich disavows the 'no property' claim.)

striving for the truth won't be just as available to the deflationist as they are on the crude account.

I'll give a fourth example of the utility of a device of infinite conjunction and disjunction, since it clearly brings out some points I want to stress. Consider some theory about the physical world, formulated with finitely many separate axioms and finitely many axiom schemas (each schema having infinitely many axioms as instances). For an example of such a theory, one can take a typical first order version of the Euclidean theory of space (which is not finitely axiomatisable). Suppose that one rejects this theory without knowing which specific part of it to reject; or alternatively, suppose that one accepts it but regards it as contingent. In the first case one will put the rejection by saying 'Not every axiom of this theory is true'; in the second case, by saying 'It might have been the case that not every axiom of the theory was true'. But the intended purpose in the first case is of course to deny the infinite conjunction of the axioms, and in the second case to assert the *possibility* of the negation of this infinite conjunction.

My reason for focusing on this example is that it shows clearly the importance of what I earlier called pure disquotational truth. Pure disquotational truth involves two important features that certain other truth concepts lack. The first is that I can understand 'Utterance u is true' only to the extent that I can understand utterance u; the second is that for me, the claim that utterance u is true in the pure disquotational sense is cognitively equivalent to u itself as I understand it. (The first pretty much follows from the second: if I can't understand u, and if an attribution of truth to u is cognitively equivalent to u, then I can't understand an attribution of truth to u.)[20] The second feature of the pure disquotational notion of truth means that this notion is of a *use-independent* property: to call 'Snow is white' disquotationally true is simply to call snow white; hence it is not to attribute it a property that it wouldn't have had if I and other English speakers had used words differently.

In ordinary English we seem to use a truth predicate that does not share these two features. It is not entirely obvious, though, that what we say can't

[20] Opponents of deflationism sometimes try to pin on it the claim that when we come to understand new sentences, or when new words and hence new sentences are added to our language, our concept of truth changes. But a deflationist can agree that on the most natural ways to individuate concepts over time, adding new sentences to the language (or to our domain of understanding) leaves the concept of truth unchanged: after all, once we have come to understand the new sentences, the truth schema dictates how the word 'true' is to be applied to them. This doesn't conflict with what is said in the text: the point there was that we don't now understand attributions of disquotational truth to sentences containing future words. (Also, there is no reasonable sense in which such attributions now have disquotational truth conditions, since what truth conditions they may come to have will depend on how the future words will be used.)

be understood indirectly in terms of disquotational truth. (More on this in §8 and §9.) In any case, these two features of pure disquotational truth make it ideally suited to serve the logical need for a device of infinite conjunction and disjunction illustrated in the examples above, particularly the Euclidean geometry example. In the first place, the only sentences we ever literally conjoin or disjoin are sentences we understand, so it is clear that a notion that is inapplicable to utterances we don't understand will serve our needs for truth as a device of conjunction and disjunction. Second and more important, the use-independence of disquotational truth is *required* for the purposes just reviewed. For if 'All sentences of type Q are true' is to serve as an infinite conjunction of all sentences of type Q, then we want it to entail each such sentence, and be entailed by all of them together. This would fail to be so unless 'S is true' entailed and was entailed by S. But the only way that can be so is if 'true' doesn't ascribe a use-dependent feature to S. Suppose for instance that Euclidean geometry is true, and that we try to express its contingency by saying that the axioms together might have been false. Surely what we wanted to say wasn't simply that speakers might have used their words in such a way that the axioms weren't' true, it is that space itself might have differed so as to make the axioms *as we understand them* not true. A use-independent notion of truth is precisely what we require.

Of course, there is another use-independent notion of truth besides disquotational truth that would be usable for these purposes: truth as applied to *propositions*, where propositions are construed as language-independent (rather than, say, as equivalence classes of utterances). But I think that pure disquotational truth is better for these purposes, for two reasons. The first and less important is ontological: it is better to avoid postulating strange entities unnecessarily. The more important reason is that unless one is very careful to limit the use made of the notion of expressing a proposition, the introduction of such a notion of proposition would beg the question in favour of inflationism.[21] There may be good arguments for inflationism, but the need to express infinite conjunctions and disjunctions can be handled with the more minimal apparatus of purely disquotational

---

[21] We can introduce a purely disquotational notion of what it is to express a proposition, with the property that claims of the form ' "*p*" expresses the proposition that *p*' are necessary truths. We can also introduce certain impurely disquotational notions of what it is to express a proposition; these are analogous to the impure disquotational views of truth that we will consider later. Deflationists about meaning-that and believing-that think that such disquotational notions of expressing are the only legitimate ones; inflationists disagree. This distinction between inflationist and deflationist notions of expressing a proposition obviously needs to be clarified, if one is going to talk in terms of propositions; I think that some of the rest of the paper suggests a way to clarify it, but I will obviate the need to discuss this by avoiding talk of propositions.

truth, and it is best to use only the more minimal apparatus as long as the need of the more powerful apparatus is unargued.

I have been arguing that inflationists as well as deflationists need some use-independent notion of truth as a device of infinite conjunction and disjunction, and that such a notion is needed only for sentences that one understands. Pure disquotational truth serves the need admirably; and I think that a deflationist should take pure disquotational truth as the fundamental truth concept. This is not to say that it is the only notion of truth available to the deflationist: in §9 I will consider the possibility of introducing a modified kind of disquotational truth, which both applies to sentences in languages we can't understand and is not use-independent. But I have argued that a deflationist needs a notion of pure disquotational truth, and I think that he should regard it as the basic notion of truth in terms of which others are to be explained.

6. DISQUOTATIONAL TRUTH VERSUS TARSKIAN TRUTH

In this section I consider the relation between Tarskian truth definitions and disquotational truth. To facilitate the discussion I will pretend that English is a language without indexicals or demonstratives or ambiguous sentences, so that we can apply talk of truth to sentence types. (I will consider what the deflationist should say about indexicality, ambiguity and the like in § 10.)

As I have explained disquotational truth, axiomatic status is given to some generalized version of the truth schema

(T) 'p' is true if and only if p.

The generalized version might be the result of prefixing the schema with a universal substitutional quantifier; alternatively, we might prefer the weaker approach involving schematic variables, mentioned earlier. (Again, I assume sufficient restrictions on the schema to avoid semantic paradoxes.) Actually, if our language contains a modal operator we need something a bit stronger, as the Euclidean geometry example of the previous section indicates: the schema (T) should be replaced by:

(NT) $\square$ ('p' is true if and only if p).

But even when the language doesn't have a modal operator, the left-hand side of (T) is to be understood as cognitively equivalent to the right-hand side. (Any view, no matter how inflationist, accepts the instances of (T) as material biconditionals.)

Tarskian approaches are somewhat different. First I should remind the reader that though Tarski was interested in explicitly defined truth predicates, he also proved a severe limitation of such explicitly defined predicates: they are available only for fragments of one's language. If we explicitly define a truth predicate in a language, not only must we exclude its application to some or all sentences of that language that contain semantic terms, we must also exclude its application to a substantial body of other sentences of the language without semantic terms but with unrestricted quantifiers. This of course limits the use of the truth predicate as a device of infinite conjunction and disjunction: for instance, we can't use it to form infinite conjunctions and disjunctions of sentences with unrestricted quantifiers, at least if arbitrarily large numbers of alternations of those quantifiers appear among the conjuncts or disjuncts. If we want to avoid such limitations on formulating infinite conjunctions and disjunctions, we should give up on the idea that our truth predicate must be explicitly defined.

Even if a Tarskian were to give up the insistence on *defining* truth, there would still be an important difference between the Tarskian approach and the full-fledged deflationary approach that takes a generalized version of the truth schema as an axiom. Central to what is usually thought of as the Tarskian approach (though perhaps it owes more to Davidson than to Tarski himself) is that truth[22] is characterized (inductively if not explicitly) in terms of compositional structure.[23] This gives compositional principles of truth a much more central role than they have on the full-fledged deflationary account. Recall the deflationist story I gave about why the word 'or' obeys the usual truth-table: the principle

If S_1 and S_2 are sentences of our language then $\ulcorner S_1$ or $S_2 \urcorner$ is true iff S_1 or S_2 is true

is built directly into the inductive characterization of truth on the Tarskian approach, whereas on the deflationary approach it is simply a consequence

[22] Or a more basic notion like satisfaction from which truth is defined.

[23] Actually even the demand for a compositional *inductive definition* must be relaxed, if we want both to get a notion of truth that applies to sufficiently many sentences that contain semantic terms and simultaneously to avoid limiting the truth predicate to sentences that contain only restricted quantifiers: the usual methods like Kripke's for defining a notion of truth that applies to sufficiently many sentences that contain 'true' require a restriction of quantifiers *even in the inductive definition* (not just in turning it into an explicit definition); that is, what is being defined isn't truth but only 'comes out true under such and such a restriction of the quantifiers'. I think that a lesson of the paradoxes is that we must go to an axiomatized truth theory rather than defining 'true', even inductively.

But this doesn't undermine the point intended in the text: for one might well demand (more or less in the spirit of Tarski or at least Davidson) that an axiomatized truth theory be built around explicit compositional axioms like 'A disjunction is true if and only if at least one disjunct is true'. A more full-fledged deflationist view would be that such compositionality has no intrinsic importance.

of the generalized truth schema (together with the principle '∀S(S is a sentence ⊃ Σp(S = "p")', on the substitutional quantifier version of the generalized schema). Something similar holds for other compositional principles, such as that a sentence consisting of a 1-place predicate and a referring name is true iff the predicate is true of what the name denotes: on a deflationist account this is simply a consequence of generalized disquotational schemas for 'true', 'true of', and 'refers' (together with principles like the one just given parenthetically, together with some obvious syntactic principles and laws of concatenation and quotation marks).[24]

Why does it matter whether such principles are built into an inductive characterization of truth or viewed as consequences of generalized disquotational schemas? One reason why it matters is that there is no guarantee that for all regions of discourse there will be such compositional principles that follow from the generalized disquotation schemas. The compositional principles for 'or' and other truth functional operators simply fall out of the logical rules of inference that govern those operators (together with the disquotational principles for 'true'); the same is basically true of other standard compositional principles (except that we sometimes need subsidiary semantic notions such as satisfaction, and disquotational principles governing them). But there is no obvious reason to think that in the case of all operators, e.g. non-extensional ones, there will be subsidiary semantic notions that yield compositional principles.

This shouldn't upset the full-fledged deflationist: for the full-fledged deflationist, such compositional principles have no particular interest in their own right; we can explain why we have them when we do, since they follow from the basic disquotational schemas whenever a substitutivity principle is part of the logic, but they are not of foundational importance. For the Tarskian they are of much more fundamental importance: they are needed in order to have a satisfactory notion of truth. This is one important way in which a Tarskian approach isn't *fully* deflationist.

---

[24] Let P be a one place predicate and N a name. By the assumptions indicated, ΣF(P = 'F') and Σa(N = 'a'). By laws of concatenation and quotation marks, it follows that ΣFΣa(P^N = 'Fa').

By syntax, ΠFΠa('Fa' is a sentence), so by the truth schema, ΠFΠa('Fa' is true iff Fa). By first order logic, we can rewrite this as ΠFΠa('Fa' is true iff ∃x(Fx and $x = a$)). But then the appropriate schemas for truth of and reference will allow us to rewrite this as ΠFΠa('Fa' is true iff ∃x('F' is true true of x and 'a' refers to x)). Combining with the previous paragraph, we get that P^N is true iff ∃x(P is true of x and N refers to x).

The step labelled 'by first order logic' implicitly assumes that N denotes, that is, that Σa(n = 'a' and ∃x($x = a$)). If this supposition is abandoned, some form of free logic must be used; the details of the free logic affect the details of the compositional principle that is derived.

A Tarskian approach may or may not be *partially* deflationist: whether it is depends on the status that is accorded the Tarskian 'truth definitions'. In particular, what (if anything) makes such a definition *correct* for a given population? For a view to count as in any serious sense deflationist, it must say either that there is no sense at all to be made of speaking of one Tarski-predicate for a population as 'correct', or that the only sense that can be made of it is based on stipulating that the *homophonic* truth predicate counts as correct *for us*.

To elaborate: it is easy to use Tarski-predicates in a theory that is in no way deflationist. One view of the significance of a Tarski truth definition (whether inductive or explicit) is as partially characterizing an *abstract language*, that is, a language viewed as an abstract entity that exists whether or not anyone actually speaks it: the language is defined by the rules governing it, including Tarskian truth rules.[25] So in addition to English there is an abstract language English*, with the same rules of grammar but different truth rules: e.g. in English* it might be that 'or' obeys the truth-table for conjunction and 'rabbit' is true of all and only the dinosaurs. Then questions about the truth conditions of a person's sentences are relocated as questions about which abstract language she speaks. An inflationist thinks that there are facts about a person's employment of her sentences by virtue of which it is one abstract language rather than another that she is speaking; such facts determine that Aristotle spoke in abstract Greek, and in the same way determine that we are speaking abstract English. The problem is to say what these facts are, and how they do the determining. But a deflationist thinks that a homophony condition guarantees that we are speaking English rather than English*, without the need of any such facts about our employment of the language.[26]

There is of course a strong suggestion of the deflationist viewpoint in Tarski himself, stemming from his famous adequacy condition on truth definitions, 'Convention T'. (I should actually say, a strong suggestion of the *partial* deflationist view, because of the points earlier in this section.) My point is only that if you de-emphasize these and focus on the truth definitions themselves, and think it is a straightforwardly factual question which truth definition is correct for a given population, then there is nothing in the least deflationist about the resulting view.

---

[25] D. Lewis, 'Languages and Language', in K. Gunderson (ed.), *Minnesota Studies in Philosophy of Science*, vii (Minneapolis, 1975), 3–35; S. Soames, 'What is a Theory of Truth?', *Journal of Philosophy*, 81/8 (1984), 411–29; R. Stalnaker, *Inquiry* (Cambridge, Mass., 1984).

[26] At least, this is so for what I've called a 'pure deflationist'. The idea of 'impure deflationism' will be considered in §9.

7. OBJECTIONS TO DEFLATIONISM

There are many different sorts of worries that one might have about deflationism. Some seem to me to be based on misunderstandings. Under this heading I would include the commonly-voiced worry that deflationism cuts language off from the world. The worry is that if I simply accept 'T-sentences' like

> 'There are gravitational waves' is true iff there are gravitational waves,

then unless the sentence on the right-hand side already has truth conditions of a more-than-disquotational sort, it has nothing to do with gravitational waves, and so the T-sentence doesn't really supply truth conditions for 'There are gravitational waves'. The response is that we do indeed need to establish a connection between the use of 'There are gravitational waves' and gravitational waves, independent of the truth schema. But deflationism allows for this (at least in the version I have sketched): it admits that among the important facts about the use of 'There are gravitational waves' are facts, stateable quite independent of disquotational truth, that relate the sentence to gravitational waves. For instance, the laws of physics are such that gravitational waves, if they exist, will cause pulses in a quadrupole antenna, and such pulses are one of the things that would increase our confidence in the sentence 'There are gravitational waves'. The objection tacitly assumed that the only kind of connection between gravitational waves and the use of 'There are gravitational waves' (other than the derivative connection that arises simply from the use of 'true' in accordance with the disquotation schema) comes in the non-disquotational assignment of truth conditions to that sentence; but this is simply false.

In contrast, many of the worries that one might have about deflationism raise deep issues. In my view the most serious worry about deflationism is that it can't make sense of the explanatory role of truth conditions: e.g. their role in explaining behaviour, or their role in explaining the extent to which behaviour is successful. Unfortunately it is a big job even to state the worry clearly, and a bigger job to answer it; I must save this for another occasion.[27] Another kind of worry about deflationism that is too big to discuss here is that it can't make the distinction between vague and non-vague discourse, or between discourse that is thoroughly factual and

---

[27] I made a rather confusing attempt to state the problem in Field, 'The Deflationary Conception of Truth', in G. MacDonald and C. Wight (eds.), *Fact, Science and Value* (Oxford, 1986), §IV and §V. I now think there is a way around the problem there raised. (Stephen Leeds helped set me straight on this.)

discourse that falls short of this in various ways. I discuss this worry elsewhere.[28]

But there remain some less serious objections that I can discuss here; discussing them will help clarify what I am taking deflationism to involve. The objections to be discussed are:

1. That deflationism can't handle the attribution of truth to utterances in other languages.
2. That deflationism gives the wrong modal properties to 'true'.
3. That deflationism can't handle ambiguous utterances, indexicals, demonstratives, and the like.
4. That it can't make sense of how we learn from others.

I think all of these can be easily answered, but it is worth spelling out how this is to be done, for my treatment will separate my version of deflationism from certain other less radical versions. I will treat these objections in order in the final four sections.

8. APPLYING 'TRUE' TO SENTENCES IN OTHER LANGUAGES

I have emphasized that a person can meaningfully apply a pure disquotational truth predicate only to utterances that he understands. This raises the question of what we are doing when we talk of the truth or falsity of sentences in other languages.

There are at least three different approaches that a deflationist might take toward talk of truth for sentences in other languages. Perhaps the most obvious—but to my mind the least satisfactory—would be to use a notion of interlinguistic synonymy: regard 'S is true' (where 'S' stands for a foreign sentence) as equivalent to 'S is synonymous with a sentence of ours that is true in the purely disquotational sense'. This option brings the semantic notion of synonymy into the characterization of truth for foreign sentences. I will call truth as so defined '*extended* disquotational truth'.

Some may object that extended disquotational truth is not a notion that a deflationist can allow himself, since it involves interlinguistic synonymy, which must be understood as involving sameness of truth conditions. I hesitate to say anything so strong; I say only that a deflationist who wants to employ a notion of interlinguistic synonymy faces a serious challenge, the challenge of showing how to make sense of it without relying on a prior notion of truth conditions. (Recall that the deflationist/inflationist contrast

---

[28] Field, 'Disquotational Truth'.

was explained in terms of whether truth conditions play a central role in semantics and the theory of content.) But perhaps this challenge can be met. If for instance one were to adopt a crude verificationism, synonymy would be just interpersonal sameness of verification conditions—assuming of course that *that* can be spelled out. On a more reasonable deflationist view, meaning will involve a variety of components: as discussed earlier, the meaning of a sentence of mine will depend on its inferential role for me, its inferential role for my fellow speakers, and its indication relations for me and my fellow speakers. So whether one of my sentences is synonymous with a sentence used by someone else (e.g., a foreign speaker) will depend on a variety of disparate facts. In that case there is no obvious way to get a useful and well-behaved synonymy relation.[29] Still, it isn't idiotic to suppose that there is an *unobvious* way to do it; so it isn't initially clear that a deflationist can't admit a useful and well-behaved notion of extended disquotational truth.

Extended disquotational truth isn't the only option the deflationist has available for talking about truth conditions for foreign sentences. A second option is more flexible: simply define what it is for a foreign sentence to be *true relative to a correlation* of it to one of our sentences: a sentence is true relative to the correlation if the sentence of ours correlated with it is true in the purely disquotational sense. This approach differs from the previous in that no claim is made that the correlated sentences are synonymous. Of course, if we accept the notion of interpersonal synonymy, we can use it to get the effect of the first option: we can say that a foreign sentence S is true in the extended disquotational sense iff there is a correlation of S to a synonymous English sentence such that S is true relative to this correlation. But the second option can be applied by those like Quine who reject a notion of interpersonal synonymy, or by those who accept it but want to consider truth relative to correlations that violate it, or by those who want to keep track of where notions like synonymy are being used and where they aren't.

I should note that even those like Quine who reject a notion of interpersonal synonymy grant that there are standards of translation: it is beyond controversy that some translations of a foreign sentence are better than others, at least for certain purposes. To translate an utterance of

---

[29] I'm inclined to think that the problem isn't just that interpersonal synonymy ('is a good translation of') is a highly vague notion, but that it isn't a straightforwardly factual notion at all, but rather an evaluative notion. Of course, a deflationist can only say this if he can make sense of the distinction between utterances that are straightforwardly factual and those that aren't, and it is commonly supposed either that this distinction cannot be drawn at all or at least that a deflationist cannot draw it. But I argue that the distinction can be drawn, even by a deflationist, in Field, 'Disquotational Truth'.

'Comment ça va?' as 'You have just passed your French exam' is to grossly violate any reasonable standard of good translation. The sceptic about interpersonal synonymy holds that though we of course have standards of translation, they are a matter of being better or worse, not of right and wrong, and also are highly context-dependent (since the purposes for which they are better or worse vary from one context to the next); and that these features together keep them from generating any useful notion of synonymy. I don't want to discuss whether this rejection of interpersonal synonymy is a reasonable position. But note that even if it is, standards of better and worse translation can be employed to partly capture the import of claims about extended disquotational truth: what we are doing when we conjecture whether some utterance we don't understand is true is conjecturing whether a good translation of the utterance will map it into a disquotationally true sentence we do understand. If 'good translation' is a highly context-sensitive and interest-relative notion that doesn't reflect an objective synonymy relation, then there is a certain non-objectivity to the question of whether the utterance we don't understand is true, but that consequence is not obviously undesirable.

(Even a deflationist who thinks there is an objective notion of synonymy for good translations to reflect will have a similar consequence to swallow. For presumably if there is an objective synonymy relation, then there could be utterances that we know don't bear this relation to any utterances we understand, and yet presumably it could still sometimes make a certain amount of sense to discuss whether such an utterance was true. An inflationist can take such a discussion at face value; but as far as I can see, the only way for a deflationist to deal with this, even if he accepts a notion of 'objective synonymy', is to appeal to context-sensitive and interest-relative standards of translation that do not reflect objective synonymy.)

In addition to extended disquotational truth and truth relative to a correlation, there is a third option for a deflationist who wants to apply 'true' to foreign utterances, and that is simply to use the concept of pure disquotational truth as originally defined in connection with the foreign utterance, without relativization. This may seem odd: didn't I say that my concept of pure disquotational truth applied only to utterances in my own language? No: I said that it was defined only for utterances that I understand. I understand the sentence 'Der Schnee ist weiss'. Following Quine[30] I hold that I can apply schema (T) to it, getting

'Der Schnee ist weiss' is true iff der Schnee ist weiss,

[30] *From a Logical Point of View* (Cambridge, Mass., 1953), 135.

which I can perfectly well understand despite its not conforming to the grammatical rules of any standard language. (If it is objected that there would be a problem had I picked a sentence with a different meaning in German than in English, my response is that in that case 'Der Schnee ist weiss' would be ambiguous for me, and there would be no problems in this case that don't arise equally for ordinary ambiguity within a language. I will discuss whether ambiguity creates a problem for deflationism in §10.)

I don't see any reason to choose between the second and third options: the deflationist can use whichever one suits his purposes of the moment. For some purposes the third option is better than the second. For instance, if I understand a foreign sentence that has no exact equivalent in English, the third option can be used to give more adequate disquotational truth conditions than the second. The third option is also more useful in certain explanatory contexts, when we want to explain a foreigner's behaviour without bringing the English language into the explanation. But the second option is often more useful than the third, in that it can in principle be used even for sentences we don't understand. Sometimes that broader application can come in handy: for instance, in trying to *come* to understand a foreign sentence we may try out several different correlations to our own sentences to see which makes most sense. And in some contexts we want to use the second option in connection with semantic or quasi-semantic notions like synonymy or acceptable translation: for instance, in a perjury trial we might want to know whether there is any acceptable translation of an utterance that makes it come out true. Finally, there are contexts in which the second option is useful even in connection with our own utterances: if we are considering a counterfactual situation in which my use of words is very different, I may be interested in the truth conditions of my sentences relative to a mapping of my language into itself that is not the identity mapping. So a deflationist should not dispense with the second option. In many contexts though I think that the third option is the most natural. It is the one that accords with my original gloss on disquotational truth: a sentence is disquotationally true iff it is true-as-I-understand-it.

I think then that the notion of extended disquotational truth should be avoided if possible: it is not obvious that a deflationist can make sense of it, it is less obvious that he needs it, and it seems better to keep the logical aspects of truth cleanly separated from any semantic and quasi-semantic elements.

9. THE MODAL PROPERTIES OF 'TRUE'

A further point about extended disquotational truth as I have defined it is that it is a concept of little theoretical utility. That is because it is a curiously hybrid notion: whether a foreign utterance is true in this sense depends on semantic facts, but whether one of our own sentences is true in this sense doesn't (since as applied to our own sentences, extended disquotational truth is equivalent to pure disquotational truth, which is use-independent). Recall that certain logical uses of the pure disquotational truth predicate 'true$_{pd}$' (for instance, the modal version of the Euclidean geometry example) require that $\square$ ('Snow is white' is true$_{pd}$ iff snow is white). So even if 'snow is white' had been used in English in pretty much the way that 'Grass is red' is actually used, 'snow is white' would still have been true in the purely disquotational sense, and hence in the extended disquotational sense as well. Moreover, if in addition grass and the German language had been as they actually are, then 'Der Gras ist rot' would have been synonymous with 'Snow is white', and hence would have been true in the extended disquotational sense too. The counterfactual supposition of a drastic change in the use of English sentences leaves their extended disquotational truth conditions the same but alters the extended disquotational truth conditions of foreign sentences! This, surely, is not a theoretically useful way to make truth conditions use-dependent.

Obviously what we would need to do, if we wanted a more useful notion of truth conditions that has semantic features built into it, is to build in such features for our own sentences as well as for the sentences of others. Inflationary theories of truth conditions do precisely this. The question is, can one do this on a theory of truth conditions with any claims to being deflationary?

There is an obvious modification of the extended disquotational approach: I don't know if a view of this sort should be called deflationary or inflationary, so I'll call it *quasi*-deflationary. It requires that we have not only a notion of synonymy, but a prior notion of meaning such that two sentences are synonymous if they have the same meaning; but meaning is to be defined independently of truth conditions. (The crude illustration would be a view according to which meanings are just verification conditions; slightly less crudely, perhaps meanings are some sort of equivalence classes of pairs of conceptual roles and indication relations; the point of using equivalence classes being of course to allow that small differences of conceptual role don't make for a difference of meaning.) Then we define quasi-disquotational truth (truth$_{qd}$) and quasi-disquotational truth conditions by:

☐ (S is true$_{qd}$ iff $\Sigma p(\exists m(m$ is the meaning of S and @(m is the meaning of 'p')) and p),

and analogously,

☐ (S has the quasi-disquotational truth conditions that p iff $\exists m(m$ is the meaning of S and @(m is the meaning of 'p'))));

where '@' is an 'actually operator' which 'temporarily undoes the effects of' the modal operator.[31] This seems to have the modal properties we desire if we want to mimic an inflationary truth predicate in making the truth of sentences use-dependent.

Indeed, it mimics it well enough so that it is natural to wonder whether it shouldn't count as an inflationary notion of truth and truth conditions. For note that according to it, a sufficient condition for having the truth conditions that snow is white is having a certain 'meaning': perhaps a certain combination of such things as conceptual role, indication relations, and the like. Why then shouldn't this count as an explication of truth conditions in terms of such things as conceptual role and indication relations?

It does nonetheless seem to me that there may be something to be said for counting a view like this as somewhat deflationary, if the idea of a meaning is explained in a sufficiently 'un-truth-theoretic' way. After all, it is compatible with this view that there be no very systematic connection between 'meanings' and truth conditions: for instance, it is compatible with this way of defining truth conditions, albeit not very plausible, that the 'meaning' of 'Snow is white or grass is green' have few systematic links to the 'meanings' of 'Snow is white', 'Grass is green', and 'or'. Note further that this view assigns truth conditions only to sentences that are synonymous with English sentences (or anyway, sentences that we understand). This points up the fact that there need be no 'natural connection' between the 'meanings' it assigns and truth conditions: the connection between the meanings it invokes and truth is supplied entirely by the disquotation schema for sentences we understand. So the view is somewhat deflation-

---

[31] See e.g. J. Crossley and L. Humberstone, 'The Logic of "Actually"', *Reports on Mathematical Logic*, 8 (1977), 11–29.

Quantification over meanings seems necessary in this definition: certainly you can't replace the right-hand side by '$\Sigma p[@(S$ is synonymous with 'p')) and p]', since this makes only the actual meaning of S relevant to whether S would be true in a non-actual context, contrary to intentions. And you can't simply take meanings to be equivalence classes of expressions under the (actual) synonymy relation: for then the proposed definition would collapse into the inadequate one just mentioned. In these remarks I'm assuming that you don't quantify over possible worlds: if you do, then you can use the relation *expression e as used in world w is synonymous with e′ as used in w′*, and take meanings to be equivalence classes of pairs of expressions and possible worlds under this equivalence relations.

ary, though just how deflationary it is will depend very much on the details of what it says about 'meanings'.

One kind of worry about views of this sort concerns whether any acceptable notion of 'a meaning' and of 'having a meaning' will do the job required. Putting aside purely ontological concerns, the main worry concerns the notion of synonymy (having the same meaning) that would be generated by any such view of meaning and the 'having' of meanings. Long ago Quine observed that it is an open question whether interpersonal synonymy and intrapersonal synonymy can be viewed as two aspects of the same general equivalence relation.[32] Obviously we employ different criteria in the two cases—for instance, in the intrapersonal case we use a speaker's willingness to substitute one expression for the other, and this criterion is unavailable in the interpersonal case—and reflection on the criteria we do use in the two cases can lead to scepticism as to how well they cohere. I won't try to elaborate this scepticism here, I simply want to note that such scepticism is possible, and that it would make it impossible to regard intrapersonal synonymy and interpersonal synonymy as both cases of the general relation of 'having the same meaning'. (In addition, the explanation of synonymy as having the same meaning requires synonymy to be an equivalence relation; this is another assumption about synonymy that has been questioned.)

I'm not sure how seriously to take these worries, but as I said in connection with extended disquotational truth, I think it advantageous to cleanly separate the semantic assumptions one is employing from the logical aspects of truth: failing to do so can easily lead to obscuring the role to which one is putting one's semantic assumptions. (I think in fact there is a serious danger of this in the case of quasi-disquotational truth conditions: it is easy to fall into trying to get them to play an explanatory role that in fact is precluded given the peculiar way they are defined. But this and other issues about explanation are beyond the scope of this chapter.) In any case, I think a full-fledged deflationist should make no commitment to a notion of interpersonal synonymy, let alone to interpersonally ascribable meanings.

Let us return now to counterfactuals like

(1) If we had used 'Snow is white' in certain very different ways it would have had the truth conditions that grass is red.

Presumably the average person would call such a sentence true. Doesn't this show that the average person is clearly not using the word 'true' in its

---

[32] *Logical Point of View*, 56; see also id., *Word and Object* (Cambridge, Mass., 1960) §9 and §11.

purely disquotational sense? And doesn't that in turn show that a version of deflationism that puts purely disquotational truth at the centre of things, and which refrains from endorsing intersubjective meanings and hence quasi-disquotational truth, is gratuitously departing from common sense? I don't think so. We could after all say that the 'cash value' of (1) is

(1*)   In considering counterfactual circumstances under which we used 'Snow is white' in certain very different ways, it is reasonable to translate it in such a way that its disquotational truth conditions relative to the translation are that grass is red;

and that this is all the ordinary person really means to assert. However, I am suspicious of this and all other claims about what the ordinary person means in making assertions involving 'true': I rather doubt that there is a consistent way to make sense of all ordinary uses of this notion. I am inclined to think that *many* ordinary uses of 'true' do fit the purely disquotational mould, though I regard the question of whether this is so as of only sociological interest. If, as may well be true, there is an ordinary meaning of (1) that (1*) fails to capture, then that would show that ordinary speakers are committed to a notion of truth that goes beyond the purely disquotational. But if we can lessen those commitments in a way that is adequate to all practical and theoretical purposes, and if in doing so we can still capture the 'cash value' of ordinary utterances as well as (1*) captures the cash value of (1), then the charge that we are 'gratuitously departing from common sense' is quite unfounded.

10. AMBIGUITY AND INDEXICALS

So far I have been a bit cavalier about whether a disquotational notion of truth applies to sentence-types or to utterances. I want it to apply to utterances, so that if an ambiguous sentence or a sentence containing an indexical or demonstrative is uttered on different occasions, we can regard some utterances of it as true and others as false.[33] One substantial worry about deflationism is whether it can accommodate this.

In dealing with this worry it is important to bear clearly in mind that talk of truth conditions as I am construing it is thoroughly non-semantic. 'True' in the purely disquotational sense means 'true as I understand it': it doesn't mean 'true on the correct understanding of it', because the idea of

---

[33] Incidentally, I remind the reader that I am counting it as an example of ambiguity if someone understands the same sentence as meaning one thing in German and something else in English: this was required by my adopting the 'third option' for dealing with sentences in other languages, discussed in §8.

a 'correct understanding' of a sentence or utterance is a semantic notion that has no place when we are discussing purely disquotational truth. If on my understanding of 'Der Schnee ist weiss' it is equivalent to '$E = mc^2$', then for me this sentence is disquotationally true iff $E = mc^2$.[34] Anyone in the grip of the Frege–Russell tradition will think that this shows that we need a notion of truth conditions very different from the disquotational one; but I don't think it at all obvious that they are right. (As I observed in §8, a deflationist can argue that there are standards of adequacy of translation that do not presuppose truth conditions, and can grant the legitimacy of saying that relative to a translation manual that meets those standards the sentence will have different truth conditions.) In any case, this *is* a feature of the purely disquotational notion, and the present question is, can this purely disquotational notion be applied to ambiguous utterances and indexical utterances?

Let's start with ambiguity. I believe that it poses little problem for the deflationist. There is a rather commonsensical story of how we process ambiguous sentences, which I assume the deflationist can help himself to: the story has it that when we come upon a two-way ambiguous sentence like 'Visiting relatives can be boring' or 'I met my lover at the bank', there are two alternative ways of processing it and using it in inferences, one corresponding to each of the interpretations; indeed, interpreting it one way rather than the other just is processing it in one way rather than the other (for instance, storing it in memory in such a way that it will be used in inferences of one kind rather than the other). When we are undecided as to how to interpret an ambiguous sentence, what we are undecided about is how to process and store it and which of the two sorts of inference to make with it. The fact that we can process and store a sentence in two different ways can be put metaphorically by saying that we attach 'inner subscripts' to lexically ambiguous elements and 'inner syntactic markers' to mark different ways of resolving the syntactic ambiguities. This metaphor allows us to talk, if we like, as if each person thinks in an ambiguity-free language. On this way of talking, to say that an utterance is disquotationally true is to say in effect that the sentence in my ambiguity-free inner language which I associate with the utterance is disquotationally true. Of course, if I am undecided how to interpret the utterance, there is no unique ambiguity-free inner sentence to use and hence no unique disquotational truth conditions will be generated. We can regard that as a case where we don't understand the utterance, so that the notion of disquotational truth doesn't apply—though of course we can also ascribe it truth conditions

---

[34] Since it is disquotationally true iff der Schnee ist weiss, and hence, by the equivalence hypothesis, iff $E = mc^2$.

relative to each of the ways of understanding it. The metaphor of the ambiguity-free language is not really playing an essential role here: I could equally well have said that I accept all instances of 'That utterance of "Visiting relatives can be boring" is true iff visiting relatives can be boring', but may process the right-hand side in either of two ways on different occasions. (I disallow inference from the right-hand side processed one way to the right-hand side processed the other way.)

Now let's turn to sentences containing indexicals and demonstratives. Here it is natural to divide up the account of truth into two stages. The first stage concerns sentence-types: here of course there is no hope of defining an unrelativized truth predicate, since sentence-types like 'I don't like her' don't have a truth-value, but we can associate a truth-value to this type relative to a pair of objects $\langle b,c \rangle$; to say that 'I don't like her' is true relative to $\langle b,c \rangle$ is simply to say that b doesn't like c. (I suppose that this isn't strictly 'disquotational' in that it involves a grammatical adjustment from 'don't' to 'doesn't', but surely we can allow the disquotationalist the machinery required for this grammatical adjustment.)

The second stage is to provide an account of unrelativized truth for sentence-tokens. Given the first stage, this simply amounts to associating objects with each of the indexical elements in the sentence, for then we can declare the token true iff it is true relative to the sequence of associated objects. How are we to do the association? If we focus only on indexicals like 'I' and 'now', there is a simple rule that would work pretty well: always relativize 'I' to the producer of the token and 'now' to the time of production. But this rule isn't invariably such a good one: consider the subway advertisement 'Stop smoking now'. At any rate, there seems to be no such simple rule for 'she', or 'that': the 'correct' object to assign, if it makes sense to talk of correctness here, depends in very complex ways on the intentions of the producer. In these cases anyway, and probably even in the cases of 'I' and 'now', we must regard all talk of the 'correct assignment' as a semantic matter which cannot appear in a deflationary account of truth conditions.

Still, nothing stops us from applying talk of disquotational truth conditions to tokens: once we remember that 'disquotationally true' means 'true-as-I-interpret-it', the obvious thing to say is that an utterance of '$p(i_1, \ldots, i_n)$' is disquotationally true (for me, that is, as I understand it) iff the sentence is true relative to the values of $a_1, \ldots, a_n$ I regard as appropriate to associate with the indexicals.[35] When I say that I 'associate values' with an

---

[35] Typically these will be the ones I take the producer of the utterance to have intended, but not always: e.g., 'now' on the sign intended to be read by various readers at different times. And since we're talking disquotational truth, the actual intentions of the producer don't matter, what matters is the reading the hearer gives.

indexical, of course, what I do is associate a mental occurrence of one of my own expressions (possibly itself indexical) with it. If I can't associate a term with an indexical in a sentence, then I can't attach disquotational truth conditions to the sentence. This is just an extension of a point made earlier for non-indexical utterances: sentences that I don't understand have no disquotational truth conditions for me.

I've said that the expression I associate with an indexical may itself be indexical: I may assign disquotational truth conditions to an utterance of 'She is here now' by thinking 'She is here now'. As with ambiguity, the deflationist needs to say something about how thoughts involving indexicals are processed, but the story is very similar to the story for ambiguity. When I think a thought involving 'she' to myself on a given occasion, that thought will typically hook up causally to a certain 'internal file drawer' of thoughts involving other singular terms, perhaps 'Sheila' and/or 'that woman I saw at the beach last Friday'. (It is possible that all the singular terms in the 'file drawer' are indexical: you can use an indexical to 'open a new file drawer'. Even when there are other terms in the 'file drawer', nothing need pick out any one person uniquely: the function of these associated terms isn't to explain how we can be referring to a certain person, if indeed we are; the function is simply to tell an obvious story of what it is for me to *regard* a given occurrence of 'she' as 'about Sheila' or 'about that woman I saw at the beach'.) Again, you could if you like say that the internal occurrences of indexicals are 'subscripted' so as to remove their indexicality; I take this to be just a dispensable manner of speaking for something better stated in terms of the internal processing.

We see that there is no special difficulty in explaining disquotational truth conditions for indexical tokens. If indexicals raise any special difficulty for deflationism, it is that for indexicals it is less believable that we don't need a more inflationist notion of truth conditions. Surely, it may be said, there will typically be a *correct answer* to the question of who another person was referring to with a particular application of 'she'; and the deflationist seems unable to accommodate this.

It seems to me though that the internal processing story does a lot to accommodate it. In a typical case where we misinterpret a token of 'she'— where we incorrectly interpret the speaker as meaning Mary when in fact she meant Sheila—we do so because of false beliefs about the speaker's internal processing: we think that her token was connected up to an internal file drawer of thoughts involving terms like 'Mary' when in fact it was connected up to a file drawer involving terms like 'Sheila'. Standards of appropriate translation are going to rule that in that case, 'Mary' is a bad translation of 'she'. The sort of facts that this brings into the standards of good translation are not in themselves semantic, so it seems hard to argue that the deflationist isn't entitled to appeal to them. Of course, it may be possible to argue that when we describe the standards of acceptable translation for indexicals in detail we will have to bring in machinery that is powerful enough to provide a reduction of the semantic notion of reference to non-semantic terms; if this is so, then the would-be deflationist is in fact turning himself into a reductionist inflationist. As I remarked earlier, the distinction between deflationism and reductionist inflationism may not in the end be altogether clear. At any rate, it certainly isn't obvious without argument that the standards of acceptable translation for indexicals give the machinery necessary to reduce the semantic notion of reference to non-semantic terms.

11. LEARNING FROM OTHERS

The final objection that I will consider is that you need an inflationist view of truth conditions to make sense of how we learn from others. Much of our information about the world is acquired from others—in particular, from their utterances, and from the beliefs we infer them to have. The notion of truth figures in this process: typically, what we do is assume that certain things the other person tells us are probably true—or that certain things we can see that she believes are probably true. It might be thought that an understanding of this process requires a non-deflationary notion of truth; or at least, that it requires more than purely disquotational truth. There are actually two distinct lines of argument that might be given for this conclusion.

The first is that since we learn from other people, including people who speak different languages, translation must somehow be involved, so that some notion of interpersonal synonymy is presupposed in the inference. If this were right it would show that pure disquotational truth, without a synonymy relation, was inadequate for these purposes: you'd need at least extended disquotational or quasi-disquotational truth, and maybe a more thoroughgoing inflationary notion, for the purpose. I'll get back to this after discussing the other line of argument.

The second line of argument purports to show that even pure disquotational truth plus synonymy isn't enough. Let's slur over the possible need for a synonymy relation, by imagining that I am learning from Charley, a speaker of my idiolect. Charley says: 'You know, on one day in 1936 there was over a foot of snow on the ground in Mobile Alabama'. Do I infer that one day in 1936 there was over a foot of snow in Alabama? For most Charleys and most circumstances, surely not. But suppose that in the past

Charley has asserted each of the following: 'You know, there are parts of Virginia that are north of parts of New Jersey'; 'You know, in 1928 the Soviet government secretly supplied arms to Chang Kai-Shek to be used against Mao'; 'You know, Leon Russell was one of the studio musicians for the Fleetwoods'. Each time I've found the claim almost unbelievable, but on checking it has turned out true. If he has never said 'You know, p' for a p that has turned out false, then I think I might well believe his claim about Mobile.

A crude way to formalize my inference is as an enumerative induction: all the sentences of a certain sort that Charley has uttered under certain circumstances that have been independently checked have been true; 'There was a foot of snow in Mobile' is a sentence of that sort uttered under those circumstances; so (in the absence of defeating evidence) probably that sentence is true. In addition to the inductive inference, we need an instance of the disquotation schema, to get from the claim about truth to the object level claim. Obviously the disquotationalist has no trouble with the last step. But the inductive part of the inference might seem more questionable. For suppose we were to try to formalize the inductive inference without use of the word 'true'. What we would get is this:

1. There are parts of Virginia that are north of parts of New Jersey.

$\vdots$

n. In 1928 the Soviet government secretly supplied arms to Chang Kai-Shek to be used against Mao.

$n+1$. Charley said 'You know, there are parts of Virginia that are north of parts of New Jersey'.

$\vdots$

$2n$. Charley said 'You know, in 1928 the Soviet government secretly suppplied arms to Chang Kai-Shek to be used against Mao'.

$2n+1$. Charley said 'You know, on one day in 1936 there was over a foot of snow in Mobile Alabama'.

Therefore (probably): On one day in 1936 there was over a foot of snow in Mobile Alabama.

A possible reaction to this inference so formulated is that it has no inductive force whatever: none of the premises have anything to do with snow or Mobile; the first n have to do with diverse topics, and the last $n+1$ have to do only with noises that Charley uttered. So, it might be argued, when we reformulate the premises and conclusion of the inference in terms of truth, this can't be the innocent reformulation that the disquotationalist says it is: for the displayed inference has no inductive force, but the refor-mulation in terms of truth does have inductive force. So the reformulated inference works by attributing a more substantive property than disquo-tational truth to Charley's utterances, a substantive property on which it is legitimate to enumeratively induce.

I have tried to set out this line of argument persuasively, but in my view it rests on a very naive theory of induction. (I'm not talking about its use of enumerative induction: I take the assumption that learning from Charley is based on an enumerative induction to be a simplifying assump-tion on which nothing important is likely to turn.) I grant that to someone who had no concept of truth whatever, the displayed inference would prob-ably have no inductive force. But that doesn't imply that we who do have a concept of disquotational truth should attach no inductive force to the very same inference (or equivalently, to the inference as reformulated in terms of disquotational truth). To be sure, our attaching force to this infer-ence does not inevitably follow from our having a disquotational truth predicate; in principle, someone could perfectly well have a disquotational truth predicate and regard it as 'unprojectable'. But the fact that we aren't like that, that we do regard it as 'projectable', doesn't seem to me to have much to do with whether the predicate is 'substantive' in the sense employed in the objection: it doesn't show that 'true' isn't just a logical predicate defined by its role as a device of infinite conjunction. (It's worth noting that someone could equally well introduce a more theoretically loaded truth predicate and find it 'unprojectable': 'grue' after all is a 'sub-stantive' predicate in the sense in question here, that is, it is not a mere logical device in the way that disquotational truth is.) Our acceptance of enumerative inductions on 'true' is presumably due to having discovered that we get useful results by doing so,[36] and such a discovery does not require that truth be anything more than what the disquotation schemas tell us.

If this is right then the second argument that learning from others is incompatible with deflationism has no force. How about the first argument, that learning from others requires an interpersonal notion of synonymy, so that pure disquotational truth by itself is inadequate to the job? This too seems wrong. Suppose Charley speaks another language, which I think I understand: anyway, I have a translation manual that I use for it. Suppose I have found out in the past that when Charley utters sentences, they usually turn out to be true as I understand them—that is, their translations turn out true, on the translation manual I use. Then we have an inductive

---

[36] We may well also have an innate predisposition to believe other people, barring evidence to the contrary; this does not affect my point.

argument that the next one will be true, on the manual I use: in this way, we can inductively argue to the snow in Mobile, as before. As far as I can see it doesn't matter in the least whether this manual accords with the genuine interpersonal synonymy relation between his sentences and ours, assuming that such talk of the correct interpersonal synonymy relation even makes sense: truth-relative-to-the-manual is the only notion we need in learning from others.

12. CONCLUSION

I repeat that there are many other arguments for the need for a more-than-disquotational notion of truth or truth conditions, some much more complicated to deal with than any given here. What I have tried to do here is simply to motivate a fairly strong version of deflationism—strong in that it does not rely even on a semantic notion of synonymy—and to sketch how such a version of deflationism can overcome various objections. I think what I have done here makes some case for what I've called 'methodological deflationism', the idea that we should assume full-fledged deflationism as a working hypothesis. That way, if full-fledged deflationism turns out to be inadequate, we will at least have a clearer sense than we have now of just where it is that inflationist assumptions about truth conditions are needed.[37]

[37] I've had helpful conversations with many people about these issues in recent years. Among those whose comments have influenced my presentation are Marian David, Michael Devitt, Paul Horwich, Barry Loewer, and Stephen Schiffer. I have also incorporated some useful suggestions by the referees for *Mind*.

NOTES ON THE CONTRIBUTORS

J. L. AUSTIN was the major figure in the movement known as 'Oxford Philosophy' in the mid-twentieth century, distinguished by meticulous attention to the niceties of ordinary language. The main works illustrating his method arose out of papers and lectures, and were published after his death. They include *Sense and Sensibilia* (1962), *How to Do Things with Words* (1962), and the collected *Philosophical Papers* (1961).

F. H. BRADLEY was the leading 'British Idealist' of the late nineteenth and early twenieth century, supporting a kind of idealism owing much to Kant and Hegel. His major works include *Ethical Studies* (1876), *Principles of Logic* (1983), and *Appearance and Reality* (1893).

DONALD DAVIDSON is Willis S. and Marion Slusser Professor of Philosophy at the University of California at Berkeley. Most of his work is in the philosophy of mind.

MICHAEL DUMMETT is Emeritus Professor of Philosophy in the University of Oxford. He was Wykeham Professor of Logic at Oxford 1979–1992, and is an Emeritus Fellow of New College. His publications include *Frege: Philosophy of Language* (1973), *The Logical Basis of Metaphysics* (1991), *Frege: Philosophy of Mathematics* (1991), *Frege and Other Philosophers* (1991), *The Origins of Analytical Philosophy* (1992), and *The Seas of Language* (1993).

HARTRY FIELD was Kornblith Distinguished Professor at the City University of New York and now teaches at New York University. He is the author of many articles on truth and semantic indeterminacy. In the philosophy of mathematics he has written *Science Without Numbers: A Defense of Nominalism* and *Realism, Mathematics and Modality*, together with numerous recent articles on objectivity and indeterminacy in mathematics and several on a priori knowledge.

GOTTLOB FREGE was a German mathematician and philosopher of mathematics, who worked all his life at the University of Jena. He pioneered the propositional and predicate calculi, and is widely regarded as the father of modern logic. Works available in English include *Translations from the Philosophical Writings of Gottlob Frege*, edited by P. Geach and M. Black (1960), *The Basic Laws of Arithmetic*, translated and edited by M. Furth

(1964), *Conceptual Notation and Related Articles*, edited by T. W. Bynum (1972), and *On the Foundations of Geometry and Formal Theories of Arithmetic*, edited by E.-H. W. Kluge (1971).

ANIL GUPTA is Rudy Professor of Philosophy at Indiana University. His publications include *The Logic of Common Nouns* (1980) and *The Revision Theory of Truth* (co-authored with Nuel Belnap, 1993).

PAUL HORWICH is Professor of Philosophy at University College London. He is the author of *Probability and Evidence* (1982), *Asymmetries in Time* (1987), *Meaning* (1998), and *Truth* (1998, second edition), from which the piece included in this volume is extracted.

WILLIAM JAMES was an American psychologist and philosopher, who worked at Harvard. He was the most eloquent spokesman of the movement known as pragmatism. Works include the two-volume *Principles of Psychology* (1890), *The Will to Believe* (1897), *Pragmatism: A New Name for some Old Ways of Thinking* (1907), *The Meaning of Truth* (1909) and *Essays in Radical Empiricism* (1912).

H. H. JOACHIM taught in the early twentieth century at Oxford, working largely in the shadow of Hegel and the British Idealists. In 1919 he was appointed to the Wykeham Professorship of Logic. In addition to *The Nature of Truth* (1906) he published work on Spinoza and translations of Aristotle. One of his undergraduate pupils at Merton College was the poet T. S. Eliot.

W. V. QUINE is the most important American philosopher of the second half of the twentieth century, and his work has been the major focus of most recent work in logic, semantics, and epistemology. Major works in the philosophy of language include the collection of papers *From a Logical Point of View* (1953), *Word and Object* (1960), *The Ways of Paradox and Other Essays* (1966), *Ontological Relativity and Other Essays* (1969), *Philosophy of Logic* (1970), and *The Roots of Reference* (1974).

F. P. RAMSEY was a Cambridge mathematician and philosopher, who died at the age of twenty seven in 1930, having made important contributions to mathematical logic, probability theory, and the philosophy of science. His major papers are collected in *Foundations: Essays in Philosophy, Logic, Mathematics and Economics*, ed. D. H. Mellor.

RICHARD RORTY is University Professor of the Humanities, Emeritus, at the University of Virginia and Professor of Comparative Literature at Stanford University. His most recent books are *Achieving Our Country:*

American Leftist Thought in the Twentieth Century and *Philosophical Papers, Volume 3: Truth and Progress*.

BERTRAND RUSSELL was the best-known English philosopher of the first half of the twentieth century. He made major contributions to all branches of philosophy. Work on logic and the foundations of mathematics culminated in *Principia Mathematica*, published in three volumes, 1910–13. Early papers on language are included in the collection *Mysticism and Logic*, and other books include *The Analysis of Mind* (1921), *The Analysis of Matter* (1927), and *Human Knowledge: its Scope and Limits* (1948).

P. F. STRAWSON FBA is Emeritus Professor of Philosophy at Oxford University and Honorary Fellow of St John's, University, and Magdalen Colleges, Oxford. His previous books include *Individuals: An Essay in Descriptive Metaphysics, Freedom and Resentment and Other Essays* (1974), and *Scepticism and Naturalism: Some Varieties* (1985).

ALFRED TARSKI was a Polish logician who spent the latter part of his working life in Berkeley. He made seminal contributions to many branches of logic and algebra. For philosophers he is best represented in the collection *Logic, Semantics, and Metamathematics* (1956).

LUDWIG WITTGENSTEIN was an Austrian who went to England to study with Bertrand Russell, and did the major part of his work in Cambridge. He is regarded by many as the greatest philosopher of the twentieth century. Major works include the *Tractatus Logico-Philosophicus* (1921), and *The Philosophical Investigations* (1953). Collections of Wittgenstein's work published posthumously include *Remarks on the Foundations of Mathematics* (1956), and *The Blue and Brown Books* (1958).

CRISPIN WRIGHT FBA is Bishop Wardlaw Professor at the University of St Andrews and a regular Visiting Professor at Columbia University in New York. He currently holds a Leverhulme Research Professorship. He is the author of *Wittgenstein on the Foundations of Mathematics* (1980), *Frege's Conception of Numbers as Objects* (1983), *Realism, Meaning and Truth* (1987), and *Truth and Objectivity* (1992).

SELECT BIBLIOGRAPHY

ADAMSON, ROBERT, *The Development of Modern Philosophy* (Edinburgh: Blackwood, 1908).

ALSTON, W. P., *A Realist Conception of Truth* (Ithaca, NY: Cornell University Press, 1996).

ALWARD, PETER, 'Correspondence on the Cheap', *Pacific Philosophical Quarterly*, 77 (1996), 163–78.

ARISTOTLE, *Metaphysics*, trans. Christopher Kirwan (Oxford: Oxford University Press, 1993).

AYER, A. J., 'The Criterion of Truth', *Analysis*, 3 (1935).

—— *Language, Truth and Logic* (London: Victor Gollancz, 1936).

ARMSTRONG, DAVID M., *A World of States of Affairs* (Cambridge: Cambridge University Press, 1997).

BARWISE, JON, and ETCHEMENDY, JOHN, *The Liar* (Oxford: Oxford University Press, 1987).

—— and PERRY, JOHN, *Situations and Attitudes* (Cambridge, Mass.: MIT Press, 1983).

BENACERRAF, PAUL, 'Mathematical Truth' *Journal of Philosophy*, 70 (1973), 661–79.

BERGSTROM, LARS, 'Quine's Truth', *Inquiry*, 37 (1994), 421–35.

BLACKBURN, SIMON, *Spreading the Word* (Oxford: Oxford University Press, 1984).

—— *Essays in Quasi-Realism* (New York: Oxford University Press, 1993).

—— *Ruling Passions* (Oxford: Oxford University Press, 1998).

BOGHOSSIAN, PAUL A., 'The Status of Content', *Philosophical Review*, 99 (1990), 157–84.

BRADLEY, F. H., *Appearance and Reality* (Oxford: Oxford University Press, 1893).

BRANDOM, ROBERT, 'Pragmatism, Phenomenalism and Truth Talk', in P. A. French, T. E. Uehling, Jr., and H. K. Wettstein (eds.), *Midwest Studies in Philosophy*, xii. *Realism and Antirealism* (Minneapolis: University of Minnesota Press, 1988), 75–93.

—— *Making It Explicit* (Cambridge, Mass.: Harvard University Press, 1994).

BURGE, TYLER, 'Semantical Paradox', *Journal of Philosophy*, 76 (1979), 169–98; repr. with a postscript in Martin (ed.), *Recent Essays*, 83–117.

CANDLISH, STEWART, 'The Truth about F. H. Bradley', *Mind*, 98 (1989), 331–48.

CARNAP, R., *Logical Syntax of Language* (London: 1937).

—— *Introduction to Semantics* (Cambridge, Mass.: Harvard University Press, 1942).

CARRUTHERS, PETER, 'Frege's Regress', *Proceedings of the Aristotelian Society*, 82 (1981), 17–32.

CLARK, MICHAEL, 'Truth and Success: Searle's Attack on Minimalism', *Analysis*, 57 (1997), 205–9.

CROSSLEY, J. and HUMBERSTONE, L., 'The Logic of "Actually"', *Reports on Mathematical Logic*, 8 (1977), 11–29.

DAVID, MARIAN, 'Truth, Eliminativism, and Disquotation', *Noûs*, 23 (1989), 599–614.

—— *Correspondence and Disquotation* (Oxford: Oxford University Press, 1994).

DAVIDSON, DONALD, *Inquiries into Truth and Interpretation* (New York: Oxford University Press, 1984).

DAVIDSON, DONALD, 'Afterthoughts, 1987', in A. Malichowski (ed.), *Reading Rorty* (Cambridge: Blackwell, 1990), 120–38.
——'The Structure and Content of Truth', *Journal of Philosophy*, 87 (1990), 279–328.
——'What is Quine's View of Truth?', *Inquiry*, 37 (1994), 437–40.
DESCARTES, *Œuvres de Descartes*, ed. C. Adam and P. Tannery (Paris: Le Cerf, 1897–1910).
DEVITT, MICHAEL, 'Dummett's Anti-Realism', *Journal of Philosophy*, 80 (1983).
——'"Realism without Truth": A Response to Bertolet', *Analysis*, 48 (1988), 198–203.
——'Minimalist Truth: A Critical Notice of Paul Horwich's Truth', *Mind and Language*, 6 (1991), 273–83.
DILLARD, PETER S., 'Radical Anti-Deflationism', *Philosophy and Phenomenological Research*, 56 (1996), 173–82.
DIVERS, JOHN, and MILLER, ALEX, 'Why Expressivists about Value should not love Minimalism about Truth', *Analysis*, 54 (1994), 12–19.
——'Platitudes and Attitudes: A Minimalist Conception of Belief', *Analysis*, 55 (1995), 37–44.
——'Minimalism and the Unbearable Lightness of Being', *Philosophical Papers*, 24 (1995), 127–39.
DREIER, JAMES, 'Expressivist Embeddings and Minimalist Truth', *Philosophical Studies*, 83 (1996), 29–51.
DUMMETT, MICHAEL, 'Truth', *Proceedings of the Aristotelian Society*, NS 59 (1959), 141–62.
——*Truth and Other Enigmas* (London: Duckworth, 1978).
——'What is a Theory of Meaning? (I) and (II)', in *The Seas of Language* (Oxford: Oxford University Press, 1983).
EDWARDS, JIM, 'Is Tennant selling Truth Short?', *Analysis*, 57 (1997), 152–8.
ETCHEMENDY, JOHN, 'Tarski on Truth and Logical Consequence', *Journal of Symbolic Logic*, 53 (1988), 51–79.
EVANS, GARETH, and MCDOWELL, JOHN (eds.), *Truth and Meaning: Essays in Semantics* (Oxford: Clarendon Press, 1976).
FIELD, HARTRY, 'Tarski's Theory of Truth', *Journal of Philosophy*, 69 (1972), 347–75; repr. in M. Platts (ed.), *Reference, Truth and Reality: Essays on the Philosophy of Language* (London: Routledge and Kegan Paul, 1980).
——'Quine and the Correspondence Theory', *Philosophical Review*, 83 (1974), 200–28.
——'The Deflationary Conception of Truth', in Macdonald and Wright (eds.), *Fact, Science and Morality*, 55–117.
——'Critical Notice: Paul Horwich's Truth', *Philosophy of Science*, 59 (1992), 321–30.
——'Disquotational Truth and Factually Defective Discourse', *Philosophical Review*, 103/3 (1994), 405–52.
FORBES, GRAEME, 'Truth, Correspondence and Redundancy', in Macdonald and Wright (eds.), *Fact, Science and Morality*, 27–54.
FREGE, G., 'On Sense and Reference', *Translations from the Philosophical Writings of Gottlob Frege*, ed. P. Geach and M. Black (Oxford: Blackwell, 1980).
——'The Thought: A Logical Inquiry', *Mind*, 65 (1956), 289–311.
FRIEDMAN, MICHAEL, 'Truth and Confirmation', *Journal of Philosophy*, 76 (1979), 362–82.

GAIFMAN, HAIM, 'Operational Pointer Semantics: Solution to Self-referential Puzzles I', in Vardi (ed.), *Proceedings*, 43–60.

—— 'Pointers to Truth', *Journal of Philosophy*, 89 (1992), 223–61.

GIBBARD, ALLAN, *Wise Choices, Apt Feelings: A Theory of Normative Judgment* (Cambridge, Mass.: Harvard University Press, 1990).

GÖDEL, K., 'On Formally undecidable propositions of *Principia Mathematica* and Related Systems, I', in *Collected Works*, i. 145–95; Ist pub. as 'Uber formal unentscheidbare Sätze der *Principia Mathematica* und verwandter Systeme, 1', *Monatshefte für Mathematik und Physik*, 38 (1931), 173–98.

—— *Kurt Gödel: Collected Works*, i, ed. Solomon Feferman *et al.* (New York, Oxford University Press, 1986).

GONSETH, F., 'Le Congrès Descartes: Questions de philosophie scientifique', *Revue Thomiste*, 44 (1938), 183–93.

GRICE, H. P., 'Meaning', *Philosophical Review*, 66 (1957), 377–88.

—— 'Logic and Conversation', repr. in *Studies in the Way of Words* (Cambridge, Mass.: Harvard University Press, 1989).

GROVER, DOROTHY L., *A Prosentential Theory of Truth* (Princeton: Princeton University Press, 1992).

—— CAMP, JOSEPH L., and BELNAP, NUEL D., Jr. 'A Prosentential Theory of Truth', *Philosophical Studies*, 27 (1975), 73–125.

GUPTA, ANIL, 'Truth and Paradox', *Journal of Philosophical Logic*, 11 (1982), 1–60; repr. in Martin (ed.), *Recent Essays*, 175–235.

—— 'Minimalism', in James E. Tomberlin (ed.), *Philosophical Perspectives*, vii. *Language and Logic* (Atascadero: Ridgeview Press, 1993), 359–69.

—— and BELNAP, NUEL, *The Revision Theory of Truth* (Cambridge, Mass.: MIT Press, 1993).

HILBERT, D., and BERNAYS, P., *Grundlagen der Mathematik* (2 vols.) (Berlin: J. Springer, 1934–9).

HILL, CHRISTOPHER, 'Rudiments of a Theory of Reference', *Notre Dame Journal of Formal Logic*, 28 (1987), 200–19.

HÖFFDING, HARALD, *The Problems of Philosophy*, trans. Galen M. Fisher (New York: Macmillan, 1905).

HOOKER, BRAD (ed.), *Truth in Ethics* (Oxford: Blackwell, 1996).

HORNSBY, JENNIFER, 'Truth: the Identity Theory', *Proceedings of the Aristotelian Society*, 97 (1997), 1–24.

HORWICH, PAUL, *Truth* (Oxford: Basil Blackwell, 1990).

—— 'Gibbard's Theory of Norms', *Philosophy and Public Affairs*, 22 (1993), 67–78.

—— 'The Essence of Expressivism', *Analysis*, 54 (1994), 19–20.

—— (ed.), *Theories of Truth* (Aldershot: Dartmouth Publishing Company Limited, 1994).

—— 'What is it like to be a deflationary theory of meaning?', in E. Villanueva (ed.), *Philosophical Issues*, v (Atascadero: Ridgeview Press, 1994).

—— 'Disquotation and Cause in the Theory of Reference', in E. Villanueva (ed.), *Philosophical Issues*, vi (Atascadero: Ridgeview Press, 1995).

—— 'Deflationary Truth and the Problem of Aboutness', in E. Villanueva (ed.), *Philosophical Issues*, viii (Atascadero: Ridgeview Press, 1997).

—— *Meaning* (Oxford: Oxford University Press, 1998).

HOSTADTER, A., 'On Semantic Problems', *Journal of Philosophy*, 35 (1938), 225–32.

HUGLY, PHILIP G., and SAYWARD, CHARLES, 'The Disquotational Theory of Truth is False', *Philosophia*, 22 (1993), 331–9.

—— 'Quine's Relativism', *Ratio*, 3 (1990), 142–9.

JACKSON, FRANK, OPPY, GRAHAM, and SMITH, MICHAEL, 'Minimalism and Truth Aptness', *Mind*, 103 (1994), 287–302.

JACOBSEN, ROCKNEY, 'Wittgenstein on Self-Knowledge and Self-Expression', *Philosophical Quarterly*, 46 (1996), 12–30.

JAMES, WILLIAM, *Pragmatism: A New Name for Some Old Ways of Thinking* (New York: Longmans, Green, and Co., 1907).

—— 'Two English Critics', in *The Meaning of Truth* (New York: Longmans, Green, and Co., 1909).

JOACHIM, H. H., *The Nature of Truth* (Oxford: Oxford University Press, 1906).

JUHOS, B. VON, 'The Truth of Empirical Statements', *Analysis*, 5 (1937), 65–70.

KAPUS, JERRY, 'Truth and Explanation', Ph.D. diss. (University of Illinois at Chicago, 1992).

—— 'The Deflationary View of Truth', *Journal of the Indian Council for Philosophical Research*, 12 (1995), 81–104.

KEMP SMITH, NORMAN, *Studies in the Cartesian Philosophy* (London: Macmillan, 1902).

KIRKHAM, RICHARD L., *Theories of Truth* (Cambridge, Mass.: MIT Press, 1992).

KOKOSZYŃSKA, M., 'Syntax, Semantik und Wissenschaftslogic,' *Actes du congrès international de philosophie scientifique*, iii (Paris, 1936), 9–14.

—— 'Uber den Absoluten Wahrheitsbegriff und einige andere semantische Begriffe', *Erkenntnis*, 6 (1936), 143–65.

KOTARBIŃSKI, T, *Elementy teorji poznania, logiki formalnej i metodologji nauk* (Elements of Epistemology, Formal Logic, and the Methodology of Sciences) (Lvov, 1929).

—— 'W sprawie pojecia prawdy' ('Concerning the Concept of Truth'), *Przeglad filozoficzny*, 37: 85–91.

KOVACH, ADAM, 'Deflationism and the Derivation Game', *Mind*, 106 (1997), 575–9.

KRAUT, ROBERT, 'Robust Deflationism', *Philosophical Review*, 102 (1993), 247–63.

KRIPKE, SAUL, 'Outline of a Theory of Truth', *Journal of Philosophy*, 72 (1975), 690–716; repr. in Martin (ed.), *Recent Essays*, 53–81.

—— *Naming and Necessity* (Cambridge, Mass.: Harvard University Press, 1980).

LAFONT, CRISTINA, 'Truth, Knowledge, and Reality', *Graduate Faculty Philosophy Journal*, 18 (1995), 109–26.

LEEDS, STEPHEN, 'Theories of Reference and Truth', *Erkenntnis*, 13 (1978), 111–29.

LEVIN, MICHAEL, 'What Kind of Explanation is Truth?', in Jarrett Leplin, *Essays in Scientific Realism* (Berkeley and Los Angeles: University of California Press, 1984), 124–39.

LEWIS, DAVID, 'Languages and Language', *Minnesota Studies in the Philosophy of Science*, vii (Minneapolis: Minnesota University Press, 1975), 3–35.

LINDENBAUM, A., and TARSKI, A., 'Uber die Beschranktheit der Ausdrucksmittel deduktiver Theorien', *Ergebnisse eines mathematischen Kolloquiums*, 7 (1936), 15–23.

LOEWER, BARRY, 'The Value of Truth', in E. Villanueva (ed.), *Philosophical Issues*, iv (Atascadero: Ridgeview Press, 1994).

MACDONALD, GRAHAM, and WRIGHT, CRISPIN (eds.), *Fact, Science and Morality: Essays on A. J. Ayer's* Language, Truth and Logic (Oxford: Blackwell, 1986).

McDOWELL, J., 'Are Moral Requirements Hypothetical Imperatives?', *Proceedings of the Aristotelian Society*, suppl. vol. 52 (1978), 13–29.

—— *Mind and World* (Cambridge, Mass.: Harvard University Press, 1994).

—— 'Knowledge and the Internal' *Philosophy and Phenomenological Research*, 55 (1995), 877–93.

—— 'Précis of "Mind and World"', in E. Villanueva (ed.), *Philosophical Issues*, vii (Atascadero: Ridgeview Press, 1996).

—— 'Reply to Gibson, Byrne and Brandom', in E. Villanueva (ed.), *Philosophical Issues*, vii (Atascadero: Ridgeview Press, 1996).

MCGEE, VANN, *Truth, Vagueness, and Paradox* (Indianapolis: Hackett, 1990).

—— 'Maximal Consistent Sets of Instances of Tarski's Schema T', *Journal of Philosophical Logic*, 21 (1992), 235–41.

MCGRATH, MATTHEW, 'Weak Deflationism', *Mind*, 106 (1997), 69–98.

—— 'Reply to Kovach', *Mind*, 106 (1997), 581–6.

MACKIE, J. L., *Ethics: Inventing Right and Wrong* (Harmondsworth: Penguin, 1977).

MARTIN, ROBERT L. (ed.), *Recent Essays on Truth and the Liar Paradox* (Oxford: Oxford University Press, 1984).

MIKEL, ANTON, 'A Problem with the Minimalist Theory of Truth', *Philosophical Papers*, 23 (1994), 137–8.

MIRAGLIA, PIERLUIGI, 'A Note on Truth, Deflationism and Irrealism', *Sorites* (1995), 48–63.

MOORE, G. E., 'The Nature of Judgment', *Mind*, NS 8 (1899), 176–93.

NAGEL, E., Review of Hofstadter, *Journal of Symbolic Logic*, 7 (1938), 90.

—— Review of Carnap, *Journal of Philosophy*, 29 (1942), 468–73.

NESS, A., '"Truth" as conceived by Those who are not Professional Philosophers', *Skrifter utgitt av Det Norske Videnskaps-Akademi I Oslo, II. Hist. -Filos. Klasse*, 4 (1938).

NEURATH, O., 'Erster Internationaler Kongress für Einheit der Wissenschaft in Paris 1935', *Erkenntnis*, 5 (1935), 377–406.

O'LEARY-HAWTHORNE, J., and OPPY, GRAHAM, 'Minimalism and Truth', *Noûs*, 31 (1997), 170–96.

PARSONS, CHARLES, 'The Liar Paradox', *Journal of Philosophical Logic*, 3 (1974), 381–412; repr. with postscript in Martin (ed.), *Recent Essays*, 9–45.

PENDLEBURY, MICHAEL, 'Facts as Truthmakers', *Monist*, 69 (1986), 177–88.

PITCHER, GEORGE, *Truth* (Englewood Cliffs: Prentice Hall, 1964).

PLANTINGA, A., 'How to be an Anti-Realist', *Proceedings and Addresses of the American Philosophical Association*, 56 (1982), 47–70.

PUTNAM, HILARY, *Meaning and the Moral Sciences* (London: Routledge and Kegan Paul, 1978).'

—— *Reason, Truth and History* (Cambridge: Cambridge University Press, 1981).

—— 'Why Reason can't be Naturalized', *Synthèse*, 52 (1982), 3–24.

—— 'On Truth', in L. S. Cauman, I. Levi, and R. Swartz (eds.), *How Many Questions: Essays in Honor of Sidney Morgenbesser* (Indianapolis: Hackett Publishing Company, 1983), 35–56.

—— *Philosophical Papers*, iii. *Realism and Reason* (Cambridge: Cambridge University Press, 1983).

—— 'Does the Disquotational Theory really solve All Philosophical Problems', *Metaphilosophy*, 22 (1991), 1–13.

QUINE, W. V., 'Truth by Convention' (1936), repr. in *The Ways of Paradox* (Cambridge, Mass.: Harvard University Press, 1976).

—— 'Two Dogmas of Empiricism', *Philosophical Review*, 60 (1951), repr. in *From a Logical Point of View*, 20–43.

QUINE, W. V., *From a Logical Point of View* (Cambridge, Mass.: Harvard University Press, 1953).
—— *Word and Object* (Cambridge, Mass.: MIT Press, 1960).
—— *Philosophy of Logic* (Englewood Cliffs: Prentice Hall, 1970).
—— *The Roots of Reference* (La Salle, Ill.: Open Court, 1974).
—— 'On the Very Idea of a Third Dogma', in *Theories and Things* (Cambridge, Mass.: Harvard University Press, 1981).
—— *Pursuit of Truth* (Cambridge, Mass.: Harvard University Press, 1990).
—— 'Pursuit of the Concept of Truth', in P. Leondardi and M. Santambrogio (eds.), *On Quine: New Essays* (New York: Cambridge, 1995).
—— *From Stimulus to Science* (Cambridge, Mass.: Harvard University Press, 1995).
RAMSEY, F. P., 'Facts and Propositions', *Proceedings of the Aristotelian Society*, suppl. vol. 7 (1927), 153–70.
—— 'The Nature of Truth', *Episteme*, 16 (1991), 6–16.
—— *On Truth: Original Manuscript Materials (1927–1929) from the Ramsey Collection at the University of Pittsburgh*, ed. N. Rescher and U. Majer (1991).
RAPPAPORT, STEVEN, 'Must a Metaphysical Relativist be a Truth Relativist?', *Philosophia*, 22 (1993), 75–85.
RESNIK, MICHAEL D., 'Immanent Truth', *Mind*, 99 (1990), 405–24.
RICHARD, M., 'Deflating Truth', in E. Villanueva (ed.), *Philosophical Issues*, viii (Atascadero Ridgeview Press, 1997).
RICKERT, HEINRICH, *Der Gegenstand der Erkenntnis; Einfuhrung in die transzendentale Philosophie* (Tübingen: Mohr, 1904).
RORTY, RICHARD, *Consequences of Pragmatism* (Minneapolis: University of Minnesota Press, 1982).
—— 'Is Truth a Goal of Enquiry: Davidson vs. Wright', *Philosophical Quarterly*, 45 (1995), 281–300.
RUMFITT, IAN, 'Truth Wronged', *Ratio*, NS 8 (1995), 100–7.
RUSSELL, BERTRAND, 'On the Nature of Truth', *Proceedings of the Aristotelian Society*, 7 (1906–7), 28–49.
—— 'Transatlantic "Truth"', *Albany Review* (Jan. 1908).
—— *The Analysis of Mind* (London: George Allen & Unwin, 1921).
—— *An Inquiry into Meaning and Truth* (London: George Allen & Unwin, 1940).
SCHIFFER, STEPHEN, 'A Paradox of Meaning', *Noûs*, 28 (1994), 279–324.
SCHILLER, F. C. S., *Studies in Humanism* (London: Macmillan and Co., 1907; New York: Macmillan, 1907; Freeport, NY.: Books For Libraries Press, 1969).
SCHOLZ H., Review of Studia Philosophica, Vol. I. *Deutsche Literaturzeitung*, 58 (1937), 1914–17.
SEARLE, JOHN R., *The Construction of Social Reality* (New York: The Free Press, 1995).
SEYMOUR, MICHEL, 'Critical Notice of Crispin Wright "Truth and Objectivity"', *Canadian Journal of Philosophy*, 25 (1995), 637–58.
SIMMONS, HOWARD, 'Circumstances and the Truth of Words: A Reply to Travis', *Mind*, 106 (1997), 117–18.
SIMMONS, KEITH, *Universality and the Liar: An Essay on Truth and the Diagonal Argument* (Cambridge: Cambridge University Press, 1993).
—— 'Deflationary Truth and the Liar', *Journal of Philosophical Logic* (forthcoming).
SIMONS, PETER, 'Vagueness and Ignorance: II', *Proceedings of the Aristotelian Society*, suppl. vol. 66 (1992), 163–77.

SMITH, MICHAEL, 'Minimalism, Truth-Aptitude and Belief', *Analysis*, 54 (1994), 21–6.

—— 'Why Expressivists about Value should love Minimalism about Truth', *Analysis*, 54 (1994), 1–12.

SOAMES, SCOTT, 'What is a Theory of Truth?' *Journal of Philosophy*, 81/8 (1984), 411–29.

—— 'The Truth About Deflationism', in E. Villanueva (ed.), *Philosophical Issues*, viii (Atascadero: Ridgeview Press, 1997).

STALNAKER, ROBERT, *Inquiry* (Cambridge, Mass.: MIT Press, 1984).

STOLJAR, DANIEL, 'Emotivism and Truth Conditions', *Philosophical Studies*, 70 (1993), 81–101.

STOUTLAND, FREDERICK, 'Realism and Anti-Realism in Davidson's Philosophy of Language (I)', *Critica Revista Hispano-Americana de Filosofia*, 14/41 (1982), 13–55.

—— 'Realism and Anti-Realism in Davidson's Philosophy of Language (II)', *Critica Revista Hispano-Americana de Filosofia*, 14/42 (1982), 19–49.

TARSKI, A., 'The Concept of Truth in Formalized Languages', in *Logic, Semantics, Metamathematics* (2nd edn.), trans. J. H. Woodger, (Indianapolis: Hackett, 1983), 153–278.

—— 'On Undecidable Statements in Enlarged Systems of Logic and the Concept of Truth', *Journal of Symbolic Logic*, 4 (1939), 105–12.

—— 'The Semantic Conception of Truth and The Foundations of Semantics', *Philosophy and Phenomenological Research*, 4 (1944), 342–60.

—— *Introduction to Logic and to the Methodology of Deductive Sciences* (New York: Oxford University Press, 1941).

—— 'The Establishment of Scientific Semantics', in *Logic, Semantics, Metamathematics*, 401–8.

—— 'Truth and Proof', *Scientific American*, 220 (1969), 63–77.

TAYLOR, BARRY, 'States of Affairs', in Evans and McDowell (eds.), *Truth and Meaning*, 263–84.

—— *Modes of Occurrence* (Oxford: Blackwell, 1985).

TEICHMANN, ROGER, 'Truth, Assertion and Warrant', *Philosophical Quarterly*, 45 (1995), 78–83.

TENNANT, N., 'On Negation, Truth and Warranted Assertibility', *Analysis*, 55 (1995), 98–104.

TENNENBAUM, SERGIO, 'Realists without a Cause: Deflationary Theories of Truth and Ethical Realism', *Canadian Journal of Philosophy*, 26 (1996), 561–90.

TOMBERLIN, JAMES E., (ed.), *Philosophical Perspectives*, vii, *Language and Logic* (Atascadero: Ridgeview Press, 1993).

TRAVIS, CHARLES, 'Meaning's Role in Truth', *Mind*, 105 (1996), 451–66.

TUGENDHAT, ERNST, *Traditional and Analytical Philosophy* (Cambridge: Cambridge University Press, 1983).

VAN FRAASSEN, BAS, *The Scientific Image* (Oxford: Clarendon Press, 1980).

VARDI, M., and KAUFMAN, MORGAN (eds.), *Proceedings of the Second Conference on Theoretical Aspects of Reasoning about Knowledge* (Los Altos: California, 1988).

VILLEGAS-FORRERA, L. (ed.), *Verdad: Logica, Representacion y Mundo* (Santiago de Compostela: University of Santiago de Compostela Press, 1996).

VISION, GERALD, *Modern Anti-Realism and Manufactured Truth* (London: Routledge, 1988).

WALKER, RALPH C. S., *The Coherence Theory of Truth: Realism, Anti-Realism, Idealism* (London: Routledge, 1989).

WALKER, RALPH C. S., 'Theories of Truth', in Bob Hale and Crispin Wright (eds.), *Companion to the Philosophy of Language* (Oxford: Blackwell, 1997).

WARNOCK, G. J., *Berkeley* (Harmondsworth: Pelican Books, 1953).

WEINBERG, J., Review of *Studia philosophica*, vol. i, *Philosophical Review*, 47 (1938), 70–7.

WEIR, ALAN, 'Ultramaximalist Minimalism!', *Analysis*, 56 (1996), 10–22.

WILLIAMS, MICHAEL, 'Coherence, Justification and Truth', *Review of Metaphysics*, 34 (1980) 243–72.

—— 'Do We (Epistemologists) need a Theory of Truth?', *Philosophical Topics*, 14 (1986), 223–42.

—— 'Epistemological Realism and the Basis of Scepticism', *Mind*, 97 (1988), 415–39.

WILLIAMSON, TIMOTHY, 'Vagueness and Ignorance: I', *Proceedings of the Aristotelian Society*, suppl. vol. 66 (1992), 145–62.

—— 'Crispin Wright's "Truth and Objectivity"', *International Journal of Philosophical Studies*, 2 (1994), 130–44.

—— 'Definiteness and Knowability', *Southern Journal of Philosophy*, 33 (suppl.) (1995), 171–91.

WRIGHT, CRISPIN, *Truth and Objectivity* (Cambridge, Mass.: Harvard University Press, 1992).

—— *Realism, Meaning and Truth* (Oxford: Blackwell, 1993).

—— 'Critical Study of Walker's *The Coherence Theory of Truth*', *Synthèse*, 103 (1995), 279–320.

YABLO, STEPHEN, 'Truth and Reflection', *Journal of Philosophical Logic*, 14 (1985), 297–349.

YAQUB, A., *The Liar Speaks the Truth: A Defense of the Revision Theory of Truth* (Oxford: Oxford University Press, 1993).

INDEX

Note: page numbers in **bold** refer to main sections.